GUIDE TO
BRITISH HISTORICAL MANUSCRIPTS
IN THE HUNTINGTON LIBRARY

GUIDE TO
BRITISH HISTORICAL
MANUSCRIPTS
IN THE
HUNTINGTON LIBRARY

HUNTINGTON LIBRARY

1982

Copyright © 1982
Henry E. Huntington Library and Art Gallery
San Marino, California

Library of Congress Card Number

ISBN 0–87328–117–9
Printed in the United States of America by Kingsport Press
Designed by Ward Ritchie

The title-page illustration shows the Great Seal of Elizabeth I (1587/88) reproduced from a manuscript now in the Huntington Library.

The preparation of this work was made possible through a grant from the Research Collections Program of the National Endowment for the Humanities.

TABLE OF CONTENTS

Foreword		ix
Preface		xi
BATTLE ABBEY COLLECTION		1
Pre-Dissolution Monastic Archive		3
I.	Accounts	3
	1. Obedientiary	3
	2. Estate and Manorial	4
II.	Court Rolls and other Court Records	4
III.	Deeds and Charters	5
IV.	Rentals and Surveys, with Related Papers	6
V.	Miscellaneous Papers	7
Post-Dissolution Family Papers		10
I.	Accounts	10
	1. Personal	10
	2. Estate and Manorial	11
	3. Foundry	11
	4. Miscellaneous	12
II.	Correspondence	12
III.	Deeds and Charters	13
IV.	Financial	13
V.	Legal	14
VI.	Estate and Local Affairs	15
	1. Court Rolls and other Court Records	15
	2. Rentals and Surveys, with Related Papers	17
	3. General	18
VII.	Personal and Family	19
ELLESMERE COLLECTION		21
I.	To 1617	26
II.	1617–1649	46
III.	1649–1686	53
IV.	1686–1701	59

V. 1701–1745   64
VI. 1745–1803   66
VII. Miscellany   67
Ellesmere Authors   70
Ellesmere Court Rolls   74
Ellesmere Deeds   75
HASTINGS COLLECTION   78
   I. Accounts and Financial Papers   82
   II. Correspondence   83
   III. Deeds   95
   IV. Inventories and Lists   102
   V. Legal Papers   104
   VI. Manorial and Local Affairs Papers   105
   VII. Maps and Plans   120
   VIII. Personal and Family Papers   123
   IX. Irish Papers   128
   X. Special Subjects   131
      1. Americana   131
      2. Genealogy   132
      3. Gentlemen Pensioners   133
      4. Indentured Retainers   133
      5. Literature   134
      6. Military Affairs   136
      7. Parliamentary Affairs   136
      8. Religious and Ecclesiastical Affairs   138
      9. Repton Charity School and Etwall Hospital   139
      10. School Exercises and Education   140
      11. Ship Money   140
      12. Transportation   141
      13. Miscellaneous   142
STOWE COLLECTION   145
Grenville Papers   148
   I. Accounts and Financial Papers   151
   II. Correspondence   155
   III. Deeds   173
   IV. Inventories, Lists, and Catalogs   173
   V. Legal Papers   176
   VI. Manorial and Local Affairs Papers   176
   VII. Personal and Family Papers   184

VIII. Special Subjects   191
   1. Admiralty Affairs   191
   2. Buckinghamshire Militia   192
   3. Elections   193
   4. Fine Arts (Pictures, Music, and Dance)   193
   5. Genealogy   194
   6. India   194
   7. Ireland   195
   8. Literature   196
   9. Parliamentary Affairs   198
   10. Photographs   199
   11. Queen Anne's Bounty Papers   199
   12. Religious and Ecclesiastical Affairs   200
   13. Schools and Education   200
   14. Transportation (chiefly Railroads)   201
   15. West Indian Estates   202
   16. Miscellaneous   202

Temple Papers   203
  I.   Accounts and Financial Papers   205
  II.   Correspondence   207
  III.   Deeds   210
  IV.   Inventories, Lists, and Catalogs   212
  V.   Legal Papers   213
  VI.   Manorial and Local Affairs Papers   215
  VII.   Personal and Family Papers   219
  VIII.   Special Subjects   223
    1. Customs   223
    2. Elections   224
    3. Foreign Affairs   224
    4. Genealogy   224
    5. Literature   225
    6. Military Affairs   225
    7. Parliamentary Affairs   226
    8. Religious Affairs   227
    9. Ship Money Papers   227
    10. Miscellaneous   228

Brydges Papers   228
  I.   Accounts and Financial Papers   230
  II.   Correspondence   231

III. Deeds 233
IV. Inventories, Lists, and Catalogs 234
V. Legal Papers 235
VI. Manorial and Local Affairs Papers 236
VII. Personal and Family Papers 239
VIII. Special Subjects 242
    1. Genealogy 242
    2. Hanaper Accounts 243
    3. Literature 243
    4. Military Affairs 244
    5. Parliamentary Affairs 244
    6. Paymaster-General Accounts 244
    7. West Indian Estates 244
    8. Miscellaneous 245
Nugent Papers 246
I. Accounts and Financial Papers 246
II. Correspondence 247
III. Deeds 247
IV. Inventories and Lists 248
V. Legal Papers 248
VI. Manorial and Local Affairs Papers 249
VII. Personal and Family Papers 250
VIII. Special Subjects 251
    1. War of 1689–91 251
    2. West Indian Affairs 252
O'Conor Papers 252
Stowe Unsorted Deeds 255
Stowe Maps and Plans 262

OTHER COLLECTIONS AND INDIVIDUAL ITEMS 275

INDEX 368

FOREWORD

Readers who have explored the first two volumes published in this four-part series, Guide to Manuscripts in the Huntington Library, are aware of the Huntington's riches in American historical manuscripts and in literary manuscripts. We expect that scholars will find comparable research opportunities in the materials recorded in the present volume, British historical manuscripts.

The *Guide to British Historical Manuscripts in the Huntington Library* is published after more than three years of intensive work in sorting, cataloging, conserving, describing, and indexing the Library's internationally known collections. The *Guide* surveys archives containing 450,000 pieces, including the Stowe, Hastings, Ellesmere, Loudoun, and Battle Abbey papers.

A final section of the guide book project, on Medieval and Renaissance manuscripts, is scheduled for completion this year and for publication in 1982. At that time, scholars around the world will have comprehensive information about one of the principal repositories of manuscript research materials on British and American history and literature.

DANIEL H. WOODWARD
LIBRARIAN

PREFACE

This *Guide* provides for the first time a comprehensive survey of the Huntington Library's research collections of British historical manuscripts, which range in date from the eleventh to the twentieth century. It supersedes two earlier accounts, "Huntington Library Collections" (*Huntington Library Bulletin* no. 1, 1931) and Jean F. Preston's "Collections of English Historical Manuscripts in the Huntington Library" (*Archives* vol. 6, 1963). Detailed descriptions of individual collections are noted in the appropriate bibliographical sections.

The four major archival collections, and the cornerstones of the Library's British historical holdings, are the Battle Abbey, Ellesmere, Hastings, and Stowe papers. Because of the variety in their range and nature, no attempt has been made to standardize their descriptions in the present *Guide;* guidelines are noted in the introduction to each of these collections under the heading "Remarks on the Following Description."

For all other collections of forty or more pieces processed before 1980, and for selected research-worthy or otherwise notable separate manuscripts not attached to any specific collection, the following information is provided:

1) Name of the collection (usually corresponding to the name of the central figure therein, in which case his birth and death dates are also given).
2) Size of the collection with range of dates of the manuscripts therein.
3) A biographical sketch of the central figure or institution of the collection, with greater emphasis usually placed on information from the collection not readily available elsewhere.
4) Subject matter of the collection.

5) A list of all persons (or corporate authors or institutions) represented in the collection by five or more pieces. It should be noted that anyone represented by fewer than five items in each of several collections will not appear in this *Guide*, although the Library may hold all together a large number of his manuscripts.
6) Brief physical description of the manuscripts in the collection.
7) Provenance (excluded for separate items).
8) Bibliography of further descriptions of the collection or separate item and of works in which substantial portions of the manuscripts have been printed. No attempt has been made to furnish a comprehensive list of all works based on the manuscripts.

Unless otherwise noted, all dates before 1752 are given in the Old Style except that the beginning of the year is taken to be January 1 rather than March 25. Peers are listed by surname, followed by their highest given title, regardless of the name or title by which they are commonly known.

The *Guide to British Historical Manuscripts in the Huntington Library* was compiled and edited under the supervision of Mary L. Robertson, Curator of Manuscripts. Kim S. Watson directed and completed the Herculean task of sorting, organizing, listing, and partially cataloging the massive Stowe and Hastings collections; she was assisted by Dorothy Popp, Elizabeth Zall, and earlier generations of Huntington catalogers. Sylvia Burd gave many hours of volunteer help in compiling an index to the Stowe deeds. The actual *Guide* entries were written by Mary Robertson, Bruce Henry, and Dorothy Popp, with the further assistance of Harriet McLoone. Special guidance at the beginning of this project was given by Virginia Rust, Associate Curator of Manuscripts, and Jean F. Preston, former Curator of Manuscripts. Further editorial assistance was provided by Jane Evans and Betty Leigh Merrell. The project was supported by a grant from the National Endowment for the Humanities.

GUIDE TO

BRITISH HISTORICAL MANUSCRIPTS

IN THE HUNTINGTON LIBRARY

BATTLE ABBEY COLLECTION
ca.3,000 pieces, 11th cent–1780

The Benedictine abbey of St. Martin at Battle was founded by William the Conqueror to commemorate his victory over Harold at Hastings. The first abbot, Gausbert of Marmoutier, was consecrated in 1076 but the church, built on the precise spot where Harold fell in battle, was unfinished when William died, and not dedicated until 1094. The Conqueror bestowed upon his abbey extraordinarily wide lay and ecclesiastical jurisdiction, focused on the banlieu or *leuga,* a circle of land one league in radius centered at the high altar. Within this liberty (geographically within but legally separate from and comparable to the Rape of Hastings in Sussex) the abbey was free of all feudal dues and customs and was enfranchised to exercise royal judicial and administrative rights independent of both shire and hundred. These privileges, imperfectly recorded at the time they were granted, were confirmed (partly on the strength of forged charters) by Henry II nearly a century later.

The original endowment included, beside the *leuga,* the six manors of Alciston (Sussex), Brightwalton (Berks.), Crowmarsh (Oxon.), Hoo [also Hou, Hoton] (Essex), Limpsfield (Surrey), and Wye (Kent), and churches at Reading, Collumpton, and St. Olave's Exeter. Royal grants of two additional manors (Bromham in Wiltshire by William Rufus and Appledram in Sussex by Henry I), a group of East Anglian churches, and numerous abbey purchases (including Icklesham, Barnhorn, and Marshal in East Sussex, and Bodiam, added to the *leuga* itself) established Battle's landed estate at ten "home manors" in East Sussex and Kent and additional "income" properties in eight other counties. During the economically troubled 14th century most of Battle's estates were farmed out, and the manors of Marley and Wode "created" to encompass and administer the remaining demesne lands within and adjoining the *leuga.* The abbey's financial position improved slightly during the 15th century and was on a sound if not overly prosperous basis by the eve of the Dissolution. The last abbot, John Hammond, surrendered his house to the crown in May 1538.

The abbey and its immediately adjacent lands, considered now as the Manor of Battle, together with most of the abbey lands in Sussex and Kent (including the additional manors of Barnhorn and Maxfield, Sussex), were sold in 1538 and 1539 to Sir Anthony Browne, Henry VIII's favorite and Master of the Horse, whose son Anthony was created 1st Viscount Montague in 1554. The property descended in the Browne family, despite a brief forfeiture for recusancy during the Commonwealth, until 1721, when the 6th Viscount sold it to Sir Thomas Webster, a prosperous London merchant who had moved into the land market some two decades before with the acquisition of Copthall in Essex. By 1725, with the assistance of a legacy from Henry Whistler, his wife Jane's grandfather, Webster also purchased the manor of Robertsbridge, Sussex, at which a profitable iron foundry had been located for over a century. He also leased the Beech Furnace ironworks in the town of Battle itself, and thereafter maintained an interest in the industry and contacts with London ironmongers. Sir Thomas was succeeded by his son Sir Whistler Webster about 1750, and thereafter the Battle estate remained in the family (with one 43-year interval in the later nineteenth century) until 1976. Since then it has been the property of the Department of the Environment.

Provenance: In 1835 Sir Godfrey Webster, 5th Bart., offered the monastic records still in his possession, together with some family estate papers, to the bookseller Thomas Thorpe, from whom they were in turn purchased by Sir Thomas Phillipps. After Phillipps' death, with the confirmation of the Court of Chancery, the Library purchased the collection through the agency of A. S. W. Rosenbach in 1923.

Bibliography: The collection is described in *Descriptive Catalogue of the Original Charters, Royal Grants, and Donations . . . and other Documents constituting the Muniments of Battle Abbey . . .* [offered for sale] by Thomas Thorpe, (London, 1835); in J. M. Vincent, "The Battle Abbey Records in the Huntington Library," *American Historical Review* 36 (1931): 63–68; in Sir William Beveridge, "Some Explorations in San Marino," *Huntington Li-*

brary Bulletin 2 (1932): 68–71; and in Jean F. Preston, "Collections of English Historical Manuscripts in the Huntington Library," *Archives* 6, No. 30 (1963): 95–96. Sections of the collection are calendared or otherwise described in *Accounts of the Cellarers of Battle Abbey 1275–1513*, ed. Eleanor Searle and Barbara Ross (Sydney University Press, 1967); Eleanor Swift, "Obedientiary and Other Accounts of Battle Abbey in the Huntington Library," *Bulletin of the Institute of Historical Research* 12 (1934): 83–101; Eleanor Swift, "The Obedientiary Rolls of Battle Abbey," *Sussex Archaelogical Collections* 78 (1937): 37–62.

Complementary collections of Battle Abbey manuscripts are located in the East Sussex Record Office and the Public Record Office, London, and are described in *A Catalogue of the Battle Abbey Estate Archives*, ed. Judith A. Brent, East Sussex Record Office Handbook No. 6 (1973) and in Great Britain. Public Record Office. *Deputy Keeper's Report VIII*, Appendix II, 139–46.

Remarks on the Following Description: The collection is particularly rich in monastic and estate accounts, court records, and deeds, but although each of these categories contains materials from both the pre- and post-Dissolution eras, the collection as a whole changes markedly in 1538. Before that time it consists of a complete monastic archive, the product of one integrated religious institution. Thereafter it consists of two major subcollections, corresponding to Browne and Webster family papers, as well as smaller groups of manuscripts pertaining to the related families of Cheke, Jorden, and Whistler. The bulk of this post-Dissolution material pertains to the Webster family, and deals with legal, financial, and estate matters. There is little correspondence.

For the categories under which this collection is described, see the Table of Contents.

PRE-DISSOLUTION MONASTIC PAPERS

I. ACCOUNTS:
  1. *Obedientiary*
      Abbey Accounts. 6 pieces, 1346–83
      Almoner's accounts. 71 pieces, 1359–1531
      Cellarer's accounts. 45 pieces, 1275–ca.1530
      Chaplain's accounts. 2 pieces, 1520–21

Sacrist's accounts. 40 pieces, 1399–1531
Seneschal's accounts. 10 pieces, 1488–1531
Treasurer's accounts. 23 pieces, 1350–1531
Miscellaneous accounts.
> Fabric Roll. 8 pieces, 1312
> Account for repairs to altar and building a new chamber. 1 piece, 15th cent.

2. *Estate and Manorial*
Battle (Beadle's accounts). 104 pieces, 1326–1527
Barnhorn (Sussex): (Chiefly bailiff, serjeant, and reeve's accounts). 101 pieces, 1325–1494
Icklesham (Sussex): (Chiefly serjeant's accounts). 34 pieces, ca.1308–90
Marley Farm (Sussex): (Serjeant's and reeve's accounts and misc.). 13 pieces, ca.1309–1511
Maxfield (Sussex): 1 piece, late 14th cent.
Pevensey Marsh (Sussex): 2 pieces, 1325, 1334
Wye (Kent): (Chiefly beadle's accounts and accounts of the deputy keeper of the woods). 21 pieces, 1326–1527

II. COURT ROLLS AND OTHER COURT RECORDS:
Battle:
Abbot's *leuga* court rolls (including views of frankpledge called here, misleadingly, "hundreds"). 47 rolls, now disbanded, for the following years:

1404–05	1479–80	1518–19
1450–51	1480–81	1519–20
1460–61	1481–82	1521–22
1461–62	1482–83	1522–23
1462–63	1493–94	1523–24
1463–64	1498–99	1524–25
1464–65	1500–01	1525–26
1465–66	1509–10	1526–27
1468–69	1511–12	1527–28
1469–70	1512–13	1530–31
1470–71	1513–14	1531–32
1473–74	1514–15	1533–34
1474–75	1515–16	1534–35
1475–76	1516–17	1535–36
1476–77	1517–18	1536–37
1477–78		

Hallmoot records. 1 roll, now disbanded, with parts of a second roll, containing entries for the following years: 1432, 1434, 1439–43, 1446, 1448–53, 1455–57, and 1459.

Gaol delivery records for the liberty of Battle. 7 pieces, for 1303, 1327 (bis), 1331, 1344 (bis), [1331<>1370].

Court book, compiled early 16th century, covering the years 1245–1532; continued contemporaneously through 1580. 1 vol.

Barnhorn (Sussex):

Hallmoot records. 17 rolls, now disbanded, containing entries for the following years: 1307, 1400–1408, 1410–13, 1461, 1470, 1472–73, 1477–85.

Marley (Sussex):

Court rolls. 22 rolls, now disbanded, containing entries for the following years: 1421–23, 1425, 1427, 1429, 1434, 1441, 1443–44, 1455, 1457, 1459–60, 1462–63, 1465, 1467–68, 1470–75, 1481, 1486–88, 1490, 1492, 1494–95, 1497, 1499–1503, 1507, 1509–16, 1519–37.

Wode [Atte Wode, Le Wode] (Sussex):

Court rolls. 7 rolls, now disbanded, containing entries for the following years: 1369, 1377, 1380, 1383, 1394, 1398, 1400, 1403.

III. DEEDS AND CHARTERS

In addition to some 900 original pre-Dissolution deeds, the collection contains two medieval cartularies of considerable interest. The first, a volume of 246 leaves made about 1330, contains copies of royal, episcopal, papal, and private grants made to the abbey from the foundation to the time of Henry III, with additions by successive abbots down to the Dissolution. The second, a volume of 138 leaves, contains copies of grants to the sacristan of the abbey or to the use of that office, and was written by sacristan John Waller in 1409–10, with additions by later sacristans down to 1511. (For detailed descriptions of these two volumes, see *Guide to Medieval and Renaissance Manuscripts at the Huntington Library.*)

The following places appear in five or more of the original deeds (many of which are of the 12th or early 13th century and bear no date):

Sussex:

Barehurst (6) n.d.-1431

Battle [including the boroughs of Sandlake, Mountjoy and Middleburgh in the town of Battle and the manors of Battle, Beech, Marley, and Netherfield in the hundred of Battle] (450) n.d.-1528

Bexhill [parish, including the manors of Barnhorn and Buckholt] (40) n.d.-1487

Bodiam (8) ca.1109–1526

Catsfield [parish, including the manor of Broomhall] (26) n.d.-1310

Etchingham (13) n.d.-1500

Guestling [parish, including Maxfield] (32) n.d.-1484

Haylesham (11) 1280–1477

Hollington (5) n.d.-1252

Hoo (12) n.d.-1464

Icklesham (18) n.d.-1516

Pevensey (26) n.d.-1492

Salehurst [including Robertsbridge] (16) n.d.-1422

Sedlescombe (17) n.d.-1471

Westham (25) 1319–1477

Whatlington (33) n.d.-1512

Willingdon (5) n.d.-1316

Winchelsea (29) n.d.-1477

Other Counties: (19) n.d.-1522

IV. RENTALS AND SURVEYS, WITH RELATED DOCUMENTS:
Battle:

Rental for the *leuga* (environs only of the town of Battle). 1252

Lists of empty tenements in town of Battle. 2 pieces, ca.1350

Rental for town of Battle. 1367

Rentals for cellarer's tenements in town of Battle. 7 pieces, ca.1387–ca.1480

Rentals for sacrist's tenements in town of Battle. 5 pieces, ca.1414–ca.1527

A paper titled "Extra leugam: Nomina eorum de quorum terris Sacrista et persona decimas quietant." Late 15th cent.

Indenture recording payment of rents to cellarer by bea-
   dle. 1457
Barnhorn (Sussex):
   Rental. 1342
   Survey. 15th cent.
   Inventory of movable goods. 1421
Hoo (Essex):
   Water-scot assessments. 4 pieces, 15th cent.-1523
Limpsfield & Prinkham (Surrey):
   Rental and extent. 1424
Marley (Sussex):
   Seneschal's rentals. 2 pieces, ca.1500, ca.1529–1530
   Indenture of stock. ca.1526?
Prinkham (Surrey): See Limpsfield & Prinkham
Miscellaneous: Extent of acreage in holdings in an un-
   identified manor(s) in ?Essex. Later 15th cent.

V. MISCELLANEOUS PAPERS

Deed of release by Robert de Baskoe to Battle Abbey of
   his claim to the service and homage of Alan the son of
   Sigar. n.d.
Feoffment by William of Munceaus [Herstmonceaux?] To Bat-
   tle Abbey of half a mark of silver yearly. n.d.
Confirmation by Henry Count of Eu of all previous grants
   to Battle. [1109< >1140]
Certificate by Bp. Richard Fitz-Neale of London that certain
   deeds for grants by Henry Count of Eu are extant in Battle's
   archives. [1189< >1199]
Agreement between the Abt. of Battle and James, son of
   William, of Northey, re making drains and drainage.
   [1235< >1261]
Agreement between Abt. of Robertsbridge and William,
   Lord of Etchingham re determination of their suits.
   1277
Quitclaim by John de Peplesham to John de Bygeneure, vicar
   of Bexhill, of his right to the body of John de Wertlesham,
   his children, and chattel. 1278
Acquittance by Thomas of Whatlington to the Abt. of Battle
   for £40. 1293
Agreement between Hugh de Dun and Alice, his daughter-

7

in-law, to abide by a judgement in a writ of novel disseisin before the justices at Lewes. n.d.

Lists of stock at Marley, Bromham, (and elsewhere?). 5 pieces, n.d.

Confirmation of a grant of rights of suit, no place given. n.d.

Recognisance for the appearance of Roger de Nottingham before the bailiff of Battle at the next Gaol Delivery. 1330

A volume of "precedents" concerning the privileges of Battle, including records of decrees and judgments by various itinerant judges. ca.1330

Subsidy assessments for the Hundreds of Guestling, Helmystrowe, Henherst, Ruthrebrugg, and Staple, and for the Half-Hundred of Bexle. 6 rolls, 1332

Quitclaims by various people to the Abt. and Convent of Battle of one or more wax tapers. 7 pieces, 1335–45

License by Edward III to the Abt. and Convent of Battle to enclose the Abbey with a wall. 1338

Pleadings on an action brought by the Abbot of Battle against William of Echyngham concerning services from lands in Whatlington. 1369–72

Prior's account of St. Mary Overies, Southwark. (incomplete). ca.1398

Bond from John Chaure of Hoo to John Swanton for 63s.4d. 1409

Text of the Statutes of Labourers, 12 Richard II and 11 Henry IV. 15th cent. copy

Commission as Justices to J. Juyn and W. Paston to take an assize of novel disseisin which Thomas, Abbot of Battle, will arraign before them by writ against Gervase Alard and others concerning a tenement in Guestling. [1417<>1435]

Pleadings on the above assize of novel disseisin concerning lands in Guestling. 2 pieces. [1417<>1435]

Requisition of Abt. of Battle to Bp. Thomas Polton of Chichester that Brother Stephen Fenesham, monk, should attend him in his episcopal visitation in the Liberty of Battle. 1432

Records of an action brought by the Abbot of Battle against Vincent Finche of Netherfield concerning impounded animals. 1428–30

Sentence by Abp. of Canterbury Henry Chichele in dispute between Abt. of Battle and Vincent Finche, Lord of the Manor of Netherfield, over tithes. 1429

Record of Escheator's inquisition concerning certain temporalities claimed by Richard Dartmouth, the new Abbot of Battle. 1437

Text of articles of impeachment presented by the Commons against William de la Pole, Duke of Suffolk. 2 contemporary copies, ca.1450?

Copy of four letters: an accusation by Lord Bonville; a denial by Thomas, Earl of Devon[shire]?; reproof to unknown addressee by Richard, Duke of York; petition to the Queen from Cecily, Duchess of York. ca.1455?

Petition of John Colcell, late sacristan, for the allowance of rents unreceived on his rental. 1462

Estreats of amercements of Court of Kings Bench concerning Battle Abbey matters. 4 pieces, 1472–98

Account of expenses and fines of Vincent Finche, seneschal, before the Courts of Justice. 1476

License by Edward IV to Maline Farnecombe to found a chantry in Winchelsea. 1478

Grant by Abt. of Battle to Simon Stephens of the wardship of John Petyr, son and heir of Richard Petyr of "The Wode" in Whatlington. 1479

Text of Acts Against Privy and Unknown Feoffments and Against Benevolences, 2 Richard II cap. 1,2. 16th cent. copy

Text of Act of Attainder against Henry Stafford, Duke of Buckingham and others, 1483. 16th cent. copy

Presentation by the Abt. of Battle of his chaplain, John Bennys, to the Rectory of Braham (*alias* Brantham) in the diocese of Norwich. 1486

Quitclaims by John A. Beche and William Lonceford to the Abt. of Battle of wax tapers. 2 pieces, 1486–88

Extracts from the Pipe Roll. 1498–1507

Depositions of witnesses concerning the chapel and tithes of Ixnyng. ca.1499?

Record of a plea of covenant transferred to court of the Abbot's Liberty at Battle, concerning tenements in Battle. ca.1499?

Certificate that the Abbot of Battle has established his rights to all assizes, fines, and amercements of himself and his tenants and other liberties within Lord Hastings' lordship. Late 15th cent.?

Answer of Robert Hollyngworth and others to the Bill of Complaint for breach of the peace brought against them by the Abbot of Battle. ca.1500

Record of a plea transferred to the Abbot's court at Battle (fragment). [1503<>1508]?

Letter of Attorney to receive £15 owed to Thomas Dogered by Thomas Stebyn. 1507

Certificate of the Commission of Array for Sussex concerning return of horse for the county. 1513

Copy of inquisition post mortem in Colchester, Essex, on the estate of John de Vere, 13th Earl of Oxford, ca.1513

Record of a plea of covenant transferred to the Abbot's court at Battle, concerning tenement in Battle. 1514

Summons by Lawrence, Abbot of Battle and other royal commissioners to the bailiff of Sir George Hastings to appear before them at Robertsbridge. 1526

A register or transcript made in the 18th century by David Casley (the King's librarian and keeper of the Cottonian manuscripts) of the Battle cartularies, the decrees re the liberties of Battle *temp.* Edward II, excerpts from the Chronicle of Battle, and extracts from other documents concerning the medieval Abbey, its government, discipline, abbots, etc. 2 vols., 1726–27

POST-DISSOLUTION FAMILY PAPERS

I. ACCOUNTS:
  1. *Personal:*

Account of personal and household receipts and disbursements of Paul Adams, steward to Francis Browne, 3rd Viscount Montague. 1 vol., 1657–58

Receipt book of wages paid to servants of Sir Thomas Webster, 1st Bart. 1 vol., 1710–30

Account books of receipts and disbursements on behalf of Sir Thomas Webster, 1st Bart., primarily for personal and household matters but including some estate receipts (chiefly of rents) and disbursements. 6 vols. for overlapping periods of years 1720–34, 1739–47.

Memorandum of the account of Sir Thomas Webster with J. Hopkins. 1 piece, 1731

Sir Thomas Webster's account of South Sea Company stock devised to him in trust for Mary, Jane, Elizabeth, Whistler, and Godfrey Webster. 1 piece, 1734

2. *Estate and Manorial:*

Account of income and expenditures at ?Battle. ca.1550

Steward's account for Ewhurst and Udimer. 1 vol., 1624–40

Steward's statements of account, most semiannual, of receipts (chiefly of rents, tithes, wood sales, and court fines) and disbursements (chiefly for taxes, building and repair work, charity, tithes, wages, and pensions) for Battle and all adjacent lands belonging to the viscounts Montague and, later, to Sir Thomas Webster, 1st Bart. Originally ca.100 separate small volumes, rebound in the 19th century into seven volumes, covering the years 1674, 1685–1706, 1708–11, 1714–36.

Thomas Coolstock's account of wood and coal for Little Brands Wood. 1 vol., 1681–82

Receipt book for James Ashenden, steward at Battle. 1 vol., 1711–30

Account of profits of the manor of Battle and Robertsbridge, belonging to Sir Whistler Webster, 2nd Bart., received by George Worge, attorney. 1 vol., 1752–62

Account of carpenters', masons', and bricklayers' work done on the estates of Sir Whistler Webster at Battle, Barnhorn, Marley, etc. 1 vol., 1754–67

Account of carpenter's work for Sir Whistler Webster. 1 vol., 1768–78

3. *Foundry:*

"Westall's Book of Pannyngrydge" [accounts of an ironmaster at ?Robertsbridge for carrying coal, sand, timber, etc., and for miscellaneous expenses]. 1 vol., 1546–47

Accounts of receipts and disbursements for furnaces [at Robertsbridge?]. 1 vol., 1722–28

Account of iron made and delivered. 1 vol., 1728–36

"Furness Book" [account of general receipts and disbursements]. 1 vol., 1729–33

Account book of a London foundry. 1 vol., 1731–32

Account of disbursements for furnace at ?Beech Farm or ?Robertsbridge. 1 vol., 1733–36

Account of Robertsbridge forge. 1 piece, 1735

4. *Miscellaneous*

Tithe-book for Hastings. 1 vol., 1651

Personal accounts of rector of All Saints Church, Hastings. 1 vol., 1725–29/30

Miscellaneous accounts, tax receipts, bills, receipts for goods and services, notes on foundry accounts, etc. 47 pieces pasted into a contemporary volume, ca.1728–35

Account book of [?rector of] All Saints, St. Clements, and other churches in Hastings showing (1) fees and marriage licenses, (2) mackerel fishery accounts, and (3) tithes. 1 vol., 1729–40

II. CORRESPONDENCE:

Anonymous, to Sir Anthony Browne's steward at Battle re employment of builders and labourers there. 1539?

Ashburnham, Thomas, to Sir Anthony Browne's chaplain, re various personal affairs. 2 letters, >1555

Browne, Thomas, to Sir Richard Ambrose re recruiting men and horses. n.d. (16th cent.)

Durant, Nicholas, to Sir Richard Ambrose re readying men and horses. n.d. (16th cent.)

[Hunlatt?], Thomas, to Sir Richard Ambrose re sending the clothes of Lord Dacres to "Byslyett."

[Crownett?], Anthony, to Sir Robert Smith re Viscount Montague's retainers. 1583

Stillingfleet, J., to Paul Joddrell re a lease. 1722

Juke, William, to Sir Thomas Webster, 1st Bart., re a forge. 1728

Morgan, John, to Sir Thomas Webster re making wire. 1728/29

Collins, Arthur, to Sir Thomas Webster, 1st Bart., re the Robertsbridge estate. 1743

Correspondence between John Churchill and Sir Whistler

Webster re the lease of furnaces at Robertsbridge. 7 letters, 1753–54

III. DEEDS AND CHARTERS:
Deeds of sale and gift, leases, mortgages, recoveries, final concords, exemplifications, and all other official conveyances of land. The following places are named in five or more deeds:
Buckinghamshire.
Bourton (14) 1639–99
Essex.
Copthall (5) 1707–32
Newbury Farm, Barking Parish (5) 1694–1749
Ongar (19) 1588–1701
Kent.
Lenham (27) 1602–88
London. (39) 1641–1778
Somersetshire.
Sandford Orcas (15) 1640–87
Sussex.
Barnhorn (25) 1660–1747
Battle (181) 1548–1776
Bodiam (26) 1558–1646
Robertsbridge (46) 1621–1774

IV. FINANCIAL:
Bonds (mainly involving Sir Thomas Webster) for the payment of monies, for the performance of covenants re conveyance of property, for good behaviour in office, etc. 32 pieces, 1588–1750
Extract from Pipe Roll re Sir Richard Minshull and payments on the manor of Gobions. 1636
Quitclaim by Elizabeth Wynn to T. Jorden of all debts. 1646
Receipts for various sums of money. 5 pieces, 1656–1735
Deeds, charter-parties, and other documents re shipping and the sale of ships or shares in ships. 13 pieces, 1683–1733
Agreement between R. Minshull and W. Blount to raise the interest rate on a mortgage. 1695

Acknowledgement of indebtedness by Henry Whistler to his daughter Elizabeth Boylston in the sum of £900. 1697

Assignments and releases of various sums of money, chiefly from legacies. 8 pieces. 1698–1741

Deed of composition of 5s. in the pound by creditors of Jeffrey Little, merchant, late of London, Sir Thomas Webster standing security. 1703

Agreements re sales of wood, chiefly involving Sir Thomas Webster. 7 pieces, 1711–31

Letter of license by Eliz. Waie *et al.* to John Pearce of Waltham, insolvent. 1723

Drafts and bills of exchange concerning Sir Thomas Webster. 3 pieces, 1727–43

Covenant between W. Northey and T. Webster re the payment of £16,400. 1727/28

Bankruptcy papers of J. Fowke and T. Burrell, founders. 3 pieces, 1736–44

James Garth's account for sorting and preparing title deeds to the Battle estate. 1 piece, 1775

V. LEGAL:

Declaration in an action of assumpsit brought by Ninian Thatcher against Abraham Thatcher. 1593

Documents re a series of lawsuits over tithes on Ongar, Essex. 6 pieces, 1594–1617

Orders and Decree by the Court of Wards and Liveries in the case of Mary and Anne Copley *v.* Josiah Tomlinson re manor of Ongar, Essex. 3 pieces, 1627

Deed of release and quitclaim by Anthony and Robert Dormer to executors of the will of Elizabeth, Lady Dormer. 1633

Writ of execution of decree in Chancery re the will of George Porter. 1641

Summons by Court of Wards and Liveries to show why injunction concerning the heirs of Ongar, Essex, should not be dissolved. 1641

Award in a dispute between T. Jorden, administrator of the affairs of T. Haddiloe, dec., and Elizabeth, relict of T. Wynn. 1645

Award in a dispute between Sir Richard Minshull of Ongar Park and Anthony Hill of High Ongar, yeoman. 1655

Schedule of actions concerning property of Minshull family. 1657–72

Articles of partnership between H. Sommers and J. Jacob to carry out the trade of dyer in Southwark. 1677

Mary Meverell's release to Godfrey Webster and George Grove of her dower rights. 1697

Order for the observance of the Lord Chancellor's order re the guardianship of H. Summers. 1700

Papers re the distribution of the estate of H. Summers, of which Godfrey Webster was the sole executor. 24 pieces, 1701–07

Sir Godfrey Webster's release to Mr. Bartholomew etc. of certain property devised by Samuel Meverell to be sold and divided among his heirs. 1717

Petition by the children of Sir Thomas Webster re the will of their grandfather, Henry Whistler. 1719

Petition by T. Webster to the Lord Chancellor for examination of Henry Whistler's will. 1719

Sir Thomas Webster's power of attorney to Edward Purser to collect rents in Hartshorne Lane, London. 1719

Papers re the transfer of Whistler Webster's interest in properties inherited from Henry Whistler. 12 pieces, ca.1734

Papers concerning the sale of the inheritance from Henry Whistler by Sir Thomas Webster. 6 pieces, ca.1734

Draft indenture between Sir Thomas Webster and Joseph and Elisha Biscoe and Samuel Hutchins re the settlement of an estate. 1739

Summary of actions re the estate of Henry Whistler. 2 pieces, ca.1744 and ca.1761

Papers in the suit of Sir Whistler Webster *v.* Sir Edmond Thomas re the will of Lady Jane Webster, relict of Sir Thomas Webster. 13 pieces, 1753<

Papers in the suit between Sir Whistler Webster and Christ's Hospital, London, re repair of a tenement. 3 pieces, 1771–74

VI. ESTATE AND LOCAL AFFAIRS:
    1. *Court Rolls and other Court Records:*
      Battle:
        Court rolls, including views of frankpledge (called "hundreds" throughout 1559 but properly identified

thereafter). 45 rolls, now disbanded, for the following years.

1541–42	1581–82	1600
1544–45	1582–83	1601
1545–46	1583–84	1602
1553–54	1585–86	1605
1554–55	1586–87	1606
1555–56	1587	1607–08
1556–57	1588–89	1608–09
1557–58	1589–90	1609–10
1558–59	1591–92	1611
1572–73	1592–93	1612
1577	1593–94	1613
1577–78	1594–95	1614
1578–79	1595–96	1615
1579–80	1596–97	1618
1580–81	1597–98	1631

Court book, compiled early 16th century, covering the years 1245–1532; continued contemporaneously through 1580. 1 vol.

Court registers (containing minutes and proceedings of manor court and court baron at Battle, including surrenders of tenantry, letters of attorney, and other related documents as evidence for the courts, bound into 6 volumes covering the years: 1631–78 (lacking 1646–55), 1677–85, 1686–96, 1697–1711, 1711–21, and 1721–37.

Court register (containing minutes of courts leet, view of frankpledge, etc., with appointments of officers, for manor of Battle bound into one volume) covering the years 1700–27.

Agmerhurst (Sussex):

Court register (containing minutes and proceedings of manor court and court baron at Agmerhurst and Barnhorn, including presentments of homage, admissions and surrenders of tenantry, appointments of officers, and other related documents as evidence for the courts, bound into one volume) covering the years 1627–1723

Miscellaneous court records. 10 pieces. 1584–1641

See also Barnhorn, below.

Barnhorn (Sussex):

Court register (containing minutes and proceedings of manor court and court baron at Barnhorn, with some early entries for Agmerhurst as well, including presentments of homage, admissions and surrenders of tenantry, appointments of officers, and other related documents as evidence for the courts, bound into one volume) covering the years 1547–1728

Miscellaneous court records (including preliminary drafts, memoranda, etc.). 17 pieces, 1560–1632

Beigham (Kent):

Miscellaneous court records (including preliminary drafts, memoranda, etc.). 7 pieces, 1553–70

Bodiam (Sussex):

Court roll, now disbanded, containing entries for the following years: 1645–46, 1648, 1650

2. *Rentals and Surveys, with Related Documents:*

Battle:

Rentals (some quitrents or leasehold rents only; most including the manor of Barnhorn). 98 pieces, for the following years: 1594, 1638, 1652, 1665, 1678–83, 1685–86, ca.1704, 1709–10, 1713–37

Extent of woods in Battle manor. 1 piece, ca.1600?

Survey of Chaunceysland in Battle. 1659

Agmerhurst (Sussex):

Rentals. 2 pieces, 1594, 1652

Barnhorn (Sussex):

See Battle *above*

Ewhurst (Sussex):

Rental, including Udimer. 1 vol., 1624/25–30

Ongar (Essex):

Rental of lands in the parishes of High Ongar and Stanford Rivers, Essex. 1696

Swinham (Dorsetshire?):

Rental. 1594

Miscellaneous:

Rental of Hastings College. 1594

Plat of the manor of Gobions, Essex. 1608

Certificates of the value of two thirds of the estate of Francis Browne, 3rd Viscount Montague, sequestered for recusancy, in Arundel and Chichester rapes, and in Lewes and Pevensey rapes. 2 pieces, 1651

Plot of a messuage called Flips-his in parishes of Marks Tay and East Thorpe (Essex). 1672

Terrier of the glebe-lands etc. of the rector of Ewhurst (Sussex). 1678

Particular of the estate of Sir Whistler Webster in East Grinstead and Worth (Sussex) and Leighfield (Surrey). ca.1760?

Particular of farm and lands at Fairlight (Sussex) belonging to Sir Whistler Webster. ca.1760?

3. *General:*

Award by Henry VIII concerning lands of Sir Roger Leukenor in Bodiam, Ilford, and elsewhere. 1542.

Decree of Lords Bailiffs of Romney Marsh concerning inheritance of lands there. 1605

License to W. Langham to deal as he will with woods on Chaunces land. 1621

Covenant between Sir Ralph Bosville *et al* suing out a writ of partition of the castle and manor of Bodiam. 1622

Covenant between J. Bracker *et al.* re lands in Bodiam. 2 pieces, 1623

Agreement between T. Alchorne, gent., and W. Jorden, yeoman, re repair of fences in town of Battle. 1626/27

Charles I. Commission to William, Lord Petre, William Lord Maynard, John Bramston, and John Wright, for distinguishing and setting forth the boundaries of the parishes of High Ongar and Stanford Rivers, Essex. 1626/27

Agreement between G. Cole and T. Wattell for the latter to keep £20 remaining due on purchase price of lands in Cokesfield and Wattlesworth until released of all claims. 1650

Lord General's tax receipt to J. Taylor for lands in Battle. 1653

Receipt to W. Pukfet for a parliamentary tax on land in Barnhorn. 1654

Release and discharge to Francis Browne, 3rd Viscount

Montague, for all arrears of rent (£550) arising out of manor and rectory of Lenham. 1656

License from Francis Browne, 3rd Viscount Montague, to T. Bunche to plough and plant certain lands in Battle. 1680

Agreement between H. Whistler and W. Pawley and Edward Dallow re the new works and construction at York waterworks. 1682

[Sir Thomas Webster's?] agreements with a bricklayer re building a house at Battle. 2 pieces, 1721

Deed of sale by Richard Hay to John, Lord Ashburnham, and Sir Thomas Webster, of furnace-bellows and other implements, at Beach Furnace in Battle. 1724

Undertaking by George de Horne to spend any money received from fire insurance on repairs to a messuage in London. 1727

Bill to Sir Thomas Webster from J. Robinson Lytton for rent and wood of Robertsbridge forge, 1736–40

Schedule of mortgages on Copthall and an estate in Derby, from Sir Thomas Webster to J. Hopkins. ca.1742

Agreement between Sir Whistler Webster and J. Churchill re repairs and carpentry work at Robertsbridge forge, with account of a rental. 3 pieces, 1754–60

Memorial of tenants of Robertsbridge to Sir Whistler Webster re navigation of the Rother river. 1760?

VII. PERSONAL AND FAMILY:

Notes and extracts from official records concerning history of Webster and Cheke families, including Pedigree of Cheke Family of Bruton, Somerset, extract from will of John Webster (1494), and copies of the wills of Hugh Webster of Chesterton (1503), John Webster of St. Margaret's Southwark (1503/04), George Webster of East Greenwich, Kent (1574), and William Webster of Eaton, Bedfordshire (1587).

Will of Margaret Drayton, late wife of Richard Drayton of Hackington. 1558, proved 1559

Will of David Drayton of Canterbury. 1623/24, proved 1623/24

Articles of the marriage settlement agreed upon between

Edward Cheek, citizen and soap-maker of London, Gabriel Whistler of Combe, Henry Whistler of London, and Mary Whistler, daughter of Henry. 1678

Will of Katherine Jorden, mother-in-law of Sir Godfrey Webster. 1690, proved 1690

Will of Thomas Jorden of London, brother-in-law of Sir Godfrey Webster. 1692/93, proved 1693

Extract from the Pipe Roll recording Sir Thomas Webster's contribution to the defense of Ulster, for which he was created baronet. 1703

Writ directing Sir Thomas Webster, as sheriff of Essex, to transfer his office to William Pett. 1704

Commission to Sir Thomas Webster as Lt. Colonel of foot, 1715

Commissions to Sir Thomas Webster as Dep. Lieutenant of Essex. 2 pieces, 1720, 1722

Will of Sir Thomas Webster, 1st Bart. 1723/24

Appointment by William Wake, Abp. of Canterbury, of Silas Drayton to curacy of Cranbrook, Kent. 1724

Will of Lady Jane Webster, widow of Sir Thomas. 1753, proved 1760

Will of Henry King of Northiam (Sussex), carpenter. 1760

ELLESMERE COLLECTION
ca.13,000 pieces, ca.1150–1803

The political and financial fortunes of the Egerton family, together with the famous collection of books and manuscripts later known as the Bridgewater Library, began with Thomas Egerton (1540–1617), the illegitimate son of a minor Cheshire knight. Educated at Brasenose College Oxford and trained in the law at Lincoln's Inn, his public career began with the office of Solicitor-General (1581–92), followed in turn by those of Attorney-General (1592–94), Master of the Rolls (1594–1603), Lord Keeper (1596–1603), and finally Lord Chancellor (1603–17).

Egerton served also as an M.P. for Cheshire (1584–87), was knighted in 1594, admitted to the Privy Council (1596), and created Baron Ellesmere (1603) and Viscount Brackley (1616). Widely respected by his colleagues as an able and honest lawyer, he was also a notable patron of literature: John Donne was for a time his secretary, John Davies dedicated a copy of "Orchestra" to him, and numerous other presentation copies of books and manuscripts were added to his growing library.

By his first wife, Elizabeth Ravenscroft, Egerton had two sons (the elder of whom, Sir Thomas Egerton, was killed in Ireland in 1599) and a daughter; his second wife was Elizabeth (More) Polsted Wolley; his third, Alice (Spencer) Stanley, was the widow of Ferdinando Stanley, 5th Earl of Derby. Although the Egerton household was normally divided between his official residence at York House in London and the manor of Harefield in Middlesex, most of the family's lands were located in Cheshire, Shropshire, and North Wales. Many of the Derby estates came into his hands by purchase or by marriage (his own to the Dowager Countess in 1600 and his son John's, a year later, to her daughter Frances Stanley, one of the three co-heirs of Earl Ferdinando).

Lord Chancellor Egerton died in March 1617 and was succeeded by his only surviving son, John Egerton (1579–1649), who was created 1st Earl of Bridgewater two months later. The 1st Earl was an M.P. (for Callington, 1597–98, and Shropshire, 1601), and was a Baron of the Exchequer at Chester (1599–1605), but was notable chiefly for his service as President of the Council of Wales (1631–42) at Ludlow Castle and for being, like his father, both a collector and a patron of literature. Milton's masque "Comus" was first presented for the Earl and his family at Ludlow. After supporting Charles I at the outbreak of the Civil War, the Earl retired to his estate at Ashridge in Little Gaddesden, Herts., and died there in 1649.

He was succeeded by his third but first surviving son John Egerton, 2nd Earl of Bridgewater (1622–86). The 2nd Earl was briefly imprisoned as a Royalist in 1651, but after the Restoration was admitted to the Privy Council (1667) and served as Lord Lieutenant of Buckinghamshire (1660–86), Cheshire and Lancashire (1670–76), and Hertfordshire (1681–86). Like his father and grandfather the Earl took an active interest in literature and compiled a catalog of the Bridgewater Library. He married Elizabeth Cavendish, a daughter of the 1st Duke of Newcastle, and devoted much effort (with only partial success) to restoring the family finances after the immense debts run up by his father. The Earl died in 1686 and was succeeded by his son, John Egerton, 3rd Earl of Bridgewater (1646–1701).

The 3rd Earl, a Whig like his father, also held local offices (he was removed from some of them by James II and reinstated by William), but served more prominently as President of the newly established Board of Trade (1696–99) and as First Lord of the Admiralty (1699–1701). He was also an M.P. for Buckinghamshire (1685–86) and later Speaker of the House of Lords (1697 and 1700) and a Lord Justice of the Realm (1699 and 1700). The Earl had no children by his first wife, Elizabeth Cranfield, a daughter of the 2nd Earl of Middlesex; and at his death in 1701 was succeeded by Scroop Egerton, his son by a second marriage, to Jane Paulet, daughter of the 1st Duke of Bolton.

Scroop Egerton, the 4th Earl and 1st Duke of Bridgewater (1681–1745), was a successful Whig courtier under Anne and George I, and was rewarded with a dukedom in 1720. He married, first, Elizabeth Churchill, a daughter of the Duke and Duchess of Marlborough, and, second, Rachel Russell, daughter of the 2nd Duke of Bedford. Bridgewater died in 1745 and was succeeded briefly by his eldest living son, John, 2nd Duke of Bridgewater (1727–48) and then by a younger son, Francis, 3rd Duke of Bridgewater (1736–1803).

The 3rd Duke, famous for his coal mines and canal building, played little role in politics and died unmarried in 1803, at which time the direct line died out and the dukedom became extinct. The earldom of Bridgewater (and most of the family estates in Buckinghamshire, Hertfordshire, Shropshire, and Yorkshire) devolved to the Duke's cousin, John William Egerton, 7th Earl of Bridgewater (1753–1823), and after his death to his brother Francis Henry Egerton, the 8th Earl (1756–1829), at whose death the earldom in turn became extinct.

Bridgewater House in London, however, together with its famous library (and other family lands, including the estates of Brackley, Northants., and Worsley, Lancs.) were left by the 3rd Duke to his nephew George Granville Leveson-Gower (afterward created 1st Duke of Sutherland), and in turn to Sutherland's second son Francis (1800–57), who assumed the surname Egerton and was created, in 1846, Viscount Brackley and 1st Earl of Ellesmere.

The Earl, a poet in his own right and a patron of scholarship, as well as a noted statesman and politician, was the first President of the Camden Society. He allowed John Payne Collier, the noted Shakespearean critic and forger, to publish both a catalog of some of the noted early books and manuscripts in the Bridgewater Library (1837) and an edition for the Camden Society (1840) of some of the more important early manuscripts (in the course of which work Collier falsified and forged certain manuscripts in the collection). Collier had also acquired approximately 2,500 18th- and early 19th-century English plays from the collection of John Larpent, Examiner of Plays, and subsequently, in 1853, sold them to the Earl. The 1st Earl married Harriet Catherine Greville in 1822, died in 1857, and was succeeded by his son George Granville Francis Egerton (1823–62). Neither the first Earl nor his descendants are represented in the present collection.

Provenance: The Bridgewater House Library was purchased by Mr. Huntington from John Francis Granville Scrope Egerton, 3rd

23

Earl of Ellesmere, in 1917, through the agency of George D. Smith and Sotheby's of London.

Bibliography: Brief summary descriptions of the Ellesmere Collection are to be found in: Historical Manuscripts Commission, *Eleventh Report, Appendix, Part VII* (1888), 126–67; *Huntington Library Bulletin No. 1* (1931) 48–51; and Jean Preston, "Collections of English Historical Manuscripts in the Huntington Library," *Archives* 6 (1963): 96–97. Selected manuscripts from the collection have been edited and published by J. Payne Collier as *The Egerton Papers. A Collection of Public and Private Documents, chiefly illustrative of the Times of Elizabeth and James I* for the Camden Society (London: 1840) and by Anthony G. Petti as *Recusant Documents from the Ellesmere Manuscripts* for the Catholic Record Society (London, 1968), vol. 60.

Twenty-seven medieval and Renaissance volumes of lasting and general significance from the collection are more fully described in *Guide to Medieval and Renaissance Manuscripts in the Huntington Library.** Post-1600 literary manuscripts are listed in *Guide to Literary Manuscripts in the Huntington Library* (San Marino: Huntington Library, 1979). For the Larpent plays, which do not appear in the following description, see Dougald MacMillan, *Catalogue of the Larpent Plays in the Huntington Library* (San Marino: Huntington Library, 1939).

The present collection should be distinguished from the "Egerton Papers" in the British Library, which were bequeathed to that institution, together with funds for additional acquisitions, by the 8th Earl of Bridgewater. Supplementary Egerton family papers (chiefly estate papers and accounts for the Brackley estate) may be found in the Northamptonshire Record Office.

Remarks on the Following Description: The Ellesmere Collection at the Huntington Library includes the personal letters and papers of the Egerton family (although there are relatively few household and estate accounts, and very few papers concerning the Bridgewater Canal), but is richer still in two other related areas: the official and semiofficial papers relating to offices held by various members of the family (most notably Lord Chancellor Egerton)

---

* For a list of these mss., see below, section 8, pp. 28–29.

and the literary manuscripts (many of them presentation copies) which comprised the family's own important library at Bridgewater House.

Prior to the purchase of the collection by Mr. Huntington, a ten-volume handlist entitled "Calendar of the Bridgewater and Ellesmere Manuscripts" was compiled at Bridgewater House. In the course of that compilation each manuscript was given a permanent reference number (either a simple number and/or, in the case of individual volumes, a combination of numbers and letters according to their Bridgewater House press-marks) and was assigned to one of numerous subject categories which were, in turn, grouped broadly into chronological periods as follows: to 1617 (the death of Lord Chancellor Ellesmere); 1617 to 1649 (the death of the 1st Earl of Bridgewater); 1649 to 1686 (the death of the 2nd Earl); 1686 to 1801 (the death of the 3rd Earl); 1701 to 1745 (the death of the 1st Duke of Bridgewater); 1745 to 1803 (the death of the 3rd Duke of Bridgewater); Miscellany ca.1200–1800. There are no 19th-century papers.

Although this organization is inconsistent with current archival practice, and the subject categories in particular often overlap, both the assigned reference numbers and the general format of the ten-volume "Calendar" have enjoyed wide currency in the intervening eighty years. We have therefore decided, reluctantly, to retain the present system while making extensive descriptive comments on each of the original subject categories as listed below.

All separate volumes are specifically noted, as are all wills and *inquisitions post mortem*. Dates, when available, are given for each item noted individually.

Following these comments are: a list of authors, both individual and corporate, represented in the collection by five or more pieces (including drafts and contemporary copies); a list of places appearing in five or more deeds; a list of court rolls in the collection.

When the collection was purchased in 1917, the Egerton family chose to retain some 1,600 manuscripts of personal or literary interest or value, but facsimiles of these items were subsequently provided to the Huntington and have been integrated into the original collection. These facsimiles are not distinguished as such in the following description.

PART I: TO 1617

PERSONAL

1. *Letters, Accounts, etc. (EL 1–433):* Personal correspondence of Lord Chancellor Egerton, his family, friends, clients, and would-be clients, on various topics including domestic and personal affairs, estate, financial, and legal matters (including proposals for marriages with his daughter), patronage, and some politics; lists and accounts (many receipted bills) of household and personal possessions (chiefly plate) and expenses; 2 checkrolls of the Egerton household; Egerton's warning to his son, the future 1st Earl, against the Dowager Countess of Derby; documents concerning another John Egerton's death in a duel with Edward Morgan in 1611.

2. *Notes for speeches and on legal and political matters (EL 434–497):* notes and memoranda, many by Lord Chancellor Egerton, on legal cases, statutes, points of law, political matters; some notes for Ellesmere's speeches in Parliament; includes two volumes of legal notes in French, arranged topically; a volume of readings by Ambrose Gilberde (on 34–35 Henry VIII c.5) and John Denshall (on 4 Henry VII c.24); an alphabetical digest of the law, with notes by Ellesmere; "John Penry's Journal," including his appeals for justice, a confession of faith, etc.

3. *Appointments and grants to Lord Chancellor Egerton (EL 498–544):* appointments to and grants of office, grants of lands, fees and annuities, etc., to Egerton by various individuals and institutions (including the crown), 1581–1607; includes half-yearly accounts of fees for faculties paid to Egerton, 1612–16.

4. *Deeds and Miscellaneous Papers (Chiefly Estate and Manorial) (EL 545–746):* deeds and various supplementary notes and legal documents chiefly concerning the Egerton estates and those of related families or associates. For lists of deeds and court rolls, see below, pp. 74–77.
Also includes a rental for Tatton (Cheshire), *temp.* Elizabeth, three *inquisitions post mortem* (for Lord Chancellor Egerton, taken 1623, Margaret the wife of Sir Fulk de Pen-

brugge, 1400, and Peter Sergeante, 1586) and eight original, copy, or draft wills (for John Bothe, Archdeacon of Hereford, 1542, William Cecil, Baron Burghley, 1598, Ambrose Dudley, 1st Earl of Warwick, 1590, Lady Mary Egerton of Ridley, 1597, Lord Chancellor Egerton, 1615, Edward Manners, 3rd Earl of Rutland, 1583, William Pymme, 1609, and William Wettenhall, 1570), notes and drafts of marriage and other property settlements concerning the Egerton family, and a few legal papers concerning suits over property (including that involving Sir Edward and Lord Francis Norreys).

5. *Rentals and Miscellaneous Papers re Land (EL 747–767):* accounts, receipts, and miscellaneous notes and memoranda concerning Egerton lands. For lists of deeds and court rolls, see below, pp. 74–77.

6. *Derby Papers (EL 768–993):* letters and papers of the Stanley family, earls of Derby, related to the Egertons through the marriages of Lord Chancellor Egerton to Alice, Dowager Countess of Derby (widow of Ferdinando Stanley, the 5th Earl) and of John Egerton, afterward 1st Earl of Bridgewater, to Frances Stanley, one of the three daughters and co-heirs of Ferdinando. Includes letters to and from various members of the Stanley family re family and business affairs; legal papers concerning proceedings in Chancery (ca.1617–19) and Exchequer (ca.1625–29) courts re lands purchased by the 1st Earl of Bridgewater from William Stanley, 6th Earl of Derby, and proceedings in the Court of Wards and Liveries in the 1630s re the property of the heirs of Ferdinando, 5th Earl of Derby; papers re various legal cases involving Alice Stanley Egerton, the Dowager Countess; a volume of copies of documents re the 5th Earl and the settlement of his estate; some material concerning the Isle of Man, of which the earls of Derby were the hereditary lords, *temp.* Elizabeth I, including books of charges at Castle Peele and Castle Rushen on the Isle of Man; notes and memoranda re Stanley lands and finances, including three rentals of the Derby estates (two undated, *temp.* Elizabeth and James I, the third 15–16 Elizabeth) and a *valor* of the possessions of Earl Ferdinando, 1593; a roll of extracts from the register of Whithorn Priory, Scotland, made in 1504.

Also includes a volume of copies of documents concerning the 5th Earl of Derby and the settlement of his estate, including the *inquisitions post mortem* of Thomas, Edward, and Ferdinando Stanley, 2nd, 3rd, and 5th Earls, the will of Edward the 3rd Earl, and lists of lands and deeds of the family.

7. *Pedigrees, family notes and verse, etc. (EL 994–1120):* pedigrees and genealogical notes concerning the Egerton, Stanley, and many other families; includes volumes of arms of gentlemen in the county palatine of Chester *temp.* James I, of pedigrees and coats of arms of the Spencer family together with those of English and European ruling families *temp.* Elizabeth, and of the Egerton and related families; two volumes of colored coats of arms for the nobility; a volume of the names of those promoted to the dignity of "equitum auratorum" for serving with the Earl of Essex in France, with pedigrees of Elizabethan and Jacobean peers; "The coppie of a Book written by Mr. Ttesremos" being an account of the various orders of nobility with sumptuary regulations, ca.1587.

Also includes occasional verse relating to affairs of the Egerton family, with volumes of verse from Nathaniel Harris (in Latin and Greek) and from Brasenose College, Oxford (in Latin) on the death of Sir Thomas Egerton, the son of the Lord Chancellor; also, a legal and historical commonplace book.

8. *Miscellaneous and Literary Manuscripts (EL 1121–1182A):* chiefly individual volumes, many dedicated to Lord Chancellor Egerton, many with original bindings, which are grouped here for convenience into the following categories:

  A. *Medieval and Renaissance volumes of significant general interest, which are described in full in the* Guide to Medieval and Renaissance Manuscripts in the Huntington Library: Chaucer's "Canterbury Tales" (the "Ellesmere Chaucer") (EL 26 C 9); Gower's "Confessio Amantis" (the "Stafford Gower") (EL 26 A 17); a collection of Middle English poetry, chiefly Lydgate (EL 26 A 13); "The Master of Game," by Edward, 2nd Duke of York (EL 35 B 63); a collection of chronicles and other works, including part of Geoffrey of Monmouth's "History of the Kings of England" (EL 34 C 9); a collection of French poetry, including Gautier de Metz, Jean de Meun, and Jacobus de Cessolis (EL 26 A 3); Sir John Fortescue's "The Governance of England and other works" (EL 34 C 18); three statute books (EL 9 H 10, 34 A 8, 34 B 23); Littleton's "Tenures" (EL 34 B 60); the "Summa Summarum" of William of Pagula (EL 9 H 3); an alphabetical index to canon and civil law (EL 34 A 5); a volume of commentaries on civil law (EL 7 H 9); a volume containing the "Modus coronationis in regno Anglie" and the "Modus tenendi Parliamentum" (EL 35 B 61); a bible (EL 9 H 4); a book of hours (EL 34 A 1); a psalter (EL 9 H 17); a gradual (EL 35 B 53); the "Processional of Dame Margery Byrkenhead" (EL 34 B 7); a martyrology and customal of the College of Boni Homines at Ashridge, Buckinghamshire (EL 9 H 15); the "Satires" of Juvenal and Persius (EL 34 B 6); the "Institutio Grammatica" of Priscian (EL 9 H 11); the "Flos Decretorum" of Johannes Hispanus and other texts (EL 7 H 8); "De Regimine Principum" of Aegidius Romanus and Nicholas Tryvet's commentaries on Boethius (EL 9 H 9); an album, now disbound, containing miniatures from Venetian *ducali*, chiefly 16th century (EL 9 H 13); a copy of Sir Philip Sidney's metrical version of the psalms (EL 35 C 39-11637).

B. *Government, Politics, and Administration:* a treatise on political science entitled "Observations," by T. B.; "Three moneths observation of the Lowe Countries especially Holland" by J[ohn] S[elden]; a treatise on the office of Lord Chancellor of England, by Francis Thynne; "The Plea betwene the Aduocate and the Ant'advocate concerning the Bathe and Bacheler knightes . . ." by Francis Thynne; a collection of notes taken out of records in the Tower of London, especially dealing with "The Kinge his oath, office, Aucthoritie, Royall and Prerogatyve"; "Summaria quedam descriptio Recordum repositorum in Archiuis Domine Rne. Elizabethe & collecta per Arthur Agarde anno domini 1602," dedicated to Egerton by Ralphe Starkey; a treatise on a revenue belonging to the Queens of England called Aurum Reginae; a copy of "Leicester's Commonwealth"; a copy of "Burghley's Commonwealth"; "Certaine observations vppon a libell published this present yeare of 1592 Intituled a declaration of the true causes of the greate troubles presupposed to be intended against the Realme of England."

C. *Law:* a volume of extracts from the statutes of Edward I; commentaries on statutes, with a list of kings from 1043 to Elizabeth I; a volume entitled "Peticiones coram domino rege ad Parliamentum . . ." [from 1290]; a legal commonplace book, including comments on various subjects arranged topically, with extracts from records, etc.; an "Indice ou Tiabla Alphabetique des Actions Recordes et Pleas mises avaunt per Monsr. Plowden et ses Comentaries . . ."; "Obseruations gathered out of Authors De iure maiestatis"; a tract comparing English and Hebrew institutions entitled "The Lawes of England"; "A short explication of some things contained in Canutus his lawes."

D. *Literature and Philosophy:* verses in Latin and Greek by R[ichard] B[rett] on the deliverance of James I from the Gunpowder Plot; a Latin poem by George "Casus" titled "Successio et Gesta Judicum Israeliticorum"; Latin verse by George Goodwin; "The Olympian Catastrophe" by Sir Arthur Gorges; "The Ho^ble, Lorde & Lady of Huntingdon's Entertainement . . . att the house of Ashby," by John Marston; "Animadversions uppon the Annotacions & Correctons of some imperfectons of impressones of Chaucers workes . . ." by Francis Thynne; "Emblemes and Epigrames" by Francis Thynne; "Parte of the fyrst parte of the Commentaries of Great Britain," by Francis Thynne; a history of England from the foundation of the world to February 1592; "Fortunia," a Latin play, 1615; a Latin verse on each English sovereign from William I to Elizabeth I; a volume of miscellaneous verses.

A prose treatise on honor by Robert Ashley; an analysis of Cicero's Manilian Oration by Thomas Bing, 1577; a volume titled "Thesis Comitiis ipsis Cantabrigie publice proposita et propugnata 5. Jul 1615" with a text by Samuel Brooke titled "De Auxilio divinae gratiae et Libero Arbi-

trio"; a Latin discourse on equivocation by Roger Fenton;
a Latin discourse on "Tranquillitas Vera" by Tobias Shaw;
a Latin treatise on quodlibetical questions by William
Wood; a commonplace book including notes or comments on quodlibetical questions; a volume titled "Bar-
laami. Vetusti et eruditi Monachi Liber de Papae princi-
patu. Auctore editionis atque interpretationis Joanne
Luido"; a volume titled "De gradibus Academicis Concio
ad Clerum, habita Cantabrigiae"; a volume of notes on
medieval metaphysics and scholasticism.

E. *Religion, the Church, and Sermons:* "A reiuewe of Dr.
Kellison's suruey of the first ground, or foundation (as
he maketh it) of religion" by Henry Bankes; a volume
titled "De disciplina Ecclesiae Primitauae" by "R[oger?]
F[enton?] Capellanus"; a treatise on six religious holidays
by Roger Fenton; a polemic titled "The church faulle"
by Thomas Jones; a translation by Thomas Master of
"Christian meditationes vppon fourc Psalmcs of Dauid"
by Philip Mornay, Lord of Plessis; a volume titled "The
rites and customes that the auncient Jewes used in their
Repentaunce . . ." by "R[ichard] B[rett]"; a treatise on
the state of religion in England by John Norden; an anti-
Catholic account of religion in various countries by Sir
Edwin Sandys; a treatise on "The perille of Pluralities,
non-residence and choppinge of Benefices" by John
Shawe, 1598; a volume titled "Refutatio Roberti Bellar-
mini et Calumniarum, quae asperguntur Remotio per
Rodolphum Ravens Oxon . . ."; a volume of biblical passages or lessons assigned to different days of the year.

"The Rehearsall Sermon 1605" by R. Barlow; a sermon
preached by Bp. John King before James I at Oatland,
1604; a sermon by Owen Neale; an anonymous sermon
on Hebrews 12:3.

F. *Miscellaneous:* a Latin dissertation on spectres by Ralph
Hutchins; a description of Milford Haven by George
Owen, 1595; two copies of "A Discorse on the Arte of
Bitting" with diagrams, by Arthur Sendaye; two copies
of "The Vse of the Mathematicall Scale, Inuented by
Jo. Speidell"; "The Fowles of Heauen," with water color
illustrations, by Edward Topsell, ca.1613; a treatise on

the ports and east coast of England, and the defenses
there; the "Ellesmere Part-books," a set of six volumes
of Italian madrigals, with music, set for different voices
(Canto, Basso, Tenore, Alto, Quinto, and Sesto), ca.1610.
Also a very few miscellaneous personal papers, including an undated description of the duties of household officials, with lists
and instructions, and a set of rules for the conduct of a noble
household.

See also Part VII, Sect. 3 below, pp. 69.

ROYAL (EL 1183–1229)

Miscellaneous letters, documents, and notes concerning the
English crown and Court, including: draft of a letter from
the Council at Windsor to the Council at London concerning
Somerset's withdrawal from Edward VI, 1549; copy proclamation of Queen Mary concerning the commission of enquiry
into claims to serve at her coronation, 1553; copy proclamation of Elizabeth I on her accession, 1558; letters to Elizabeth
concerning her intended invasion of Scotland (1560) and other
political matters, including a working draft of Parliament's
petition to the Queen to carry out sentence on Mary Queen
of Scots, 1586; copies, drafts, and some original letters re the
Earl of Essex's rebellion; Deed of Association of Lincolns Inn
for the defense of Queen Elizabeth, signed and sealed by
87 persons, ?1584; letters and papers concerning James I and
Prince Henry; notes re the proposed union of Scotland and
England; James I's speech to Parliament of 1621.

Separate volumes include: a list of public officials, nobility,
churches and livings, officers of the law courts, etc., *temp.*
Elizabeth I [1579<>1587]; the order of the coronation of
James I and Queen Anne at Westminster Abbey; a brief dis-
course on the union of Scotland and England, addressed to
James I.

OFFICIAL

1. *Crown grants, appointments, etc. (EL 1230–1481):* chiefly
drafts and copies, stemming from Egerton's legal work (as
Solicitor-General, Attorney-General, Lord Keeper, and Lord
Chancellor), of royal grants of lands and offices, pardons, licenses, commissions, charters, etc.; includes petitions to the

crown for confirmations of grants, letters to Egerton (several from Walsingham, Burghley, and Cecil) concerning grants and patronage, and royal warrants to Egerton as Lord Keeper or Chancellor for issuing commissions, appointments, etc.; some papers re concealed lands; sections of legal documents concerning Wollaston, Northamptonshire; two volumes of registers of signed bills, privy seals, commissioners warrants, etc., received by Lord Chancellor Egerton and passed under the Great Seal, 1609–11 and 1611–13.

2. *Creation of honors (EL 1482–1515):* copies and drafts, again related to Lord Chancellor Egerton's official work, of charters of creation of various earldoms (many 1606–07) and other titles of honor (including some copies of 15th- and 16th-century letters patent); an index of letters patent granting honors, lands, etc. to Prince Henry, son of James I, ca.1610–11.

3. *Crown lands and affairs (EL 1516–1589h):* papers concerning various aspects of crown lands, particularly letters (many from Egerton to Burghley) and papers (including surveys, accounts of sales, etc.) re commissions of 1589 and 1599 for the sale of crown lands; notes and copies of documents re lands held by other members of royal family (e.g. the jointure of Henry VII's queen, Elizabeth of York); some notes and accounts of revenues owed to crown from royal lands, including a copy of Edmund Dudley's book of accounts of money received on behalf of crown, 1504–08; a report on the decay of royal revenues and suggestions for remedying this through escheats, liveries, wardships, etc., *temp.* Elizabeth; deeds, accounts, and court rolls for manors in the lordship of Bromfield and Yale. For lists of deeds and court rolls see below, pp. 74–77.

4. *Foreign Affairs (EL 1590–1678):* brief tracts, reports, notes, and letters relating to foreign affairs, particularly Anglo-Spanish relations and Spanish activities in Europe, *temp.* Elizabeth and James I, including documents re the Court of Admiralty proceedings at suit brought against English piracy by the Spanish ambassador ca.1611–13; extracts from and notes on various diplomatic treaties (with France 1572 and 1596; with the Netherlands *temp.* Elizabeth); notes and letters of instruc-

tion to Lord Chancellor Egerton re preparing commissions concerning foreign affairs; letter and report concerning Sir Thomas Bodley's missions to the Netherlands in the 1590s; papers re Francis Cherry's embassy to Moscow in 1598; reports and letters to John Egerton, later 1st Earl of Bridgewater, from English diplomats and other agents abroad, chiefly from Richard Daniell (9 letters, from Vienna, Ratisbon, Paris, 1613–14) and Henry Tweedy (5 letters, from Italy, ca.1606–15).

Separate volumes include: "Ye Compleat Ambassador," being instructions for Sir Francis Walsingham, sent by Elizabeth to the French king, 1570; "The Suddaine and ill digested opinions of G. L." concerning Spain's offer of a treaty with Queen Elizabeth; 3 copies of "An Epistell directed unto the Lords and States of the Empire of Germany written 1564, yet principallie unto the Lord or Earle of Embden," one bound with Bacon's "Certaine observacions upon a Libell published . . . 1592 intituled a Declaration of the true causes of the great troubles pre-supposed to be intended against the Realme of Englande"; a commonplace book of copies of letters, documents, tracts, etc. re Anglo-European (chiefly Anglo-Spanish) affairs, *temp.* Elizabeth and James I.

5. *Admiralty (EL 1679–1681):* a short report on the state of the English Navy in 1584; letter from Sir John Popham and Lord Chancellor Egerton re Sir Thomas Williams' suits in the Court of Admiralty and other courts, 1590; copy of the letters patent creating Lord Howard of Effingham Lord High Admiral of England, 1585.

6. *Colonies (EL 1682–1683):* copy of a report attributed to Battista Antonelli, addressed to Philip II, concerning Spanish fortifications in the West Indies, 1594; Capt. Peter Wynne's letter to John Egerton, (later 1st Earl of Bridgewater) from Jamestown, Virginia, including a description of that settlement, 1608.

7. *Militia (EL 1684–1698):* commissions to Lords Lieutenant and their deputies, chiefly for Buckinghamshire; notes on a statute (2 & 3 Edward VI, cap. 2) re runaway soldiers; notes and lists of men fit to bear arms in various places.

8. *Ireland (EL 1699–1747):* letters, reports, commissions, and articles (many drafts) concerning the resettlement of Munster after Desmond's rebellion, 1586–87; a few privy seal warrants to Lord Chancellor Egerton for issuing letters patent concerning Irish affairs; documents and accounts re the Plantation of Ulster, 1610–13; the exemplification by Henry VI of the Irish "Modus tenendi Parliamentum." Separate volumes include: "A Briefe Declaration of the Gouernment of Irelande opening many Corruptions in the same," 1594; Francis Bacon's "Certaine Considerations touching the Plantations in Ireland," 1609; E. S[pencer?]'s "Suruey of the present estate of Ireland Anno 1615."
See also Part III, Official, Sect. 9 below, pp. 57–58.

9. *Wales (EL 1748–1765):* letters and papers chiefly relating to legal affairs in the Council of Wales and to appointments to office in Wales; includes copies of instructions given by Queen Elizabeth to the Council of Wales in 1601 and to Edward la Zouche, Lord Zouche, as President of the Council of Wales, 1602; copy of a speech given by Robert Cecil in the year 43 Elizabeth concerning the Welsh Council; report on a debate and speech given by James I in 1608 on the royal prerogative in relation to the question of jurisdiction in the Welsh marches.

10. *Manors etc. in Flint and Denbigh (EL 1766–1861):* chiefly deeds and miscellaneous papers concerning Egerton and other lands in Flint and Denbigh. For a list of deeds see below, pp. 75–77.

Also includes legal papers re Lord Chancellor Egerton's interest in the rectory of Gresford, the *inquisition post mortem* for Peter Stanley, 1539, a rental of the lands in Denbigh and Merioneth of John Salisbury, the Queen's ward, 1601, and an inventory of the goods and chattel, with particulars of lands, of Sir Robert Salisbury, deceased, 1601.
See also Personal, Section 4 above, pp. 26–27.

11. *Scotland (EL 1862–1873):* letters addressed to Lord Chancellor Egerton on Scottish affairs; speeches (by Egerton and Francis Bacon) and notes on speeches (by Sir Edward Coke,

Sir George Snigg, and Sir David Williams) on Calvins Case, or the case of the *post-nati*, 1608; list of acts hostile to England passed by the Scottish parliament.

12. *Border Affairs (EL 1874–1890):* documents concerning various aspects of affairs on the Anglo-Scottish borders, chiefly *temp.* Elizabeth I, including: a petition to the Privy Council from the town of Berwick with notes on their case; papers re the charges against Ralph Lord Eure as Lord Warden of the Scottish Marches; instructions given by Queen Elizabeth to the Council in the North, 1595, with various reports and drafts for commissions and instructions to be given to the Council; warrants to Egerton for appointments to be made to offices in the Scottish Marches; copy of a letter from Elizabeth I to James VI (afterward James I of Great Britain) as King of Scotland, reproaching him for border raids, 1596, with a copy of his answer.

13. *Jersey and Guernsey (EL 1891–1912):* letters to Lord Chancellor Egerton on legal matters involving Jersey and Guernsey, chiefly concerning the Queen's rights there, and a report by Egerton and Sir Walter Mildmay on this subject, 1584; letters and notes for a case involving the governor (Sir John Peyton) and bailiff (John Herault) of Jersey, ca.1616; a volume containing copies of reports, orders, articles, letters, petitions, etc. re the island of Guernsey and adjoining islands, chiefly 1580–87; a volume containing "The Ecclesiasticall Discipline as it hath been used synce the Church was reformed by the ministers elders and deacons of the Isles of Guerneze, Jerze, Serch and Alderney established," ca.1597.

14. *Universities (EL 1913–1977):* letters, requests for patronage, and complaints addressed to Lord Chancellor Egerton as Chancellor of Oxford, including in particular those from Christ Church re electing a dean, and those re the "town and gown" disputes of 1611; includes also accounts of disputations at Oxford and notes concerning scholarships and fellowships at each of thirteen colleges at Oxford, ca.1610?; a volume titled "Concio Ad Clerum habita Oxoniae Maij 24° 1598."

15. *Ecclesiastical Affairs (EL 1978–2030):* drafts and copies of a few Parliamentary statutes concerning religion; papers concerning the establishment of a Choir College at Hereford Cathedral; institutions to rectories; documents concerning the establishment and jurisdiction of the High Commission, and the controversy surrounding it ca.1608–11. Includes as a separate volume the "petition" of Maurice Gruffyn to Lord Chancellor Egerton and Chief Justice Sir John Popham against simony and other ecclesiastical abuses.

16. *Religious Persecutions (EL 2031–2076):* consists entirely of disbound pages from a volume of extracts from John Foxe's *Actes and Monuments* (chiefly Books VII and VIII).

17. *Recusants (EL 2077–2197a):* examinations by Sir John Popham and others of recusants, and of John Penry, with notes and letters concerning official action against recusancy, including a volume of examinations for the period February–May 1593; certifications or *significavits* from various bishops (Chichester, Coventry & Lichfield, Ely, Gloucester, Hereford, Lincoln, Norwich, Rochester, Salisbury, Winchester) and the Archbishop of Canterbury for the delivery of recusants (listed) in their dioceses to secular powers, 1601. Separate volumes include a discourse "provinge the Lawfulnes of the Othe of Allegiance," by John Goode; "An Humble Supplication [pro-Catholic] to her Majestie in aunswere of a late Proclamation," 1592; an account of various Protestant tenets and heresies, arranged alphabetically; a list of recusants indicted in Oxfordshire, 2–10 James I; a report of "The Case of Praemunire, or, the conviction and attainder of Robert Lalor, priest," 4 James I.

18. *Coinage and the Mint (EL 2198–2285a):* notes and records on the organization and procedures of the Royal Mint; few accounts of monies coined, profits, etc.; copies of earlier grants of office to warden, master, worker of monies, etc.; treatises, letters, and suggestions of Gerard de Malynes concerning money, coinage, and Mint affairs; several papers concerning the transportation of gold out of England, the debased coinage of the 1590s (and how to improve it), and plans to coin

debased coins for Ireland ca.1598–1601; a few notes re the value of various coins, and a volume by Francis Hoffman giving the value of exchange of coins in different countries.

19. *Trade and Monopolies (EL 2286–2469):* drafts, notes, and other papers concerning legal cases involving merchants, guilds, and customs farms; notes, accounts, and records of importing and exporting goods, giving prices, quantities, etc.; notes on and extracts from statutes and proclamations regulating trade; drafts of leases and licenses granting rights to import, export, collect customs, etc., with relevant correspondence; reports and recommendations (chiefly brief and anonymous) on various aspects of English trade and mercantile companies (especially the Merchant Adventurers); letters and documents re the unsuccessful suit of Edward de Vere, 17th Earl of Oxford, for the farm of the Cornish tin mines. Separate volumes include a brief treatise in support of the Merchant Adventurers and "The Vsurer Reformer," a tract against usury attributed by Lord Chancellor Egerton to Sir Thomas Chaloner.

20. *Subsidies and Taxation (EL 2470–2513):* notes and copies of documents re the collection of subsidies; miscellaneous undated lists of men in Middlesex and Buckinghamshire to be rated for loans under the privy seal; accounts of collection of subsidies in the hundreds of Northwich, Esbury, Broxton, and Worall, ca.1589; warrants for levying subsidies, *temp.* Elizabeth & James I; 5 subsidy rolls for James I of subsidies levied on all above rank of baron, 1606–10; accounts of Arthur Maynwaring as collector of three payments on subsidies of 3 James I; a note of assessments for subsidies, with lists of [?justices of the peace] for each of the English counties, 1609.

21. *Strangers (EL 2514–2519):* extract of returns of the 7113 aliens living in and around London, 1593; undated complaints against merchant strangers living and trading in England (*temp.* Elizabeth or James I); record of the number of aliens in various trades and professions, 1593.

22. *The Poor (EL 2520–2527):* notes on statutes and procedures affecting the poor, rogues, vagabonds, etc.; a volume of orders for setting "Roges and ydle persons to woorke" in London, 1597.

23. *Mines (EL 2528–2530):* letter from Sir Francis Walsingham to Egerton re a commission for the assistance of dealers in northern copper mines, 1586; letter from Egerton to Lord Burghley concerning Ralph Bowes' mines and debts, 1592; undated draft commission from Queen Elizabeth to the Earl of Huntingdon, Bishop of Carlisle, and others concerning royal mines in the North.

24. *Fens (EL 2531–2535):* undated notes and draft grants re draining fen land, and the method of conveying fen lands; abstract of a legal case involving rights of common on Erles Fenn in Lincolnshire.

25. *Forests and Hunting (EL 2536–2546):* warrants for commissions dealing with royal game in Buckinghamshire (1566), archery (1596), and the office of Master of the Hawks (1608); a schedule of the divisions of the Forest of Rockingham, Northants., with officers and grantees thereof, *temp.* Elizabeth; includes a volume containing "A Declaracion of the Statute De Charta de foresta collected for the moost part out of Master Trehern's Readinge vpon the sayd statute, aᵒ 12 H.8," "Lectura Mʳⁱ Treherne de statuto de vsura edit. aᵒ 11 H.7 ca.8," extracts from Adam Blackwood, extracts from Pleas of the Forest, writs, inquisitions, etc., and Lord Chancellor Egerton's loose notes.

26. *Parliamentary Affairs (EL 2547–2624):* copies of and extracts from rolls and, later, journals of Parliament (sporadically, from Edward II on); drafts of parliamentary bills dealing with sumptuary legislation (1576), the courts of Justices of the Forest (1576), and an explanation of the statute of 18 Elizabeth for confirmation of grants made to and by the Queen; proposals for (legislation concerning?) outlawries and possible royal profits therefrom, undated, and reordering of the state of the realm, 1559; copies of, or extracts from, speeches delivered by Queen Elizabeth in 1601 (her "Golden Speech"), James I in 1607 and 1616 (to the judges in Star Chamber), Sir John Croke (Speaker of the House of Commons) in 1601, Sir Walter Mildmay in 1581 and 1584, Sir Edward Phellips in 1614 (not given in Parliament), and Sir Christopher Yelverton (Speaker of the House of Commons) in 1597 and 1598;

lists of statutes on various topics; warrants for the preparation of writ of summons to Parliament; a list of royal proclamations, divided into groups by type, Edward I–Henry IV; a memorandum by Lord Chancellor Egerton of "Things to be Considered of before a parlem^t to be called," 1615; a dissertation on the laws and records of England, dedicated to Lord Chancellor Egerton; draft by Egerton endorsed "Memorialles for Judicature. Pro Rege. Pro Bone publico." *temp.* James I. Miscellaneous notes and documents re parliamentary affairs.

Separate volumes include: a collection of speeches in Parliament and the Star Chamber, some by Sir Nicholas Bacon, 1558–71; a collection of speeches by the Lord Keeper (Sir Nicholas Bacon) *temp.* Elizabeth; "An Exposicion of the Kynges Prerogative" and "A Discourse upon the exposicion and understandinge of Statutes" dedicated to Nathaniel Bacon by Sir William Stanforde, 1548; and "The Priuiledges or speciall rights belonging to the Baronage of England" by John Selden.

27. *Privy Council (EL 2625–2628):* copy of "Instructions for the Counsellors appointed to heare and determine the Requests made either to the King or to his Privy Counsell," 1551; copy of a commission to certain counsellors to hear and determine suits preferred to the King or Privy Council, so as to expedite the hearing, 1551; proposals (chiefly mercantile and economic) "for redresse of the state of the Realme," *temp.* Elizabeth; Lord Chancellor Egerton's notes on the opinion of the Council on holding a parliament and raising money, 1615.

28. *Exchequer (EL 2629–2651):* notes on past and present procedures in the Exchequer; several legal documents in suits and other conflicts involving Chidiocke Warder, Clerk of the Pells (especially against Vincent Skinner), 1580–90s; a few letters and other papers concerning appointments to office in the Exchequer. A copy of "Gervasii Tilberiensis de necessariiz Scaccarii obseruantiiz Dialogus" presented to Lord Chancellor Egerton by William Lambarde, 1598.

29. *Star Chamber (EL 2652–2805):* notes and extracts from Star Chamber records re precedents, jurisdiction, procedure,

fees, judgements; few petitions, letters, notes, briefs, particulars, etc. re various cases in Star Chamber (including proceedings against Edmund Campion and case between Edward Dymock and Henry Clinton *or* Fiennes, 2nd Earl of Lincoln); documents re the clerkship of William Mill; papers re serjeant John Hele and the accusations brought against him at the time of Egerton's successful opposition as candidate for the office of Master of the Rolls; letters to Egerton re various Star Chamber affairs and offices; 36 cause lists (chiefly *temp.* James I; one for 1632), many with Egerton's notes; miscellaneous notes and papers dealing with Star Chamber affairs.

Separate volumes include: three compilations of transcripts and extracts from Henrician Council registers (compiled in the later part of the 16th century); compilation of letters and speeches in Star Chamber relating chiefly to Spanish affairs and Anglo-Spanish relations, *temp.* Elizabeth and James I. *See also* Part II, Official, Sect. 13, "Star Chamber" below, p. 52.

30. *Official Matters in the Courts of Law (EL 2806–3042a):* appointments and drafts of appointments of various persons to offices in Chancery; lists and accounts of fees of various offices or for various procedures in courts of law; copies and drafts of oaths taken by various officials; a few notes and papers concerning procedures in Chancery; documents in the dispute between the Six Clerks and the Examiners in Chancery; letters from Thomas Sackville, Baron Buckhurst (afterward 1st Earl of Dorset) and other papers re the office of his client and cousin John Parker in Chancery, ca.1594; letters to Lord Chancellor Egerton requesting patronage or other favors involving Chancery; notes and documents concerning the jurisdictional disputes within and among the courts of law; petitions and other documents concerning charges against Richard Orrell, usher of Chancery, for misdemeanors in office, ca.1600; papers re the objections of the Clerk of the Hanaper to farming out fees for writs; some few documents re the jurisdictional dispute between Lord Chancellor Egerton and Sir Edward Coke. Miscellaneous letters and papers concerning Chancery, including a schedule of small writs issued 33–34 Elizabeth; a collection of the number of writs

made by the Cursitors 34–37 Elizabeth, with names and terms of County Cursitors; "Ordinances provided in Easter Terme Anno 39 Elizabeth by Sir Thomas Egerton . . . [*et al.*] for the remedie of sundry abuses . . . ," concerning the Court of Requests, 1597; a defense of the Court of Requests by Sir Julius Caesar in a paper endorsed "Touchinge the prohibitions and habeas corpus graunted out of the comon pleas, to stay sutors from pleading in ye Court of Whitehall," 1600; an undated list of Doctors of Law in London in term time; an undated list of "Petitions towching Chancery" [Chancery Register].

Separate volumes include an Entry Book of warrants to Chancery in 12 James I and a "Collection as well of all the Kings Maties offices and fees in any the Courtes at Westminster, as of all the offices and fees of his Maties honorable howshold. Togeth^r wth all fees apertaineinge to Captaines and souldio^rs, haueinge charge of Castells, Bullwarkes, and fortresses w^thin ye Realme of England. And likewiese ye offices and fees of his highnes hono^rable howses, Parkes, forrestes, and chases w^thin ye said Realme."

31. *Dockets (EL 3043–5646):* ca.2,600 dockets for the preparation of documents to be issued under the Great Seal, 1592–96, which time Sir John Puckering was Lord Keeper of the Great Seal.

32. *Papers relating to Legal Proceedings (EL 5647–6161):* numerous letters and papers concerning lawsuits involving members of the Brereton family, including: suits involving Dame Jane Brereton (16th century) and Richard and Sir William Brereton (*temp.* Charles II); the case of Richard Brereton *v.* Francis Sherington *et al.* in the Court of the Duchy of Lancaster and in Star Chamber over lands at Stanistreet, Worsley, *temp.* Elizabeth; the case of Richard Brereton *v.* Sir Robert Worsley, in the Court of the Duchy of Lancaster; the case of Richard Brereton of Worsley *v.* Thomas Worsley *et al.* in Star Chamber concerning a forcible entry into Ellenbrook Chapel, 1591; papers concerning the tenure of the manor and lordship of Worsley in Lancashire.

Also papers concerning other legal cases, including those of: Roland and Bridget Egerton *v.* Edward Egerton; the alleged crimes of Thomas Coo, especially as they involved Sir Robert Newdigate and Edward Cage, ca.1600–11; the lands of the Earl of Arundel (chiefly Arundel Castle and Forest) and the case of Sir John Arundel of Treryes *v.* John Arundel of Gwarnacke, chiefly *temp.* Elizabeth; the lands and heirs of William Dacre, 3rd Baron Dacre of the North, and re Lady Anne Dacre; and petitions for assistance from Arthur Hall, imprisoned in the Fleet.

Miscellaneous notes and documents stemming from Lord Chancellor Egerton's legal activities for the Crown (1580s onward), including: occasional petitions, bills of complaint, answers, interrogatories, extracts from the Plea Rolls, briefs, orders of the court, etc.; Egerton's miscellaneous notes on legal matters before him, with subsidiary or supplemental lists, valuations, notes, etc.; some notes on cases before courts other than Chancery; notes of jurisdictional conflicts between Sir Edward Coke and Lord Chancellor Egerton. Also includes 2 sheets of legal notes or extracts from Yearbooks for Henry VI.

Separate volumes include: a volume of notes on proceedings in the Court of Kings Bench 1–35 Edward I, written in a Tudor hand; compilation of extracts from Robert Keilway's *Reports, temp.* Henry VII and VIII; 15th-century register of writs; two copies of a volume of copies or compilations of various legal documents, including commissions, warrants, licenses, etc., *temp.* Elizabeth, partly written by Lord Chancellor Egerton; a report of the arguments in the case in Chancery between Thomas Sackville Lord Buckhurst (afterward 1st Earl of Dorset) and the executors of the Lady Ann Dacre, with another volume of copies of the bill and answer with other documents relating to the suit and a volume containing the schedule of the questions at issue and the arguments in the case, 1594; a treatise on the descent of the Barony of Abergavenny.

33. *Miscellaneous (EL 6162–6202d):* a commonplace book compilation of copies of various political, religious, legal, and miscellaneous papers, including some verse, historical notes, sermons, treatises, *temp.* late Elizabeth or early James I; a compilation of lists of central and local officers, peers, ships

in the navy, forts and castles on the coast, schedules of musters and ordnance, fugitives, etc., *temp.* Elizabeth (after 1578); an undated volume containing a "Catalogus Nobilium siue magnatum Anglie" and "Consanguinitas Regis Hispanie," etc.

34. *Commissions of Array (EL 6207–6209):* 16th-century copies of Commissions of Array for 10 Edward I and 1403.

35. *Judges (EL 6209–6216):* draft commissions for hearing suits of prisoners in the Kings Bench, with letter from Lord Burghley to Lord Chancellor Egerton (and his reply) on the same topic, 1585; letter to Egerton from Sir Francis Walsingham re commission to send condemned prisoners to the galleys, with copy to relevant commission, 1586; Privy Council letter of instruction to Egerton concerning a commission of oyer and terminer for the North, 1603; "A note of various Warrants and Commissions issued to Lord Keepers and others" in 1 Edward VI, 1 Mary, and 1 Elizabeth.

36. *Lollards (EL 6217–6218):* a note of commissions against heretics issued in Richard II's reign, and of the statute 3 Richard II cap. 5 and its subsequent repeals and revivals, with comment; abstract of writs of 1 Henry V directed against heretical preaching and for a reward for taking Sir John Oldcastle.

37. *London (EL 6219–6222):* letters to Lord Chancellor Egerton (from the Duke of Lennox) re receivership of London and Middlesex (1603) and from the Privy Council re issuing a commission to hear the controversy between the City and the Tower of London (1606); copy of a commission to inquire into royal title to certain lands in White Friars (1617); copies of medieval documents concerning London (a commission of 9 Edward I re amercement of aldermen; account of submission by London aldermen to the king 9 Edward II); copies of pardon of Gerard Salueme 10 Edward II and appointment of commission to enquire into oppression by sheriffs, 12 Edward II.

38. *Lord Cobham (EL 6223):* Privy Council letter to Lord Chancellor Egerton requiring him to make out writs of execu-

tion, endorsed by him "For the L. Cobham L. Graye, Sir Gryffin Markham. By Cuthbert Strongfleete."

39. *Sir John Perrot (EL 6224–6229):* four letters from Lord Chancellor Egerton to Burghley re the investigation of and proceedings against Sir John Perrot, 1590–92; letters to Egerton re Perrot's land, 1609.

40. *Sir Walter Ralegh (EL 6230–6232):* Privy Seal to Lord Chancellor Egerton and others to order Ralegh to give over Durham House to the Bishop of Durham, 1603, with Ralegh's reply; letter from Ralegh to Sir Robert Carr (afterwards Earl of Somerset), ca.1608.

41. *Sir Christopher Hatton (EL 6233–6236):* reports and accounts of his lands and legal affairs, including draft of a grant to him of gold brought back to England by Sir Francis Drake.

42. *Papers relating to the Passing of Bills by Immediate Warrant (EL 6237–6238):* Warrants to Lord Chancellor Egerton signed by Elizabeth (1596) and James I (1604) restraining the passing of Bills by immediate Warrant.

43. *Commission for Sewers (EL 6239):* petition to Lord Chancellor Egerton from two London aldermen and others re stopping a commission for sewers pending royal action on bill of the petitioners relating to sewers, *temp.* Elizabeth.

44. *Oath of Allegiance (EL 6240):* Privy Council letter to Lord Chancellor Egerton requesting him to issue commissions to mayors and bailiffs of certain seaports (named in a schedule) to administer the Oath of Allegiance to suspected persons coming into the country, 1608.

45. *Sumptuary Laws (EL 6241):* Proclamation of Queen Elizabeth concerning apparel, 23 July, 1597.

46. *Soldiers, Arms, Etc., in Lancashire (EL 6246–6308):* letters, orders, notes, and other papers re levying troops in Lancashire for various services, chiefly 1582–89; notes of assessments for soldiers arrayed at Ormeschurch (undated); copy of Presentment of Jurors in Salford Hundred re horses and arms; directions for drilling.

PART II: 1617–1649

PERSONAL

1. *Letters, etc. (EL 6309–6666):* personal and domestic correspondence of the 1st Earl and Countess of Bridgewater and their family and circle on various topics, including: the marriage of their daughter Elizabeth with Sir Robert Cecil's son David, legal aspects of the marriage settlement, and consequent financial, legal, and domestic affairs of the young couple; disposition of the estate of Robert Spencer, 1st Baron Spencer of Wormleighton, particularly as it concerns legacies to his daughters; the dispute concerning the will of Peter Warburton and the wardship of his heir, related through Warburton's wife Elizabeth to the 1st Earl of Bridgewater; the creation of the earldom of Bridgewater in 1617; patronage and requests for favors; general politics; estate and financial matters; letters to and from servants (particularly Richard Harrison) with domestic and financial instructions.

Also a few lists and inventories of clothing, "A Catalogue of my Ladies [Countess of Bridgewater?] Bookes at London," 1617–32, a few building and estate accounts, an undated rental of the 1st Earl's lands in Flint and Denbighshire and a rental of tenements in Snape, the journal of David Evans, Bridgewater's steward, concerning legal and other affairs, 1629–31, and the will of William Noy.

Also includes letters and papers of the Herbert family, related to the Egertons through the marriage of the 1st Earl of Bridgewater's daughter Mary to Richard Herbert, 2nd Baron Herbert of Cherbury, particularly as they relate to the marriage settlement and Herbert lands in Wales. Also rentals and surveys of Herbert lands in Montgomeryshire (1598), Monmouthshire (1628), and Anglesea (1630, 1636–37).

Also notes and particulars of other Egerton family properties, including: two court rolls for Idsall, *alias* Snufnall, Shropshire, for 1622 and 1632–33; 23 small court rolls (view of frankpledge only) for Wilderley, *temp.* James I–Charles I; rentals for High Legh, Nether and Over Knutsford, Northope, Northwich, Ollerton, and Plumley, *temp.* Charles I and undated; and notes and documents in suits between the Dowager Countess of Derby (and the 1st Earl of Bridgewater, her son-in-law and stepson) and Sir Edward Kynaston, over lands in Ellesmere and Hordley, Shropshire, *temp.* James I and Charles I.

2. *Accounts (EL 6667–6692):* miscellaneous accounts of personal and household expenses (for travel, clothes, provisions, funerals, wages, etc.) for the period 1620–49.

3. *Deeds and Miscellaneous Papers (Chiefly Estate and Manorial) (EL 6692a–6830e):* deeds, rentals, court rolls, and various supplementary notes and legal documents chiefly concerning Egerton estates and those of related families or associates. For lists of deeds and court rolls, see below, pp. 74–77.

Also includes occasional accounts, bonds, notes and memoranda, commissions from the 1st Earl of Bridgewater to his estate agents to make leases, etc.; receiver's accounts of the possessions late belonging to the Duke of Suffolk in Leicestershire, Lincolnshire, Nottinghamshire, Suffolk, and Yorkshire in 1–3, 6, 9–10 Elizabeth and other papers and legal documents in proceedings concerning title to the Duke's estates, some of which were later granted to the 1st Earl of Bridgewater; papers in the case in Star Chamber between Henry Stanley, 4th Earl of Derby and the commoners of Eighthundred Fen, ca.1580s; documents re a dispute over tithes of the parsonage of Rostherne, Cheshire, 1616–37.

4. *Notes, inscriptions, verses, etc. relating to the Egerton family (EL 6831–6855):* chiefly epitaphs and memorial inscriptions, death and burial certificates, etc, re the deaths of the 1st Earl of Bridgewater's wife and children, including a volume of Latin and English verses by Robert Codrington, M. A., on the death of Frances (Stanley) Egerton, Countess of Bridgewater.

5. *Miscellaneous Treatises, Sermons, and other Literary Manuscripts (EL 6856–6897):* chiefly individual volumes, some dedicated to the 1st Earl of Bridgewater, and some with original bindings, grouped for convenience here into the following general categories:

A. *Literature and Philosophy:* a commonplace book of poems by John Donne; a copy of the masque "Comus" by John Milton, presented at Ludlow Castle in 1634; "A Game at Chess," by Thomas Middleton; treatises titled "Scholia super prophetium Jonae" and "Ars Cabalistica" by Nathaniel Flick, 1630; "Obseruations of State and military affaires for the moste parte collected out of Cornelius Tacitus, by Th. Gainsforde," 1612; "Queene Ester's Hali-luiahs and Hamans Madrigalls expressed in a sacred poem, with the translation and illustration of the 83 Psalme" by Francis Lenton, 1635; a history compiled from records and chronicles titled "Oceanus Brittanicus, or Narrowe Seas," 1614<; a treatise on Boethius; a volume containing a treatise on logic or rhetoric, texts titled "De generibus peomatum" and "In Quintum Horatium de Arte Poetica," and [class notes? from William Hart, 1623, titled] "De Arte Rhetorica."

B. *Politics and Government:* a journal or log kept by Sir Kenelm Digby, Dec. 1627–Feb. 1628/29, containing directions to his fleet, an account of his fight with the Venetians at Scanderoon, etc.; three copies of John Selden's "Judicature in Parliament"; a copy of "The State of Christendom" by Sir Henry Wotton; a manuscript copy of a printed book (published in York in 1643?) titled "A plaine Case or Reasons to convince any . . . which side to take in this present Warre."

C. *Religion and the Church:* "A Proposition of a Bloodlesse Strategem" (a treatise against Cardinal Bellarmine) by Geoffrey Burdon; a treatise titled "The Faultie Fauorite" by Ralph Crane, 1631/32; "Certaine Collections [of prayers and devotional literature] of the Right honble. Elizabeth, late Countess of Huntingdon, for her owne private vse, 1633"; a dissertation on a theological work by [Bp. Richard?] Montagu, by "J. S."; an argument in defense of a work by [Bp. Richard?] Montagu, against which a charge of Arminianism had been brought; a treatise titled "Defensiuncula Fidei Catholice opposita impugnationi viri clarissime A. W. de formali caussa Justificationis," 1617.

D. *Sermons:* a sermon preached at Whitehall 14 March

1622/23 by Dr. Bell Canckwell; six brief volumes of sermons by John Carter, two of them at the funeral of the
Countess of Bridgewater and one at the funeral of Lady
Frances Stanley, 1636; the sermon preached at Little
Gaddesden, Herts., at the funeral of the 1st Earl of Bridgewater, 1649, by "T. F."; a sermon preached at St. Paul's
15 October 1626 by Matthew Griffith; a sermon preached
at Ludlow, 24 September 1637, by "T. L."; "An Elegiack
Comemoration" for Mr. Josiah Shute, rector of the parish
of St. Mary Woolnoth in Lombard Street, delivered by
Mr. Povey [1643]; a sermon preached at Theobalds before
the King by Dr. Rawlinson, 19 December 1619; a volume
containing two sermons by Dr. Skynner; a sermon
preached at Ludlow 1639; a sermon preached before the
King on Innocents Day; a volume containing copies of
several sermons by various persons.

E. *Miscellaneous:* "Rules How to compose" by Giovanni
Coprario [John Cooper]; "Int^t & Valuation Tables" endorsed "Mr. Richard Delamaine 1 March 1637."

OFFICIAL

1. *Foreign Affairs (EL 6898–6916):* letters, documents, drafts,
notes and memoranda, etc. concerning the 1621 treaty with
Denmark, war in the Palatinate, Anglo-Dutch relations, and
the expedition to the Isle of Ré. Includes a volume containing
"A Treatise about Impositions" [a historical account of British
wars and foreign policy] and a "Treatise about an office for
Compositions for Alientations."

2. *Parliamentary Affairs (EL 6917–6958):* notes of proceedings
in the Parliaments of 1620, 1624, and 1640; petitions to Parliament and notes re petitions; copies of, or notes on, speeches
in Parliament by James I, Charles I, John Pym (against Abp.
Laud), and Sir Benjamin Rudyerd; notes on impeachment
proceedings against Thomas Wentworth, 1st Earl of Strafford;
a list of the members of Parliament, May 6, 1625. Separate
volumes include two copies of Henry Elsyng's treatise on
parliamentary statutes entitled "Expeditio Billarum Antiqua," 1632.
See also Sect. 12, below, pp. 52.

3. *Trade (EL 6959–6968a):* notes and legal papers concerning the proceedings between the Goldsmiths' Company and John Reynolds, Common Assayer, ca.1620s; notes on the commission for granting charters to brewers and masters, 1636.

4. *Taxation (EL 6969–6979):* notes and extracts from documents concerning subsidy collections and loans; a letter of complaint to the 1st Earl of Bridgewater from Richard Harries re the assessment of Ship Money in Shropshire, 1635. Separate volumes include a collection of speeches on Ship Money in Hampden's Case and a collection of "The Arguments of the Judges concerning Ship-Mony" in Hampden's Case, 1638. *See also* Sect. 12 below, p. 52, for a similar volume.

5. *Coinage and the Mint (EL 6980–6997):* notes and papers concerning the value of English coins; accounts of monies coined and of trials of the pyx, 1620s–1632.

6. *Ecclesiastical Affairs (EL 6998–7001):* an undated paper concerning the petition of Kings College, Cambridge, for additional patronage; an attack on Abp. Laud by Hd. Blair, 1640; a plan by Richard Daye to increase royal revenues through perpetual annuities from the church, 1629; letter from Bishop Edmund Griffith of Bangor to the 1st Earl of Bridgewater re rights to a living, 1634.

7. *Admiralty (EL 7002–7040):* various notes and papers concerning the Navy; records of lost or captured ships; legal papers in the lawsuit of Captain Thomas King against Humphrey Slaney, heard in the Admiralty Court, concerning shares in a prize taken by a ship, and apparently at some stage referred to the 1st Earl of Bridgewater and others for arbitration, 1627–30. Also two volumes containing a report on the state of the Royal Navy, with recommendations, by a royal commission, 1626.

8. *Ireland (EL 7041–7060):* brief reports, treatises, notes, and petitions dealing with Irish affairs; notes and documents concerning the Ulster Plantation and the settlement of Londonderry; notes on the titles of various individuals to Irish lands; a copy of the Scottish Commissioners' petition against Straf-

ford, 1640. Separate volumes include a 17th-century copy of Edmund Spenser's "Vewe of the present state of Ireland" and a short biographical dictionary of Irish peers, *temp.* Charles I.

See also Part III, Official, Sect. 9 below, pp. 57–58.

9. *Wales (EL 7061b–7607):* official and private papers stemming from the 1st Earl of Bridgewater's work as Lord President of the Council in the Marches of Wales, 1631–42, including: numerous lists of sheriffs, and of names to be presented for pricking as sheriffs, and of names fit to be sheriff, with letters to the 1st Earl asking to be excused from the office of sheriff; lists of escheators for the Marches, and of persons fit to be escheators; lists, schedules, etc. of military officers and military supplies in individual Welsh hundreds; miscellaneous lists of Welsh names for various purposes; a few Privy Council letters of instruction to the 1st Earl, authorizing commissions, etc.; documents re the collection of money in Wales for the repair of St. Paul's Cathedral; papers re the jurisdiction of the Council of Wales, particularly in English shires; notes and documents re individual legal cases and suits heard by the Council, particularly Vaughan *v.* Vaughan, the rape of Margery Evans, and Hugh Osborne *v.* Crompton; papers and accounts re the 1st Earl's residence at Ludlow Castle (provisioning of, diets at, etc.); requests for patronage addressed to the 1st Earl; miscellaneous reports, memoranda, letters, etc. re specific Welsh and local affairs.

Separate volumes include 64 Books of Hearing, or entry books, for the legal terms of the Council in the Marches of Wales (a few being first drafts), 1632–42.

See also Part VII, Sect. 3 below, p. 69.

10. *Crown Lands (EL 7608–7612):* copy of an act *temp.* James I to explain a statute of 18 Elizabeth concerning grants to the crown by ecclesiastical bodies, with notes on a 1621 act dealing with grants to the crown between 13 and 25 Elizabeth; list of all grants made to Queen Elizabeth by deans and chapters, masters of colleges, and hospitals between 13 and 26 Elizabeth; unsigned declaration re royal grant of land to Endymion Porter, 1630s.

11. *Militia (EL 7613–7710)*: instructions and memoranda re musters, including those from the Privy Council, county officials, etc., chiefly during the 1630s; letters and other papers re the opposition to paying the muster master's fees in Shropshire, and re Sir John Corbett's petition to the House of Commons against the 1st Earl of Bridgewater in the matter of the Shropshire Muster Master's fees, with the resulting impeachment of the Earl before the House of Lords, 1640–41.

12. *Charles I (EL 7711–7877)*: notes and other documents concerning proposals for the marriage of Charles I (while Prince of Wales); letters, documents, notes, and other papers concerning the relations between Charles I and Parliament, particularly re the Petition of Right and the Grand Remonstrance, and during the Civil War; letters, reports, notes, copies of acts and speeches, etc., dealing with relations between Charles I and Scotland, particularly re the Solemn League and Covenant and the negotiations with the Scottish Commissioners in 1640–41; a long series of 51 newsletters from John Castle ("de Sacro Bosco") to the 1st Earl of Bridgewater at Ludlow during the years 1638–40, with information about politics, the Court, London, etc.; a similar series of 9 newsletters sent to the Earl by Roger Holland in 1640, dealing chiefly with the proceedings at York and in Parliament.

Separate volumes include a collection of copies of letters from Charles I to the Prince of Wales concerning the Treaty of Newport, November, 1648, and a collection of reports of proceedings in Kings Bench and Exchequer Chamber in the Ship Money case.

13. *Star Chamber (EL 7878–7921)*: letters, documents, and notes re various individual Star Chamber cases; 27 Star Chamber Cause Lists, giving names of plaintiffs and defendants and the nature of the suit, 1631–35 (with 3 additional Cause Lists *temp.* Lord Chancellor Egerton and James I). Also a treatise on the Court of Star Chamber by William Hudson, dedicated to the 1st Earl of Bridgewater by "J. E."

14. *Official Matters in the Law Courts (EL 7922–7929c)*: miscellaneous notes re the grant to Sir Robert Lloyd of a patent for ingrossing wills and inventories; memorandum of charges

against Lord Chancellor Francis Bacon, with notes in the hand of the 1st Earl of Bridgewater re explanations and confessions; copies of a letter from Charles I, and petitions of Francis Burton, concerning fraud by clerks of the Exchequer, 1628–31, with note of King's further directions, 1631. Also a treatise on "The Office of Executors" by Thomas Wentworth.

15. *Legal Proceedings (EL 7930–7968):* letters, petitions, briefs, etc. on various legal matters, including notes and orders for specific cases (Love's *v.* Doyley, Eure *v.* Lorte, and cases involving the Egerton family); includes a Star Chamber cause list with notes by the 1st Earl of Bridgewater, chiefly re the prosecution of various people for slandering Lord Keeper Thomas Coventry, 1630.

16. *Colonies (EL 7969–7970):* abstract of the patents re the Massachusetts Bay Co.

17. *Miscellaneous Papers (EL 7971–8007a):* notes and records of Court ceremonial occasions; vouchers, receipts, and bonds of 1st Earl of Bridgewater and receipts for money due to Lady Alice Hastings; two copies of "A Lre intituled from the Diuill to the Pope" purporting to have been translated from the Dutch, found in the hands of a widow of Okingham and sent to the Privy Council, 1627; a schedule of the names of all the vestry and quest men in the parish of St. Giles without Cripplegate, London, 1634. Also a commonplace book containing copies of political discourses and treatises.

PART III: 1649–1686

PERSONAL

1. *Letters, etc. (EL 8008–8189):* personal and domestic correspondence and other papers of the 2nd Earl of Bridgewater, his family, and circle of friends and associates, on a wide range of subjects, including: the 2nd Earl's household and domestic affairs; his estates and relations with his tenants; and the threatened sequestration of those estates during the Commonwealth; his debts and general financial affairs; the marriage of the 2nd Earl's son to the daughter of Lionel Cranfield,

3rd Earl of Middlesex; the second marriage of Bridgewater's son; patronage and requests for favor; the 2nd Earl's will and its subsequent administration; bonds, receipts, accounts, etc. relating to Thomas Savage, *styled* Viscount Colchester during the 1670s.

Individual items of interest include an inventory of the goods of the 2nd Earl at Ashridge, 1663; orders for his household servants; a genealogical table of the Egerton family from the time of Lord Chancellor Egerton to 1676; three rentals (1655–57) and two court rolls (amercements only, 1655 and 1659) for the manor of Wollaston, Northamptonshire; a volume containing notes of sermons and reflections by the 2nd Earl, 1645–50; four sermons by Robert Hitchcock (the Earl's chaplain); a sermon by "Mr. Hooker" on Abak. 1:4; three additional sermons indexed by the 2nd Earl; and a collection entitled "The Soules Banquet" made up of hymns, etc. written by Ralph Crane, Francis Davison, and other gentlemen and dedicated to the 2nd Earl

2. *Deeds and Miscellaneous Papers (chiefly Estate and Manorial) (EL 8190–8270k):* deeds, rentals, letters, petitions, notes, and other miscellaneous papers related to Egerton family lands and tenants (particularly in Cheshire and Flint), marriage settlements of the Egerton family (particularly the marriage between Lady Alice Egerton and Richard Vaughan, 2nd Earl of Carbery). For a list of deeds, see below, pp. 75–77.

3. *Lawsuits (EL 8271–8341):* bills of complaint, answers, briefs, judgements, notes, and other papers chiefly relating to actions for debts of the 1st Earl of Bridgewater, brought at or after the death of the 1st Earl, and to the sale of various estates to raise money during and after the Commonwealth. The principal cases involved are Love *v.* Bridgewater, beginning 1651; Frances Randolph *v.* Bridgewater, beginning ?1650; and 3rd Earl of Middlesex *v.* Lady Elizabeth Cranfield (the ward and subsequently daughter-in-law of the 2nd Earl of Bridgewater). Includes copies or abstracts of the wills of Lionel Cranfield, 1st Earl of Middlesex, and James Cranfield, 2nd Earl of Middlesex.

4. *Epitaphs, Certificates, Occasional Verse, etc. (EL 8371–8375 and many unnumbered):* chiefly individual volumes, grouped here for convenience into the following general categories:

A. *Literature:* "Pedantius," a Latin play by Dr. Thomas Beard; a translation of the life of Alexander Severus of Aelius Lampridius by John Egerton, afterward 2nd Earl of Bridgewater; "The Banish'd Shepherdess," a poem dedicated to the Dowager Queen by Cosmo Manuche; "The Character of a Trimmer," by George Savile, 1st Marquis of Halifax; "Certaine Observations or Maxims of State by the late Marq. of Hal - - - x," with a supplement by a "Mr. Cha. M."

B. *Politics and Government:* "Carolina Threnodia" by Sir Thomas Herbert; a treatise on the duties of a Counsellor by "T. Kinge"; "A Catt may look at a King," a treatise on kings concluding that England ought to be a commonwealth

C. *Religious and Devotional Literature and Sermons:* of "Meditations on the generall Chapters of the Holy Bible" by Elizabeth, Countess of Bridgewater; "True Copies of certaine loose Papers left by the Right Honble. Elizabeth, Countess of Bridgewater. Collected and transcribed together here since her death, anno Dni. 1663"; "A Collection of all those places of the Holy Scriptures which may be found in more bookes of the Holy Bible then one," in the hand of the 2nd Earl of Bridgewater; a treatise on "The morality of the fourth Commandment" by Samuel Wilson; a volume of devotional treatises and prayers.

A sermon preached at Ashridge before the Earl of Bridgewater by Robert Hitchcock; "Visitation Sermon" by George Burhope; a sermon on Luke 9:55 by "Mr. Fowler."

D. *Miscellaneous:* "The Vision," a poetical description of Ashridge by Marie Burhope, daughter of the vicar of Ashridge; a copy of "The R^t. Honble Richard [Vaughan] Earle of Carberry his Advice to his Soun," 1651; a catechism translated from the Latin into English by "my sonne J. B." [i.e., the 2nd Earl of Bridgewater]; a copy by the 2nd Earl of Bridgewater of Sir Walter Ralegh's advice to his son; a description of "His Maties Dialls in

White-Hall Garden"; a "Book of Arms" enlarged and corrected by the 2nd Earl of Bridgewater, 1669; an oration given by Dr. Henry Stanley in London on the occasion of the anniversary of the death of William Harvey, 1658.

OFFICIAL

1. *Parliamentary Affairs (EL 8396–8446):* notes, memoranda, copies and extracts from official documents, letters, etc., dealing with post-1660 parliamentary affairs, in particular the impeachment proceedings against Edward Hyde, 1st Earl of Clarendon, and Thomas Osborne, Earl of Danby (afterward 1st Duke of Leeds); notes and extracts concerning proposed bills and other legislation; notes on proceedings in Parliament January–February 1674, July and August 1680, March 1681, and August 1685.

Separate volumes include: a collection of records concerning the impeachment of the Earl of Clarendon; a record of proceedings in Parliament 7 November 1693 through 24 April 1694; "Remembrances for Order and Decency to be kept in the Upper House of Parliament by the Lords when his Majesty is not there . . ." (the "Lords Standing Orders"), ca.1700; a 17th-century copy of the "Modus Tenendi Parliamentum," noted as being a description of the way in which Parliament was held in the time of Edward the Confessor, prepared at the command of William the Conqueror.

2. *Foreign Affairs (EL 8447–8507):* letters, notes, and other papers concerning foreign ambassadors and relations with Spain, the British seige of Tangiers (including 33 reports on the siege from Sir Palmer Fairborne, 1680), and the Dutch Wars (including several letters to the 2nd Earl of Bridgewater from C. Herbert).

3. *Trade (EL 8508–8517):* petitions to Parliament and other papers concerning economic legislation; copies of the letters patent appointing Commissioners for the Council of Trade (of which 2nd Earl of Bridgewater was one), October 1668, with instructions for the Commissioners; account (in French) of grievances concerning English trade in Sweden, with notes by Sir Leoline Jenkins; a volume containing a petition to

the House of Commons by the laboring porters of London concerning competition from other societies of porters, 1620.

4. *Militia (EL 8518–8535):* letters, accounts, and miscellaneous papers concerning the Buckinghamshire and Hertfordshire militia and the 2nd Earl of Bridgewater's Lord-Lieutenancy of those two counties, *temp.* Charles II and James II. Separate volumes include a Book of Orders of the Deputy-Lieutenants for the Buckinghamshire militia, 1677–1715, a muster book for the county of Buckinghamshire, 1673, and an "Index to the Act for the ordering the forces in the several Counties of this Kingdom, made 14to Caroli 2^{di} . . ."

5. *Admiralty (EL 8533–8537):* lists of English ships during the Dutch Wars, ca.1665–66, including "The Order of ye Battle of his Maties fleet May 15th 1665"; considerations re the appointment of the Duke of York (later James II) as Lord High Admiral. Includes a small volume listing the wages of naval officers and men, the cost of victuals, the weight of ordnance, and an estimate of the ordinary charges of the Royal Navy, June 1660–June 1661.

6. *Dissenters (EL 8538–8546):* petitions, articles and miscellaneous papers concerning Thomas Porter, parson of Whitchurch, Shropshire, and his attacks on the government, 1654; copies of letters and official papers concerning non-conformist ministers.

7. *Recusants (EL 8547):* an account of proceedings in Parliament, January 8, 1673/74, against recusants.

8. *Ecclesiastical Affairs (EL 8548–8557):* letters, notes, and papers re individual livings; notes of acts for "better securing the Protestant Religion" and for "composing differences in Religion"; an account of the examination of Henry Compton, Bishop of London, re his proceedings against John Sharp; brief poems on transubstantiation and on a clerical "cabal"; a report of the Ecclesiastical Commissioners, 1688.

9. *Ireland (EL 8558–8562):* copy of the protest by 2nd Earl of Bridgewater and others, 1667, against a bill to restrain

the importation of cattle from Ireland; drafts of letters to be signed by Charles II concerning "the transplanted persons in Conoght"; instructions for the "Viewers" sent to the "Dyery" to consider a plan for plantations there, with their answer; compilation of extracts from official records, Edward I–Henry VI, concerning English interest and jurisdiction in Ireland; undated suggestions of the Queen's Solicitor for Ireland (Sir John Davies?) re collecting revenue, land tenure, accounting, etc.

10. *Wales (EL 8563–8564):* two unsigned letters of complaint concerning abuses and corruption of the law courts at Ludlow, 1665.

11. *Subsidies (EL 8565–8566):* notes on the value of annual subsidies and on levying them; a commission for the collection of the subsidy in Buckinghamshire, 1671.

12. *Coinage and the Mint (EL 8567–8570):* three accounts of trials of the pyx, 21 Jan. 1673, 14 Feb. 1674, and 14 June 1679; undated account of value of various foreign coins, *temp.* Charles I?

13. *The Poor (EL 8571):* undated proposal for dealing with poverty by providing more responsible vestrymen.

14. *Mines (EL 8572):* copy Privy Seal for an annuity to Sir George Charnock for discovering royal interest in "aalome" mines at Mulgrave and elsewhere, 1675.

15. *Miscellaneous Papers (EL 8573–8596):* an abstract of a petition to Parliament re Lincolnshire fens, *temp.* Charles I or Commonwealth; account of the ceremonies at creation of Knights of the Bath, April 1661; account of a legal case involving Thomas White's pursuit of a privateer, on board which were discovered William Penn and other gentlemen; account of the case of William Bishop, discharged by Charles II from post of Serjeant at Arms; copy letter from 2nd Earl of Bridgewater to Sir Francis North, with North's reply, concerning the return from Brackley and Scarborough respecting the Act for regulating corporations, 1680; a few bonds, receipts, and accounts for 2nd Earl of Bridgewater and Lady Alicia Hastings; a volume containing an alphabetical list of towns

in Buckinghamshire, by hundreds, 1662; miscellaneous notes and papers.

PART IV: 1686–1701

PERSONAL

1. *Letters and Miscellaneous Personal Papers (EL 8598–8947):* few letters to and from the 3rd Earl of Bridgewater and his family and circle on personal, family, and financial matters, and re patronage; draft of death certificate and of memorial inscriptions for Elizabeth Cranfield Egerton, 1st wife of the 3rd Earl of Bridgewater; bills and receipts for personal, household, and some estate expenses of 3rd Earl of Bridgewater and his family; a checkroll of servants' names and quarterly wages of the household of (the 3rd Earl?), September 29, 1690; court rolls for the manor of Wollaston, Northants., 1693, 1695–98, and 1702–03; miscellaneous deeds and other documents concerning the descent, tenure, and rents of Bridgewater House at the Barbican in London, chiefly 1650–93; a polling book for Buckinghamshire, 1698 and 1700; a volume containing a copy of the motion in the House of Commons by Robert Price concerning the grant of the lordships of Denbigh, Bromfield, and Yale.

Numerous literary manuscripts, chiefly political and occasional verse, including four commonplace books of political and satiric verse, *temp.* Charles II, James II, and William and Mary; sermons by George Burhope, chaplain to the 3rd Earl, preached at the opening of the new chapel at Ashridge, 1699 and by "Mr. Moore" on Acts 24:16. Other separate volumes include: a consolatory discourse written by George Burhope for the 3rd Earl upon the death of his two eldest sons in London, 1687, and "The Compleat Keeper or The Young Woodman's Guide" by Patrick Bamford.

2. *The Herbert Papers (EL 8948–8950a):* copy of the will of Henry Herbert, 4th Baron Herbert of Cherbury, 1690, and a note concerning its effect; deed of settlement and note on settlement at marriage of the Hon. Alice Herbert with John Burrard, 1696.

59

See also Part II, Personal, Sect. 1, p. 46 above, for other Herbert Family papers.

3. *The Bolton Papers (EL 8951–9014):* letters, legal documents, and other papers concerning the affairs of Charles Paulet, 1st Duke of Bolton, the father-in-law of the 3rd Earl of Bridgewater. In particular: sixteen letters from the 1st Duke of Bolton to the 3rd Earl of Bridgewater concerning politics, his own health, and personal and family matters, 1693–98; letters from the 2nd Duke of Bolton to Scroop Egerton, later 1st Duke of Bridgewater; a copy of the 1st Duke's will; the various suits and countersuits re the settlement of the Duke of Bolton's estate, especially those between the Countess of Bridgewater and her brother Charles Paulet, 2nd Duke of Bolton; the marriage settlement of Lord William Paulet.

4. *The Wrey Papers (EL 9015–9091):* manorial papers (accounts, rentals, surveys, memoranda, etc.) of the estates of the Wrey family in Cornwall, Devon, and Caernarvonshire, and of the estates of Sir William Williams in Caernarvonshire and Anglesey, including rentals and accounts for the Vaynol Estate (Caern.), 1697–1701, Wanting (Berkshire), 1696–1701, Worlington (Devon), 1696, and the Williams estates, 1698–99; papers relating to the lawsuits between Wrey and Williams, Wrey and the Earl of Bridgewater, and Lauze and Wrey, including copies of the will of Sir William Williams, 1695; financial and estate papers relating to the affairs of Sir Bourchier Wrey (the 3rd Earl of Bridgewater was apparently one of the trustees of his will), including a copy of Wrey's will, 1694, and of the will of an ancestor, Sir Christopher Wrey, 1589; correspondence between Lady Wrey and the 3rd Earl concerning her son, ca.1697–1700, and correspondence between Bridgewater and others of the Wrey circle.

OFFICIAL

1. *Admiralty (EL 9092–9413):* official papers stemming from the 3rd Earl of Bridgewater's offices as First Lord of the Admiralty, 1699–1701, and as president of the commission for hearing Admiralty appeals, including: petitions to the 3rd Earl, the Admiralty, or the Crown concerning naval affairs; the

3rd Earl's notes and memoranda on Admiralty affairs and particularly on individual cases brought before the commissioners for hearing Admiralty appeals, chiefly 1692–93; notes and papers concerning the protest of the 3rd Earl and others to the Admiralty's directions to Sir George Rooke, 1694; reports, lists, memoranda, etc. re officers, seamen, ships, and the general conditions of the Navy, chiefly 1699–1701; reports to the Admiralty from Peregrine Osborne, Marquis of Carmarthen (afterward 2nd Duke of Leeds) during the summer of 1695 concerning actions at Plymouth, Kinsale Harbour, Cork Harbour, and elsewhere at sea. Includes a volume of drafts of forms of warrants, commissions, record books, instructions for different officials, accounts of naval officials, etc., *temp.* 3rd Earl of Bridgewater and later.

2. *Recusants (EL 9414–9439):* correspondence of the 3rd Earl of Bridgewater (chiefly in his capacity as Lord Lieutenant of Buckinghamshire?) concerning the seizure of the arms and horses of Catholics, 1695, Catholics who would not take the Oath of Allegiance, 1696, and the general affairs of Catholics in Buckinghamshire.
See also Sect. 3, Militia, below.

3. *Militia (EL 9440–9570):* letters and papers stemming from the 3rd Earl of Bridgewater's office as Lord Lieutenant of Buckinghamshire during the 1690s, including: circular letters and other instructions to deputy-lieutenants, chiefly concerning Catholics and impressed seamen; lists of officers and men of the Buckinghamshire militia and of deputy-lieutenants; orders for payment, and receipts for pay, to Buckinghamshire militia officers and men, with some receipts for payments for goods; a few Privy Council letters of instruction to the 3rd Earl concerning a plot to kill the King, the seizure of arms and horses of Catholics, and the impressment of seamen.
See also Sect. 2, Recusants, above.

4. *Colonies (EL 9571–9872):* letters and papers stemming from the office of the 3rd Earl of Bridgewater as President of the Board of Trade, 1696–99, including: notes by the 3rd Earl on a wide range of colonial affairs (chiefly concerning North America and the West Indies) such as trade, fishing, piracy,

colonial and English military activity and preparedness,
French military activity, colonial governors and government,
and complaints against it, the disposition of ships at sea, and
the proposed union of New York and New England; legal
papers concerning cases arising in the colonies and appealed
to England; notes and papers, including depositions, many
sent by or through Governor Sir Francis Nicholson of Maryland, concerning privateers and runaway seamen in the
American colonies, with correspondence between Nicholson
and the Board of Trade; reports to the 3rd Earl from colonial
governors Nicholson, Nathaniel Blakiston, and Richard Coote,
1st Earl of Bellamont, and from other colonial officials; a few
notes concerning trade in Europe. Includes a volume of copies of various documents concerning transactions between
England and France relating to Hudson's Bay.

5. *Trade (EL 9873–9881):* notes, reports, drafts, etc. dealing
with the state of English trade.

6. *Ireland (EL 9882–9886):* miscellaneous papers relating to
Ireland including: James II's speech to Parliament in Ireland,
May 15, 1689; an agreement re the surrender of Limerick,
1691; a notice to the King by Parliament of abuses in Ireland,
1692; charges by the Earl of Bellamont and James Hamilton
(?afterward 6th Earl of Abercorn) concerning abuses in Irish
administration, 1693.

7. *Foreign Affairs (EL 9887–9890):* miscellaneous papers including: a letter to William III from the Spanish Ambassador,
Don Pedro Ronquillo, informing him that the French had
entered Luxembourg, 1687/88; report by Daniel Finch, 2nd
Earl of Nottingham, 1689, on the Anglo-Dutch treaty and
progress of the war; an account of an Anglo-Dutch naval
engagement against France, June 30, 1690.

8. *Law Courts (EL 9891–9895):* copies or drafts of an act, *temp.*
William and Mary, for regulating the royal household and
the courts of justice; copy of "Orders for regulateing proceedings in the Courts of Equity and for the better ascertaininge
of the law," *temp.* William and Mary; a volume containing
some pages of accounts by Charles Morgan, 1694–96, and

particulars of fees, offices, oaths and duties of all the officials of the Exchequer.

9. *Coinage (EL 9896–9900):* two reports of trials of the pyx, 1697, 1699; letter from William Bridgeman to the 3rd Earl giving notice of a Council meeting and the trial of the pyx, 1697; a list of "Coynes wanting," and a list of coins with their values.

10. *Ecclesiastical Affairs (EL 9901–9902):* a note of alterations in the Prayer Book; copies of proceedings at vestry meetings for St. James' Westminster regarding the rebuilding of the church, January 1695–96.

11. *London Waterworks (EL 9903–9904):* notes on the case of Craven Howard concerning the new waterworks in London, 1694–98.

12. *Office of Land Credit (EL 9905–9908):* a list of the Lords Visitors of the Office of Land Credit (one of whom was the 3rd Earl of Bridgewater); notes of meetings and an explanation of the intentions of the Undertakers in the Office of Land Credit, 1696.

13. *Parliamentary Affairs (EL 9908a–9930a):* a brief account of speeches of the King and the Lord Chancellor at the prorogation and dissolution of Parliament; notes concerning the legality of acts of the Convention Parliament, 1690; copies of the Declaration of Right and other parliamentary acts; notes on the trial for murder of Charles Mohun, 5th Baron Mohun, 1693; copy of a speech by John Sheffield (afterward 1st Duke of Buckingham and Normanby) on a bill concerning freedom of elections and impartial proceedings in Parliament, 1692; notes on a speech on the Triennial Bill intended to have been given by John Smith, 1694; a volume containing the speech of the Attorney-General in the House of Commons against the bill charging Sir Charles Duncombe, ca.1698; a copy of the Lords Standing Orders, ca.1697.

14. *Jersey and Guernsey (EL 9931–9937):* notes and documents in the legal case of Daniel Messeruy *v.* Charles Dumaresq and James Corbet concerning debts on the estate of the late Maximillian Messeruy, ca.1690s, and notes re other cases in-

volving inhabitants of the island of Jersey *temp.* William III; notes re the 1693 Order in Council concerning customs in Guernsey.

15. *Miscellaneous (EL 9938–9985d):* a series of thirty-six anonymous newsletters sent to the 3rd Earl of Bridgewater at Ashridge, June–November 1694, chiefly political in nature; miscellaneous notes on legal cases; a pay warrant for royal huntsmen and the Master of the Hounds, etc., 2 William and Mary.

PART V: 1701–1745

PERSONAL

1. *Letters and Miscellaneous Personal Papers (EL 9986–10080):* estate and financial letters and papers re the affairs of Scroop Egerton, 4th Earl and 1st Duke of Bridgewater, and his family, including mortgages, marriage settlements, deeds, papers concerning building at Bridgewater House in London, documents concerning the Bolton Estate Trust; letters and a few accounts concerning the family, domestic, and financial affairs of John Leveson-Gower, 1st Baron Gower, and his son John Leveson-Gower, 1st Earl Gower; legal and genealogical papers concerning in part the claim of the Duke of Atholl to the Barony of Strange, ca.1736; includes an account book for Lady Gower and Lady Cheyne, 1718–19 and an inventory of the household goods of Jane (Paulet) Egerton, Dowager Countess of Bridgewater.

OFFICIAL

1. *Jacobites and the Militia (EL 10081–10096):* lists of justices of the peace and deputy lieutenants for Buckinghamshire, ca.1700 and 1702; nine letters of instruction from the Privy Council to the 1st Duke of Bridgewater as Lord Lieutenant of Buckinghamshire, re impressed seamen, seizing arms and horses of Catholics and other potentially disaffected persons, and the expected Jacobite invasions of 1708 and 1715.

2. *Foreign Refugees (EL 10097–10100):* Privy Council letter to the 1st Duke, and his answer, re ordering charitable assis-

tance for German Protestant refugees, 1709; two reports to the 1st Duke from Buckinghamshire justices of the peace on the same topic.

3. *Prince George of Denmark (EL 10101–10109):* orders and other papers concerning the funeral procession of Prince George of Denmark, the consort of Queen Anne, 1708; an "appraisment" of the value of the horses of the late Prince.

4. *Militia (EL 10110, nos. 1–47):* circular letters of instruction from the Privy Council Office to justices of the peace, and from the 1st Duke (as Lord Lieutenant of Buckinghamshire) to his deputy lieutenants, re seizing the arms and horses of Catholics, especially in 1705, and re tendering the Oath of Allegiance; reports to the 1st Duke from Buckinghamshire justices of the peace, including lists of men, in accordance with the above instructions; appointments by the 1st Duke to commission in the Buckinghamshire militia, 1715; includes a volume containing schedules of British forces in Minorca, Gibraltar, Annapolis Royal, and Placentia, with the King's orders for their establishment at certain rates, 1731.

5. *Frampton Papers (EL 10110a–c):* a deed of agreement between the Duke of Newcastle and John Asgill re the enclosure of Eighthundred Fen, 1706; two deeds re the holdings therein of Jane (Paulet) Egerton, Dowager Countess of Bridgewater, 1706.

6. *Miscellaneous (EL 10111–10259):* estate and personal papers including: approximately 130 household and estate vouchers for, and accounts of, monies received for heriots and tithe rents, spent on Court dinners, victuals, tradesmen and laborers, newspapers, postage, clothes and books, household furnishings, etc., for the 1st Duke of Bridgewater and his family, 1700–43 (chiefly 1712–29); a recommendation from several Buckinghamshire gentlemen of Sir Edmond Denton and Mr. Hamden as parliamentary candidates, 1712/13; copy of an undated letter from the Lord Lieutenant of Norfolk (?Robert Paston, 1st Earl of Yarmouth) concerning shire elections; copies of a few letters concerning the feud between George I and the Prince of Wales; account of entry fines at three of the

1st Duke of Bridgewater's manorial courts (at Whitchurch, Doddington, and Marbury), 1727–28; a summary of profits from rents, etc. due from the executrix of Alexander Duncombe, Mich. 1728; a check roll of servants for one half year, 1714; a steward's account for April 1722, and another household account for October–December 1714.

PART VI: 1745–1803

1. *Miscellaneous Letters and Papers (EL 10260–10313):* various personal and financial papers concerning the 2nd and 3rd Dukes of Bridgewater and their families, including: papers re the settlement of the estate of the 1st Duke; a few letters concerning the 3rd Duke's canal project and his dispute with Sir Richard Brooke over lands for the canal, 1775; rolls of officers and monthly returns of the Sutherland Fencible Regiment and other volunteer regiments, 1797; a series of 22 receipts for special rates allowed tenants in Chertsey, Surrey, for repairing their parish church (1806–07); a catalog of engraved gems or intaglios and an inventory of the Duke's plate; a statement of the expenses of Sutton's Hospital (Charterhouse), 1754–65.

Also five brief volumes of accounts (chiefly for domestic repairs and upholstery, in London and elsewhere) for Granville Leveson-Gower, 1st Marquis of Stafford, and his son George Granville Leveson-Gower (afterward 1st Duke of Sutherland), 1798–1805.

2. *Parliamentary Affairs (EL 10314–10316):* a copy of the Poll Book of the hundred of Cutleston, Staffordshire, 1747; two printed copies of parliamentary acts.

3. *Canals (EL 10317–10329):* chiefly notes and papers re the 3rd Duke of Bridgewater's parliamentary bill for a canal across the Irwell, and the clash with the previously existing Mersey and Irwell Navigation canal; notes of examinations of witnesses in the Committee of the Commons on the Duke's bill for a canal to the Hempstones, 1762.

4. *Foreign Affairs (EL 10330–10333):* minutes of a Privy Council meeting concerning Minorca, 1770, and a "memorial" (in

Spanish) attributed to Thomas Townshend concerning poverty in that island; a letterbook of diplomatic dispatches,
chiefly from Sir Benjamin Keene, the British envoy to Portugal, addressed to the Duke of Newcastle and the Duke of
Bedford, with copies of related letters and documents, 1748;
a letterbook of diplomatic dispatches, chiefly from Sir James
Gray, British resident at Venice, to the Duke of Bedford and
then to Robert Darcy, 4th Earl of Holdernesse, with copies
of related letters and documents, 1751.

5. *Waldegrave Papers (EL 10334–10388a):* papers arising from
the 3rd Duke of Bridgewater's trusteeship (with 1st Duke
of Sutherland and Thomas Gilbert) of George Waldegrave,
5th Earl Waldegrave, ca.1789–1791, including: correspondence between Thomas Gilbert and Lady Waldegrave re the
Trust; letters and documents concerning the 1791 Act for
draining and dividing lands at Sedgmoor, Somerset; deeds
and other estate papers, chiefly for Navestock, Essex (including two rentals, 1719 and 1766) and lands in Somerset (including a rental for Radstoke, Somerset, 1789–90).

6. *Marine Square Papers (EL 10389–10433):* abstracts of title
deeds, rentals, accounts, and other miscellaneous papers relating to Marine Square (Wells Close Square) in Middlesex,
chiefly 1740–50s; includes a copy of the will of Thomas Wilkins,
1747.

7. *Vouchers (EL 10434–10439):* bills for wine, brickmaking,
and farm repairs, 1760s.

8. *Privy Seal Warrants (unnumbered):* approximately 1,000
Privy Seal warrants from the tenure of the office of Keeper
of the Privy Seal by Granville Leveson-Gower, 2nd Earl
Gower and 1st Marquis of Stafford, in 1755–57 and 1784–94.

PART VII: MISCELLANY (ca.1200–1800)

1. *Cheyne Papers (EL 10440–11146):* official, legal, financial,
estate, and a few family papers of the Cheyne family, and
in particular of William Cheyne, Baron Cheyne and 2nd Viscount Newhaven (1657–1738), including: accounts and other
papers re the duties and office of Clerk of the Pipe, 1670–

1727, with two of Lord Cheyne's account books as such, 1703–06 and 1711–25; accounts, correspondence, and other papers concerning Lord Cheyne's trusteeship (with others) of his nephew Evelyn Pierrepont, 2nd Duke of Kingston, ca.1726, with reports from Kingston's tutors during a tour of Europe, 1726–27; letters and papers relating to elections involving the Cheyne family, and in particular to the Buckinghamshire election campaign of 1713–14; deeds and miscellaneous estate papers involving Cheyne lands, chiefly in Buckinghamshire and at Chelsea, Middlesex, including court rolls for Drayton Beauchamp, Bucks., with Willesthorne, Herts. (1690–1721), and papers re the sale of land to Chelsea Hospital, 1686–1707.

Also included are: a copy of the will of Sir Thomas Cheyne, 1558; an account book for Francis Cheyne, sheriff of Buckinghamshire, 1589–90; a personal account book for Jane Cavendish, 1635; a volume containing copies of patents, appointments, etc., re the Customs Office, ca.1670s; a tax book for Acton, Middlesex, 1672; an account book of the Customs for the City of London, 1677–78; an account of the Buckinghamshire Quarter Sessions for 1702; three volumes of personal or estate accounts (1669–73, 1679, 1707).

2. *Miscellaneous Papers relating to Lands (EL 11147–11633):* chiefly deeds (many medieval), with other estate and manorial papers, legal and financial documents, and a few letters and accounts, concerning lands or interest in lands held by the Egerton and other families in Cheshire, Staffordshire (principally Dilhorne and Fossbrook), Warwickshire (principally the lead mines at Hilton and Murton), Wales (principally the manor of Ridley in Denbighshire), and elsewhere. For lists of deeds and court rolls, see below, pp. 74–77.

Also legal notes, briefs, and other papers, chiefly from the time of Lord Chancellor Egerton, relevant to legal cases involving lands (principally in Berkshire, Buckinghamshire, and Hertfordshire).

Includes returns of concealed lands in Berkshire, Buckinghamshire, Devon, Flint, Gloucestershire, Herefordshire, Middlesex, Monmouthshire, Somerset, Suffolk, Sussex, Wiltshire, and Yorkshire, 1584–85; copies of the *inquisitions post mortem* of Hugh de Redich, 1448, Sir John Bromley, 1486, and

Agnes Pigot, n.d.; copies of the wills of John Boydell, n.d. (16th century?) and Thomas Blewitt, 1702; and 18th-century poll book for Scisdon Hundred, Staffs.

3. *Literary and Miscellaneous Manuscripts (EL 11634–11821):* political, satirical, and occasional verse; two plays in heroic couplets ("Henry the Fifth" and "Mustapha") by Roger Boyle, 1st Earl of Orrery; sermons, including a short volume titled "The Everlasting Covenant" (a sermon on Romans 10:9); a volume containing a sermon on 2 Samuel 12:14; a volume titled "A dutiful advisement to beware of the Puritanes by the Papistes and of the Papistes by the Puritanes, with the names of such 'auctors' and authorities as are used in this booke,"; a treatise addressed "To the reader of Doctor Tillesleyes Animadversions one of the historye of tithes"; a volume containing an account of Ashridge College by Browne Willis; a treatise on diseases of horses, translated from the Italian of Romano Merchadine by William Hunnis, titled "Closet for Ferrers"; a three-volume "History of Arms" containing painted coat of arms with brief accounts of families or individuals of Italy and Burgundy, ?19th century; a scrapbook compiled in the ?18th century containing engravings of English monarchs and other personalities, chiefly of the 17th century, with drawings of heads, portraits, statues, etc.

Also papers and briefs concerning 19th-century proceedings between Lord Francis Egerton (afterward 1st Earl of Ellesmere) and James Southern, one of the Bridgewater Trustees, and others; accounts of, and a few letters concerning, estate affairs of George Granville Leveson-Gower, 1st Duke of Sutherland, 1787–97, with a note on successive earls of Sutherland; a few miscellaneous letters and legal papers concerning various trusts of the Egerton family.

Also an important series of "English Shrievalty Papers" including pricked Sheriff Rolls for 1631, 1632, 1633, and 1635; bills of nomination of sheriffs for 1632, 1634, and 1635, sent to the 1st Earl of Bridgewater as Lord President of the Council in the Marches of Wales; lists of sheriffs chosen 1636 and 1637.

4. *Wardley Hall Papers (EL 11822–12047):* miscellaneous papers, chiefly financial, legal, and manorial, of the Downes

and Sherington families and their circle, including: two commonplace books and an account book of John Downes, ca.1630
and n.d.; account book of Roger Downes, 1605–36 and Ellen
Worsley, 1603–30; 17th-century deeds involving Roger
Downes and others of his family for lands in Lancashire; bills,
answers, briefs, petitions, letters, and other supplementary
legal papers for lawsuits in the Duchy of Lancaster Court
and in Star Chamber between Thurstan Tildisley and Gilbert
Sherington over lands in Wardley and elsewhere, 1560s–90s,
and for other related suits involving the Sherington and Tildisley families.

Also includes: a book of Law Reports, 40–41 Elizabeth; a
list of Lancashire gentlemen who compounded for knighthood, 1632; a series of receipted bills and accounts for Thomas
Savage, *styled* Viscount Colchester, for the 1680s; miscellaneous coal accounts, 1683.

ELLESMERE AUTHORS
The following authors (including corporate and institutional entries) are represented in the collection by five or more pieces,
including drafts, contemporary copies, and reasonable but uncon-
firmed attributions. Royal grants, commissions, and appointments
are entered under the name of the individual monarchs.

Abbot, Abp. George (6)
Acton, William (5)
Allen, Francis (5)
Altham, Edward (12)
Anderson, Sir Edmund (7)
Anne, Queen of Great Britain (6)
Bacon, Francis, 1st Viscount St. Albans (18)
Bacon, Sir Nicholas (5)
Betts, George (11)
Brydgeman, Sir John (15)
Brydges, Grey, 5th Baron Chandos of Sudeley (6)
Buckinghamshire. Militia (5)
Burton, Edward (6)
Carlile, T. (5)
Carter, John (6)
Cartwright, Richard (8)
Castle, John (51)

Cecil, David, 3rd Earl of Exeter (11)
Cecil, Elizabeth (Egerton), Countess of Exeter (12)
Cecil, Sir Richard (7)
Cecil, Robert, 1st Earl of Salisbury (24)
Cecil, William, 1st Baron Burghley (22)
Chapman, Robert (7)
Chapman, Thomas (5)
Charles I (30)
Charles II (19)
Cheyne, Gertrude (Pierrepont), Viscountess Newhaven (42)
Cheyne, William, 2nd Viscount Newhaven (commonly *styled*
   Lord Cheyne) (70)
Cookman, John (9)
Coke, Sir Edward (11)
Collier, John Payne [forgeries by] (11)
Coo, Thomas (30)
Coote, Richard, 1st Earl of Bellamont (12)
Cromp, Thomas (16)
Dale, Hugh (5)
Daniell, Richard (10)
Day, John (15)
Delamaine, Richard (9)
DeVere, Edward, 17th Earl of Oxford (7)
Devereux, Robert, 2nd Earl of Essex (6)
Drake, John (11)
Duncomb, Fr[ancis] (13)
Ecclestone, Henry (37)
Edward III (10)
Edward VI (7)
Egerton, Frances (Stanley), Countess of Bridgewater (13)
Egerton, Francis, 3rd Duke of Bridgewater (7)
Egerton, Jane (Paulet), Countess of Bridgewater (5)
Egerton, John, 1st Earl of Bridgewater (ca.210)
Egerton, John, 2nd Earl of Bridgewater (ca.50)
Egerton, John, 3rd Earl of Bridgewater (ca.240)
Egerton, Scroop, 1st Duke of Bridgewater (26)
Egerton, Thomas [fl. 1670s] (5)
Egerton, Thomas, 1st Viscount Brackley (ca.300)
Elizabeth I (ca.300)
Evans, Elizabeth (5)

Fairbarne, Mary (Norrington) (9)
Fairborne, Sir Palmer (33)
Gilbert, Thomas (5)
Great Britain.
    Admiralty (31)
    Board of Trade (5)
    Chancery [*See also* Court of Chancery] (21)
    Chancery. Six Clerks (7)
    Commission for Charitable Uses (10)
    Commissioners for the Sale of Crown Lands (12)
    Commissioners for the Subsidy (6)
    Courts
        [Admiralty?] (11)
        Chancery (16)
        Court of the Council in the Marches of Wales (85)
        Court of the Duchy of Lancaster (10)
        Exchequer (18)
        Kings Bench (7)
        Star Chamber (48)
        Wards and Liveries (59)
        Other and unidentified (ca.80)
    Exchequer [*See also* Court of Exchequer] (22)
    Exchequer. Pipe Office (16)
    Parliament (55)
    Parliament. House of Commons (22)
    Parliament. House of Lords (21)
    Privy Council (65)
    [Privy Seal Office?] (ca.2,600 dockets, see above p. 42)
    Royal Mint (19)
Griffiths, Sylvanus (8)
Hall, Arthur (6)
Harrison, Richard (33)
Hastings, Lady Alice (8)
Heale, John (5)
Henry VI (5)
Henry VII (7)
Henry VIII (12)
Herbert, C. (6)
Herbert, Richard, 2nd Baron Herbert of Cherbury (11)

Hickman, N. (19)
Higgs, Dan (7)
Holland, Roger (17)
Hornby, Charles (7)
Hoskyns, J. (6)
James I (88)
James II (7)
Joyce, William (5)
Keene, Ed. (6)
Lambarde, William (5)
Legh, Dorothy (6)
Leigh, Humphrey (5)
Lloyd, Sir Marmaduke (18)
Lummis, J. (6)
Malynes, Gerard de (10)
Martin, Sir Richard (9)
Mary I (5)
Maryland, Provincial Court of (5)
Mason, [George?] (7)
Maynwaring, Arthur (59)
Merchant Adventurers Co. (6)
Mildmay, Sir Walter (9)
Mill, William (5)
Milward, Sir Thomas (6)
Moseley, James (7)
Mutton, P. (5)
Neale, Francis (6)
Nicholson, Sir Francis (14)
Norreys, Sir Edward (7)
Norreys, Francis, 2nd Baron Norreys of Rycote (7)
Osborne, Peregrine, 2nd Duke of Leeds (23)
Osborne, Thomas, 1st Duke of Leeds (5)
Oxford University [not including individual colleges] (8)
Oxford University, Vice Chancellor (9)
Paulet, Charles, 1st Duke of Bolton (18)
Paulet, Charles, 2nd Duke of Bolton (7)
Pierrepont, Evelyn, 1st Duke of Kingston (11)
Platel, Peter (27)
Popham, Sir John (30)
Price, Priscilla (6)
Randolph, Ed. (5)

Randolph, Ed. (5)
Ravenscroft, William (8)
Reynolds, John (5)
Robarts, John (9)
Sackville, Thomas, 1st Earl of Dorset (8)
Savage, Thomas, *styled* Viscount Colchester (10)
Scotland. Commissioners for Treating with England,
    ca.1640 (8)
Sherrington, Gilbert (6)
Shropshire. Grand Jury (7)
Sparke, Noel (8)
Spencer, Sir Edward (5)
Stanhope, Edward (6)
Stanley, Henry, 4th Earl of Derby (13)
Throckmorton, Sir Robert (5)
Thynne, Francis (5)
Tibbets, T. (7)
Tourneur, Timothy (22)
Tweedy, Henry (5)
Vaughan, Richard, 2nd Earl of Carbery (6)
Venables, Thomas (5)
Villiers, George, 1st Duke of Buckingham (6)
Walrond, Edward (7)
Walsingham, Sir Francis (33)
Warder, Chidiocke (5)
Webb, John (5)
Wenlock, William (5)
Whitbe, Thomas (11)
Willis, Browne (18)
Wrey, Lady (14)
Wymarke, Edward (5)

ELLESMERE COURT ROLLS
All of the court rolls in the collection (including views of frank-pledge or lists of fines and amercements only, and other incomplete rolls) are listed below:

Buckinghamshire:

Drayton Beauchamp (with Willesthorne, Herts.) (7) 1690,
    1694, 1696, 1703, 1716/17, 1718, 1721
Ivingho (with Pitstone) (3) 1615–16

Cheshire:
  Cholmondeston (1) 1629
Denbighshire:
  Bromfield and Yale [a lordship of 16 manors in Denbigh and Flint, including among others Abenbury, Burton, Iscoyd Morton, Pickhill, Ruabon, and Wrexham] (14) 1375 (Wrexham only), 1412–13 (Wrexham only), 1510–11, 1516, 1519–20, 1522, 1525–26, 1534, 1564, 1569–70, 1569–70 (Forest Court?), 1620–21, 1621–22, 1627
Hertfordshire:
  Rickmansworth (with Watford) (2) 1573–80
  Watford (1) 1632
  Willesthorne. *See* Bucks. Drayton Beauchamp
Lincolnshire:
  Frampton (alias Earleshall) (8) 1590–94, 1597, 1636–39, 1639–44, 1648–54, 1649–57, 1659–63, and Court Book, 1561–1603
  Mumby (4) 1531–32, 1594–95, 1600–01, 1625–26
  Skirbeck (with Leake) (10) 1585–86, 1599–1600 (bis), 1600–01, 1617, 1618–20, 1621, 1624–25, 1628–29, 1631–32
Northamptonshire:
  Wollaston (35) 1616–24, 1629–31, 1641–42, 1645, 1650, 1655, 1659, 1695–98, 1700, 1702–03, 1708, and Court Book (now disbanded) 1558–90
Shropshire:
  Idsall (*alias* Snufnal) (2) 1622, 1632–33
  Whitchurch (1) 1537–38
  Wilderley (23) 1617–31
Warwickshire:
  Sutton Maddock (1) 1628

ELLESMERE DEEDS
The following places appear in five or more deeds (including leases, mortgages, fines and recoveries, and any other legal instruments conveying land or rights over land; also including drafts or copies):
Buckinghamshire:
  Drayton Beauchamp (8) 1681–1719

Cheshire:
   Alstanton (with Nether-and Overalstanton) (6) 1443–1572
   Broom Hall (6) 1443–1577
   Brotherhulme (9) 1452–1666
   Chester. Brewershaugh (28) 1284–1650
      Whitefriars (17) 1575–1651
   Cholmondeston (39) ca. 1280–1686
   Clutton (43) ca.1290–1604
   Cuddington (11) ca.1310–1462
   Golbourne David (5) 1549–1606
   Haughton (6) 1339–1604
   Holford (5) 1445–1510
   Hoole (21) 1338–1651
   Lower Kinnerton (8) 1549–1650
   Lyme (7) 1546–76
   Malpas (8) 1319–90
   Middlewich (6) 1572–1603
   Nantwich (6) 1566–1606
   Nether Knutsford (20) 1484–1675
   Ollerton (10) 1341–1675
   Pickmere (5) 1445–1510
   Ridley (6) 1346–1651
   Rostherne (10) 1484–1675
   Tatton (9) 1501–1675
   Tilston (12) ca.1300–1510
   Torpurley (12) ca.1310–1604
   West Kirby (14) 1583–1667
   Worleston (12) 1483–1597
Denbighshire:
   Gresford (5) 1598–1658
   Hem and Hewlington (13) 1570–1653
   Holte (5) 1610<–1653
   Marsley Park (6) 1634–51
   Ridley (10) 1561–1604
Flintshire:
   Coleshill (21) 1563–1652
   Mold (*alias* Moughnutesdale) (9) 1651–75
   Northope (14) 1584–1671
Lancashire:
   Barton (6) 1606–79
   Monton (14) 1578–1687

76

Pemberton (14) 1515–1683
Swinton (9) 1561–1634
Wordeley (5) 1597–1678
Lincolnshire:
Frampton (*alias* Earleshall) (14) 1557–1680
Mumby (9) 1583–1648
Skirbeck (9) 1583–1680
London:
Bridgewater House (15) 1341–1694
Other (11) 1587–1687
Middlesex:
Chelsea (24) 1611–1712
Monmouthshire:
Caerleon (5) 1636
Northamptonshire:
Brackley (10) 1574–1686
Halse (7) 1580–1664
Wollaston (ca.95) 1593–1634
Shropshire:
Bildwas (5) 1632–46
Somersetshire:
Curry Rivel (7) 1566
Staffordshire:
Dilhorne (including Fossbrook) (116) ca.1220–1620
Ipstones (5) 1633–1703
Warwickshire:
Astley (23) ca.1260–1657
Westmoreland:
Murton-cum-Hilton (6) 1676–ca.1750
Yorkshire:
Flaxfleet (5) 1615–45
Scotland:
Whithorn Priory. Roll of extracts from cartulary of medi-
eval deeds, 1504
Ireland:
Killeshin (5) 1670–1701

HASTINGS COLLECTION
ca.50,000 pieces, ca.1100–1892

For over four hundred years the Hastings family (variously barons Hastings, Botreaux, Hungerford, Loughborough, and Moleyns, earls of Huntingdon, Pembroke, and Moira, and marquesses of Hastings) played a major role in English political life and exercised wide local influence in Leicestershire and numerous other English counties.

Already an important medieval local power with lands in Leicestershire, the family rose to national prominence with William Hastings, 1st Baron Hastings (1430?–83), a staunch Yorkist whom Edward IV ennobled in 1461 and appointed to numerous local and national offices (including that of Lieutenant General of Calais in 1479). He was executed for treason in 1483 for refusing to support Richard III's bid for the throne, but his lands and title were restored to his son Edward, the 2nd Baron (1466–1507) by Henry VII. Edward married Mary Hungerford, *suo jure* Baroness Hungerford, Botreaux, and Moleyns; she brought those titles and extensive West Country lands into the Hastings family.

Their son George (1488–1544) was a successful if extravagant courtier and favorite of Henry VIII and was created 1st Earl of Huntingdon in 1529. He was a privy councillor, but played little active role in central politics although he helped to suppress the Pilgrimage of Grace in 1536. He married Anne Stafford Herbert, a sister of the 3rd Duke of Buckingham, and died at Stoke Poges, Bucks., although the family seat had long since been established at Ashby de la Zouch in Leicestershire. His son and heir Francis, the 2nd Earl (ca.1514–60), supported the Duke of Northumberland against Somerset and, briefly, Lady Jane Grey, but quickly regained Queen Mary's confidence, possibly because of his marriage to Catherine Pole, a daughter of Lord Montague and niece of Cardinal Pole. He was appointed Lord Lieutenant of Derbyshire (1552–60), Leicestershire (1554–60), Rutland (1550–59), and Warwickshire (1554–59), and added the extensive Beaumont lands in Leicestershire to the family's growing wealth.

Henry Hastings, the 3rd Earl (ca.1536–95), was an active Puritan and politician who served as Lord President of the North for over twenty years, was a joint-custodian of Mary Queen of Scots, and held the lord lieutenancies of Leicestershire, Rutland, Yorkshire, Northumberland, Cumberland, Westmoreland, and Durham at various times during Elizabeth's reign. Through his mother the 3rd Earl could claim legitimate Yorkist descent and was supported by many Protestant nobles in his claim to succeed to the throne at the death of Elizabeth, but the Queen survived him, and his younger brother George, 4th Earl of Huntingdon (ca.1540–1604), had less interest in upholding the claim. George married Dorothy, the daughter of Sir John Port of Etwall, Co. Derby, and enjoyed local office and influence but little national importance. More famous at the time was Sir Francis Hastings (1546?–1610), another younger brother of the 3rd Earl and, like him, a noted Puritan; he was active as a Protestant propagandist author and sat in six Elizabethan parliaments.

The 4th Earl was succeeded by his grandson Henry Hastings, the 5th Earl of Huntingdon (1586–1643), who served as Lord Lieutenant of Leicestershire (1607–42) and Rutland (1614–42) and married Elizabeth Stanley, one of the daughters and co-heirs of Ferdinando, 5th Earl of Derby (and thus sister-in-law of John Egerton, 1st Earl of Bridgewater). Their son Ferdinando Hastings, 6th Earl of Huntingdon (1609–56) was an M.P. for Leicestershire in 1625 and 1628–29, succeeded his father in 1643, and held a commission in Cromwell's army although apparently took no active role in the Civil Wars. He married Lucy, the daughter and heir of Sir John Davies, the poet and influential Attorney-General for Ireland. More active during the wars was his younger brother Henry Hastings (d. 1667), a staunch Royalist who held Ashby for the King until 1646, and whose privately raised troops harried Cromwell's troops in and around Leicestershire. He was created Lord Loughborough in 1643, eventually accompanied Charles II into exile, and returned with the Restoration to serve as Lord Lieutenant of Leicestershire. After the siege and destruction of Ashby Castle, the main branch of the family removed to Donington Park, Leicestershire, where the 6th Earl was succeeded in 1656 by his young son Theophilus.

Theophilus Hastings, 7th Earl of Huntingdon (1650–1701), was a firm Tory and Royalist who held under James II the offices of Chief Justice in Eyre South of the Trent, Lord Lieutenant of Leicestershire and Derbyshire, and Colonel of the 13th Foot. He was deprived of his offices at the Revolution, and twice imprisoned briefly, but died peacefully in London in 1701 and was succeeded by his son by a first wife, Elizabeth Lewis. This son, George Hastings, 8th Earl of Huntingdon (1677–1705), served briefly but with distinction under Marlborough, died unmarried in 1705 and was succeeded by his half-brother (by the 7th Earl's second wife, Frances [Fowler] Needham Hastings, aftw. De Ligondez) Theophilus, the 9th Earl (1696–1745).

An anti-Walpole Whig who held no major offices and played little role in national politics, the 9th Earl is more famous for his wife Selina (the daughter of Washington Shirley, 2nd Earl Ferrerrs), who founded a Methodist sect known as "The Countess of Huntingdon's Connection," was an active patroness of evangelical clergymen, and popularized Methodism in aristocratic circles. She died in 1791, surviving all four sons including Francis, the 10th Earl (1728–89), at whose death without children the earldom remained dormant for nearly 30 years while the various Hastings baronies (of Hastings, Botreaux, Hungerford, and Moleyns) devolved on the 10th Earl's sister and heir-general Elizabeth.

Elizabeth married in 1752 John Rawdon, 1st Earl of Moira (d. 1793). Their son Francis (1754–1826), who assumed the surname Rawdon-Hastings in 1790, had served with distinction in America during the Revolution and succeeded his father as 2nd Earl of Moira in 1793. His military and political careers were capped with an appointment as Governor-General of Bengal (1813–22), where he both consolidated and reformed British government in India, and for which he was created 1st Marquis of Hastings in 1817. He had married, in 1804, Flora Mure-Campbell, *suo jure* Countess of Loudoun, and was succeeded by his son George Augustus Francis Rawdon-Hastings (1808–44), 2nd Marquis of Hastings and, after the death of his mother, Earl of Loudoun.

The marquessate of Hastings became extinct after the deaths of their two sons (Paulyn Reginald Serlo Rawdon-Hastings, 3rd Marquis, and his brother Henry Weysford Charles Plantagenet Rawdon-Hastings, 4th Marquis), while the earldom of Loudoun descended to the surviving daughter of the 2nd Marquis, Edith Maud Rawdon-Hastings (1833–74), who married Charles Frederick Clifton in 1853. He later took the surname Abney-Hastings (after inheriting the Abney estates at Willesley), and after her death was created 1st Baron Donington. Their son, Charles Edward Abney-Hastings (afterward Rawdon-Hastings), died without children in 1920, when the various Hastings baronies fell into abeyance, while the earldom of Loudoun devolved onto his niece Edith Maud Abney-Hastings [formerly Huddleston] (1883–1960).

The earldom of Huntingdon, in abeyance since the death of the 10th Earl in 1789, was successfully claimed thirty years later by Hans Francis Hastings, a distant cousin and naval officer, who as the 12th Earl began the current line.

Provenance: The Hastings Collection was purchased by the Huntington Library in January 1927 from Maggs Bros. of London, who had acquired the papers from Edith Maud Abney-Hastings, Countess of Loudoun. A small group of ca.100 miscellaneous Hastings manuscripts was purchased from Lady Edith Maclaren in 1977.

Bibliography: Many (but by no means all) of the Hastings manuscripts are calendared in extensive detail in the Historical Manuscript Commission's four-volume *Report on the Manuscripts of the Late Reginald Rawdon Hastings, Esq.* (London: H.M.S.O., 1928–47), based on a survey prepared at the Public Record Office largely before 1914. Many of the royal charters and other important individual items were described, and often reproduced in facsimile, in the six-part Maggs sale catalog, *The Huntingdon Papers* (1926). A "Summary Report on the Hastings Manuscripts" was published by the Library in *The Huntington Library Bulletin* 5 (April 1934): pp. 1–67. Claire Cross has edited *The Letters of Sir Francis Hastings, 1574–1609* for the Somerset Record Society, Vol. 64 (1969).

A supplementary collection of approximately 3,500 letters written by American and English Methodists and others to Selina, Countess of Huntingdon, between 1760 and 1791 are located in the Archives of Cheshunt College (formerly Trevecka College), Cambridge.

Remarks on the following description: The Hastings papers are distributed among, and described under, the headings listed in the Table of Contents.

Papers concerning Ireland (including those which came into the collection with the marriages of Lucy Davies to the 6th Earl of Huntingdon and of Lady Elizabeth Hastings to the 1st Earl of Moira) are described separately, although the estate and financial papers have long since been integrated into the main runs of manuscripts and are not here distinguished.

Scottish papers coming into the collection with the marriage of Flora Mure-Campbell, Countess of Loudoun, to the 1st Marquis of Hastings, were restored to the Loudoun Collection, with which they properly belonged in the past, and are now described under that entry.

I. ACCOUNTS AND FINANCIAL PAPERS
ca.20,000 pieces, 1281–1891

The following category consists of estate, household, and personal accounts, bills, receipts, acquittances, annuities, bonds, obligations, defeasances, legal expenses, insurance papers, bank papers, income tax papers, bankruptcy papers, and other general finanical papers dealing with the Hastings and related families (particularly those of the Rawdons, earls of Moira, and the Shirleys, earls Ferrers, beginning in the last third of the 17th century).

Estate material includes accounts of building and repairs, stables, gardens, woods, laborers' wages, and general estate expenses. There are extensive 17th- and 18th-century accounts for mills at Donington and Loughborough, and coal accounts for the Moira Colliery and other collieries at Oakthorpe and Melbourne, 1606–1890. (Rentals, compotus rolls, and other major manorial accounts are filed with the *Manorial and Local Affairs Papers* of Section VI.)

Household material includes accounts of provisioning, furnishings, building and repairs, servants' wages, and general household expenses. Of particular interest are: an account of the wages of the household servants of Henry, 3rd Earl of Huntingdon, March–September 1564: an account of the monthly expenses at York Castle during the presidency of the Council of the North of Henry, 3rd Earl of Huntingdon, 1584–85; summaries of household expenses at Ashby, 1598–99; a declaration of account of the clerk of the household at Ashby, 1614; a volume of steward's household accounts at [Castle Donington?] April–June, 1628, including daily lists of provisions consumed; a volume of the household expenses of Alice, Countess of Derby, at Harefield House, 1634–35; a volume of the household accounts of Henry, 5th Earl of Huntingdon, 1638–43.

Personal material includes accounts for traveling expenses (meals, transportation, etc.), clothing, other personal necessities, miscellaneous expenses, and general financial statements. Of particular interest are: lists of debts of various earls of Huntingdon, 1553, 1596, 1597, 1612, 1614, and 1620; accounts of the administration of the estates of Henry, 3rd Earl of Huntingdon, 1597, and of George, 4th Earl of Huntingdon, 1606, including accounts of all goods, chattels, and debts; a volume of receipts and expenditures by Thomas Harvey on behalf of Henry, 5th Earl of Huntingdon, 1606–13; booksellers' bills, 1635–38, 1638–40, 1693–94, and 1744–45; an abstract of the 8th Earl of Huntingdon's expenses from 1689 to 1702; a few accounts for the 7th Earl as Colonel of his regiment, 1685–88.

From 1770 to 1800, there are fairly regular series of yearly bundles of accounts grouped under the headings "repairs," "court charges," "salaries and pensions," "my Lord's private account," and "London accounts."

The accounts are distributed chronologically as follows:

     13th century: 1 piece
     14th century: ca.25 pieces
     15th century: ca.30 pieces
     16th century: ca.80 pieces
     17th century: ca.1,550 pieces
     18th century: ca.10,250 pieces
     19th century: ca.8,000 pieces

See also p. 311 below.

II. CORRESPONDENCE

ca.13,900 pieces, 1477–1892

Consists of the political, military, personal, and business correspondence of the Hastings family and their circle. There is less political material after 1660, and the majority of the business correspondence belongs to the 19th century. Among the topics covered are:

Political: official correspondence of the 3rd and 4th Earls of Huntingdon as Lords Lieutenant of Leicestershire, Rutlandshire, and other counties, dealing with Anglo-Scottish affairs (especially during the time the 3rd Earl was Lord President of the North), the imprisonment of Mary Queen of Scots, the levying and transporting of troops for foreign service and the drilling of county trained bands, compositions for knighthood, purveyance, recusants and their detection and punishment, subsidies and other levies; 17th-century correspondence between the earls of Huntingdon and the deputy lieutenants of Leicestershire and Rutland, and other county officials, concerning elections, appointments, levies, surrenders of charters, etc.; correspondence of the 7th Earl of Huntingdon with Lady Huntingdon during his imprisonment at Plymouth in 1688, with fellow Tories during the exile of James II in France, and with friends and officials during his imprisonment in the Tower. Also 78 newsletters, chiefly to the earls of Huntingdon, and chiefly during the period 1670–92.

Military: letters from Henry Carey, 1st Baron Hunsdon, and others to the 3rd Earl, concerning troops on the Scottish border, 1581; correspondence of Henry Hastings, Baron Loughborough, as high sheriff and colonel of a regiment of horse for Charles I; correspondence of the 7th Earl as Colonel of the 13th Regiment of Foot, with the officers and men of his regiment, 1685–88; also some material on the American Revolution, the Peninsular War, and the Napoleonic Wars in general, with accounts of battles and army movements.

Personal and Business Affairs: correspondence of the Hastings family and their friends, relatives, agents, and business associates concerning family and social news, the administration of the Hastings estates, relations with tradespeople and creditors, the charitable foundations of the family (including Etwall Hospital, the hospital at Stoke Poges, Dilhorne and Repton Schools, and gifts to Oxford and Cambridge), and the plantations in America; also includes small groups of Shirley and Ferrers family letters.

The following persons or institutions are represented by 5 or more letters or other papers (including drafts and contemporary copies):

Abney, Sir Edward (12)
Abney-Hastings, Charles Frederick (formerly Charles Frederick Clifton), 1st Baron Donington (30)

Abney-Hastings, Edith Maud (Rawdon-Hastings), Baroness
  Donington & *suo jure* Countess of Loudoun (19)
Adam, William (6)
Adderley, J. (6)
Alexander, H. (12)
Alexander & Co. (firm) (18)
Alington, Hildebrand, 5th Baron Alington of Killard (5)
Allan, Robert & Son (firm) (15)
Anderson, J. & F. (firm) (95)
Angouleme, Louis Antoine, Duc de (6)
Armstrong, Thomas (14)
Atkinson, Charles (13)
Atkinson, John (6)
Atkinson, Joseph (32)
Atkinson, Joseph & John (firm) (9)
Augustus Frederick, Duke of Sussex (14)
Ayleway, Robert (8)
Bache, Thomas (5)
Bagnold, John (6)
Barckman, P. (7)
Barlow, William, Bp. (5)
Barnetts Hoare Company (12)
Barradall, Edward (9)
Barrington, William Wildman, 2nd Viscount Barrington (19)
Barretto, Joseph (5)
Barrodale, Thomas (16)
Bartrum, Thomas (89)
Barwell, Henry (5)
Bayly, Thomas E. (70)
Beaumont, Sir Henry, 2nd Bart. (16)
Benson, Martin (5)
Bigland, Ed. (9)
Bittleston, Thomas (5)
Blake, John (87)
Blake, Thomas John (9)
Blathwayt, William (7)
Blennerhassett, Eliza (5)
Bloomfield, Benjamin, 1st Baron Bloomfield (7)
Bold, Peter (15)
Bonneville, Marie de (12)

Bowes, Robert (7)
Bret, Daniel (17)
Breval, D. (6)
Brisbourne, Isaac (14)
Brome, James (7)
Brookes, Job (8)
Brookes, Theophilus (11)
Burgridge, Thomas (8)
Byron, Richard, 2nd Baron Byron of Rochdale (5)
Campbell, Arthur (5)
Carey, Henry, 1st Baron Hunsdon (5)
Carleton, Thomas (9)
Carte, Samuel (6)
Carte, Thomas (5)
Carter, Lawrence (13)
Carver, Christopher (5)
Chaplin, Robert (10)
Charles I (34)
Charles II (6)
Cheyne, George (32)
Clarke, Sir Gilbert (7)
Clerke, Beatrix, (6)
Clifton, Lady Alice Hastings (8)
Clifton, Augustus Wykeham (9)
Clifton, Sir Gervase, 1st Bart. (6)
Clifton, Hetty (Treves) (5)
Cobbe, Lady Elizabeth Beresford (10)
Cocchi, Antonio (7)
Colles, F. (7)
Cooke, Sir Miles (5)
Coote, Richard, 1st Baron Coote of Coloony (10)
Cotton, Rowland (7)
Coutts, Thomas (6)
Coutts & Company (firm) (17)
Cradock, John (7)
Cradock, John & Thomas (firm) (8)
Cradock, Norrice (5)
Cradock & Son (firm) (12)
Cripps, James (6)
Croft, Bridgett (61)

Crowle, William (9)
Crowley, Theodosia (6)
Crozier, George (5)
Cunninghame, James (7)
Curzon, Lady Mary Assheton (5)
Curzon, Richard William Penn (8)
Dalby, Henry (5)
Dalby, Thomas (25)
Davall, J. B. (6)
Davies, Sir John (8)
Davison, Noll, Templer & Co. (5)
Davys, Ferdinando (51)
Davys, John (a) (40)
Davys, John (b) (9)
Davys, Matthew (22)
Davys, Tristram (10)
Davys, William (5)
Dawson, Edward (111)
Dewes, W. (9)
Dickinson, Robert (25)
Dighton, Christopher (20)
Dixie, Wolston (5)
Donovan, Jeremiah (17)
Douglas, Lady Eleanor (Tuchet) Davies (12)
Doyle, Sir Francis Hastings (5)
Dudley, Robert, Earl of Leicester (5)
Dugdale, Sir William (12)
Eames, John (18)
Edmonds, Lady Sarah (Harington) Hastings Kingsmill Zouche
   (5)
Edward Augustus, Duke of Kent & Strathern (52)
Edwards, Elizabeth (6)
Edwards, Templer & Co. (firm) (6)
Egerton, Alice (Spencer) Stanley, Viscountess Brackley &
   Countess of Derby (12)
Egerton, Thomas, 1st Viscount Brackley (7)
Eglington Iron Co. (firm) (5)
Elizabeth I (17)
Ellis, Edward (10)
Ernest Augustus, Duke of Cumberland (7)

Evans, John (290)
Everard, Robert (13)
Faulkner, E. (244)
Finch, Heneage, 1st Earl of Nottingham (5)
Fisher, James Hurtle (32)
Fitzgerald, Lady Charlotte Adelaide Constantia (Rawdon) (9)
Fitzgerald, Hamilton (5)
Fletcher, George (5)
Forbes, Arthur, 1st Earl of Granard (5)
Forbes, Selina Frances (Rawdon), Countess of Granard (9)
Fortescue, Francis (5)
Frecheville, John (7)
Frederick Augustus, Duke of York (22)
Gailhard, Jean (9)
Gardiner, William (20)
Geddes, George H. (22)
George IV (10)
German, G. (20)
German, William (495)
Gery, John (54)
Gibson, James (9)
Gillett, F. C. (13)
Glasse, George Henry (17)
Great Britain.
    Commissioners for the Subsidy? (19)
    Lord Steward's Department (18)
    Privy Council (144)
    War Office (5)
Greenwood, Cox & Co. (firm) (10)
Grey, Henry, 1st Baron Grey of Groby (5)
Hamilton, Sir Francis, 1st Bart. (7)
Handley & Durant (firm) (119)
Hastings, Lady Christiana (13)
Hastings, Lady Elizabeth (42)
Hastings, Elizabeth (Lewis), Countess of Huntingdon (47)
Hastings, Elizabeth (Stanley), Countess of Huntingdon (46)
Hastings, Ferdinando, 6th Earl of Huntingdon (31)
Hastings, Lady Flora Elizabeth Rawdon. *See* Rawdon-Hastings

Hastings, Flora (Mure-Campbell) Rawdon-, Marchioness of Hastings and *suo jure* Countess of Loudoun. *See* Rawdon-Hastings

Hastings, Lady Frances (15)

Hastings, Francis Rawdon-, 1st Marquis of Hastings and 2nd Earl of Moira. *See* Rawdon-Hastings

Hastings, Sir Francis (25)

Hastings, Francis, 10th Earl of Huntingdon (79)

Hastings, Gabriel (11)

Hastings, George, 4th Earl of Huntingdon (13)

Hastings, George, 8th Earl of Huntingdon (20)

Hastings, Sir George (5)

Hastings, George [1729–43, son of 9th Earl] (5)

Hastings, George [fl. 1818, claimant to the earldom of Huntingdon] (8)

Hastings, George Augustus Francis Rawdon-, 2nd Marquis of Hastings. *See* Rawdon-Hastings

Hastings, Henry, 3rd Earl of Huntingdon (65)

Hastings, Henry, 5th Earl of Huntingdon (143)

Hastings, Henry, 1st Baron Loughborough (31)

Hastings, Henry [fl. 1684–88, a captain in the 7th Earl's regiment] (35)

Hastings, Henry [b. ca.1644, son of Henry Hastings of Humberston, Leics.](5)

Hastings, Henry [fl. 1686] (5)

Hastings, Henry [fl. 1733–46, of Newhall & Ledstone?] (54)

Hastings, Henry [fl. 1754–87, in the London Customs House] (8)

Hastings, J. (10)

Hastings, Knyvett (14)

Hastings, Lucy (Davies), Countess of Huntingdon (88)

Hastings, Lady Mary (10)

Hastings, Selina (Shirley), Countess of Huntingdon (18)

Hastings, Theophilus, 7th Earl of Huntingdon (252)

Hastings, Theophilus, 9th Earl of Huntingdon (13)

Hastings, Warren (79)

Hatton, C. (7)

Heath, Robert (23)

Hemington, Robert (107)

Hendrie, Robert (321)
Henshawe, William (6)
Herbert, Henry, 10th Earl of Pembroke & 7th Earl of Mont-
gomery (6)
Hill, Joseph (15)
Hill, Robert (5)
Hill, Thomas (16)
Hoare, Benjamin (5)
Holden, Robert (6)
Hooten, Henry (5)
Hope, J. (9)
Hopton, Robert (9)
Hotham, Sir Charles, 6th Bart. (5)
Hotham, William, 1st Baron Hotham (6)
Howe, Mary Sophia Charlotte (Kilmansegge), Viscountess
Howe (5)
Ibbetson, James (7)
Ingham, B. (7)
Ingham, Robert (13)
Iveson, John (107)
Jackson, Charles (7)
Jackson, John (11)
Jacob, Sir John, 3rd Bart. (5)
Jacques, Anne (7)
Jacques, Gervase (152)
James I (11)
James, Charles (452)
J'anson, Brian (5)
J'anson, John (6)
Johnson, Richard (10)
Johnston, Nathaniel (66)
Jolliffe, Lady Mary (Hastings) (34)
Jolliffe, Sir William (15)
Jones, Alexander (12)
Jones, James (25)
Joynes, John (8)
Karnes, Susanna (8)
Kendall, John (7)
Kent, William (7)
Kirwan, Lady Victoria Mary Louisa (Rawdon-Hastings) (8)

Knight, Gowin (7)
Lacey, Charles (5)
Langham, Sir James (25)
Laplace, C. (6)
Lascelles, Talbot (5)
Latham, John (5)
Leake, William (5)
Leedham, Thomas (14)
Leicester. Mayor & Aldermen (11)
Leicestershire. Deputy Lieutenants (14)
Leke, Mary Lewis, Countess of Scarsdale (26)
Leke, Robert, 3rd Earl of Scarsdale (19)
Leman, J. Curtis (5)
Leveson, Anne Venables (10)
Levinge, Sir Richard, 1st Bart. (5)
Levinge, Samuel (5)
Ligondez, Frances Fowler Needham Hastings de (5)
Liguire, Mary (5)
Lindsey, Theophilus (19)
Lister, Nicholas (14)
Lloyd, John (27)
Louis Phillippe I, King of France (12)
McCarthy, Felix (8)
McClintock, Robert (6)
MacCulloh, Elizabeth (41)
MacDonald, Thomas (7)
McDonall, W. (12)
MacFarlan, [   ] (6)
McHugh, Dominick (5)
Mackie, Robert (221)
McMahon, Sir John, 1st Bart. (15)
Mammatt, Edward (254)
Mammatt, Edward F. (38)
Mammatt, John (6)
Man, Edward (5)
Mann, Sir Horace, 1st Bart. (11)
Marshall, John (10)
Martin, William (16)
Mason, William (7)
May, Sir Humfrey (5)

Maynwaring, Katherine (8)
Middleton, John (6)
Miles, Samuel (10)
Miles, William Augustus (6)
Milward, Robert (6)
Molloy, James Scott (11)
Monck, George, 1st Duke of Albemarle (60)
Monsley, William Eaton (11)
Morgan, Charles (17)
Morgan, John (5)
Morley, James (39)
Mousley, William Eaton (11)
Muddiman, Henry (16)
Murray, David, 2nd Earl of Mansfield (53)
Murray, John Fisher (5)
Nash, J. (5)
Needham, Mary (Shirley), Viscountess Kilmorey (11)
Needham, Thomas, 9th Viscount Kilmorey (8)
Nicholas, Sir Edward (29)
Nickolls, Robert Boucher (6)
Noble, Francis (7)
Ogilvie, William (20)
Onslow, Denzell (7)
Onslow, Sarah Foote Lewis (8)
Palmer, Charles F. (8)
Peat, Thomas Henry (233)
Pelham, Catherine Cobbe (5)
Pelham, Henry (8)
Percy, Hugh, 2nd Duke of Northumberland (13)
Pestell, Ellis Shipley (5)
Pestell, Thomas (6)
Petour, Vasse Le (5)
Phillipps, Ambrose (6)
Piddocke, Leonard (11)
Pierce, Thomas (8)
Pitman, Frederick (35)
Pole, Cardinal Reginald (10)
Pratt, Charles (8)
Rawdon, Elizabeth (Hastings), Countess of Moira (32)
Rawdon, John, 1st Earl of Moira (8)

Rawdon-Hastings, Lady Flora Elizabeth (27)
Rawdon-Hastings, Flora (Mure-Campbell), Marchioness of
   Hastings and *suo jure* Countess of Loudoun (71)
Rawdon-Hastings, Francis, 1st Marquis of Hastings and 2nd
   Earl of Moira (159)
Rawdon-Hastings, George Augustus Francis, 2nd Marquis of
   Hastings (22)
Reid, Andrew (8)
Ridge, John (9)
Ridley, Nevile (31)
Rodgers, John (13)
Russell, Lord Wriothesley (15)
Rutland. Deputy Lieutenants (13)
St. Denis, [?] de (6)
St. George, Oliver (6)
Salusbury, Thomas (12)
Scargill, John (12)
Segrave, A. (5)
Segrave, Charles (6)
Selwin, Charles (5)
Sewell, Stephen John (5)
Sharpe, John (10)
Shaw, Sa[?] (5)
Sheeron, John (6)
Shirley, Laurence (6)
Shirley, Lewis (8)
Shirley, Mary (Levinge), Countess Ferrers (6)
Shirley, Robert, 1st Earl Ferrers (5)
Smallman, R. (62)
Smart, Ithiel (10)
Smith, William Edward (446)
Smith & Mammatt (firm) (814)
Smith, Mammatt & Hale (firm) (175)
Smithsby, J. (44)
Somodevilla y Bengoechea, Zenó de, Marqués de la Ensenada
   (6)
Stanhope, Arthur (40)
Stanhope, Charles [1655–1712, of Mansfield Woodhouse,
   Notts.] (25)
Stanhope, Charles [d. 1759, son of above] (6)

Stanhope, Charles [1673–1760, Secretary of the Treasury] (5)
Stanhope, Philip, 1st Earl of Chesterfield (13)
Stanhope, Philip Dormer, 4th Earl of Chesterfield (48)
Stanhope, Philip, 5th Earl of Chesterfield (19)
Stanley, Hans (25)
Staveley, Christian (5)
Stavely, William (13)
Stillingfleet, John (5)
Stoughton, Thomas (6)
Stuart, Sophia Frederica Christina (Rawdon-Hastings), Marchioness of Bute (12)
Sturt, Charles (6)
Thacker, Godfrey (8)
Tidcombe, John (9)
Townesend, George (5)
Tylee, Edward (16)
Tyler, Francis Henry (7)
Vane, Lucy (Jolliffe), Viscountess Vane (14)
Venables, Catherine (Shirley) (6)
Vernon, George (13)
Wade, George (13)
Walkinshaw, Catherine (7)
Walsingham, Sir Francis (19)
Watson, Bp. Thomas, (69)
Webster, J. (10)
Wedderburn, Alexander, 1st Earl of Rosslyn (5)
Wentworth, Anne (Johnson), Countess of Strafford (17)
Wheler, Lady Catherine Maria (Hastings) (10)
Wheler, Granville (32)
Wilkinson, Abraham (7)
Willes, Samuel (11)
William IV (31)
William Frederick, 2nd Duke of Gloucester & Edinburgh (19)
Williams, Frances (5)
Williams, John, Archbishop of York (6)
Wilmot, Nicholas (5)
Wood, Peter (7)
Wood, William (6)
Woodhouse, John Thomas (111)

Woodhouse, Jonathan (50)
Woodruffe, Benjamin (22)
Wotton, Thomas (7)
Wright, Sir Nathan (5)
Wrightson, Michael (5)
Yelverton, Barbara (Yelverton) Rawdon-Hastings (5)
Yelverton, Sir Hastings Reginald (7)
Young, John (5)

III. DEEDS
ca.4,800 pieces, 12th–19th centuries
The following category consists of legal instruments conveying land or rights over land, including deeds of grant, gift, or sale, leases, releases, bargains and sales, mortgages, fines (final concords) and recoveries, quitclaims, surrenders of rights, confirmations, exemplifications, letters of attorney for delivering or receiving seisin, and licenses of alienation. Over half of the deeds relate to Leicestershire, where the Hastings family had their principal estates after the 15th century; well over half of the deeds predate 1600.* There are many fine royal, ecclesiastical, corporate, and personal seals.

The places listed below by county appear in five or more deeds (the exact number being given in parentheses); the beginning dates are the earliest that can be ascribed, although many of the undated deeds belong to the 12th or early 13th centuries.
Berkshire:
Charlton (8) 1317–85
Englefield (18) 1568–1672/73
Hill (7) 1306–55
Hungerford (36) 1273–1469
Inkpen (5) 1334–39
Sanden (12) 1306–39

---

* In addition to the deeds summarily listed below (nearly two thirds of which were omitted from the Historical Manuscripts Commission's *Report*), there are approximately 1,000 unsorted late 18th- and early 19th-century deeds (those of the 18th century chiefly concerning the exchange of lands made between Francis Rawdon-Hastings, 1st Marquis of Hastings, and his wife, Flora Mure-Campbell, *suo jure* Countess of Loudoun), and another approximately 200 unsorted deeds (many fragmentary, fragile, drafts, or office copies) dating from the 16th to the 18 century.

Buckinghamshire:
Beachendon (5) 1469/70–1537/38
Brill (9) 1332–1569
Chearsley (7) 1469/70–1536
Cippenham (9) 1330–1591
Datchet (6, including 5 on a short cartulary) 1331–37, 1460
Ditton (8, including 6 on a short cartulary) 1337–1469/70
Eton (5) 1469/70–1590/91
Fulmer (6) 1331–1590/91
Ilmer (6) 1504/05–1537/38
Ludgershall (15) 1313–1536
Stoke Poges (11) 1337–1590/91
Cambridgeshire:
Fen Ditton (22) 1269–1320
Fulbourn (7) 1344–1411/12
Teversham (5) n.d.–1304
Cornwall:
Botreaux Castle (Boscastle) (8) 1385–1607/08
[Bottlet]? (10) 1369–1574
Minster (5) 1413–1562
Penhele (9) 1349–1563
Uny Lelant (6) 1349–1537/38
Worthyvale (8) 1369–1574/75
Derbyshire:
Dale [Abbey] (5) 1569–1609, 1754/55
Egginton (5) 1611–36
King's Newton (6) 1487–1698
Measham (6) 1450–1621
Melbourne (26) 1487–1794
Netherseal (7) 1609–98
Osleton (5) 1469/70–1569
Repton (6) 1541–69
Smisby (37) 1328–1754
Swarkestone (7) 1346/47–1445
Devonshire:
Clyst Gerred (5) (n.d.–1227)
Diptford (28) 1432–1574/75
Langford (7) 1369–1574/75
Linnacombe (5) 1331–1348/49

South Pool (5) 1432–88, 1585
Stokenham (10) 1409–1586
Dorset:
Canford [Magna] (14) 1567–1617
Puddletown (5) 1575/76–1788
Hampshire:
Christchurch (10) 1540–85/86
Hertfordshire:
Pirton (6) 1608/09–1645
Ware (13) 1549–74
Leicestershire:
Alton (26) 1339/40–1630
Anderchurch (7) 1351–1527
Anstey (6) 1294–1598
Appleby [Magna] (14) 1262–1712
Ashby de la Zouch (284) 1301–1771
Aylestone (12) 1282–1312
Baggrave (7) 1274–1319
Bagworth (24) 1313–1571/72
Barlestone (6) 1395–1606
Barrow-upon-Soar (149) 1241/42–1788
Belton (45) 1345–1788
Belvoir (7) 1464–75
Blackfordby (27) 1414/15–1754
Boothorpe (5) 1565–1649
Botcheston (5) 1464–1625
Bottesford (5) 1469/70–1475
Brascote (10) 1348/49–1600
Braunstone (28) 1312–1591
Breedon (21) 1427–1631
Carlton Curlieu (7) 1361–1549
Castle Donington (105) 1234–1790
Charley Chase (10) 1633–1726
Charnwood Forest (30) 1342–1788
Cossington (6) 1331/32–1516
Dalby (8) 1381–1568/69
Desford (7) 1463–1557
Donisthorpe (7) 1325/26–1539
Enderby (30) 1329–1593

Framland Hundred (13) 1318–1788
Hathern (14) 1504–1698
Isley Walton (5) 1440–1547
Kilby (6) 1368–1537/38
Kilwardby (19) 1286–1513
Kilworth (5) 1399–1517
Kirby Bellars (9) 1300–60
Kirby Muxloe (149) 1247–1621
Kirkby Mallory (17) 1299–1503
Knighton (6) 1322–1540
Knightthorpe (6) 1561–79
Leicester (73) 1285–1622
Leicester Forest (11) 1241/42–1413/14
Long Whatton (37) 1319–1705
Loughborough (457) 1281–1796
Lubbesthorpe (31) 1312–1615
Lutterworth (4) 1477/78–1606
Market Bosworth (9) 1508/09–1589
Market Marbrough (6) 1330–1476/77
Mountsorrel (19) 1324/25–1650
Newbold Verdon (14) 1419/20–1616
Newton Harcourt (12) 1423–1568/69
Oadby (5) 1370–1482
Oakthorpe (27) n.d.–1786
Orton Quartermarsh (7) 1330–1492
Orton Saucey (22) 1310/11–1566
Osbaston (9) 1316/17–1621
Osgathorpe (51) 1318/19–1788
Packington (36) 1303–1788
Pipewell (10) 1316–1428/29
Prestwold (6) 1434/35–1547
Quorndon (83) 1274–1589
Ravenstone (21) 1284/85–1625
Redmile (6) 1464–75
Rotherby (9) 1316–1472
Serlethorpe (6) 1400–1546
Shackerstone (20) 1272–1572
Sheepshed (79) 1278–1576
Sileby (14) 1325/26–1574
Stoney Stanton (15) 1492–1788

Stoughton (5) 1370–1556
Swannington (8) 1323–1686/87
Thornton (21) 1295–1537/38
Thringstone (56) 1230–1712
Tonge (14) 1294–1457
Whitwick (24) 1342–1788
Wistow (14) 1247–1537/38
Woodcote (24) 1316–1428/29, 1619
Woodhouse (10) 1312/13–1589
Woodthorpe (15) 1384–1579
Worthington (5) 1419/20–1527

Lincolnshire:
Woolsthorpe (6) 1464–75

London: (21) 1352–1584/85

Middlesex:
Edmonton (6) 1472/73–1505
Finchley (5) 1488–1527

Norfolk:
Gissing (5) 1247

Northamptonshire
Ashley (5) 1469/70–1475
East Farndon (13) 1363–1461
Sibbertoft (7) 1382/83–1476/77
Stoke Albany (9) 1464–84
Sutton (8) 1464–84
Welford (50) 1225–1581
Wilbarston (7) 1469/70–1484

Northumberland:
Kirkharle (8) 1323–58
Slaley (10) 1328–32/33
Styford (9) 1319–79

Nottinghamshire:
Bonnington (49) 1246/47–1487
Eastwood (10) 1391–1565
Kingston [-on-Soar] (10) 1311–63
Leake, East (16) 1402/03–1788
Leake, West (45) 1226–1742
Sutton (24) 1246/47–1487
Sutton Bonnington (5) 1537/38–1539

Oxfordshire:
> Henley-on-Thames (20) 1332–1599

Somerset:
> Aller (22) 1360–1626
> Cadbury, North (21) 1460–1586
> Cadbury, South (9) 1537/38–1596
> Clapton (8) 1460–1596
> Feltham (9) 1318–1452/53
> Frome (5) 1313–79
> Hatherleigh (8) 1460–1596
> Holton (7) 1460–1586
> Kilmersdon (5) 1532–89
> Maperton (10) 1265/66–1596
> Newton St. Loe (9) 1413–1564
> Pensford (5) 1468/69–1565
> Publow (10) 1413–1565
> Queen Camel (8) 1357–1420
> Somerton (5) 1518/19–1593
> Wootton Courtney (7) 1488–1562

Staffordshire:
> Caverswall (7) 1422/23–1677
> Tutbury (9) 1475–1682

Sussex:
> Chiltington [West?] (8) 1344–1411/12
> Hastings (8) 1469/70–1695
> Nutbourne (7) 1344–1411/12
> River (7) 1344–1411/12

Warwickshire:
> Burton Hastings (6) 1436/37–1537/38
> Drakenage (12) 1318–1511/12
> Woodcote (6) 1464/65–1537/38

Wiltshire:
> Chippenham (8) 1322–1544
> Clevancy (5) 1251–1401
> Great Cheverell (9) 1356–1535
> Heytesbury (28) 1282–1535
> Lea (7) 1508–75
> Little Cheverell (6) 1413–1468/69
> Maiden Bradley (5) 1359/60–1490
> Mildenhall (5) 1313–1490

Norridge (10) 1283–1447
Norton Bavant (7) 1283–1353
Orcheston St. George (8) 1349–1563
Orcheston St. Mary (6) 1349–1447
Rowden (5) 1460–1544
Teffont Evias (27) 1293–1378
Thoulstone (11) 1283–1447
Tytherington (5) 1364–1535
Upton (6) 1348–80
Upton Scudamore (46) 1283–1447, 1535
Warminster (20) 1317–1537/38

Worcestershire:
Little Malvern (8) 1280–1505

Yorkshire:
Aldbrough (9) 1302/03–1378/79
Allerston (6) 1247–1548
Bewick (7) 1302/03–1488
Bolton Percy (9) 1464–88
Colden (6) 1302/03–78/79
Drypool (15) 1302/03–1378/79
Farmanby (7) 1275–1504
Halsham (5) 1302/03–1378/79
Hedon (18) 1275–1380
Huddleston (10) 1282/83–1355
Ledsham (12) 1654/55–1787
Ledston (18) 1654/55–1787
Leppington (6) 1302/03–1371
Lillings Ambo (15) 1322–1578
Little Weighton (5) 1302/03–1369
Newton (7) 1242–1467
Pickering (10) 1390/91–1504
Rawdon (52) 1324/25–1520, 1741
Rimswell (8) 1302/03–1358
Sheriff Hutton (9) 1546/47–1577
Stoneferry (5) 1366–84
Sutton (25) 1297?–1562/63
Thornton Dale (13) 1275–1504
Tunstall (5) 1302/03–1342
Walkington (5) 1101<–1302/03
Wauldby (6) 1302/03–1369

Willerby (19) 1302/03–1363
Wold Newton (5) 1379–1463
France:
Calais (12) 1350–1495/96
Ireland:
Co. Down (14) 1610–1718, 1779
Co. Dublin (11) 1641–1759
Co. Fermanagh (13) 1625/26–1673/74
Co. Louth (12) 1635–1712
Co. Meath (18) 1608–1761
Co. Tyrone (18) 1607–1671/72

IV. INVENTORIES AND LISTS

125 pieces, 1596–ca.1875

The following category consists of inventories, lists, and schedules (some with appraised values) of various categories of goods (linens, furniture, books, pictures, armor, plate, etc.), household and farm implements, papers (deeds, court rolls, other writings), and miscellaneous items belonging, chiefly, to the Hastings family.

Some of the more important or interesting items are listed chronologically below.

An inventory of the goods of Henry, 3rd Earl of Huntingdon, at York, 1596
An inventory of the furniture at Ashby Castle, 1596
An inventory of armor at Donington, 1633
An inventory of the household goods of Henry, [5th?] Earl of Huntingdon at Donington Park, 1633
An inventory of the Earl of Huntingdon's armor, 1633
An inventory of the household stuff of the Earl of Huntingdon at Donington Park, 1639
An inventory of the goods delivered to George Walker for the use of John [Bramhall], Bishop of Derry, 1640
An inventory of the goods of Henry, Earl of Huntingdon at Donington Park, evaluated, 1644
An inventory of the goods of the earls of Northumberland and Warwick and Oliver St. John, executors to the late Earl of Essex, 1646
An inventory of the goods of Sir Robert Shirley at Stanton Herald, evaluated, 1657

An inventory of the goods of Sir John Lewis at Ledstone, 1671

An inventory of the goods of Lucy, Countess of Huntingdon, at Ashby House, 1678

An inventory of the goods at Donington Park House, 1687

An inventory and appraisal of the goods of Theophilus, 7th Earl of Huntingdon, room by room, stable, park, gold, jewels, plate, money, etc., 1701

An inventory of the goods at Donington of Theophilus, Earl of Huntingdon, 1705

A catalogue of Sir John Rawdon's medals, 1718

Inventory of Lord Ferrers' goods sent from Astwell House, 1723–26

Personal estate taken by Theophilus Hastings, 9th Earl of Huntingdon, 1728<>1746

An inventory of the goods of the Earl of Huntingdon in the house in Savil Street, St. James Parish, 1740

Catalog of books given to George Hastings, ca.1740?

List of books of Theophilus, Earl of Huntingdon, ca.1740?

Inventory of the goods at Ledstone House, 1741

List of paintings by Italian Masters, [compiled by? owned by?] Francis Hastings, 10th Earl of Huntingdon, ca.1753

Inventory of furniture and household goods at Ledstone Hall, 1759

Inventory of the goods of the Earl of Huntingdon at Donington Park, 1788

Inventory of paintings at Donington Park, 1793

Pictures at Donington Park, 1798

Loughborough sale catalog, 1809

Auction catalog of furniture, glasses, pictures, books, and prints from the Earl of Moira's mansion, 1813

Catalog of paintings at Donington Park, 1813<

Inventory of effects of the Earl of Moira at Donington Park, 1818

List of maps of Lord Hastings, 1821

A catalog of furniture at Donington Park, 8 vols. 1827

An appraisement of the goods of the Marquis of Hastings, 1830

A list of tapestry at Loudoun Castle, 1860

An inventory of articles belonging to the Marquis of Bute at Loudoun Castle, 1869

V. LEGAL PAPERS
ca.600 pieces, 1329?–19th century

The following category consists primarily of papers from approximately 110 legal cases, most of them involving the Hastings and Rawdon families and their associates and most of them belonging to the 17th century. Many of the cases are far from complete, containing only draft briefs, extracts, opinions, fines, interrogatories, petitions, or mere notes and memoranda. The majority of the cases are concerned with land: disputes over inherited properties and mortgaged lands, legacies and settlements, rights of succession, manorial disputes, etc. Also included are miscellaneous legal papers.

The following people appear in five or more cases as either plaintiff or defendant:

Hastings, Ferdinando, 6th Earl of Huntingdon (5)
Hastings, Henry, 5th Earl of Huntingdon (9)
Hastings, Theophilus, 7th Earl of Huntingdon (10)
Hastings, Theophilus, 9th Earl of Huntingdon (7)

Among some of the more interesting, important, or complete cases are:

5th Earl *v.* Sir Henry Shirley, re libellous remarks and for hunting on the Earl's grounds. 1626–28
Sir Archibald and Lady Eleanor Douglas *v.* the 6th Earl re the estate of Sir John Davies. ca.1626–29
Sir Arthur Rawdon, 2nd Bart. of Moira *v.* Ursula (Stawell) Conway Sheffield, Countess Conway and Marchioness of Normanby, re the estate of the Earl of Conway. 1683
Tenants of Loughborough (Leics.) *v.* the 6th Earl re Loughborough mills, 1649–1651, with a similar case involving the 7th Earl. 1696–98

Among the miscellaneous items of general legal interest are: a claim to the lands of Margaret, Lady Hungerford, ca.1470; a list of actions comprising the charges of felony, murder, robbery, etc., n.d. [16th cent.?]; petition of Roger Kelly to the Lord President and Council of the Province of Munster, ca.1611; an exemplification made 1624 of a quo warranto proceeding of 1282; a petition to Sir Arthur Hesilrige, 1635; a list of cases to be heard in Star Chamber during the Michaelmas term, 1638; a note re the appearance in court of Thomas Hodgeson and John Walker in a case involving the liberties and privileges of the Corporation of Liverpool, 1644; a copy of "Dr. Burnet's defence," ca.1687; a case whether certain privateers sailing under Letters of Marque from James II might be tried as pirates by William III, 1692/93; information of Capt. Francis Russell *et al.* in the Coke-Ash murder case, 1686; the petition of Lord Falkland for his son Lucius Cary (afterward 2nd Viscount Falkland), imprisoned for challenging Sir Francis Willoughby to a duel, ca.1630; a dispute re a university fellowship, n.d. 17th cent.?; the opinion of Theobald Wolfe on the will of Henry Petty, 1st Earl of Shelburne, 1773; copy of a letter re the lunacy of Nicholas Ward, 2nd Viscount Bangor, 1781; opinion on the will of Francis, 10th Earl of Huntingdon., 1791; and two lists of judgements against the Marquis of Hastings, 1790–1809 and 1813.

Also: ca.80 pieces of unsorted 19th-century legal papers (chiefly 1800–58) concerned primarily with estates of Marquis of Hastings and the Rawdon family.

VI. MANORIAL AND LOCAL AFFAIRS PAPERS
ca.6,000 pieces, 13th–19th centuries

The following category consists of documents pertaining to individual manors, parishes, towns, and other specific localities. Included are: court rolls (including views of frankpledge) and books, suit rolls and bills of presentment, fines and amercements, and other papers concerning manorial courts; papers concerning justices of the peace and local sessions; rentals, customals, compotus rolls, fee-farm rents, rent receipts, and other papers concerning rents and manorial finances; valors, extents, surveys, and terriers; papers concerning enclosures; documents concerning towns, town councils, and other corporations; documents pertaining to the land tax and other local taxes; papers concerning parish affairs, such as tithes, advowsons, presentations, and appointments of minor church officials; appointments to manorial and other local offices; petitions dealing with local matters; documents pertaining to local markets, fairs, schools, hospitals, buildings, tolls, etc. Over one half of the material pertains to Leicestershire. There are approximately 250 pieces of Irish interest. All places represented in this section* are listed below, by county, together with the number of pieces, inclusive dates, and notice of all court rolls, suit rolls, rentals, surveys, compotus rolls, and *selected* significant individual items or groups of items. Following this are listed significant individual items or groups of items pertaining to more than one county.

Berkshire:

Bray: 1 piece, 1431

Englefield: 3 pieces, 1629–n.d. [17th cent.]

Theale Hundred: 1 piece, 1580

Court roll (1): 1580

Tilehurst: 2 pieces, 17th cent.

Buckinghamshire:

Aston with Ilmer: 1 piece, 1350

Court roll (1): 1350

Brill: 6 pieces, 1349–1493

Court rolls (5): 1349, 1432, 1454, 1491, 1493

Cippenham: 4 pieces, 1339–1574

Court rolls (2): 1430–53, 1562–74

Ditton: 3 pieces, 1365–1414

Compotus rolls (3): 1365–66, 1407–08, 1413–14

Grove, with Linslade and Hapton: 1 piece, 1831

Stoke Poges: 20 pieces, 1430–17th cent.

Court roll (1): 1430

Also includes papers re the Stoke Poges Hospital

Water Eaton: 1 piece, 1612

General: Receivers' accounts for Bucks. lands, 1583–88

Cheshire:

General: tax lists for the poor, the church, etc., 1694

Cornwall:

Bodmin: 1 piece, 1626

Boscastle: 3 pieces, 1468–[16th cent.?]

Includes book of fines for Boscastle, Penhele, Hendra, & Bottlet, with totals for Cornwall, Somerset, and Devon, 1552–53

Coddiford Farleigh: 1 piece, 1555

Court roll (1): 1555

---

* Excluding numerous rent and tax receipts, and bills of presentment attached to suit rolls.

Lanteglos, with Polruan: 1 piece, 1542
    Court roll (1): 1542
Minster: 1 piece, 1439
Newland: 2 pieces, 1546–54
    Court rolls (2): 1546, 1554
Pengelly, with Trengoff: 1 piece, 1557
    Court roll (1): 1557
Polruan: 1 piece, 1555
    See also Lanteglos, above
Trevigowe: 1 piece, 1554–55
    Court roll (1): 1554–55

Cumberland:
Inglewood Forest: 1 piece, 15th cent.

Derbyshire:
Derby: 20 pieces, 1474–1689
    Includes papers re the Corporation of the city 1687–88
Egginton: 1 piece, 17th cent.
Gresley: 4 pieces, 16th cent.–1838
High Peak: 1 piece, 1474
Killamarsh: 2 pieces, 1674–75
Measham: 2 pieces, 1625–31<
Melbourne: 55 pieces, 1401–ca.1800
    Court rolls (28): 1461–76, 1528–50, 1557–58, 1574–75, 1634–38, 1700, 1723, 1729, 1737, 1748, 1756 (2), 1759, 1764, 1765, 1770, 1772, 1775 (2), 1776, 1777, 1785 (3), 1791, 1792 (2), 1794
Netherseal: [formerly in Leicestershire], 1 piece, 1696
Normanton: 2 pieces, 18th cent.
Sinfin: 2 pieces, ca.1800–02
Smisby: 6 pieces, ca.1694–1812
Winster: 1 piece, 1762
Woodthorpe: 1 piece, 1814
General: 3 pieces, 1723–ca.1800

Devonshire:
Diptford: with Carswell: 1 piece, 1281
Stokenham: 10 pieces, 1568–ca.1615
    Rental (1): 1568
    Customal roll (1): 1577
General: 1 piece, 1635
    Inquisition as to the holders of Knights Fees, 1635

Dorset:
  Hilton: 2 pieces, 1552–55
      Court rolls (2): 1551–53, 1554–55
  Newton Montagu: 3 pieces, 1344–1523
      Court rolls (3): 1344, 1523
  Puddletown: 6 pieces, 1581–1790
      Includes papers re advowsons and past presenta-
      tions, 1581–1639
Essex:
  Felstead: 1 piece, 1566
  Waltham Forest: 1 piece, 1487
Flint:
  Mold: 8 pieces, ca.1756
      Includes papers re the case of Mold Rectory and
      advowson, ca.1756
Hampshire:
  Christchurch: 1 piece, 1573
  Ringwood: 3 pieces, 1365–1550
      Court roll (1): 1549–50
      Extent and customary, 1365
  Ripley: 1 piece, ca.1600
      Survey, ca.1600
  Rockford Moyles: 1 piece, 1423
      Rental of the lands of William Lord Botreaux, 1423
  Somerford: 1 piece, 1558
Hertfordshire:
  Shenley: 1 piece, 19th cent.
  Ware: 1 piece, 19th cent.
Lancashire:
  Lytham: 1 piece, 19th cent.
Leicestershire:
  Alton: 1 piece, 1675
  Anstey: 1 piece, 17th cent.?
  Ashby de la Zouch: ca.180 pieces, 1269–1847
      Compotus roll (1): 1469
      Court rolls (72): 1430–31, 1480–81, 1566–67, 1571–72,
          1674–79, 1679, 1682, two each year (1683–1714) [with
          the following exceptions: none for 1684, 1693; three
          for 1692, 1701, 1710; four for 1698]; one n.d.
      Court books (3): 1665–72, 1672–79, 1680–86

Rentals (12): 1574–85, 1628, 1661, 1662, 1664/65, 1697,
1729 [with Loughborough, Normanton, Packington, and Whitwick], three for 1806–07 [two of them
including Castle Donington], 1812, 1813–14
Surveys (2): 1697, 1729
Also includes: a volume of the Penal Laws of Ashby
de la Zouch, 1620–1714; Churchwardens' accounts,
1626–36; Overseers of the Poor accounts, 1628–34;
paper concerning the rights and privileges of
Ashby Church and vicar [1693<>1711?]; papers re
the enclosure of Ashby Woulds, 1767–1812; papers
re Ashby and Ivanhoe Baths, ca.1813–ca.1824
Bagworth: 2 pieces, 1484–1568
Court rolls (2): 1484–85, 1568
Barrowcoate?: 1 piece, 1721
Barrow-upon-Soar: 23 pieces, 1314–1817
Court rolls (4): 1389, 1520, 1568, 1571
Rentals and rent rolls (5): 1537 [19th cent. copy],
1638–39, 1641–42, 1642–43, 1769
Suit roll, with Quorndon and Woodhouse (1): 1817
Survey (1): 1769
Belton: 3 pieces, 1796–1810
Blackfordby: 12 pieces, 1685–1855
Rental and survey, with Boothorpe (1): 1776
Also includes papers re tithes, tithe lists (1705–06,
n.d.), and tithe book (with Boothorpe, 1775)
Boothorpe: *See* Blackfordby above
Braunstone: 1 piece, 1550
Breedon, with Wilson and Tonge: 3 pieces, 1768–
1806
Brokesby: 1 piece, 15th cent.
Burton Overy: 3 pieces, 1724–53
Survey (1): 1724
Castle Donington: ca.100 pieces, 1439–1815<
Churchwardens' Accounts (1 vol.), 1574–88
Compotus roll (1): 1491
Court rolls (5): 1464–65, 1466–1583
(extracts): 1485–1564, 1572–74, 1591
Rentals and rent rolls (2): 1600–05, 1661
Survey (1): n.d. (18th cent.)

Also includes: 2 volumes of land tax assessments, 1764–82; papers re enclosures, 1778–83; notes and sketches re building and landscaping at Donington Park, 18th cent.–1808; roll of signatures of all parishioners of Castle Donington welcoming Lady Edith Maud Hastings on her accession, 1858

See also Ashby de la Zouch, above

Charnwood Forest: 10 pieces, 18th–19th centuries
Includes papers re the enclosure of the Forest, 1804–ca.1811

Cold Newton: 2 pieces, 1680–81

Coleorton: 2 pieces, 1704 & n.d. (18th cent.)
Suit roll, with Ravenstone (1): n.d. (18th cent.)

Cossington: 3 pieces, 1729 & n.d. (18th cent.)
Court roll (1): 1729

Donington: *See* Castle Donington

Donisthorpe: 1 piece, 1813–18

Enderby: 4 pieces, 1443–1585
Court rolls (4): 1443, 1565, 1579, 1585

Evington: 1 piece, 1565
Court roll (1): 1565

Framland Hundred: ca.150 pieces, 13th cent.–1809
Court rolls (49): 1436, 1704, 1712, 1713–14, 1728, two each year 1729–59 [with the following exceptions: none for 1739, 1742, 1756–57; one only for 1730, 1737, 1741, 1744–45, 1750, 1752–59], 1769 (2).
Rent roll (chief rents) (1): n.d. (early 18th cent.)
Suit rolls, usually with bills of presentment (45): n.d., 17th cent., 1745, yearly 1770–1809 [with the following exceptions: none for 1782; two for 1770, 1772, 1800, 1805]

Hathern: 2 pieces, 17th–18th centuries
Survey (1): n.d. (17th cent.)

Heather: 1 piece, 1625

Holwell: 1 piece, 1753

Hoton: 19 pieces, 1539–1760
Court rolls (17): 1667, 1729 (2), 1730, 1731, 1732, 1733, 1735, 1736, 1738, 1740, 1749, 1751, 1753, 1755, 1757, 1759

Hugglescote: 1 piece, ca.1731

Kegworth: 19 pieces, 1699–1701
Kettleby: 1 piece, 1368
Kibworth (deanery of): 1 piece, 1528
    Court roll (1): 1528
King's Norton: 1 piece, 1349
Kirby Muxloe: 4 pieces, 1316–ca.1613
Kirkby Mallory: 2 pieces, 1300–ca.1320?
Leicester, City of: 32 pieces, 1400–1832
    Compotus rolls (2): 1399–1400 (for the Honour of Leicester), ca.1596
    Court book of Leicester Castle (1): 1595–97
    Also includes proposed regulations for the Corporation, ca.1685; lists of aldermen, etc., 1572–73, 1688; papers re the election of M.P.s for Leicester
Leicester Forest: 36 pieces, 1519–1628
Loughborough: ca.375 pieces, 1376–1818
    Compotus rolls (10): 1376–77, 1398, 1427–28, 1439–40, 1440, ca.1450, 1467–68, 1471<, 1472–73, 1477–78
    Court rolls (128): 1397–98, 1402–03, 1403–04, 1405, 1406–07, 1409, 1411–12, 1429–30, 1435–36, 1455–56, 1459–60, 1486, 1488–89, 1492–93, 1494–95, 1496–97, 1501–02, 1503–04, 1504–05, 1505–06, 1507–08, 1530–31, 1558–64, 1574, 1619, 1624, 1645, 1654, 1655, 1675, 1675–78, 1692, n.d., 17th cent., yearly 1717–1809 [with the following exceptions: none for 1731, 1741–49, 1770–77; two for 1729, 1732, 1752, 1755, 1761, 1782, 1784, 1786–88, 1791–95, 1803, 1805–08]
    Court books (3), 1599–1602, 1607–12, 1685–86
    Rentals (32): n.d., 14th cent., 1489–90, 1527, ca.1550, 1559 (2), 1620, 1624–34, 1644–45, 1645, 1663, 1715, 1728, 1729 (6), 1730 (3), 1731 (2), 1747, 1752, 1792 (2), n.d., 18th cent. (2), 1804, 1806
    Surveys (6): 1559, 1620, ca.1746, 1790, ca.1790, 1807
    Also includes: lists of tenants; Enclosures Book, 1760, and other enclosure papers, 18th cent.; Bylaws, rules, orders and pains made by Jury at Court Leet and Court Baron, 1797; papers re Land Tax, ca.1800–20
Lubbesthorpe: 3 pieces, 1603–04
    Rental (1), 1604

Markfield: 5 pieces, 1741<–1796
Melton Mowbray: 9 pieces, 1501?–1693
    Court rolls (5): 1501?, 1677, 1679, 1679?, 1681
    Suit roll (1): 1692
Mountsorrel: 9 pieces, 17th cent.–1825
Newbold Verdon: 1 piece, 1599
    Rental (1): 1599
Newton Harcourt: 3 pieces, 1412–38
Newtown Linford: 1 piece, ca.1713
Oakthorpe: 10 pieces, 1395–ca.1800
    Survey (1): 1592
Orton Saucy: 1 piece, 16th cent.
    Extent or survey (1): 16th cent.
Osgathorpe: 3 pieces, 17th–18th centuries
Owston: 1 piece, 17th cent.
Packington: ca.135 pieces, 1515–1797
    Court rolls (83): 1515 (2), 1571, 1583–84, 1593–94, 1689,
        yearly 1699–1791 [with the following exceptions:
        none for 1700–01, 1705, 1734–35, 1744, 1754–55,
        1771–84; two for 1729, 1730, 1733, 1736]
    Rentals (14): 1631–1641, n.d., 17th cent., ca.1740
    Survey (1): n.d., 17th cent.
Quorndon: 6 pieces, 1767–1816
    Survey (1): 18th cent.? with comparisons
        with 1559
    Suit roll (1): 1814
    See also Barrow-upon-Soar
Ratby: 1 piece, 1615
Ravenstone: 1 piece, 1651
Ragdale: 1 piece, 1669
Redmile: 1 piece, 1470–71
Rotherby: 1 piece, 1746
Shelton: 1 piece, 1520
Sparkenhoe Hundred: 1 piece, 17th cent.
Stanton under Bardon: 3 pieces, 1628–53
Stoney Stanton: 12 pieces, 16th cent.–1814
    Rentals (3): 1768, 1775, 1803
    Survey (1): 16th cent.?
Swannington: 1 piece, 1730

Swithland: 2 pieces, 1650
    Court rolls (2): 1650
Thringstone: 1 piece, 18th cent.?
Thrussington: 1 piece, 1636
Tonge: *See* Breedon, above
Whitwick: 3 pieces, 17–18th centuries?
Wigston Magna: 1 piece, 1520
Willesley: 1 piece, 1858
Wilson: *See* Breedon, above
Winchester Fee (Honour of): 4 pieces, 1417–1561
    Court rolls (3): 1417, 1475–79, 1561
Wistow: 1 piece, 1368
Woodhouse: 1 piece, 19th cent.?
    See also Barrow-upon-Soar, above
General, ca.115 pieces, 1607–19th cent.
    Includes: Rental and Customary of the lands of the Knights Templar in Rothley and elsewhere in Leics., 13th cent.; Names of those who contributed money to be lent to the King, 1611; Entry Book of patents for the commission of the Lieutenancy of Leicestershire, and official correspondence to and from Henry, 5th Earl of Huntingdon as Lord Lieutenant, 1 vol., 1613–27; lists of J.P.s (1625, 1688); Book of statutes and punishments, ca.1625; names of the head constables of the hundreds, 1637; list of taxes (tithes?) paid by the clergy, arranged by deanery, 1669–85; lists of inhabitants and [rents?] arranged by hundreds, n.d. (17th cent.); other lists of inhabitants, officers, etc.

Lincolnshire:
Aslackby: 1 piece, 1475–76
    Court roll, with Authorpe and Dowsby (1): 1475–76
Authorpe: *See* Aslackby, above
Dowsby: *See* Aslackby, above
Laughton: *See* Ropsley, below
Pinchbeck: 1 piece, n.d. (18th cent.)
Rippingale: 3 pieces, 1435–82
    Compotus roll (1): 1435–36
    Court rolls (2): 1473–74, 1481–82

Ropsley: 3 pieces, 1466–80
    Court rolls (2): 1474, 1480 (with Laughton)
    Rental (1): 1466
General: 2 pieces, 1472–78
    Compotus rolls of the bailiffs of William Lord Hastings for lands in Lincolnshire (2): 1472–73, 1477–78
London: 4 pieces, 1637–85
    See also Maps and Plans (plans and the Report of the Select Committee on improving the Port of London, ca.50 pieces, 1799–1803)
Middlesex:
    Enfield: 1 piece, n.d. (18th cent.)
    Hornsey: 1 piece, 1778
Norfolk:
    Howe: 1 piece, 1725–26
    Yarmouth: 1 piece, 1781
    General: 3 pieces, 1722–1861
        Rentals (2): 1722–26 (for the lands of Lady Elizabeth Hastings), 1723–24 (for Howe, Shotesham, Brooke, Mundham, and Poringland)
Northamptonshire:
    Astwell: 2 pieces, 1721–22
        Rental (1): 1721
    Bulwick: 1 piece, 1587
        Rental roll of the lands of Edward Lord Zouche (1): 1687
    Rockingham Forest: 1 piece, 1466
    Sulby: 1 piece, 1591
    Syresham: 1 piece, 18th cent.
Northumberland:
    Berwick-on-Tweed: 1 piece, 16th cent.
Nottinghamshire:
    Arnold: 1 piece, 1480–81
        Compotus roll (1): 1480–81
    Leake, East: 22 pieces (most with West Leake), 1527–1804
        Includes papers re enclosures, 18th cent., and re Land Tax assessments, 1776–80
    Leake, West: 2 pieces, 1640–1743
    Ratcliffe-upon-Soar: 1 piece, 1617

Sherwood Forest: 4 pieces, 1203–1475
Welbeck: 1 piece, 1477
Whatton: 1 piece, 18th cent.?
    Rental (1): 18th cent.?

Rutland:
Belton: 1 piece, 1563
    Court roll (1): 1563
Forest of Rutland: 6 pieces, 1203–1566
Lee Lodge: 1 piece, 1567
Leighfield Forest: 2 pieces, 1555–81
Oakham: 1 piece, 1461

Somerset:
Aller & Aller Moor: 34 pieces, 15th–18th centuries
    Court Book (1): 1571–73
    Rentals (5): 15th cent., 1564, 1573–76, 1576, 1742–43
    Survey (1): 16th cent.?
    See also Somerton, below
Cadbury: 1 piece, 1388–89
    Court roll (1): 1388–89
Hinton: 1 piece, 1327
Holton: 1 piece, 1452–53
    Court roll (1): 1452–53
North Cadbury: 1 piece, 1401–02
    Court roll (1): 1401–02
Shepton Montague: 2 pieces, 1335–39
    Court roll (2): 1335–36, 1338–39
Somerton: 10 pieces, 1349–1574
    Court rolls (9): 1349, 1376–77, 1390–91, 1392–93, 1447–
        48, 1562 (with Aller), 1565–66 (with Aller), 1571–
        72, 1573–74
    Rental (1): 1572
South Cadbury (Cadbury Castle): 1 piece, 1442–43
    Compotus roll (1): 1442–43
Wellow: 1 piece, 1341–53
    Court roll (1): 1341–53

Shropshire:
Ludlow: 1 piece; 17th cent.
    Notes re Council of the Marches of Wales held at
        Ludlow, n.d., 17th cent.
Market Drayton: 1 piece, 1558?

Staffordshire:
    Cheadle: 1 piece, 18th cent.?
    Dilhorne: 5 pieces, 1581–1841
        Rent roll of the lands of Dilhorne School (1), 1581
    Stafford: 1 piece, 1683
    Stockley Park: 1 piece, 18th cent.
    Tamworth: 1 piece, 1727
    Tutbury (Honour of): 2 pieces, 1472–1529?
Sussex:
    East Marden: 1 piece, 1446
    Hastings (Rape of): 6 pieces, 1429–1672
        Lathe Court rolls (3): 1429–30, 1434–35, 1475–76
    General: 3 pieces, 1548?
Warwickshire:
    Arrow: 1 piece, 17th cent.
    Eatington (*alias* Ettington): 9 pieces, 1711–23 & n.d. (18th
    cent.)
        Rentals (2): 1711
    Mancetter: 4 pieces, 1391–n.d. (15th cent.)
    Woodcote: 1 piece, 1408
        Court roll (partial, with survey or extent) (1): 1408
    General: 2 pieces, 1482–1710
Wiltshire:
    Boscombe: 1 piece, 1328
    Bradford: 1 piece, 1430
    Heytesbury: 1 piece, 1401
    Horningsham: 1 piece, 1420
    Lea: 1 piece, 1569
        Court book (1): 1569
    Mildenhall: 1 piece, 1490
    Somerford: 2 pieces, 1561–65
    Upton Scudamore: 1 piece, 1399
    General: 2 pieces, 1411–1545–46
Worcestershire:
    Daylesford: 1 piece, ca.1800
    Lalton Farm: 1 piece, 1525–37
        Court roll (1): 1525–37
    Ombersley: 1 piece, 1441
        Rental (1): 1441

Yorkshire:
 Allerton: 4 pieces, 1376–1671?
  Court rolls (3), 1376, 1379?, 1383
 Bilsdale: 1 piece, 1678
 Bolton Percy: 1 piece, 1478–79
  Compotus roll (1): 1478–79
 Collingham: 3 pieces, 1697–1737
  Survey (1): 1737
 Eske: 1 piece, 1604
  Extent (1), 1604
 Harwood: 3 pieces, 1664–75
 Hedon: 2 pieces, 13th cent.-1370
 Knaresborough: 3 pieces, 1548–67
 Leake: 1 piece, 1527
 Ledsham: 88 pieces (most with Ledstone), 1739–89
  Rentals (9): 1759, 1767, [1770<>1780], 1784, 1787, 4
  n.d. (18th cent.)
 Ledstone: 10 pieces, 1739–91
  Rentals (4): 1785, 1789, 2 n.d. (18th cent.)
 Malton: 1 piece, 14th cent.?
 Newby: 1 piece, 19th cent.?
 Rawdon: 2 pieces, 1296, 1831
 Slingsby: 1 piece, 1560
  Survey (1): 1560
 Storthwaite: 1 piece, 1364
 Thorp Arch: 2 pieces, 1743–44
  Rental (1): 1744
 Wheldale: 1 piece, 1739
 Wike: 1 piece, 1619
 General: 22 pieces, 1675–18th cent.
  Rent rolls for the Earl of Huntingdon's estates (2):
  1690, 1694–1700
Pieces pertaining to lands in more than one English County:
 ca.330 pieces, 1277–19th cent.; chiefly dealing with rents
 and rentals, and profit and management of Hastings es-
 tates.
  Minister's account (1): of the lands of Elizabeth,
  Countess of Oxford, 1533–37
  Compotus rolls (3): of lands of Sir William Hastings,

1474–75; of "Salisburysland," 1506–07; of all lands
of James Blount, 6th Baron Mountjoy, 1554–55

Rentals and rent rolls (38): of lands in Leics., Lincs.,
14th cent.?; of lands of William Lord Botreaux,
ca.1425; of lands of William Lord Hastings, 1466–
67, 1473–74, 1475–76; of the lands of Nicholas
Montgomery, 1481–87; of lands confiscated from
Margaret, Countess of Salisbury on her attainder
and execution, 1541–42; of various towns in five
counties, 1577–79, 1579, 1599; of Ashby, Loughborough, and Melbourne, 1647; of estates of Earl of
Huntingdon, 1689; chiefly of estates of the earls
of Huntingdon, 1703–04, 1705–06, 1706, 1708, 1710,
1711, 1712, 1713, 1714, 1715, 1716, 1718, 1727, 1728
(2), 1728–29, 1729 (4), 1730–31, 1740, n.d., 18th
cent. (4)

Surveys (3): of the lands of Henry, 3rd Earl of Huntingdon, in [Leicester and Devon?], 1562; of the
manors of Ashby, Loughborough, Packington, Castle Donington, and Melbourne, 1645; of lands of
the Duke of Buckingham, 18th cent.

Valors (4): of lands of William de Botreaux, 1421; of
the lands of Richard Hastings, Lord Willoughby,
1488; of the lands of Lady Mary Hastings and Hungerford, n.d. [15th cent.?]; of the lands of Francis,
2nd Earl of Huntingdon, 1543–44

Also includes: Account roll of the stewards and bailiffs of William Lord Hastings for lands in various
counties, 1468–69; Receivers account of Thomas
Langham, receiver of Francis, 2nd Earl of
Huntingdon, for lands in various counties, 1545–
46

Also: ca.800 pieces unsorted fee farm rents, in original bundles, 18th cent.

ca.630 pieces unsorted papers re land taxes, many
in original bundles, 17–18th cent.

ca.285 pieces re land sales, many in Loughborough, 16–19th cent. (chiefly 19th cent., printed)

ca.200 pieces unsorted 19th cent. papers, many
printed

Ireland:
    Co. Antrim: 4 pieces, 1657–1741
    Co. Armagh: 8 pieces, 1662-n.d. (17th cent.)
        Rental (1): 1662
    Co. Cork: 2 pieces, 1612–13
    Co. Down: 25 pieces, 1639–1745
    Co. Dublin: 34 pieces, 1641 <–1821
        Rentals (4): 1674, ca.1758, 1821 (2)
    Co. Fermanagh: 89 pieces, 1604-n.d. (18th cent.?)
        Rentals and rent rolls (37): 1633–66, 1637 (with Ty-
            rone), 1641–70, 1671 (for Lisgoole)
        Survey of the lands of Ferdinando Lord Hastings:
            1638. Includes Tyrone
    Co. Galway: 1 piece, 1666
    Co. Kerry: 2 pieces, 1641–73
    Co. Kilkenny: 1 piece, 1603<
    Co. Leix (formerly Queen's County): 1 piece, 1617
    Co. Limerick: 2 pieces, 1612–68
    Co. Londonderry: 3 pieces, 1641–64
        Includes a Particular of those estates forcibly taken
            from their holders, 1641; rental of the lands of the
            Bishopric of Derry, 1664
    Co. Louth: 5 pieces, 1636-n.d. 17th cent.?
    Co. Meath and West Meath: 21 pieces, 1558?-n.d. (18th
        cent.?)
        Rent rolls (2): of Sir John Rawdon's lands, in-
            cludes Dublin, 1723: of the Earl of Moira's lands,
            1768
        Surveys (3): of John Rawdon's lands, 1716; of Rath-
            molyan and of Killmoon parish, n.d. (18th cent.)
    Co. Monaghan: 1 piece, 1693
    Co. Sligo: 3 pieces, 17th cent.
    Co. Tyrone: 17 pieces, 16th cent.?–17th cent.
        Rentals (2): n.d. (16th cent.?); of the Countess of Hun-
            tingdon's estates, 1661–66
    Co. Wexford: 17 pieces, ca.1660-n.d. (17th cent.)
        Rentals (4): 1661, 1664–65, 1665 rent roll of the Duke
            of Albemarle's lands, 1669–70
        Survey (1): of the Duke of Albemarle's lands, 1669
    Co. Wicklow: 6 pieces, 1667–ca.1790?

General: 41 pieces, 1608-n.d., (18th cent.)
    Rentals (2): 17th cent.
    Survey (1): of the Earl of Moira's estates, 1781
    Also includes: lists of inhabitants according to their
    religion, 17th cent.; religious census, 1716

VII. MAPS AND PLANS
ca.135 pieces, ?16th–19th centuries
The following category consists primarily of estate and field plans
relating to lands of the Hastings family in the 18th and 19th centuries. There are a few plans of buildings or other architectural
or mechanical details, a few plans relating to canals or proposed
canals (noted separately below), and a few printed items (chiefly
of European lands).

Derbyshire:
    Overseal
        Plans of Reservoir Colliery, 1889
    Sinfin
        Map of enclosure allotment, n.d. (18th cent.)

Gloucestershire:
    Cheltenham?
        Plan of a tank for watering Sir [Home?] Popham's
        garden, n.d. (19th cent.)

Huntingdonshire:
    Huntingdon
        Plan of lands owned by the Earl of Huntingdon in
        the parish of St. Mary, n.d. (18th cent.)

Lancashire:
    Lytham
        Diagram with measurements of the Chancel of Lytham Church, n.d. (19th cent.)

Leicestershire:
    Ashby de la Zouch
        Plans etc. of Ashby Place taken when Mr. George
        Hastings [later the 4th Earl?] proposed to build
        there. 8 pieces, ca.1600?
        Plan of an intended canal, with observations,
        ca.1790?
        Plan and purchase note for Ashby Would, ca.1800
        Plan of Ashby Estates. 2 pieces, 1813
        Plan of lands purchased by H. V. White, 1817

Plan of Fountain in Ivanhoe Baths, ca.1824?

Plan of school site and surrounding area, n.d. (19th cent.)

Canal plan, n.d. (19th cent.)

Castle Donington:

"A map of the mills, Islands, and Ponds at Castle Donington," (with color), n.d. (16th cent.?)

Plan of the parish (pasted onto a deed), ca.1673

Charnwood Forest:

Plan of the allotments sold to T. N. Philips by the Earl of Moira, n.d. (18th cent.)

Leicester Forest:

"Mapp taken of the Launds in Leicester Forest," n.d. (early 17th cent.?)

Loughborough:

Field plans, 2 pieces, 1790

Plan of Loughborough Moor, ca.1790?

Field plans, ca.1792?

Plan of Loughborough Moor, ca.1792?

Plan of certain holdings, ca.1792?

Plan of Nether meadow and Foothill field, ca.1792?

Plan of Tatmarsh fields and allotments, ca.1792?

Plan of Park Field and Sealthorp closes, ca.1792?

Willesley:

Diagram and measurements of the front elevation of the Altar Tomb erected in Willesley church in memory of Sir Charles Hastings, Bart., n.d. (18th cent?)

General:

Field plans, 6 pieces, n.d. (18th cent.)

Garden plans re "Newton Corner," n.d. (18th cent.)

Map of Leicestershire, n.d. (19th cent.)

Plan of [Union] Lodge Farm, n.d. (19th cent.)

Plan of buildings proposed from Murphy's Corner to the Jolly Miller [Leics.?], n.d. (19th cent.)

Plan of lands at Barratt Mill, n.d. (19th cent.)

Estimation of Barrat Pool flood gates, n.d.

London:

Plans to accompany the Report of The Select Committee for the improvement of the Port of London (including plans for the new bridge). ca.50 plans, 1799–1803

Yorkshire:
>   Ledsham (with Ledstone):
>   >   Field plans, 7 pieces, 1759
>   Ledstone:
>   >   Plan of that part of the Earl of Huntingdon's estate at Ledstone through which the intended canal from Leeds to Selby is to pass, n.d. (18th cent.?)

Ireland:
>   Dublin:
>   >   Plan of Moira House and adjoining ground, surveyed and laid out in lots for building, 1806
>   Louth:
>   >   Map of the Barony of Louth, 1707
>   Meath (with West Meath and East Meath):
>   >   Map of the "Manor and lands of Castletowne of Moylough in ye Parish of Rathmullen, Barony of Moysenragh and County of Meath," n.d. (early 18th cent.?)
>   >   Survey map of Trammont?, n.d. (18th cent.?)
>   >   Survey of the Manor, towns, and lands of Rathmolyan, East Meath, n.d. (18th cent.)

America:
>   Two maps, with surveys, of lands in East Florida granted to John Rawdon, 1st Earl of Moira, 1768

France:
>   Map of the area around Touloun, n.d. (19th cent.)

Maps and Plan concerning Canals or Proposed Canals
>   Plan of fields with ownership and size through which the Leicester Navigation should go, n.d.. [18th cent.?]
>   Map of intended canal from Cheshire to Derbyshire, n.d. (18th cent.?)
>   Map of rivers and streams falling into the River Trent at or near Burton, 1796
>   Plans for the Harbour at Ardrossan and the canal from there to Glasgow (paperbound volume with 3 maps), 1805
>   Plans for canal route and dock-side buildings (with a letter from John Mammatt to the Marquis of Hastings), ca.1838
>   Plan of [canal route?] through Hillmorton and Clifton parishes, ca.1838

Plan of the Navigation of a Canal as it is intended to
go by the estate of Charles Hudson (printed), ca.1838?
Map of Midlands canals, n.d. (19th cent.)
[Canal plans?], 2 pieces, n.d. (19th cent.)
See also Ashby (Leics.) and Ledstone (Yorks.) above
Miscellaneous and Unidentified Maps and Plans
Map of an unidentified seaport, 1637
Description and plan of a mosaic table made entirely
from Derbyshire stone specimens, 1830
Sketch of certain dock yard buildings, ca.1838?
Map of the proposed road from Oakthorpe Pits to Moira
Colliery, 1871
Description and sketch of a Casolette, n.d. (19th cent.)
"Plan de L'ordre d'une Bibliotheque Divertissante et Cu-
rieuse," n.d. (19th cent.)
Plans for the Reservoir Colliery in Overseal District (on
the Leics./Derbs. border). 3 pieces, n.d.
Also 11 additional unidentified plans, including those for
pieces of furniture, farms (one with brewery?), houses,
a wine cellar, and the ground plan of a heating system,
all undated, presumably 19th cent.
Printed items:
Map of Switzerland (W. Faden, 1773)
Map of the Mouths of the Nile with the scene of Action
in Egypt (John Wallis, 1798)
Map of Portugal (W. Faden, 1797)
Plan of the Harbour at Cadiz, as surveyed by Don Vincent Tofino de San Miguel in 1789 (Published 1805)
Map of the Northern Part of Russia in Europe, exhibiting
the Seat of War (Laurie & Whittle, 1812)
Engravings of designs for the new Register Office in Ed-
inburgh, 2 pieces, n.d. (19th cent.)

VIII. PERSONAL AND FAMILY PAPERS
ca.760 pieces, 13th–19th centuries
The following category consists of a wide variety of papers relating to individual members of the Hastings family and to their
relatives, peers, associates, and occasionally tenants or servants.
Included are wills, notes on legacies, letters of administration,
settlements of estates, inquisitions (especially *inquisitions post
mortem*), marriage settlements, jointures, appointments to various

offices (directed either to or by the Hastings family), royal mandates to specific persons, petitions, grants of wardship, summonses to Parliament, powers of attorney, pardons, personal memoranda, inscriptions from statues and funeral monuments, and miscellaneous papers concerning the family and their activities. The vast majority of the material is evenly distributed throughout the 16th, 17th, and 18th centuries.

All wills and *inquisitions post mortem,* with additional selected documents of interest or significance, are listed chronologically below by sub-category.

Wills:

1346	Sir Ralph Hastings (copy)
1347	Sir Hugh de Hastings (late copy)
1377	John de Meaux
1397	Sir Ralph de Hastings (late copy)
1415	William de Botreaux, Baron Botreaux
1450	William Heyley of Brill
1455	Sir Leonard Hastings
1459	Robert Hungerford, 2nd Baron Hungerford
1476	Margaret, Lady Hungerford and Botreaux (2 copies)
1481	William Lord Hastings (3 copies)
1503	Katherine, Baroness Hastings
1506	Edward, Lord Hastings (with abstract and extract)
1532	John Blackgreff
>1533	Mary (Hungerford) Hastings Sacheverell
1534	George Hastings, 1st Earl of Huntingdon
1544	Francis Hastings, 2nd Earl of Huntingdon
1544	George Hastings, 1st Earl of Huntingdon (abstract only)
1550	Anne (Hastings) Stanley, Countess of Derby
1553	William Hubbard
1556–57	Sir John Port (3 copies)
1558	Sir Thomas Hastings (contemp. copy)
1560	Francis Hastings, 2nd Earl of Huntingdon (5 copies)
1561	Edward Lord Hastings of Loughborough
1566	Margaret Hubbard, of Southwold, Staffordshire (contemp. copy)

1591	William Stokes
1597	William Stokes (a nuncupative will, with related papers)
1603	Sir Edward Norreys
1606	Dorothy (Port) Hastings, Countess of Huntingdon
1607	Henry Blagrave
1608	Thomas Hackstall
>1610	Francis Hastings (with draft)
1625	Sir Robert Spencer
>1626	Sir John Davies
1630	Sir Hugh Losse
1634	William Noy
1656	Ferdinando Hastings, 6th Earl of Huntingdon (2 copies with an extract)
1656	Lucy (Davies) Hastings, Countess of Huntingdon
1665	Henry Hastings, Lord Loughborough (2 copies)
1667	Alice Clifton
1670	Edward Buersall
1670	Thomas Harley (extract only)
1670–71	Sir John Lewis (with later codicil)
1673	Thomas Heckstall
1675	Peter Venables
1680	Sir George Rawdon (with later wills for 1682, 1683, and 1684)
1683	John Heckstall
1689	Gabriel Hastings
1690	Theophilus Hastings, 7th Earl of Huntingdon (with later will and copies for 1698)
1704	George Hastings, 8th Earl of Huntingdon (two copies, with two later copies for 1705)
1712	Brilliana Rawdon
1713	Joseph Simmons (2 copies)
1715	John Graham
1723	Felina Rant
1724	Theophilus Hastings, 9th Earl of Huntingdon (with extract from will of 1746)
1733	Abraham Chambers
1739	Elizabeth Hastings

1742	Laurence Shirley
1756	Sir Dudley Ryder
1760	Leona Fasbrooke
1761	Selina (Shirley) Hastings, Countess of Huntingdon (3 copies and extract, with a later will for 1763)
1768	Mary (Lepell) Hervey, Lady Hervey
1770	Mary Adcock
1778	Catherine Spooner
1779	Francis Hastings, 10th Earl of Huntingdon (5 copies, 1 abstract, 1 extract, with a later will for 1789)
1781	Thomas Smith [of Packington, a salt carrier]
1787	John Elliott
1793	John Rawdon, 1st Earl of Moira (copy)
1794	Archibald Kennedy, 2nd Earl of Cassillis (extract only)
1795	William James
1795	Thomas Pering (copy)
1798	Lydia Matchitt
1800	Mary James
1800	Sir John Call
1803	Nathaniel Ryder, Baron Harrowby
1806	Nathaniel Middleton
1825	Granville Hastings Wheler
1836	George Rawdon-Hastings, 2nd Marquis of Hastings
1854	Sir Charles Abney Hastings

Inquisitions Post Mortem:

1329	Johanna Wake. Wilton, Wiltshire
1331	Roger Poges
1362	Thomas Courteney (two)
>1377	Henry de Erdington. Barrow-upon-Soar, Leicestershire
1391	Simon Pakeman. Leicester
1393	William Botreaux. York
1406	Peter Courteney. Broughton, Hampshire
1434	Elizabeth Botreaux. South Cadbury, Somerset
1440	John de Moleyns
1445	Reginald de Motton

1447	Walter Hungerford
1465	Robert Lord Hungerford. Ashburton, Devon
1478	Agatha Cawode. Harlford, Buckinghamshire
1482	James Cawode. Harlford, Buckinghamshire
1488<	Thomas Burgh
1505	John Osborne
1507	John Osborne. Orcheston St. George, Wiltshire
1530	John Bothe
1544	George Hastings, 1st Earl of Huntingdon (2 copies and draft)
1561	Francis Hastings, 2nd Earl of Huntingdon. Leicester (and extent)
1565	Exemplification of the *i.p.m.* of George Duke of Clarence
1588	Thomas Waterton. Wakefield, Yorks.
1588	Michael Rawdon (certified copy)
1596	Peter Barnewell
1607	George Hastings, 4th Earl of Huntingdon. Leicester

Additional significant or interesting items:

Summonses to Parliament for: William Lord Hastings, 1461, 1462; Edward, Lord Hastings, 1482, 1487, [1503], 1506; George, Lord Hastings, 1509, and as Earl of Huntingdon, 1536; Francis, 2nd Earl of Huntingdon, 1555; Henry, 3rd Earl of Huntingdon, 1586; George, 4th Earl of Huntingdon, 1597, 1604; Henry, 5th Earl of Huntingdon, 1623, 1625; Theophilus, 7th Earl of Huntingdon, 1678, 1679, 1680, 1682, 1686, 1688, 1690, 1698; George, 8th Earl of Huntingdon, 1702; Theophilus, 9th Earl of Huntingdon, 1715, 1723, 1731; Francis, 10th Earl of Huntingdon, 1754, 1761;

Extracts from Parliament rolls (1461–81, 1485–1503) and House of Lords Journals (1509–43, 1545–55, 1547–59, 1559–93, 1597–1604, 1605–41, 1640–45, 1676–88, 1701–03, 1722–64) chiefly re various members of the Hastings family. Many are 19th-century copies, presumably prepared to substantiate the claim to the earldom of Huntingdon of Hans Francis Hastings (subsequently the 12th Earl)

Numerous pardons, grants of office, and commissions issued by Mary I to Francis, 2nd Earl of Huntingdon, and to Sir Edward Hastings.

A volume of extracts from various grants to Sir John Davies, 1609–17

Oath of allegiance to Charles I, with 23 signatures, 1625

Memoranda book of Lucy, Countess of Huntingdon, containing notes on the Scriptures, 1 vol. [1630< >1679]

Memoranda books of Theophilus, 7th Earl of Huntingdon, containing notes on the Scriptures, 5 vols. ca.1660, 1663–64, ca.1665–66

Notes and papers re the interrogation and imprisonment of Theophilus, 7th Earl of Huntingdon, May-June 1692

IX. IRISH PAPERS

ca.2,400 pieces, 1583–1751

The following category consists of letters and papers, official and personal, pertaining to Ireland and Irish affairs during the 16th–18th centuries. Most of the material, which consists of the papers of the Rawdon family and their relatives in the Graham and Bramhall families, came into the Hastings Collection with the marriage of Lady Elizabeth Hastings to John Rawdon, 1st Earl of Moira, in 1752; a smaller group of papers, belonging to Sir John Davies, Attorney-General of Ireland, probably came into the collection with the marriage of his daughter Lucy to the 6th Earl in 1623.

The papers are strongest in information about the political and ecclesiastical affairs of the 17th century, and include: warrants, recognizances, and examinations made by Sir George Rawdon as a justice of the peace, covering such events as the Rebellion of 1641, Colonel Blood's plot to take Dublin Castle, and the expected invasion by France in 1667; political and ecclesiastical correspondence of Abp. John Bramhall (both as Speaker of the Irish House of Lords and as Bishop of Derry and Archbishop of Armagh, 1633–66); correspondence of George Monck, 1st Duke of Albemarle, and his agents and associates with Sir George Rawdon concerning his affairs in Ireland, family, public news, etc., 1660–70; correspondence of Edward Conway, 1st Earl of Conway, to Sir George Rawdon, 1st Bart., and his family concerning their own family and business affairs (strongest after 1665); military correspondence and other papers of Edward Conway's regiment, of which George Rawdon was the major, chiefly 1648–49.

Of particular interest are approximately 100 pieces (including ca.33 large vellum rolls) concerning Irish Concealed Lands, including inquisitions returned to Dublin by the Commissioners for Defective Titles during Sir John Davies' tenure of the offices of Solicitor-General and Attorney-General, with warrants or fiants for grants of forfeited Irish lands, signed by the Lords Deputy and addressed to Davies, ca.1605–20. Other significant individual items include: Sir Josias Bodley's Survey of the undertakers and servitors planted in Ulster, 1613; "A booke of the jayle delivery" taken before Davies and Justice Lowther at a General Sessions for the County of Monaghan, 1617; particulars of the cities, walled towns, castles, forts, and strongholds, with the territories held by the Protestants and by the rebels at the time of the cessation of arms in Ireland, 1643.

The following persons or institutions are represented by five or more letters or other papers (including drafts and contemporary copies):

Baily, William (5)
Baker, George (7)
Beaumont, George (15)
Boyle, Abp. Michael (27)
Boyle, Richard, 2nd Earl of Cork (7)
Boyle, Roger, 1st Earl of Orrery (27)
Bramhall, John, Abp. (44)
Bramhall, Sir Thomas (6)
Butler, James, 1st Duke of Ormonde (21)
Cary, Sir George. *See* Ireland. Lord Deputy
Charles II (10)
Chichester, Arthur, 1st Baron Chichester. *See* Ireland. Lord Deputy
Church of Ireland (5)
Clarges, Sir Thomas (11)
Clifton, Sir Richard (39)
Coghill, Sir John (70)
Conway, Edward, 1st Earl of Conway (231)
Conway, Edward, 2nd Viscount Conway (8)
Conway, Francis (11)
Dance, Thomas (7)
Ellis, Edmond (14)
Farewell, Thomas (48)

Forbes, Arthur, 1st Earl of Granard (11)
Forward, John (14)
Foulis, Robert (7)
Fuller, William (7)
Fulwar, Abp. Thomas (11)
Graham, Agnes (5)
Graham, Lady Isabella (23)
Graham, J. (7)
Graham, Sir James (27)
Graham, Joghery (5)
Graham, William, 8th Earl of Menteith (34)
Ireland.
    Commissioners (6)
    Lord Deputy (5)
    Lord Deputy (Cary, Sir George) (13)
    Lord Deputy (Chichester, Arthur) (135)
    Lord Deputy and Council (5)
    Lord Lieutenant (6)
    Lords Justices (5)
    Lords Justices and Council (6)
    Parliament (6)
Jacob, Sir Robert (5)
James I (22)
Jervis, Sir Humphrey (5)
Jones, Henry (6)
Kennedy, M. (7)
King, Robert (6)
Lake, Sir Edward, Bart. (10)
Lane, George (6)
Laud, William, Abp. (20)
Leslie, John (6)
Leslie, Robert (5)
Lock, Matthew (18)
MacDonnell, Rose (6)
Margetson, James (5)
Marsh, Francis (9)
Maxwell, Robert (15)
Monck, George, 1st Duke of Albemarle (60)
Montgomery, Hugh, 1st Earl of Mount-Alexander (12)
Morley, George (7)

Mossom, Robert (7)
O'Neill, Henry McToole (5)
O'Neill, Phelim (61)
Parker, John, Abp. (20)
Parnell, Thomas (31)
Prior, Thomas (29)
Pullen, Samuel, Abp. (10)
Rawdon, Sir Arthur (7)
Rawdon, Dorothy (7)
Rawdon, Lady Dorothy (Conway) (20)
Rawdon, Sir George (54)
St. John, Oliver, 1st Viscount Grandison (33)
Sheldon, Gilbert (8)
Skeffington, Sir John (5)
Smith, Hugh (5)
Stanhope, John (6)
Stanhope, Thomas (88)
Symes, Thomas (7)
Ussher, James, Abp. (13)
Wild, George, Bp. (30)

X. SPECIAL SUBJECTS

1. *Americana: 43 pieces, 1610–1823*

There are three main groups of American material in this category. The first contains papers concerning the Virginia Company of London, in which the 5th Earl of Huntingdon "adventured" £120 in return for 1,000 acres of land in the new Virginia Plantation, and includes (among other items): a contemporary copy of the names of some of the "adventurers" of the Virginia Company, together with their subscriptions, 1610–11; three "Bills of Adventure," or share certificates, issued to the 5th Earl by the Company, 1610–13; the Company's note of "what quantity of ground shale be sett forth for an adventuror to Virginia," [1613]; the 5th Earl's power of attorney to Nicholas Martiau and Benjamin Blewett to manage his Virginia estates, 1620; and a document by William Davys endorsed "My Lord's case for lands in Virginia," [1644].

The second group contains papers concerning the investments of John Rawdon, 1st Earl of Moira, in Florida lands, and includes: a copy of a scheme "for the Establishment of

Trade and Navigation, in all the Sea Ports of His Majesty's New Dominions in America [i.e., Florida]," ca.1763; two warrants by James Grant to survey lands in East Florida granted to the Earl of Moira, 1767; a map and survey of each of two plots of land in East Florida granted to the Earl of Moira, 1768; and papers concerning the claim of William Legge, 4th Earl of Dartmouth, to land in Florida, 1823.

The third group contains material concerning the military aspects of the American Revolution, in which Francis Rawdon-Hastings, Lord Rawdon (afterward 1st Marquess of Hastings) served with distinction from 1775 until the summer of 1781, and includes: Sir Henry Clinton's commission appointing Lord Rawdon Brigadier-General, 1781; an address to Lord Rawdon, as commander of the King's forces in South Carolina, by certain inhabitants of Charleston, 1781. There are also approximately 70 letters in the Hastings Correspondence section, most of them addressed to the 10th Earl of Huntingdon (including 19 from Lord Rawdon, 1775–80) concerning American affairs and the War, including information about the battles of Bunker Hill, Long Island, White Plains, and Kip's Bay, and the Charleston Expedition of 1776.

2. *Genealogy: ca.110 pieces, 15th–19th centuries*
Genealogical papers (many undated) tracing the descent of the family of Hastings, the earldoms of Huntingdon and Moira, the marquessate of Hastings, and the baronetcy of Rawdon, along with birth, death and marriage certificates (or copies of certificates) notices of christenings, and copies of epitaphs and monumental inscriptions, chiefly concerning the Hastings family.

Genealogical papers (most undated) for other families, including those of: de Clare, Davies, earls Ferrers, barons Grey de Ruthyn, Homet, Hubbard, Jolley, La Zouche, Levinge, Mure, Peverell, barons Strange, and Touchet lords Audley.

Pedigrees for various individuals, including those for: Thomas Mowbray, the dukes of Suffolk, King Gustavus Adolphus of Sweden, and Augustus Caesar.

Among the important or interesting individual items are:
An illuminated genealogical roll of the kings of England from Egbert to Henry IV, early 15th century

An emblazoncd genealogical roll of the Hastings family from the time of Sir Henry Hastings (d. 1250) to that of the children of Sir Hugh, 15th Baron Hastings, ca.1540

Biographical notes by Theophilus Hastings, 7th Earl of Huntingdon, concerning his father Ferdinando, the 6th Earl, and Sir John Davies. ca.1674?

Autobiography of Theophilus Hastings, 7th Earl of Huntingdon, with draft and notes, n.d.

Sir William Dugdale's autograph manuscript volume entitled "Historicall and Genealogical collections of the family of Hastings, Earls of Huntingdon, extracted from original deeds, charters . . . and other authentik evidences. . . ," 1677. With preliminary notes for the history, many in numbered sets.

3. *Gentlemen Pensioners: 46 pieces, 1660–88*
Papers concerning the Band of Gentlemen Pensioners, of which Theophilus, 7th Earl of Huntingdon, was appointed Captain by Charles II in 1682. Included are: lists of the names of the Band (1682< and 1686), and of the captains since the institution of the Band (1683); a note by John Belasyse, 1st Baron Belasyse of Worlaby, concerning the duties of the Captain (1682); "Orders for the weekley waiting of the Band. . ." (1685); a note concerning the precedence of the Captain over the Gentlemen of the Bedchamber (ca.1678?); an account of Lewis Kirke, paymaster (1663) and a report on the revenues concerning the Band submitted by John Lawrence to the Lords Commissioners of the Treasury (1683); and various grants, appointments, petitions, and other papers concerning the Band and its members.

4. *Indentured Retainers: 69 pieces, 1461–83*
Indentures of service of 71 retainers of William, Lord Hastings, with a list of the retainers and a statement of their obligations and those of Lord Hastings.

All but four of these documents were known to William Huse Dunham and are the subject of his *Lord Hastings Indentured Retainers, 1461–83*, vol. 39 of the *Transactions of the Connecticut Academy of Arts and Sciences* (1955), where twenty-six of the indentures are transcribed in full.

5. *Literature: ca. 100 pieces, 17th–19th centuries*
Papers of literary merit or interest, chiefly poetry, including compositions by various members of the Hastings family. The papers are listed chronologically below.

Kinder, Philip. "Eugenia sive genealogica chronolgraphica Impp. Regum Principum. . ." 1628<

Makin, Bathsua. Poem on the death of Henry, Lord Hastings. 1649<

Latin epitaphs for Sir John Davies and his wife, Lady Eleanor, which Lucy, Countess of Huntingdon, had engraved on her parents' tombstones. 1652<

Acrostic verse on Theophilus, 7th Earl of Huntingdon [1656<>1701] (fragment)

Epitaph for a "beloved Husband" who died 1661.

A volume of anecdotes, sayings, etc. dedicated to Lady Christiana Hastings. (In Italian). ca.1665?

A volume of prayers and scriptural quotations collected by Elizabeth, late Countess of Huntingdon, for her own use. 1676

Satire addressed to Lord Ferrers, beginning "As Colon drove his sheep along. . ." 1676

Political ballad of 13 stanzas beginning "Would you send Kele to Portugal. . ." ca.1685

Faye, Thomas. Poem of 26 lines beginning "Excellent Lady, you are, so all good. . ." n.d. (17th cent.)

Matthews, Mathew. Poem of 24 lines beginning "Because my paper Noble Lord doeth doe. . ." n.d. 17th cent.

"The Ghost of Honest Tom Rosse," a poem of 25 lines. n.d. (17th cent.)

A volume containing a vocabulary list or index, probably to a classical text. n.d. (17th cent.)

Political ballad of 29 stanzas beginning "Our nolrey and Councell both. . ." n.d. (17th cent.)

A poem on the Land Tax and Poll Tax, addressed to the Countess of Huntingdon. n.d. (17th cent?) (endorsed "Time K. Willm.")

Crudeli, Tommaso. "Cicalata Accademica" (a discourse on poetry, in Italian). ca.1738

A small booklet of poetry titled "Il Bellicoso." 1744

Two unbound quires of poetry titled "Componimenti Satirici eruditi" (in Italian). ca.1750–60?

Poetry in the hand of Francis, 10th Earl of Huntingdon. 3 pieces, ca.1752–89

Hastings, Francis, 10th Earl of Huntingdon. Copy of an epitaph made on a cask of wine by Dr. Caleb Harding. ca.1753

"Epilogue to the Eunuch, spoken by Pythias, Bringing in the Marriage Bill." 1753

List of poems of Petrarch and Ariosto. ca.1753?

Hastings, Francis Rawdon, 1st Marquess of Hastings. Translation of the first chorus of Sophocles' "Antigone." ca.1765

[Bradbury, Silas?]. An ode to Thomas Abney of Willesly, written by his tutor, 1770

Poem to Thomas, Viscount Wentworth (in Latin) beginning "Quis hic est, alto qui arduus incedit gradu. . ." [1774<>1815]

"Matri triumphanti, Filiae militantis deserium," a Latin poem beginning "Non quod te prognata fui, mea vita, tuisque. . ." n.d. (18th cent.)

"Laudenhill," a poem of six stanzas beginning "A swain who nothing knew of love. . ." n.d. (18th cent.)

Hawker, Robert Stephen. "The Silent Tower of Botreaux," (extract only). n.d. (18th cent.?)

Italian canzonetta, with music, n.d. (18th cent.)

Ellis, S. "Verses on Miss Fanny Prat." n.d. (18th cent.?)

"To Dr. Askew. On the Buckle Verses, in Lloyd's Chronicle," a poem of 13 lines beginning "This blundering Rhimer tells a sad silly story. . ." n.d. (18th cent.?)

Ballad beginning "I promised Silvia to be true. . ." n.d., 18th cent.?

Poem or epitaph to the "Honble. R. D. Esqr," n.d. (18th cent.?)

Rawdon-Hastings, Lady Flora Elizabeth. Poetry: translations, originals, fragments, etc. ca.60 pieces. 1812–ca.1838

Rawdon-Hastings, Francis, 1st Marquis of Hastings. "Mine-Even-Song," a poem of 3 stanzas. ca.1826

"Chanson" (in French). n.d. (19th cent.?)

6. *Military Affairs: 85 pieces, 1477–1823*

Official and other papers, chiefly concerning the military activities of various members of the Hastings family. Included are: military commissions and appointments (many for Leicestershire forces); warrants and instructions to Lords and Deputies Lieutenant; county muster rolls and lists (including 7 for Leicestershire, 1597–1602; and for Rutlandshire, 1614, 1638–39, ca.1680s); regimental lists and returns for the 7th Earl of Huntingdon's regiment (ca.1670s, 1685, ca.1680s), for the 12th Regiment of Foot (1822), and for the 20th Infantry Regiment (1823); other miscellaneous lists (including: of the fleet under the command of Prince Rupert, n.d. (17th cent.), and of Derbyshire militia officers, ca.1685); and a few accounts (including a note of the yearly muster charges, 1619, and two weekly pay accounts for the Derbyshire militia, 1686).

Other miscellaneous items of interest are listed chronologically below:

> "Certaine propositions made unto King James as it was thought by Sir Robert Dudley, Knight." ca.1612?
> Sir Robert Bruce Cotton. "The danger wherein the kingdome now standeth and the Remedyes." 1628
> A relation of the fight between the King of Sweden and the Emperor's Army. 1632
> "Sum publick mar[ine?] affairs about Dunkirk" (in French). 1650
> List of English and Dutch ships lost and damaged, and of loss and injuries of personnel, in the Dutch War. 1665?
> A report concerning the forces in Tangier. [1676<>1683?]
> Rules and directions for Regiments of Foot. 1685
> "Records collected by Sir Robert Cotton . . . [re?] Raisings of forces at Country's Charge." n.d. (17th cent.)
> Note of the expense of building men of war in England. ca.1722

7. *Parliamentary Affairs: ca.130 pieces, 1532–19th cent.*

Official and other papers concerning Parliament, chiefly during the 17th century. Included are a variety of lists: returns of members (1554, 1603, 1614, 1621, 1625, 1626, 1628); Scottish members of Parliament, 1617<; the Lords Committees for the customs and privileges of the House, 1621; the Lords, 1625; "certaine noble men that . . . a messenger of the chamber brought the writt of sumons for the Parliament . . . unto," 1628; those to whom a commission to prorogue Parliament is to be addressed, 1686; and "the Lords who entered their discents to the vote that the Crown is become vacant," 1689. Also petitions or copies of petitions (to the Crown from the Commons, 1610, ?1620, 1621, 1626, 1673; from the Lords, ?1566, 1610, 1626, 1679; and from both Houses, 1625, ?1628; together with some royal responses).

Also speeches or notes on speeches delivered in Parliament (by William Barlow, Bp. of Lincoln, 1610; James I, 1624; Sir Thomas Crewe, 1624; Charles I, 1626, 1640; Thomas Coventry, 1st Baron Coventry and Lord Keeper, 1628; George Villiers, Duke of Buckingham, 1628; John Pym, 1640; Sir John Glanville, 1640; Sir Harbottle Grimston, 1640; Lucius Cary, 2nd Viscount Falkland, 1640; Francis Rose?, 1640; Edward Hyde, 1st Earl of Clarendon, 1667; Theophilus Hastings, 7th Earl of Huntingdon, ca.1688; also a volume of copies of speeches and notes on proceedings, 1610–24; speeches concerning Sir Giles Mompesson, 1621; and of the Lord Treasurer and Lord Chancellor, ?1621).

Also copies or drafts of acts (some printed), both private and public; accounts and notes on proceedings and transactions in Parliament, or of issues concerning Parliament, many made by or for Theophilus Hastings, 7th Earl of Huntingdon.

Among other individual items of interest or significance are:

"Articles commended by the King's majestie for the Lower House to Consider of." 1610

[Sandys, Sir Edwin]. Report to the Commons on the conference with the Lords concerning impositions. 1614

"A Book of Proxies [of the House of Lords] from the 25 of k[ing] H[enry] the 8th [through 12 James I]." ca.1616

Submissions to the Lords by Sir Francis Bacon and by Thomas Howard, 2nd Earl of Arundel. 1621

Copy of the charges brought against the Duke of Buckingham, 1626, and of his answers to charges. ?1628

2 copies of the "Lords Standing Orders." 1629<, 1690

The "Names of the Lords spirituale and temporall that granted their proxies and to whom, 16 Car I." 1640

The Commons address for war with France, sent up to the Lords 1678, with [an attendance list? division list?] for the Lords.

See also p. 127, above.

8. *Religious and Ecclesiastical Affairs: 66 pieces, 1558–1847*

There are two general types of material in this category. The first consists of personal religious papers, chiefly of the Hastings family, including prayers, meditations, sermons, scriptural notes, etc., chiefly from the 17th century and chiefly by or involving Lucy (Davies) Hastings, Countess of Huntingdon, and Theophilus, the 7th Earl of Huntingdon. Included are: the Countess's "A Methode for Private Devotion," ca.1650, "Notes and observations taken out of the whole Duty of man. . . ," 1665, and memorandum book of scriptural notes; Henry, the 5th Earl's "A prayer for the Parliament," 1634, and "A short meditation upon the ill newes of a tolleration. . . ," 1622; the 7th Earl's "A Briefe forme of Devotion," 1676, "A forme of private devotion Morning and Evening," 1691, and other prayers and notes; a "First Sermon" by Peter Smith, n.d. (17th cent.); a paper by Lady Eleanor Douglas headed "Bathe Daughter of BabyLondon—woman sitting on seven mountains," >1670; and other miscellaneous and often anonymous devotional pieces.

The second type of material concerns ecclesiastical matters of public interest, both local and national. Included here are: a copy of Cardinal Pole's directions for the payment of money to Thomas Teysdey from a reestablished Battle Abbey, 1558; an injunction of Elizabeth I addressed to Abp. Parker commanding that no head or member of any college or cathedral church be allowed to have his wife or other woman dwell there, 1561; a copy of the "Bill for the Reformation of the Ecclesiasticall Lawes," 1559; a volume containing a defense of the conduct of Puritan ministers, possibly written by Thomas Cartwright, with an answer, and with a copy of a letter from Abp. Grindal to the Queen concerning the number of preachers; legal papers concerning ecclesiastical affairs (including an examination of William Hance, priest, taken by Francis Hastings as J.P. for Leicestershire, 1582, a paper titled "Notts and Leicester Case relating to ye people called 'Quakers,' ca.1685, papers re the proceedings of the Ecclesiastical Commission, of which the 7th Earl of Huntingdon was a member, 1686–88); copies of Parliamentary Bills or Acts concerning religion; a few undated and miscellaneous notes and papers concerning Catholics; and Charles Drelincourt's "An Abridgment of controversy or a summary of the errors of the Church of Rome,"k0 1666.

Other miscellaneous items include: a list of pluralities in Leicestershire, 1610; English translations of three papers by Cardinal Richelieu on "The Supremacy of the Pope," "Of the Scriptures of Tradition," and "Of the sacrifice of the Eucharist propitiatorie," 1635; a copy of instructions from Charles II concerning his religious intentions after the Restoration, ca.1660; the names of all the cathedrals and collegiate churches in England, ca.1670?; an undated 17th-century "Directory for the Abridgement of Sermons" by I. M.; an undated 17th-century paper concerning "The Forme of Government used in the Kirk of Scotland"; a "Copie of the paper found in King Charles II's strong box concerning controversy," 1685; and an undated "Account of the yearly Tenthes of ye Clergy in every Diocese of England as they are in Dr. Heylins help to History."

9. *Repton Charity School and Etwall Hospital: ca.100 pieces,*
1557–1841

Legal, financial, and administrative papers concerning the two charitable institutions of Repton School and Etwall Hospital, established in Derbyshire by Sir John Port in 1557. Included are: rentals for the lands of the endowments (1622, 1629, 1633, and 1636) with other notes on rents, surveys and lists of lands; legal papers from lawsuits concerning Repton and Etwall (particularly that of ca.1613–20 involving Henry, 5th Earl of Huntingdon, *v.* Sir John Harpur, the [trustee? administrator? of the lands] and that of 1705–10 involving Lady Elizabeth Hastings' right to the governorship of Repton and Etwall); notes on the warrants for the granting of leases;

petitions from staff (e.g. for salaries) and inhabitants or would-be inhabitants of Repton or Etwall, many addressed to Henry Hastings, 5th Earl of Huntingdon; and various rules and regulations for the administration of the institutions.

Also included are 9 pieces concerning Dilhorne School, chiefly concerning the appointment of schoolmasters there, 1646–99.

See also Hastings Deeds, for Repton, and correspondence of Henry Hastings, 5th Earl of Huntingdon, and Philip Stanhope, 1st and 2nd Earls of Chesterfield, among others, for additional material concerning these institutions.

10. *School Exercises and Education: ca.400 pieces, 1600–1835*
School or tutorial exercises, educational commonplace books and notebooks, notes on history and other subjects, and miscellaneous educational material probably belonging to various members of the Hastings family. Included are: twelve 17th-century volumes of extracts from various histories, including those on the Punic Wars, Plutarch, the "Life of Tarquin," the Assyrian Empire, Richard Knolles' history of the Turks, Ralegh's history of the world, the "Annales" on the Roman occupation of Britain, medieval European history, etc., together with numerous smaller papers of historical notes and extracts; numerous language exercises, principally of Francis Hastings, the 10th Earl, in Greek, Latin, Italian, and French; notes on logic by Theophilus Hastings, 7th Earl of Huntingdon; a geometrical commonplace book based on John Speidel, 1623<; a list of Italian books worthy to be read, ca.1754; a list of French books on Astronomy, ca.1770; a volume of short discourses dealing with subjects such as virtue, women, beauty, marriage, honor, etc., out of "Du Verger's booke etituled 'Admirable events and Morall Relacons,'" 1647.

11. *Ship Money: 9 pieces, 1635–38*
Copies and transcripts of legal opinions and other papers concerning Ship Money. Included are:

A volume of the arguments of Oliver St. John, Sir Edward Littleton, and Sir John Bankes on Ship Money. 1635

A copy of a letter from Charles I to the judges of Kings Bench, Common Pleas, and the Exchequer, concerning Ship Money, and their opinions on the same. 1636

"The Coppie of his Majesties queries concerning the pay-
inge towards the Shipps unto the Judges and there
answeares therunto." 1637

A large volume of transcripts of the opinions of several
judges and justices concerning Ship Money, with "cer-
tein necessary quaerees uppon perusall of theise arguments." 1637–38

Individual copies of the opinions of Sir George Crooke,
Sir Thomas Jones, Sir Richard Hutton, Sir John Denham, and Sir Humphrey Davenport. 1638

12. *Transportation: 35 pieces, ca.1765–ca.1871*

Miscellaneous papers concerning canals, rivers, and roads,
including: notes on canals or proposed canals linking the rivers Tame, Avon, Severn, Weaver and Mersey (1765–66), in
Leicestershire (n.d., 18th cent.), in Worcestershire (n.d., 18th
cent.?), and from the Weaver Navigation in Cheshire to Wil-
den in Derbyshire (n.d., 18th cent.); a copy of a petition to
the House of Commons from the Committee of the Proprietors of the Coventry Canal Navigation, 1768<; proxies from
Francis, 10th Earl of Huntingdon, to Edward Dawson, as one
of the proprietors of the River Soar Navigation from the River
Trent to Loughborough, 1776–90; an account of and calls due
on Lord Rawdon's shares in the Leicestershire Navigation,
ca.1793; a list of subscribers to the loan for Ashby Canal, 1801;
several copies of the prospectus for the Burton-upon-Trent
and Moira Canal, 1840; and a copy of the Act for making
and maintaining a Navigable Canal from the Coventry Canal
to Ashby, Ticknall, and Cloudhill, (n.d., 19th cent.)

Also a few papers concerning rivers (including notes on
the problems of water levels in the River Trent and the ability
of the dam at King's Mills to accommodate certain boats,
ca.1796, and notes opposing the making navigable of the River
Trent and Tame in Staffordshire, n.d., 18th cent.) and turnpike
and other roads (including an account of the trustees of the
Turnpike road between Loughborough and Cavendish
Bridge, 1779, a discussion of monies to be spent on roads in
Melbourne by the Commissioners for enclosure, 1789, and
a resolution made at a meeting of the trustees of the Tamworth and Harrington Bridge Turnpike Road re a bridle path
through Castle Donington, 1842).

See also numerous maps and plans of proposed canals in Hastings Maps & Plans, above, pp. 122–23.

13. *Miscellaneous Manuscripts: ca.400 pieces, 14–19th centuries*

A wide variety of material which does not fit into any of the above categories, or which does not immediately appear to be connected with the Hastings family or their circle. Many pieces are incomplete or fragmentary, and many are anonymous.

Some of the more important or unusual items are listed chronologically below in three groups: material of political significance; material concerning India and the East, probably from the time of the 1st Marquis of Hastings; material of general interest

Political:

> A volume of transcripts of charters, fines, pleadings, inquisitions, etc. re Richard Duke of Gloucester (aftw. Richard III). ca.1550
>
> A copy of the confession of William Andrew, servant to Sir Everard Digby, of his involvement with those convicted in the Gunpowder Plot. 1605
>
> Proposals for the creation of the rank of Baronet. ca.1610?
>
> "The Contents of the Lords of the Councells letters about the Constitution." 1622
>
> Privy Council order for the Lords Lieutenants of the shires to nominate their deputies. 1625
>
> Copy of instructions to Justices of the Peace in all English and Welsh counties. 1626
>
> Copy of a Privy Council warrant to [Sir?] Baptist Hickes, collector for the loan to the King in Middlesex. 1626
>
> "The names of the Commissioners for the encrease of the kings yearly revenue and the raysinge of mony for his present supply. . ." 1626
>
> "The gests of his ma[jestie]s progresse." 1633
>
> An account of a naval battle. 1683
>
> List of those created peers by Charles II. 1684
>
> "The names of those who took the othes and tests in Chancery." 1685

List of persons pardoned for taking office without having taken the Oaths of Supremacy and Allegiance and the Test of the Sacraments. [1686–88?]

Memorandum re the indictment of Aaron Smith of London for writing "seditious and malicious instructions for one Stephen Colledge who was indicted and tried for high treason at Oxford." 1692

"Instructions to be exactly and effectivally observed and followed by his Majesty's Commissioners for the loan of money unto his Majesty." n.d. (17th cent.)

Account of the accession of Charles II. n.d. (17th cent.)

Formula for the Oath of Supremacy and Allegiance, n.d. (17th cent.)

Orders for proper behavior upon entering the royal chapel and privy chamber. n.d., 17th cent.

"Reasons humble offered for the restrayings the great number of parks etc. in this Kingdome and the bringing those that are allready made under the Stamp of the Royall Prerogative." n.d. (17th cent.?)

India and the East:

Pottinger, Henry. Translations of confessions regarding the death of a woman in India. 1818

Minutes of the Court of Directors of the East India Co. 1819

Resolution of [the Court of Directors?] of the East India Co. 1819

A letter of appreciation from the inhabitants of Singapore to Francis, Marquis of Hastings, upon his departure. 1822

A memorial to the chairman and the Court of Directors of the East India Company for the management of affairs in India. 1823

A resolution from the British inhabitants of Madras, India. 1824

An address by the Asiatic Society to Francis, 1st Marquis of Hastings. 1824?

Eight volumes written in [Arabic?]. 19th cent?

List of the villages in Pergunnahs. 19th cent.

Statistical queries and replies re the [Sylhet?] district, 19th cent.

Chart and memoranda on the military positions of the Deccan. 19th cent.

List of maps, plans, etc. relating to India. 19th cent.

Table showing the capacities, populations, etc. of the Pergunnahs of Singbhoom, with a chart of the country around Chouta Nagpere. 19th cent.

Other:

"Orders for Swanes printed by the kings permission for all those that are upon any great water or streame." 1610

List of the chief cities and towns in England and Wales, with the "magistracie of the same, and howe many severall families have borne the titles of those places taken out of Speeds Mappes." 1620

The arms of the several corporations in England. ca.1620?

A petition from linen weavers concerning an act re the making of linen cloth. 1663<

Notes from volumes of Cranmer's memoirs. 1696?

Recipes, menus, prescriptions, etc., 17th–18th centuries. ca.120 pieces

A volume of accounts of the executors of Sir Isaac Newton. 1727

Notice concerning the collection of money by the S.P.C.K. for the poor of Salzburg. 1732

Traballefi, Jo. Gaetano. List of statues bought by Francis, Earl of Huntingdon. 1755 (in Italian)

Lists of papers read at the Royal Society with discourse concerning the French Academy of Science. 1769–70

An account of Henry Howard, Earl of Surrey, in a joust in 1540. 18th cent.?

Campbell, John. "Post mortem examination of the Dowager Marchioness of Hastings. . . ," 1840

STOWE COLLECTION
ca.350,000 pieces, ca.1175–1919

The Stowe Collection, largest by far of any in the Library, consists of the papers of the Grenville, Temple, Nugent, and Brydges families, related through the 18th-century marriages which brought each of them to the famous house at Stowe in Buckinghamshire. It also includes a much smaller group of papers of Charles O'Conor (1764–1828), the Irish scholar and Catholic priest who came to Stowe in 1798 as chaplain and librarian.

Spanning nine centuries, the papers begin and end, appropriately, with the Grenvilles. Established at Wotton Underwood in Buckinghamshire by the 12th century, the family gradually amassed a considerable landed estate in that county. With the marriage in 1710 of Richard Grenville (1677–1727) to Hester Temple, sister and heiress of Richard Temple, Viscount Cobham, the Grenvilles assured their acquisition (at the death of Cobham in 1749) of the extensive Temple lands in Buckinghamshire and Warwickshire, as well as of Stowe House itself, on which the Temples had lavished such care in the preceding hundred years. The grandson of this union, George Grenville, later created Marquis of Buckingham, married in 1775 the heiress Mary Elizabeth Nugent, thus bringing to the growing Grenville fortunes the Irish, Cornish, and Essex estates of her father Robert Nugent, Earl Nugent. Their son Richard Grenville, afterward 1st Duke of Buckingham and Chandos, made the family's third great marriage alliance of the 18th century by marrying in 1796 Anna Elizabeth Brydges, daughter and heiress of James Brydges, the 3rd and last Duke of Chandos. With the addition of the Brydges lands (chiefly in Hampshire, Middlesex, and Somerset) and money, the Grenvilles' estates and fortunes reached a high point, matching the political eminence they had achieved in the later 18th century. The 19th century witnessed a gradual decline, despite the magnificence of life at Stowe. The 2nd Duke of Buckingham's extravagance and profligacy brought the family to bankruptcy in 1848, and much of the lands and personal property had to be sold; his son, the 3rd Duke, retrieved something from the disaster, and enjoyed a modest political career, but died without male heir. His eldest daughter married into the Morgan (afterward Morgan-Grenville) family, a small group of whose papers form a brief postscript to the present archive. Stowe House itself is now a school.

Source: the collection was sold in 1921 by Lady Mary Morgan-Grenville, Baroness Kinloss of Stowe, and purchased for the Huntington Library through Frank Marcham and the Museum Bookstore, London, in 1925.*

Bibliography: the massive size of the collection has naturally inhibited comprehensive description. The best modern summary is found in Jean F. Preston, "Collections of English Historical Manuscripts in the Huntington Library," *Archives* 6 (1963): 97–101. A brief partial summary, limited chiefly to Buckinghamshire material, was compiled by J. G. Jenkins and published as *A Handlist of the Stowe Collection in the Huntington Library* for the Buckinghamshire Record Society (1956). (The stack locations and box numbers given by Jenkins are now outdated.)

Only a small fraction of the Grenville papers have been published *in extenso*. Some of the political correspondence of the late 18th and early 19th centuries, and part of the private diary of Richard Grenville, 1st Duke of Buckingham and Chandos, were edited by the 2nd Duke and published by Hurst and Blackett, London, as: *Memoirs of the Court and Cabinets of George III, 1782–1810,* 4 vols. (1853–55); *Memoirs of England During the Regency, 1811–20,* 2 vols. (1856); *Memoirs of the Court of George IV, 1820–30,* 2 vols. (1859); *Memoirs of the Court and Cabinets of William IV and Victoria,* [1830–60], 2 vols. (1861); and *The Private Diary of Richard, Duke of Buckingham and Chandos,* 2 vols. (1862).

* A small group (ca.60 pieces) of additional miscellaneous Grenville, Temple, and Brydges papers was acquired from Frank Marcham between 1939 and 1951. Other additions to the Stowe Collection, acquired after 1925, are noted below in the appropriate sections.

Some of the Temple papers concerning Ship Money have been published, unsatisfactorily, in *Ship Money Papers and Richard Grenville's Notebook*, edited by Carol G. Bonsey and J. G. Jenkins for the Buckinghamshire Record Society (1965). (The Library does not have Richard Grenville's notebook, which is in the Buckinghamshire Record Office.)

Major supplementary collections of Stowe manuscripts (chiefly accounts, deeds, and other estate papers) are located in the Buckinghamshire Record Office, the Northamptonshire Record Office, and the Library of the University of Reading.

The present collection should be distinguished from the Stowe Collection in the British Museum, which consists of the manuscripts collected by (but not usually pertaining to) the 1st Marquis of Buckingham and the 1st and 2nd Dukes for the library at Stowe, including the Astle Collection purchased by the Marquis in 1804, many of the ancient Irish manuscripts of Charles O'Conor's grandfather, Charles O'Conor of Belanagare, and other collections and individual pieces. These manuscripts were sold in 1849, following the bankruptcy of the 2nd Duke, to Bertram Ashburnham, 5th Earl of Ashburnham, from whose estate they were eventually purchased by the British Museum in 1883. They are cataloged in *Stowe Manuscripts in the British Museum*, 2 vols. (London, 1895–96), which excludes the Irish manuscripts which have been deposited in the Library of the Royal Irish Academy in Dublin.

Remarks on the following description: the collection is organized to preserve the separate family groups, and is described accordingly under the headings of Grenville, Temple, Nugent, Brydges, and O'Conor Papers, following brief biographical sketches of each of the families. Within each family subcollection the same principles have been applied as those in use in the Hastings Collection description: papers are divided generally into the archival classes of accounts, correspondence, inventories, lists and catalogs, legal papers, manorial and local affairs papers, and personal and family papers. For the types of documents included in each of these classes, see the appropriate introduction to each in the Hastings description. In addition, smaller collections of papers dealing with specific "special subjects" have been kept separate, and are described accordingly. All of the Stowe maps and plans, and most of the deeds, were not sorted by family and have therefore been described in a concluding "Stowe General" section. Of the remaining unsorted papers, those dated later than 1750 and not immediately linked to any of the five families have generally been assumed to belong to the Grenvilles, and are listed as such here. It is probable, finally, that some of the papers belonging properly to one family group have migrated into those of another. As the reasons for these migrations are now unknown, and may well have included intentional selection while the material was still at Stowe, no attempt has been made at present to restore papers to their original order.

For the categories under which the papers of the various families are described, see the Table of Contents.

Grenville Papers (ca.300,000 pieces)

Although firmly established at Wotton Underwood in Buckinghamshire by the 12th century, the Grenville family* achieved little beyond local recognition as lesser gentry until the 17th, when Richard Grenville (1611?–65) emerged as Sheriff and Deputy-Lieutenant of the county and as a Parliamentary soldier in 1643–44. In 1710 a later Richard Grenville (1677–1727) married Hester Temple (1690–1752), sister and heiress of Richard Temple, Viscount Cobham, of Stowe; she was created Countess Temple in her own right upon the death of Cobham in 1749. The family then took up residence at Stowe, which became the center for three remarkable generations of aristocratic politicians and statesmen. The eldest son of Richard and Hester, Richard Grenville (1711–79), afterward Grenville-Temple, succeeded his mother as 2nd Earl Temple in 1752; he served as First Lord of the Admiralty (1756–57) and Lord Privy Seal (1756–61), supported Pitt (who had married Grenville's sister Hester), patronized John Wilkes, and joined his brother George in leading the Grenville faction in English politics. He married Anne Chambers (d. 1777) in 1737, and died in 1779 leaving no direct male heirs. A younger brother, Henry Grenville (1717–84), was Governor of Barbados.

---

* The Buckinghamshire Grenvilles should be distinguished from the Cornish family of that name, of Stow, Kilkhampton, and from Sir Richard Grenville of "Revenge" fame.

Another of Earl Temple's brothers, George Grenville (1712–70), is perhaps the most famous of the family; he served as M.P. for Buckingham (1740–70), Treasurer of the Navy (1756–62), First Lord of the Admiralty (1762–63), Secretary of State (1762–63), and Prime Minister and Chancellor of the Exchequer (1763–65). Under his ministry the Stamp Act was enacted, and he remained active in politics throughout the 1760s as "The Gentle Shepherd." Grenville married Elizabeth Wyndham (d. 1769) in 1749. Of their younger sons, Thomas Grenville (1755–1846) sat in Parliament (1780–84 and 1790–1818), led diplomatic missions to Vienna in 1794 and Berlin in 1799, and served as First Lord of the Admiralty and President of the Board of Control in 1806–07. He was also a notable book collector, and his bequest of these to the British Museum formed the Grenville Library there. His younger brother William Wyndham Grenville (1759–1834) was also an M.P. (1782–90), Chief Secretary for Ireland (1782–83), Vice-President of the Board of Trade (1786–89), Home Secretary (1789–90), President of the Board of Control (1790–93), Foreign Secretary (1791–1801), and Prime Minister as the head of the "Ministry of All Talents" (1806–07). He married Anne Pitt (d. 1864), daughter of Thomas Pitt, 1st Baron Camelford, and was created Baron Grenville in 1790.

The eldest surviving son of George Grenville, and brother of Thomas and William Wyndham, was George Grenville (1753–1813), afterward Nugent-Temple-Grenville, who succeeded his uncle in 1779 as Earl Temple and was created Marquis of Buckingham in 1784. He served as Lord Lieutenant of Buckinghamshire from 1782 until his death, and as Lord Lieutenant of Ireland (1782–83 and 1787–89). In 1775 he married Mary Elizabeth Nugent (d. 1812), daughter and coheiress of Robert Nugent, Earl Nugent; she was created Baroness Nugent in 1800.

The head of the next generation was their eldest son, Richard Nugent-Temple-Grenville (1776–1839), afterward properly Temple-Nugent-Brydges-Chandos-Grenville (but hereinafter shortened simply to Grenville), a Commissioner of the India Board (1800–01), Joint Paymaster-General and Vice-President of the Board of Trade (1806–07), and Lord Lieutenant of Buckinghamshire from 1813 until his death. He was created 1st Duke of Buckingham and Chandos in 1822. He married in 1796 Anna Elizabeth Brydges (1779–1836), *suo jure* Baroness Kinloss, the daughter and heiress of James Brydges, 3rd and last Duke of Chandos.

Although the social status of the family was now distinguished, and their house and gardens at Stowe (to which many of the major architects, landscape gardeners, and other artists of the 18th century had contributed much effort and talent) were justly famous, their political and financial position was waning. Richard Grenville, 2nd Duke of Buckingham and Chandos (1797–1861), was an automatic leader of the agricultural interest in the House of Commons (where he sat until his father's death), and gave his name to the Chandos Clause of the Reform Bill of 1832, but paid more attention to lavish entertaining at Stowe and in London, and to his beloved troops of Buckinghamshire militia. The expense of these interests, the ruinous cost of a royal visit by Victoria and Albert to Stowe in 1845, and his inability to economize or to supervise the administration of his wide-spread estates, brought the 2nd Duke to bankruptcy in 1847–48 with debts of over £1,000,000. His son the Marquis of Chandos (afterward the 3rd Duke), as the result of an agreement with his lawyers and creditors, in 1847 assumed the debts as well as control over the Grenville estates and finances. Many of the outlying estates, and the personal contents of Stowe itself, were sold in 1848, but the core of the estate was preserved. The 2nd Duke's wife since 1819, Mary (Campbell) Grenville (d. 1862), a daughter of the 1st Marquis of Breadalbane, obtained a legal separation from him in 1850 and he died in near poverty, a pensioner of his son, in 1861.

Richard Grenville, 3rd Duke of Buckingham and Chandos (1823–89), restored solvency and some order to the family fortunes, and inherited the Grenville interest in politics. He was a Conservative M.P. (1846–57), President of the Council (1866–67), Colonial Secretary (1867–68), Lord Lieutenant of Buckinghamshire (1868 until his death), and Governor of Madras (1875–80). He married first, in 1851, Caroline Harvey (d. 1874) and second, Alice Anne Graham-Montgomery, who after his death in 1889 married the 1st Earl of Egerton.

The 3rd Duke had no sons; at his death the dukedom became extinct, while the earldom of Temple of Stowe and the viscountcy of Cobham devolved on indirect male heirs. Stowe itself, with the remaining but much reduced family estates, passed to the 3rd Duke's eldest daughter Mary Grenville (1852–1944), *suo jure* Baroness Kinloss, who married in 1884 Major Luis Morgan, afterward Morgan-Grenville. Following World War I, in which her son Richard, Master of Kinloss, was killed in action, she arranged for the sale of Stowe and its contents.

I. GRENVILLE ACCOUNTS AND FINANCIAL PAPERS
ca.225,000 pieces, ca.1700–1920

The Grenville family accounts are so voluminous, and so varied, that no brief summary can provide an adequate description. Roughly, they consist of the estate, household, personal, legal, commercial, and other financial papers of the Grenville and related families from 1749,* when they inherited Stowe, through the beginning of the 20th century. Approximately half of the papers in this category are estate accounts for Stowe, Wotton Underwood, and other Buckinghamshire lands, and these are strongest for the period from 1749 through the bankruptcy of the 2nd Duke of Buckingham and Chandos in 1847–48. Thereafter legal and financial papers proliferate alongside continuing runs of estate, household, and personal accounts. In addition to individual pieces, there are over 200 bound volumes of accounts (of varying detail and completeness); both are presented in very summary fashion below.

1. *Estate Accounts*
    A. *Buckinghamshire (ca.120,000 pieces):* chiefly for Stowe, with additional material for Wotton and other Grenville lands. Included are both regular summarized accounts (kept by estate officials for presentation at weekly, fortnightly, monthly, and longer intervals) and individual bills, receipts, pay vouchers, etc. for such aspects of estate expense as: estate, farm, garden, and building labor (planting, sowing, threshing, digging peat, "welling," mending fences and walls, weeding, trimming, carpentry, glazing, masonry, digging tree holes, making drains, cartage, road work, etc.); livestock (sheep and cattle sales, sheep shearing, sales of wool, fat, skins, etc.); dairy (fowl,

---

* Although there are a handful of earlier items (19 pieces, 1454–1699), it would be misleading to include them in the above bracketing dates. In general, Grenville accounts from the time before the family moved to Stowe are not at the Library.

milk, eggs, etc.); kilns and bricks; grain, straw, seeds, etc.; stables, barns, saddles, harnesses, blacksmiths, etc.

There are also some 15,000 pieces pertaining to wood and timber production and sales, chiefly at Stowe and Wotton, and approximately 34,000 pieces concerned primarily with repair work, including accounts of work done by firms or individual tradesmen (plasterers, bricklayers, masons, carpenters, etc.) and for their supplies (wood, marble, brick, lead, etc.).

Also included are receipts and accounts for rents, tithes, and local taxes and levies.

B. *Other Counties (ca.52,000 pieces):* accounts and other papers similar to those for Buckinghamshire, for Grenville holdings in Cornwall (1,400 pieces, 1775–1890), Derbyshire (340 pieces, 1813–65, chiefly for mines and mineral properties), Dorsetshire (1,600 pieces, 1749–98 and 1877–85), Essex (2,700 pieces, 1777–1825, chiefly for Gosfield Hall), Hampshire (25,000 pieces, 1795–1860, chiefly for Avington), London and Middlesex (7,900 pieces, 1741–1890, including Pall Mall House, Chandos House in Cavendish Square, and Little Stanmore), Northamptonshire (150 pieces, 1774–1844, chiefly Astwell), Somerset (10,100 pieces, 1762–1861, chiefly for Keynsham, Rodney Stoke, and Dodington), Warwickshire (2,400 pieces, 1743–1828, chiefly for Burton Dassett and Moreton Morell), and Ireland (700 pieces, 1840–67).

Among the more important separate volumes of accounts are:

> Wood account books [for various estates, chiefly in Buckinghamshire, both single and collective]. 42 vols. 1735–1824
>
> Stowe and Wotton home bargain books. 2 vols. 1741–61
>
> Wotton rent accounts. 3 vols. 1741–1840
>
> Burton Dassett account book kept by Leonard Lloyd. 1 vol. 1742–55
>
> Pollicott rent accounts, 1 vol. 1743–50
>
> Pollicott estate account book. 1 vol. 1744–72
>
> Brill rent accounts. 1 vol. 1746–50

Stowe granary books. 3 vols. 1748–96
Stowe rent and tax accounts. 3 vols. 1750–71
Burton Dassett rent accounts. 1 vol. 1755–71
Buckinghamshire estates day books. 16 vols. [not consecutive]. 1762–1838
Miscellaneous estates accounts. 32 vols. [not consecutive]. 1768–1859
Stowe and Wotton kiln account. 1 vol. 1769–97
Stowe garden accounts. 1 vol. 1770–75
Stowe and Wotton repairs accounts. 1 vol. 1771–92
Incidental accounts. 3 vols. 1776–1809
Moreton Morrell day book. 1 vol. 1781–93
Laborers' account books. 18 vols [not consecutive]. 1783–1873
Garden labor accounts. 1 vol. 1827–39
Stowe House repairs accounts kept by John Boorer. 3 vols. 1841–45
Buckinghamshire estates repairs accounts kept by Thomas Beards. 3 vols. 1842–70
Wotton garden book. 2 vols. 1865–73
Stowe garden books. 5 vols. 1881–85

See also Grenville West Indies Estates papers, p. 202, for additional accounts.

2. *Household Accounts (ca.35,000 pieces)*

Chiefly for Stowe (ca.19,000 pieces) and Wotton Underwood (ca.13,000 pieces), with additional miscellaneous material for London and other establishments. Included are receipts, bills, house stewards' and housekeepers' accounts, and other records for servants' wages and livery, food, drink, coal, candles, entertainment, linens, plate, domestic labor (laundry, cleaning, mending, sewing, etc.), tradesmen (chimney sweeps, glazing, etc.), kennels, stables, horses, harnesses and coachmaking, and miscellaneous housekeeping expenses.

Among the more important separate volumes of accounts are:

London furniture repair book. 1 vol. 1733–62
Meat account. 1 vol. 1751–56

Household account books [chiefly for Stowe, also some entries for Wotton, Avington, London]. 8 vols. [not consecutive]. 1769–1844

Household account book exclusively for Avington, Hampshire. 1 vol. 1817–34

Account of servants' wages. 2 vols. 1808–47

See also Grenville Personal Papers, p. 190, for related volumes.

3. *Personal Accounts (ca.18,000 pieces)*

Approximately half (ca.8,400 pieces) of the papers in this section pertain to the general personal expenses of the Grenville family for goods (clothing, jewelry, wigs, perfume, swords and firearms, pipes and tobacco, newspapers, books, stamps, art objects, etc.), services (tailors, embroiderers, medical and veterinary services, travel and transportation, etc.), gifts, charities (including Stowe school and Stowe and Wotton Clothing Clubs), payments or receipts of annuities, legacies, jointures, official fees, and ceremonial expenses. There are a few later accounts for the Morgan family.

The remainder (ca.9,600 pieces) of the material concerns the legal and financial expenses of the family, including bonds and acquittances, banking papers (ca.6,800 pieces, with Coutts & Co., Morland & Co., and other firms), insurance accounts (with receipts, policies, premiums, etc.), and expenses for lawsuits, legal advice, and other legal services (chiefly from Robson, Lightfoot, & Robson, Currie & Williams, and Manning & Dalston).

Among the more important separate volumes of accounts are:

Grenville-Temple, Richard, 2nd Earl Temple. Accounts. 1 vol. 1732–79

Legal accounts with the firm of Robson, Lightfoot, & Robson [later known as Lightfoot & Co.] 10 vols. 1787–58

Accounts of receipts and payments. 3 vols. 1847–48

Account of payments for interest and annuities. 1 vol. 1847–53

Insurance book with Norwich Union Fire Insurance
Society. 1 vol. 1858

II. GRENVILLE CORRESPONDENCE
ca.30,000 pieces, 1572–1919

The largest single collection of letters in the Library, this category
consists of the personal, political, estate, and business correspondence of the entire Grenville family; it is strongest from the time
of Richard Grenville–Temple, 2nd Earl Temple, to that of Richard
Grenville, 3rd Duke of Buckingham and Chandos, or roughly
for the period 1740–1880.

No brief summary can give any adequate idea of the range
of topics and people involved, and the following items are noted
only because of the relative wealth of letters concerning each.

Among the personal correspondence, the longest runs of letters
are those addressed to: George Grenville, 1st Marquis of Buckingham; Richard Grenville, 1st Duke of Buckingham and Chandos,
and to his wife, the Duchess Anna Eliza; Duchess Mary (the wife
of the 2nd Duke, who wrote 722 letters to her); the 3rd Duke;
and Richard Morgan-Grenville, Master of Kinloss; there are numerous letters concerning the Campbell family (particularly the
1st and 2nd marquises of Breadalbane) and the Morgan-Grenvilles.

Political correspondence (and some official papers) are particularly strong for: Richard Grenville–Temple, 2nd Earl Temple;
the Hon. George Grenville (especially concerning the American
colonies, the West Indies, and diplomatic affairs); Henry Grenville,
Governor of Barbados (especially concerning Anglo-French relations in the West Indies, 1747–52); the 1st Marquis of Buckingham
(especially concerning Irish affairs and the Buckinghamshire Militia); Thomas Grenville (especially concerning Admiralty matters
and diplomacy, particularly the diplomatic missions of 1794 and
1799); the 3rd Duke of Buckingham and Chandos (particularly
concerning Madras, India, the Colonial Office, the Privy Council
Office, and the Buckinghamshire Militia); and George Manners
Morgan (again, concerning the Buckinghamshire Militia). There
are lesser but still important collections of letters for: William
Wyndham Grenville, Baron Grenville; Sir William Henry Fremantle; and Charles Watkins Williams Wyn.

Estate and business letters include extraordinarily long runs of letters to the various family estate agents and officials and to their lawyers and financial agents, including to stewards Thomas Beards, Thomas Crawfurd, and George Parrott, and to the firms of Currie & Williams and of Robson, Lightfoot & Robson; much of this correspondence deals with the bankruptcy of the 2nd Duke. There are also extensive runs of letters to each of the 1st, 2nd, and 3rd Dukes of Buckingham and Chandos; those to the 3rd Duke deal in part with railway development, specifically with the London and Northwestern Railway, the Aylesbury and Buckinghamshire Railway, and the Wotton Tramway.

In addition to the individual letters in this category, there are 49 separately bound volumes of private and official letterbooks, as listed below:

Beards, Thomas:
> Letterbook (from the steward to 2nd and 3rd Dukes of Buckingham and Chandos and others). 8 vols. 1844–69

Grenville, George (the Prime Minister):
> Secret and Confidential letterbooks of diplomatic correspondence (chiefly with Denmark, the Hague, Hamburg, and Prussia). 8 vols. 1761–62
> Letterbooks (chiefly to political associates and placeseekers). 2 vols. 1763–70

Grenville, George, 1st Marquis of Buckingham:
> Letterbook as LordLieutenant of Ireland. 4 vols. 1782–83

Grenville, Mary (Campbell), Duchess of Chandos:
> Letterbook (copies of letters, with comments, to and from her husband, the 2nd Duke, whom she divorced). 1 vol. 1847–49
> Letterbook (copies of letters to and from her brother, Lord Breadalbane, re her husband, the 2nd Duke). 1 vol. 1848
> Letterbook. 1 vol. 1848–50

Grenville, Richard, 1st Duke of Buckingham and Chandos:
> Letterbook. 1 vol. 1806–09
> Letterbook, mostly political. 1 vol. 1808–09
> Letterbook, mostly political. 1 vol. 1818–23
> Letterbook. 1 vol. 1823–27
> Letter-press copy letterbook. 1829–32

Letterbook (of in-letters, chiefly from George Parrott and
co-trustees of the Grenville estates). 1 vol. 1836–38
Grenville, Richard, 3rd Duke of Buckingham and Chandos:
Letterbook. 1 vol. 1855–57
Letterbook as Colonial Secretary. 2 vols. 1867–68
Letterbook as Colonial Secretary. 4 vols. 1868
Letterbook as Governor of Madras. 3 vols. 1878–80
Grenville, Thomas:
Official letterbook. 2 vols. 1798–99
Miscellaneous letterbook. 2 vols. 1799
Letterbook. 1 vol. 1806 (July–September)
Index to private letters as President of Board of Control.
1 vol. 1806
Letterbook. 3 vols. 1806–07

The following persons or institutions are represented by ten or
more separate letters (not including the letterbooks):
Abbott, John A. (13)
Acott, William (20)
Addison, John C. (26)
Agriculturalist Cattle Insurance Co. (20)
Alderson, Edward S. (14)
Andrews, William (17)
Arbor (James) & Son (17)
Arundell, Mary Anne (Grenville), Baroness Arundell (15)
Astle, Thomas (30)
Atcheson, Henry (68)
Bacon, James (15)
Baker, Arthur Octavius (192)
Baker, Thomas (d) (12)
Baker & Sons (13)
Baldwin, Thomas (14)
Ball, Ambrose Edward (26)
Barker, George (28)
Barker & Bowker (34)
Barker, Bowker & Peake (224)
Baron, Charlotte Anne (14)
Baron, John S. (10)
Barrett, Richard (34)
Barrington, Percy, 8th Viscount Barrington (17)

Bartlett, Eliza H. (24)
Baugham, William (20)
Baynes, Edward Robert (115)
Bearcroft, Henry (12)
Beards, John Thomas (254)
Beards, Thomas (552)
Beer, William Jones (16)
Bennett, G. C. (11)
Bennett, George (22)
Berkeley, Sir George Cranfield (13)
Bernard-Morland, Sir Scrope, 4th Bart. (100)
Bircham & Co. (16)
Birt, J. (21)
Blencowe, B. R. (14)
Boehm, Sir Joseph Edgar, 1st Bart. (10)
Bonham, James (10)
Boodle & Partington (26)
Boucher, James (31)
Boughton, Thomas Rutland (26)
Box, Philip (14)
Boys & Tweedie (10)
Brise, Joseph (15)
Britton, Thomas (27)
Bromley, Thomas (22)
Brooks & Beal (10)
Brounton, Robert (10)
Browne, Robert (22)
Bruce, Thomas, 7th Earl of Elgin and 11th Earl of Kincardine
    (11)
Bryon, William (12)
Buckingham Cattle Assurance Association (11)
Budd, Thomas William (55)
Bulfett, W. W. (14)
Bulkeley, Thomas James Warren, 7th Viscount Bulkeley of
    Cashel (13)
Bull, H. (13)
Bull, Humphrey (659)
Bunce, William (22)
Burge, William (41)
Burke, Sir Henry Franham (11)

Burton, John (98)
Calvert, Reginald? (53)
Campbell, Eliza (Baillie), Marchioness of Breadalbane (25)
Campbell, Sir James, Bart., of Inverneil (19)
Campbell, John, 2nd Marquis of Breadalbane (15)
Campbell, Mary Turner (Gavin), Marchioness of Breadalbane (30)
Cardwell, Edward, Viscount Cardwell (64)
Carmichael, David Fremantle (21)
Carne, Charles (14)
Carpimall Co. (12)
Cecil, Robert Arthur Talbot Gascoyne, 3rd Marquis of Salisbury (10)
Chabot, Louis William de Rohan Chabot, Vicomte de Rohan (26)
Chamberlain, Sir Neville Bowles (15)
Chaplin, Acton (54)
Chapman, T. S. (21)
Chester, Charles Montagu (57)
Chesterman, H. (13)
Chilcott, Charles (35)
Clark, W. C. (24)
Clarke, R. (45)
Clarke & Medcalf (12)
Coates, John (15)
Cochrane, Sir Alexander Forrester Inglis (12)
Codd, Thomas Hudson (12)
Codrington, Richard (17)
Coker, J. (15)
Coles, George (12)
Collingwood, Cuthbert, Baron Collingwood (24)
Congreve, Sir William, 2nd Bart. (14)
Corry, Isaac (11)
Cory, Henry (28)
Cotterill & Sons (11)
Coutts & Co. (288)
Cowley, J. W. (20)
Coxe & Chambers (24)
Craufurd, Sir James Gregan, 2nd Bart. (20)
Crawfurd, Thomas (506)

Crawter, Henry [fl. 1843–54, land agent for Mercers Co.] (79)
Crawter, Henry [fl. 1855–73, nephew and successor of the above] (67)
Crawter, John (10)
Cripps, Francis (10)
Cripps, Fredrick (11)
Cripps, John (20)
Crook, Charles (21)
Crook, E. (23)
Cross, William (62)
Currie & Williams (1,136)
Dacres, James Richard (10)
Dalziel, George (51)
Daniel, John (11)
Dardis, William (53)
Darling, James Stermonth (11)
Davids, C. H. (17)
Davidson & Syme (19)
Davis, Hewitt (27)
Dawes & Sons (21)
Dayrell, Edmund (11)
Deane, George (10)
De la Palue, [   ] (15)
Deverell, Thomas (15)
Disraeli, Benjamin, 1st Earl of Beaconsfield (14)
Dodwell, Joseph (30)
Doggett, William (40)
Doig, R. (10)
Duckworth, Sir John Thomas, 1st Bart. (10)
Dudley, John (38)
Dudley, Samuel B. (16)
Duncan, Jonathan (12)
Dunnett, D. (50)
Durley, John (11)
Eales, John (11)
East, Sir Edward Hyde, 1st Bart. (105)
East, Sir James Buller, 2nd Bart. (33)
Eden, Morton, 1st Baron Henley (25)
Eden, William, 1st Baron Auckland (10)
Edwards, R. F. (10)

Egerton, Hubert D. (11)
Eggar, Thomas (28)
Elliott, Joseph (11)
Ellis, H. Leslie (15)
Ellis, J. H. (22)
Elphinstone, George Keith, Viscount Keith (29)
Eyre, William Thomas (11)
Fagel, Jacob, Baron (20)
Farquhar, Robert Townsend (20)
Farrers & Co. (16)
Fellowes, John (353)
Ferguson, D. (11)
Fessey, John (11)
Field, Edward (28)
Field, Francis (11)
Field, William (19)
Field & Bignold (62)
Figg, Joseph (11)
Finlay, Alexander (23)
Fishbourne, Joseph (102)
Fishbourne, William (108)
Fitch, Joseph (28)
Fitch, Matthew (12)
Fitzgerald, Richard Purefoy (25)
Fooks, Chadwick, Arnold & Chadwick (12)
Forman, John N. (13)
Fortescue, Hugh, 2nd Earl Fortescue (10)
Fowler, John Kersley (46)
Fowler & Co. (25)
Fowler, Harris & Taylor (13)
Fox, George Frederick (13)
Frankton, John (83)
Fraser, Alex (16)
Fraser, Charles (10)
Freeman, Edward (12)
Freeman, Thomas (15)
Freer, Blunt & Co. (12)
Fremantle, John (61)
Fremantle, Louisa Elizabeth (Nugent), Baroness Cottesloe (11)
Fremantle, Sir Thomas Francis (34)

Fremantle, Thomas Francis, 1st Baron Cottesloe (47)
Fremantle, Sir William Henry (269)
French, M. H. (25)
French, Samuel (35)
French, William Henry (10)
Freshfield & Sons (20)
Frogatt, William (20)
Fuller, John (40)
Gardner, Phoebe Sophia (14)
Gardner, T. W. (39)
Garlike, Benjamin (71)
Garrett, Richard (11)
Gathorne-Hardy, Gathorne, 1st Earl of Cranbrook (12)
Gay, George (14)
George III (31)
George, Sir Rupert, Bart. (15)
George, Thomas (17)
Gibbons, William Edward (15)
Gibson-Craig, Dalziel & Brodie (75)
Gill, Thomas W. (30)
Girdwood, James (122)
Girdwood, John (41)
Glass, Elliot & Co. (16)
Goodall, John (64)
Goodall, Samuel (66)
Goold, William (17)
Gordon, Joseph (12)
Gore-Langton, Lady Anne Elizabeth Mary (Grenville) (59)
Gore-Langton, William Henry Powell (20)
Goss, Thomas G. (44)
Graham & Son (13)
Gray, C. E. (37)
Great Britain.
    Admiralty (129)
    Board of Control (23)
    Inland Revenue Department (29)
    Navy (26)
    Navy Office (54)
    Parliament. House of Lords (28)
    Privy Council (16)

Privy Seal Office (151)
Queen Anne's Bounty Office (19)
Revenue (10)
Tithe Commission (59)
Treasury (10)
War Office (87)
Great Western Railway (17)
Green, Francis (28)
Green, William (21)
Grenville, Anna Elizabeth (Brydges), Duchess of Buckingham
& Chandos (274)
Grenville, Sir Bevil (21)
Grenville, Caroline (Harvey), Duchess of Buckingham &
Chandos (196)
Grenville, Lady Caroline Jemima Elizabeth (40)
Grenville, George (56)
Grenville, George Nugent, 2nd Baron Nugent (32)
Grenville, George . . . 1st Marquis of Buckingham (300)
Grenville, Henry (106)
Grenville, Mary (Campbell) . . . Duchess of Buckingham &
Chandos (287)
Grenville, Mary Elizabeth (Nugent) . . . Marchioness of Buck-
ingham (14)
Grenville, Richard . . . 1st Duke of Buckingham & Chandos
(563)
Grenville, Richard Plantagenet . . . 2nd Duke of Buckingham
& Chandos (1,390)
Grenville, Richard Plantagenet Campbell . . . 3rd Duke of
Buckingham & Chandos (1,763)
Grenville, Thomas (573)
Grenville, William Wyndham, Baron Grenville (560)
Grenville-Temple, Richard, 2nd Earl Temple (137)
Greville, Arthur E. (10)
Greville-Nugent, Rosa Emily Mary Anne (Nugent), Baroness
Greville (10)
Grey, Charles, 2nd Earl Grey (37)
Griffin, Edward (31)
Griffin, James (22)
Griffin, John [agent for Grenville family] (129)
Griffin, John [of Brillsbury Hall, ?Bucks.] (30)

Griffin, Richard, 2nd Baron Braybrooke (14)
Grimsteed, James (14)
Groom, James (17)
Grose, Matthew (49)
Gurden, William (19)
Gurney, Henry (47)
Gutteridge, Daniel (11)
Gutteridge, Joseph (16)
Hadaway, Lady Anne . . . (Grenville) (12)
Haiden, Robert (14)
Halifax Groving Deck Co. (11)
Hall, Frederick (13)
Hall, Laurence (40)
Hall, Robert [of Avington, Hants.] (16)
Hall, Robert [of Easton Lodge, ?Hants.] (10)
Hallowes, R. (33)
Hamilton, Mary Gavin (Pringle) Baillie (13)
Hankin, Philip James (10)
Hanson, John (29)
Harding, G. R. (11)
Hardum, James (38)
Harper, Edward [of Ashendon, Bucks.] (16)
Harper, Edward [of Wotton, Bucks.] (11)
Harper, J. T. (20)
Harriot, George (10)
Harris, James (13)
Harris, James, 1st Earl of Malmesbury (16)
Harrison, J. (55)
Harrison, James (15)
Harrison & Son (32)
Harvey, Anne (Hotham) (33)
Harvey, Lady Magdalen Breadalbane (Pringle) Anderson (20)
Harvey, Robert (19)
Harvey, Sir Robert Bateson, 1st Bart. (39)
Harvey, Sir Robert Grenville, 2nd Bart. (66)
Hatch, Thomas (13)
Havers, Richard (17)
Hayward, William (19)
Hazel, E. W. (15)
Hearn, Henry (12)

Hearn & Nelson (88)
Hedges, Joseph (13)
Hibbert, Frederick Drummond (10)
Higham, John (11)
Hindes, Richard (27)
Hinsby, Maria (11)
Heare, Charles & Co. (180)
Hobart, George Bertie Benjamin (31)
Hobart, Robert, 4th Earl of Buckinghamshire (15)
Hobley, Richard (11)
Hodgkins, William (11)
Hollier, John (12)
Home, Thomas (93)
Hood, William (42)
Horwood, Edward (22)
Horwood, Thomas (30)
Hotham, John William (248)
Houshton, James (16)
Howard, Henry [fl. 1683, of London] (27)
Howard, Henry [fl. 1821–26, employed on Avington estate] (26)
Howard, Henry [fl. 1841–48, of St. Cross, Winchester; surveyor and auctioneer] (162)
Howard, Henry [fl. 1848–55, son of surveyor] (27)
Howard, Joseph (20)
Howes, Percival & Ellen (11)
Hubbard, J. G. (31)
Hudleston, William (13)
Hull, Christopher (31)
Humfrey, F. (13)
Humphreys, Ambrose (51)
Hutt, Robert (16)
Inglis & Leslie (14)
Inns, P. (86)
Insurance Companies. Various (190)
Jago, George William Stephen (143)
Jago, Robert (18)
Jago, Thomas Dalby (165)
James, John (29)
James, Thomas (28)

Jenkin, Alfred (48)
Jenkin, Pearse (52)
Jenkin, William (11)
Jervis, John, Earl of St. Vincent (31)
Johnson, Thomas (14)
Johnson Brothers (11)
Johnston, Farquhar & Leech (19)
Jones, John (24)
Jones, Ralph A. (491)
Jones, W. (60)
Joyce, Medbury (25)
Karslake, Crealock & Karslake (11)
Kay, James (126)
King, D. P. (44)
King, James (13)
Lacey, William (10)
Lambert, Nathaniel G. (26)
Lancaster, E. (18)
Landor, Henry Eyres (11)
Lands Improvement Company (147)
Langton (Thomas) & Sons (24)
Lardner, Edmund (11)
Law, Tindal & Hussey (18)
Lawford (E. J. H.) & (J.) (75)
Lawford & Houghton (74)
Lawrence, Charles William (24)
Ledbrooke, Tobias (201)
Leeman & Clark (11)
Leer, William (43)
Leigh, Lady Caroline (Brydges) (11)
Leigh, Julia Judith (Twisleton) (14)
Levy (Charles) & Co. (36)
Ley, Richard (17)
Lipscomb, Lawrence (27)
Littlewood, Thomas Y. (33)
Loder, Sir Edmund Giles, 2nd Bart. (22)
Loftus, Anna Maria (Dashwood), Marchioness of Ely (21)
Loftus, Lady Anna Maria Ellen (15)
London & County Bank (17)
London & County Joint Stock Bank (27)

London & Northwestern Railway (85)
London. International Health Exhibition. 1884 (13)
Loveridge, William (11)
MacDonald, [   ] (11)
McFarland, Lady Maria Gertrude (Van Kemple) (13)
Madras (India). Native inhabitants (22)
Madras (India). Native rulers (60)
Madras (India). Public Works Department (12)
Malins, J. B. (41)
Manning & Dalston (64)
Mansfield, Daniel (10)
Marshall, George? (40)
Martyn, Catherine Horner Strangeways (Pearson) (25)
Martyn, Mary Anne Fonnereau (10)
Mason, Charles [fl. 1820–25, of London] (27)
Mason, Charles [fl. 1848–51, timber merchant?] (23)
Meehan, Thomas (10)
Mcggy & Chalk (12)
Mercers Company (18)
Meynell & Copleston (11)
Michael, James (10)
Miller, John (10)
Mold, John (13)
Morgan, Chandos Stuart Temple Henry (12)
Morgan, George Manners (97)
Morgan, Thomas Chandos Chardin (41)
Morgan-Grenville, Luis Ferdinand Harry Courthope (13)
Morgan-Grenville, Mary . . . *suo jure* Baroness Kinloss (30)
Morgan-Grenville, Richard George Grenville, Master of Kin-
    loss (43)
Morgan-Grenville-Gavin, Thomas George Breadalbane (32)
Morlands, Auriol & Co. (57)
Morrice, George (57)
Morrice, J. (19)
Morrison, J. (10)
Morton (Francis) & Co. (87)
Morton (Henry J.) & Co. (54)
Moss (S.) & Co. (47)
Mould, Frederick? (44)
Mould, William (130)

Mountague, F. W. (46)
Mousley & Barber (90)
Mumford, J. Aubrey (30)
Mumford & Son (44)
Munday, John (25)
Murray, Eustace Clare Grenville (44)
Murray, Thomas (12)
Napier, James (32)
Nash, W. J. (16)
Nelson, George (33)
Nevill, H. (10)
Norris & Sons (10)
North, William H. (18)
Norwich Union Fire Insurance Societies (39)
Nugent, Sir George, 1st Bart. (40)
Nugent, George Thomas John, Marquis of Westmeath (21)
Nugent, Lady Maria (Skinner) (79)
Osborn, James (14)
Osborne, Ward & Co. (17)
Oxford University.
    All Souls College (25)
    Christ Church College (42)
    Lincoln College (58)
    New College (11)
    Queen's College (21)
    Various Colleges (100)
Oxlade, Jonathan (10)
Oxley, John (14)
Oxley & Son (134)
Page, Thomas (173)
Pakington, John Somerset, 1st Baron Hampton (10)
Palmer, W. J. (73)
Palmer, William (15)
Panin, Nikita Petrovich, Count Panin (26)
Parfitt, Edmund (54)
Parker, J. H. (27)
Parker, Samuel (111)
Parker, William (19)
Parker, Hayes, Barnwell & Twisden (23)
Parkinson, John (13)

Parslow, Thomas (13)
Partridge, W. G. (28)
Parrott, Edmund (20)
Parrott, George (595)
Parrott, Joseph [fl. 1765–1809; steward of Stowe] (289)
Parrott, Joseph [fl. 1849–62, of Aylesbury, Bucks.] (24)
Parsons, John (10)
Paul, John (26)
Paxton, Jonas (48)
Paxton, Robert (24)
Payne, John (48)
Peel, Sir Robert, 2nd Bart. (22)
Pellew, Sir Edward, 1st Viscount Exmouth (14)
Penton, Thomas (29)
Perry, Jane (19)
Phillimore, Joseph (17)
Phillips, Henry (82)
Pickering, J. (10)
Pigott, George Grenville Wandesford (80)
Pilgrim, C. (16)
Poole, John (73)
Popham, Sir Home Riggs (19)
Powys, Thomas Littleton, 4th Baron Lilford (13)
Praed, Helen (Bogle) Mackworth (24)
Pratt, John Jeffreys, 1st Marquis Camden (12)
Pratt, Walter Caulfeild (51)
Price, John (15)
Pringle, Lady Elizabeth Maitland (Campbell) (67)
Probets, William (13)
Proby, John Joshua, 1st Earl of Carysfort (18)
Puckle, Henry (33)
Puget, Peter (10)
Rae, R. R. (11)
Read, Thomas (33)
Reeves, Edmund (36)
Revile & Thorne (24)
Rickett, Thomas (55)
Ridgeway, William (20)
Ringrose, George H. (17)
Robarts, A. G. (19)

Robertson, Duncan (16)
Robinson, George (16)
Robinson, Sir William Rose (14)
Robson, Edward (421)
Robson, John (299)
Robson, Lightfoot & Robson (200)
Rogers, (12)
Rogers, Martha (11)
Rogier, Charles (14)
Rolfe, Benjamin (13)
Ross, Lady Anne (10)
Ross, Sir James Clark (48)
Ross, William (18)
Roundell, H. (17)
Rowe, J. Grindley (265)
Rowell, James (21)
Roy, John (14)
Royal Agricultural Society of England (50)
Rummens, Francis (37)
Ryde, H. T. (13)
Sabin, John Edward (125)
Sainsbury, William (16)
St. Paul's (London). Dean and Chapter (24)
Salmon, George (20)
Sandars, Charles (14)
Sandars, Francis (15)
Sanders, Henry (10)
Saunders, James (12)
Savage, T. W. (44)
Sawbridge, J. S. (10)
Sayer, Henry (12)
Scammel, William (86)
Sellick, Thomas (13)
Shailer, T. H. (131)
Shefford, John D. (25)
Shepperd, Samuel (11)
Simmons, J. Lintern (14)
Simmons, John (54)
Small, Edward H. (10)
Small, Henry (187)

Smith, Henry (356)
Smith, Thomas (10)
Smith, Thomas H. (90)
Smith, William James (254)
Smith & Roberts (17)
Smith & Small (49)
Smith & Son (16)
Smithfield Club (15)
Snee, Edmund (11)
Southam, John (10)
Southee, Robert (11)
Spence, John (16)
Spencer, George John, 2nd Earl Spencer (43)
Stamford, Heinrich Wilhelm von (33)
Standbridge & Kaye (16)
Stanhope, James Hamilton (19)
Stansby, James W. (79)
Staples, Abel (11)
Stewart, Robert (76)
Stone, Edward (22)
Stuart & Maxwell (11)
Sweet & Sutton (38)
Symes, Thomas (27)
Talbot, James, 3rd Baron Talbot of Malahide (11)
Tatham, Thomas James (12)
Taylor, William (119)
Terry, E. (24)
Terry, John (30)
Terry (E.) & Son (31)
Thornbrough, Sir Edward (10)
Thorpe, Henry (43)
Thurlow, William (19)
Tibbetts, William Holliday (31)
Tindal, Acton (29)
Tindal, Thomas (70)
Tindal & Baynes (164)
Tods, Murray & Jamieson (10)
Toogood, William (33)
Truss, Thomas (12)
Tucker, Benjamin (10)

Tuxford & Sons (15)
Tyley, Charles (17)
Urren, Edward S. (17)
Uthwatt, E. A. (12)
Vane, Charles William, 3rd Marquis of Londonderry (61)
Varcoe, Henry (23)
Verney, Sir Harry, 2nd Bart. (28)
Vernon, G. C. (12)
Viccars, Richard (14)
Waldegrave, William, 1st Baron Radstock (10)
Walford, W. (20)
Ward, Robert Plumer (27)
Warner, W. P. (15)
Warren, Sir John Borlase, Bart. (11)
Watkins, Hooper, Baylis & Baker (28)
Webb, D. H. (10)
Webb, Robert (13)
Weedon, John (12)
Wellesley, Arthur, 1st Duke of Wellington (68)
Wellesley, Richard, Marquis Wellesley of Norragh (35)
Wells, Thomas (42)
Wethered, Owen Peel (30)
Wethered (Thomas) & Sons (38)
Whatley, Thomas (14)
White, Archibald (40)
Whitney, James (20)
Whitton, William (39)
Whitworth, Charles, Earl Whitworth (49)
William I, King of the Netherlands (26)
Williams, Henry (26)
Williams, Thomas J. (14)
Willmere, John C. (29)
Wilson, John (40)
Windham, William (32)
Wing, Abraham (18)
Witherell, S. D. (10)
Wood, Charles Harris (21)
Wood, Edward H. (16)

Woodham, John (12)
Woodward, William (18)
Wotton Tramway (86)
Wynn, Charles Watkin Williams (258)
Wynn, Sir Henry Watkin Williams (12)

III. GRENVILLE DEEDS (PARTIAL LISTING)
ca.750 pieces, 12th century–ca.1640
The main body of Grenville deeds are listed below, pp. 255–262, among the Stowe Unsorted Deeds. The present category contains a group of medieval and 16th-century deeds (with a few related manorial and personal papers) known collectively as the "Grenville Evidences," together with three 16th and 17th century cartularies. Of these three volumes the first, written by Richard Knight in 1599, contains a "Copie of certeyne olde charters" concerning Stowe and Dadford. The second volume, of 1611, contains "An Abstracte of many evidences of Richard Grenviles, the deedes themselves beinge in his custodie," and includes a cartulary of Wotton Underwood deeds bound with extracts from Dudgale concerning the Grenvilles. The third volume, written about 1640, is a copy of the Wotton cartulary made for and annotated by Richard Grenville.
　　There are deeds for the following places:
　　Buckinghamshire:
　　　　Cottisford (6) 1208–50
　　　　Dadford (69) 1198<–1488 and undated
　　　　Long Crendon (107) 1189<–1563 and undated
　　　　Woodham (7) 1273–1475 and undated
　　　　Wotton Underwood (541) ca.1250–1508 and undated
　　Other Counties:
　　　　Kent, Northamptonshire, Oxfordshire,
　　　　Staffordshire, Sussex, and Warwickshire: 16
　　　　deeds in all, *temp.* Henry II-1438

IV. GRENVILLE IVENTORIES, LISTS AND CATALOGS
ca.500 pieces, 1586 and 1701–1921
The inventories and catalogs in this category deal primarily with the personal effects and possessions of the Grenville family during the 19th century, and include lists of books, works of art (paintings,

engravings and prints, statuary, and objets d'art), household goods (plate, china, furniture, linens), personal possessions (jewelry, some clothing, horses), and general inventories. Many of the fullest inventories were made in connection with the enforced sale of the contents of Stowe House in 1848–49 following the bankruptcy of the 2nd Duke. There are a few inventories of the possessions of other people or estates connected to the Grenvilles.

Some of the catalogs are printed, and many of the individual lists and inventories are quite fragmentary. Some of the more interesting pieces are listed below by subject.

Book and Library catalogs:

1761<   Catalog of a library [at Stowe?], 3 vols.

1783   Alphabetical catalog of the Library in the Dressing Room at Stowe [by George Grenville, 1st Marquis of Buckingham?]

1845   Rules for, and catalog of, the Parish Lending Library at Stowe, by the Society for Promotion of Christian Knowledge

>1848   Catalog of the library at Stowe (incomplete, letter "A" only, but 71 pp.) by William Smith James

1863   Excerpt from inventory of books of the late John Campbell, 2nd Marquis of Breadalbane, at Taymouth Castle, Scotland, and 21 Park Lane, London

1875   Alphabetical list of the books of Richard Grenville, 3rd Duke of Buckingham and Chandos

Art:

ca.1815   Catalog of prints and engravings at Stowe House [by Richard Grenville, 1st Duke of Buckingham and Chandos?]

1830   Alphabetical print catalog of Richard Grenville, 1st Duke of Buckingham and Chandos

1848   Inventory of the pictures at Biddlesden Park, Bucks. [a copy of 1894 made in connection with the will of George Manners Morgan]

1851   List of paintings removed from Avington House

ca.1862   Inventory of the pictures and other works of art of the late John Campbell, 2nd Marquis of Breadalbane, at Taymouth Castle, Scotland, and at 21 Park Lane, London

Household Goods:

1739–64   Inventories and lists of plate, china, etc. at Stowe, Wotton Underwood, and London, ca.26 pieces

1839   Inventory of household furniture at Stowe House

1848   Catalogs of the sales by auction of the china, wine, silverplate, and furniture of the 2nd Duke of Buckingham and Chandos

General Inventories:

1586   Inventory of the goods and chattel of Edward "Greenvile"

1813   Inventory and valuation of Gosfield Hall, Essex

1847   General inventories of the effects of the 2nd Duke of Buckingham and Chandos at Avington House, London, and Wotton House

1871   Inventory of the effects of Richard Grenville, 3rd Duke of Buckingham and Chandos

Miscellaneous:

1782   Inventory and valuation of articles at Dublin Castle and Phoenix Park transferred from William Henry Cavendish-Bentinck, 3rd Duke of Portland, to George Grenville, 1st Marquis of Buckingham, at the latter's becoming Lord Lieutenant of Ireland

1827–29   Register of seeds, plants, minerals, marbles, etc. from the European trip of Richard Grenville, 1st Duke of Buckingham, aboard the yacht "Anna Eliza"

1873   Inventory of implements, tools, machinery, etc. at Stowe Home Farm

1903   List of heirlooms (including family portraits, the Temple diamonds, plate, etc.) under the will of the 3rd Duke of Buckingham and Chandos (a typewritten copy)

V. GRENVILLE LEGAL PAPERS
ca.2,200 pieces, 18th–19th centuries

Of the 60 identified lawsuits for which papers survive in this category, the vast majority belong to the 19th century, were heard in Chancery, and concern land. There are a few cases concerning Grenville and other debts, heard in Kings Bench, and a few miscellaneous cases.

The only persons appearing in five or more cases, as either plaintiff or defendant, are the three Dukes of Buckingham and Chandos: the 1st Duke in 22, the 2nd Duke in 11, and the 3rd Duke in 5.

The remainder of the Grenville legal papers (ca.1,600 pieces) are unsorted, but deal in general with other legal affairs of the Grenville and Breadalbane families, and include legal opinions and advice, lists and schedules of documents, abstracts, marriage settlements, etc. Most of this material dates from the 19th century.

VI. GRENVILLE MANORIAL AND LOCAL AFFAIRS PAPERS
ca.32,000 pieces, 1209–1918

Over nine tenths of the papers in this category pertain to Buckinghamshire, and most of those fall within the period 1750–1889, during which the Grenvilles were at Stowe. There are a few early (pre-18th century) papers, chiefly for Wotton Underwood and Ashendon, but earlier records for many of the places listed here may be found in the *Temple Manorial and Local Affairs Papers*.

Listed below by county are: all places represented by 5 or more pieces (excluding individual receipts and accounts for rents, tithes, taxes, and local levies in Buckinghamshire, which number well over 25,000), with covering dates and selected items of interest; all court rolls; all rentals; and selected additional miscellaneous items of interest or importance.

   1. *Places represented by five or more pieces:*
      Buckinghamshire:
         Ashendon: 88 pieces, 1444–1913
            Includes: a list endorsed "Nomina villarum in tribus hundreds de Ashendon," 1599–1609; particular and valuation of estate at Ashendon belonging to

the Rector and Scholars of Lincoln College, Oxford, 1853

Aston Abbots: 15 pieces, 1748–1849

Aston Clinton: ca.250 pieces, 1702-n.d. (19th cent)

Aylesbury: ca.200 pieces, 1695-n.d. (19th cent.)

Biddlesden: 50 pieces, 1835–1912

Includes part of an undated 19th cent. history of Biddlesden

Bierton: 12 pieces, ca.1750–1841 (some with Hulcot)

Brill: 17 pieces, 1801–1913

Buckingham: 96 pieces, 1554–1914

Includes: a copy of Queen Mary's charter of incorporation for the town of Buckingham, 1554; names of the clerks of the peace (Custodii Pacis) for the borough and parish, 1686; letters and petitions re the replacement by James II of Jonathan Seaton with Henry Robinson as mayor, contrary to the charter of the corporation, 1687–88; lists of the peers, bishops, gentlemen, and clergy who signed the parliamentary petition in favor of the county town of Buckingham, 1748; opinions and other legal papers concerning a case involving the Mercers Company and the corporation of Buckingham, 1750; an abstract of the churchwarden's expenses for Buckingham, ca.1770

Chearsley: 16 pieces, n.d. (18th cent.)–1838

Cheddington: 26 pieces, 1787-n.d. (19th cent.)

Dadford: 5 pieces, 1736–1912

Dorton: 10 pieces, 1760-n.d. (19th cent.)

Ewelme: 5 pieces, 1681<–1856

Foscott: 8 pieces, 1712<–ca.1841

Includes a list of the poor of the parish, 1839

Gawcott: 45 pieces, 1752–1913

Includes a valuation of the tithe, 1777–1804

Ham: 27 pieces, 1611<–1848

Long Crendon: 27 pieces, 1620–1914

Ludgershall: 5 pieces, 1777–1863<

Maids Moreton: 50 pieces, 1759–1894

Oakley: 9 pieces, 1819-n.d. (19th cent.)

Pollicott (Great and Little): 44 pieces, 1501–1871
 Includes: particulars and valuation of the estate belonging to the Rector and Scholars of Lincoln College, Oxford, 1853; return of children "capable of attending school" at Pollicott, 1856
Prebend End: 5 pieces, 1801–n.d. (19th cent.)
Radclive-cum-Chackmore: 13 pieces, 1730–1867
Stowe: ca.300 pieces, 1734–1918
 Includes 13 volumes of notebooks of the Clerk of the Works for Stowe and Wotton, containing architects and builders notes, etc. 1866–86
 N.B.: most of the over 25,000 receipts for rents, taxes, tithes, local levies, etc., are for lands in and around Stowe; no attempt has been made to describe them in detail here. *See also* Grenville Accounts and Financial Papers for much more material concerning building, gardening, repair work, tenants, etc. in and around the Stowe estate.
Thornborough: 13 pieces, 1749–1814<?
Tingewick: 15 pieces, 1773-n.d. (18th cent.)
Waddesdon: 11 pieces, 1705–1884
 Includes a description of the "hamlet" of Waddesdon, with Woodham, 1755
Weedon: 18 pieces, 1703–1845
Westbury: 24 pieces, 1209–1799
Westcott: 8 pieces, 1741–1913
Weston Turville: 14 pieces, 1798–1839
Winchendon (Upper and Lower): 17 pieces, 1753–1838
Wotton Underwood: ca.700 pieces, 1273–1908
 Includes: a two-volume copy of the Wotton parish register, 1599–1801; a "Poor Book" for Wotton, 1763–70; a volume of copyletters for prizes awarded to tenants at Wotton, with lists of prizes and tenants, 1856–65; 13 volumes of notebooks of the Clerk of the Works for Stowe and Wotton (see entry under Stowe, above); a valuation list of the parish of Wotton, n.d. (19th cent.); a list of tombs in the Wotton church, by [Richard Morgan–Grenville, Master of Kinloss]?, 1908

Cornwall:
  Mevagissey: 5 pieces, 1826–59
  St. Mawes: ca.340 pieces, 1609–1889
    Includes: lists of freemen with the right to vote,
    1789–1830; Declaration of the Mayor or Portreeve
    for St. Mawes [Nicholas Jennings], 1831
  Tolcarne: 5 pieces, 19th cent.
  Tregavethan: 8 pieces, 1752-n.d. (19th cent.)
  Treleven: 9 pieces, ca.1810–59?

Dorset:
  Dean: 24 pieces, 1765–66
  Tarrant Grenville: 19 pieces, 1763–98?
    Includes an account of Thomas Wyndham's estate
    with lists of tenants, values, etc., 1767
  Tarrant Launceston: 11 pieces, 1763–96
  Tarrant Monkton: 13 pieces, 1768–99?
  Tarrant Rushton: 31 pieces, 1765–77?

Essex:
  Bocking: 19 pieces, 1809–11
  Gosfield: 70 pieces, 1793-n.d. (19th cent.)
    Includes a summary account of parish dues paid,
    1817

Hampshire:
  Andover: 21 pieces, 1776–78
  Avington: 20 pieces, 1771-n.d. (19th cent.)
  Easton: 7 pieces, 1621-n.d. (19th cent.)
  Itchen Abbas: 8 pieces, 1812–47

Middlesex:
  Enfield: 5 pieces, 1813–29?
  Kingsbury: 6 pieces, 1814-n.d. (19th cent.)
  Stanmore (Great and Little): 10 pieces, 1775-n.d. (19th
    cent.)

Northamptonshire:
  Astwell: 31 pieces, ca.1774–1848 (most with Falcutt)
  Syresham: 5 pieces, n.d. (18th cent.)

Oxfordshire:
  Finmere: 21 pieces, 1745–ca.1857
    Includes: a list of inhabitants, divided into two
    groups (the poor and others), 1745–46; a descrip-
    tion of Finmere Warren House, 1764.

Somerset:

Batcombe: 6 pieces, 1774-n.d. (19th cent.)

Cheddar: 33 pieces, 1795–1859

Compton Martin: 5 pieces, 1760–1832

Dodington: 35 pieces, 1764–n.d. (19th cent.)

Keynsham: 83 pieces, ca.1813–61

Includes report on the coal mines under the estate of the Duke of Buckingham, 1847

Lilstock: 10 pieces, 1764–1829

Pawlett: 6 pieces, 1736<-n.d. (19th cent.)

Priddy: 28 pieces, 1811–ca.1859

Rodney Stoke: 57 pieces, n.d. (18th cent.)–ca.1859

Stogursey: 11 pieces, 1764-n.d. (19th cent.)

Westbury: 32 pieces, 1788–ca.1859

Warwickshire:

Burton Dassett: 80 pieces, 1745–1828

Knightcote: 17 pieces, 1745-n.d. (19th cent.)

Moreton Morrell: 62 pieces, 1757–ca.1792

Northend: 13 pieces, 1745–82

Ireland:

Co. Clare: 60 pieces, >1801–48

Co. Leix: 48 pieces, 1817–ca.1849

Co. Longford: 45 pieces, 1804–48

Co. West Meath: 63 pieces, >1801-n.d. (19th cent.)

2. *Court Rolls and other court papers:*

Buckinghamshire:

Ashendon: rolls, some drafts (most with Great and/or Little Pollicott) for: 1651, 1664 (2), 1668 (2), 1669, 1670 (2), 1674 (2), 1691 (2), 1701.

Aston Abbots: rolls for 1748, 1750, 1754, 1756, 1757, 1760, 1763, 1766, 1767, 1772; draft court book, 1843–49

Aston Clinton: draft court rolls, misc. court papers, presentments, etc., ca.130 pieces, 1740–1826

Aylesbury: copies of fines received at courts baron, with Bierton, Broughton, and Stanley. 1815–37, 1839–42. 2 vols.

Dadford: copy of court record, 1736

Hardwick: extracts from court rolls, 1703–93

Maids Moreton: court minutes, presentments, and copyhold admissions, 8 pieces, 1759–1808

Pollicott (Great and/or Little): rolls [some drafts, many with Ashenden] for 1651 (3), 1664 (4), 1668 (2), 1669 (2), 1670, 1674 (2), 1691 (4), 1701 (2), 1702

Radclive-cum-Chackmore: court records, 4 pieces, 1730–68; notes from court rolls, 1768<

Weedon: extracts from court rolls, 1703–93

Westbury: copy of court record, 1736

Wotton Underwood: rolls for 1273, 1312–17, 1366, 1379, 1380, 1381, 1430–31, 1432 (3), 1436, 1443, 1444, 1475 (2), 1487, 1488 (2), 1490, 1498, 1501; court Baron presentments, 1752

Cornwall:

St. Mawes: a two-volume copy of court rolls 1609–1738; court leet papers, including views of frankpledge, presentments, etc., ca.125 pieces, 1739–1830; also "Instructions for holding the Court Leet," 1816

Hampshire:

Easton: draft court book, 1621–89

Middlesex:

Little Stanmore: notes on court proceedings, 1775–98

Staffordshire:

Chartley: roll for 1647

3. *Rentals:*

After 1750 rentals for individual Grenville estates are more than plentiful (well over 1,000 for Buckinghamshire alone), sometimes sketchy and not always clearly identified. No attempt has been made to list them individually here. There are pre-1750 rentals for Ashendon Hundred (1444), Wotton Underwood (1411, three for 1430, 1459, two for 1732–33, 1743–44, 1745–46, and 1749–50), and for the estates of Viscount Cobham in Buckinghamshire and Warwickshire (1733),

There are general rentals for most or all of the full range of Grenville lands (i.e., those of the Marquis or later Dukes of Buckingham) for the following years: 1792, n.d. (late 18th cent.), ca.1812, 1819, 1830–31, 1831, 1837, and 1847–52. There are also rentals for the estates of George Grenville (in Buckinghamshire and Warwickshire, 1795–96), of G. Morgan (at Biddlesden Park, 1835–40), and for the "Stowe Estate," 1889–1900.

4. *Additional Items of Interest:*
   Buckinghamshire:

1714–15?	Oath of allegiance to George I for Buckinghamshire, with list of names subscribed
1717	George I's precepts for Justices of the Peace for Buckinghamshire
ca.1730	An account of the church of Hart-well St. Mary, with records of the Lee, Hampden, and other families
1780	An account of the proceedings at the county meeting held at Aylesbury
1794	Rules and regulations for the Winslow Association, "for the more effectual bringing to justice and punishing all offenders against our persons & property . . ."
1797	A volume titled "Commission of the Peace," with names arranged alphabetically
1798<	A list of "the several Manors within the County of Buckingham with the names of the Lords and their gamekeepers . . ."
1799–1801	A volume of land tax assessments for various parishes, with penciled notes of 1856
1811	Rules and regulations for an Association for Quainton for the better protection of property against thieves and robbers (printed)
1826	Parochial returns to a circular from the 1st Duke of Buckingham and

Chandos asking for details for a county history. Parishes responding include: Alseley, Cholesbury Chalfont St. Peter, Clifton Reynes, Hedgerley, Holton, Leckhampstead, Little Harwood and Shucklow, Long Crendon, Marsworth, Newton Blossomville, Pitchcott, Radclive, and Stoney Stratford

1841   List of jurors for Assizes

1843   A description of the Fountain Inn at Steeple Claydon

1850?   A proposal to collect examples of Buckinghamshire handicrafts and industry for display at the Great Exhibition of 1851

1857–88   Quarter Sessions agenda papers, ca.60 pieces

1860–88   Calendars of prisoners to be tried at Quarter Sessions and Assizes, ca.100 pieces

1865–78   Papers concerning the cattle plague and the Contagious Diseases Act, chiefly from Quarter Sessions

1868   Draft lists of the names of Justices of the Peace, judges, etc., for Buckinghamshire

1869–91   Lists of magistrates for the county

1872   Lists of Deputy-Lieutenants for the county

1872   Licensed House returns

Cornwall:

1764   The constitution of the borough of Lostwithiel

1787   A paper on the general state of the Cornish copper mines

Gloucestershire:

1743   The argument of Mr. Sergeant Foster, Recorder of the city of

Bristol, regarding the legality of pressing

Hampshire:
    1776   A paper re the procedure for choosing a mayor for Winchester

London:
    n.d. 19th cent.   Instructions for getting a patient into "Bethlem" Hospital

Northamptonshire:
    1882   A list of the county magistrates, according to the date of qualification

General:
    ca.1828   A schedule of lands, with values, of the Duke of Buckingham and Chandos, by a settlement of May 3, 1828

    1866–67   Weekly returns of the Cattle Plague Inquiry, with related papers, ca.65 pieces

See also Grenville West Indian Estates papers, p. 202.

VII. GRENVILLE PERSONAL AND FAMILY PAPERS
ca.1,400 pieces, 1419–1918

Well over nine tenths of the material in this category belongs to the 18th and 19th centuries. In addition to numerous wills and marriage settlements, and related legal notes and papers, there are extracts from parish registers for individual births or burials, numerous diaries, journals, and commonplace books, household records for Grenville establishments at Stowe, Wotton Underwood, London, and elsewhere, speeches and other representations for various occasions, papers concerning the agreements between the 2nd and 3rd Dukes of Buckingham and Chandos at the time of the former's bankruptcy, and numerous newspaper clippings concerning various members of the Grenville family.

Listed below in chronological order are all wills, *inquisitions post mortem*, marriage settlements, diaries, journals and commonplace books, household volumes, and additional selected items of interest or importance.

Wills:

1419	Richard Grenville
1455	Christiana (Launceline) Grenevyle
1553	George Greenfield
1553<	Edward Grenville
1577	Sir Gerard Crocker
1618	Richard Grenville
1644	Edward Stone
1654	Walter Sweete
1656	Richard Courtney
1657	Sir James Palmer
1658	Mary Sheppeard
1660	Susanne Grenville
1663	Audrey (Duncombe) Grenville
1665	William Wartter
1666	John Greene
1671	Peter Beck
1676	William Jeffes
1678	Francis Hills
1684	Robert Irish
1693	John Newnham
1696	Edward Becke
1696	Ralph Mountague
1697	John Perkins
1698	John Jeffes
1704	Henry Smith
1707	John Miller
1707	Edward Wilson
1712	Thomas Hiccock
1712	Dorothy James
1714	John Perkins
1716	John James
1717	Joan Wigg
1724	Mary Brown
1724	Thomas Bacon
1725	Thomas Fellowe
1727	Samuel King
1733	Bridget Hiccock
1735	Edward Hudson
1739	Joseph Corbett

1741   Anne (Chambers) Grenville
1742   Nathaniel Bacon
1744   Mary Moore (extract only)
1744   Elizabeth Smith
1746   Paul Fellowe (extract only)
1750   Robert Boughton
1752   Jasper Corbett (extract only)
1754   William Brookes
1754   Joseph Brookes
1755   Thomas Mills
1756   Susannah Tull
1760   William Tuder
1760   William Andrewes
1761   Drope Gough
1761   Rice Fellowe
1762   John King
1762   Anne Blundell
1763   Thomas Berry
1763   John Taylor
1766   William Villiers, 3rd Earl of Jersey
1767   Richard Green
1767   William Corbett
1767   Thomas Bett
1768   Thomas James Selby
1769   John Saunders
1770   George Grenville (with draft of 1769)
1771   John Ware
1772   William Collins
1772   John Chapman
1777   Richard Grenville-Temple, 2nd Earl Temple
1780   Matthew Fortescue, 2nd Baron Fortescue
1788   Thomas Scott
1791   Henry Cockerill
1791   William Jackson (extract only)
1792   Joseph Markham
1794   Richard Dayrell
1795   Gerard Dutton Fleetwood (extract only)
1796   Ann Lovell
1797   George Cheshire
1798   Robert Byrne

1799   John Dixon
1800   Anna Eliza (Brydges) Grenville, Duchess of Buck-
         ingham and Chandos (with another will of 1828)
1812   William Hale
1812   George Nugent-Temple-Grenville, 1st Marquis of
         Buckingham
1813   Richard Grenville
1813   Richard Shuttleworth
1813   Samuel Hall
1814   William Falke Grenville
1815   Richard Low
1820   George Bradford
1822   John Malsbury Kirby (extract only)
1822   Letitia Sarah Cribbs (abstract only)
1822   Henry Cockerill
1824   James Bernard
1824   James Grenville, 1st Baron Glastonbury
1826   William Butcher
1830   Sir Scrope Bernard-Morland
1832   William Ray
1833   Richard Temple Nugent Brydges Chandos Gren-
         ville, 1st Duke of Buckingham and Chandos
         (with later wills of 1836 and >1839)
1838   Thomas Cannon
1838   Chandos Leigh, 1st Baron Leigh
1838   William Clark
1841   Richard Arkwright (extract only)
1841   William Burbidge
1842   Mary Anne (Grenville) Arundell, Baroness Arun-
         dell of Wardour
1843   Mary Turner (Gavin) Campbell, Marchioness of
         Breadalbane
1845   Thomas Grenville (extract)
1845   George Manners Morgan
1845   Sarah (Harvey) Paine
1846   Alexander Baring, 1st Baron Ashburton
1847   John Campbell, 2nd Marquis of Breadalbane
1847   Richard . . . Grenville, 3rd Duke of Bucking-
         ham and Chandos (with later drafts of 1848 and
         1874)

1853   Sir Robert John Harvey (extract only)

1853   Francis Barchard (with abstract of 1856)

1855   Mary (Campbell) Grenville, Duchess of Buckingham and Chandos

1856   Richard . . . Grenville, 2nd Duke of Buckingham and Chandos

1858   Abraham George Robarts (abstract only)

1862   George King

1863   Robert Harvey

1864   Thomas Martin (epitome only)

1870   John Paine

1873   Henry Charles Morgan

1875   George Brigstocke

1886   Sir Robert Loder, 1st Bart. (abstracts only)

1886   Sir George Manners Morgan (epitome only)

1908   Thomas Chandos Chardin Morgan

Inquisitions Post Mortem:

1609   Sir Thomas Palmer

1624   Thomas Antrobus

Marriage Settlements:

1514   George Flemyng and Katherine Rockford

1559   Richard Grenville and Marie Gifford

1647   Nowell Powell and Winifred Lewes

1648   Philip Palmer and Phoebe Palmer

1659   Thomas Beck and Avis Gurney

1690   John Beck and Anne Griffin

1713   James Fermor and Mary Throckmorton

1725   Richard Uthwatt and Elizabeth Andrewes

1735   Alexander Dallway and Margaret Andrewes

1737   Richard Grenville-Temple, 2nd Earl Temple, and Anne Chambers

1738   Daniel Finch, 7th Earl of Winchelsea, and Mary Palmer

1754   William Pitt and Lady Hester Grenville

1775   George Grenville, 1st Marquis of Buckingham, and Mary Elizabeth Nugent (with drafts and abstracts)

1777   Richard Drope Gough and Ann Lyndon

1782   Hugh Fortescue, 1st Earl Fortescue, and Hester Grenville

1792   William Wyndham Grenville and Anne Pitt

1796   Richard . . . Grenville, 1st Duke of Buckingham and Chandos, and Anna Eliza Brydges (with later copies)

1811   James Everard Arundell and Mary Anne Grenville

1813   George Nugent-Grenville and Anne Poulett

1819   Richard . . . Grenville, 2nd Duke of Buckingham and Chandos and Mary Campbell

1820   James Morin and Harriet Grenville

1882?   Col. George Hadaway and Lady Anne Grenville

1884   George Manners Morgan's epitome of settlements to be signed on marriage of Luis Morgan-Grenville and Mary Grenville

Diaries, Journals, and Commonplace Books:

Brigstocke, Mary Harriette Player
> Diary. 1834

Grenville, Anna Eliza (Brydges), Duchess of Buckingham and Chandos
> Diaries. 9 vols. 1807–34 (not all years)
> Commonplace Book. ca.1811–32
> Commonplace Book. 1812<

Grenville, Caroline (Harvey), Duchess of Buckingham and Chandos
> Diary and notebook. 2 vols. 1857

Grenville, Mary (Campbell), Duchess of Buckingham and Chandos
> Commonplace Book (England and Italy). 1812–31
> Journal of her tour through France to Geneva. 1816 (incomplete)
> Diary and notebook of Italian travels. ca.1818
> Diary. 1825–39
> Brief engagement diaries. 19 vols. 1826–49
> Diary and Commonplace Book. 1844–46
> Scrapbook, ca.1860

Grenville, Richard, 1st Duke of Buckingham and Chandos
> Political journal with copies of speeches and letters. 1811–16
> Journal aboard a vessel in the English Channel at the close of the war. 1814
> Personal and political diary. 1823

Diary (chiefly politics and travel). 1827–28
Notes on Mt. Etna, Sicily. ca.1828
"Monte Nuovo-Puzzuoli" (geographical notes on the
    Bay of Naples). 1828
Notes on mineralogy and geology. ca.1830
Grenville, Richard, 2nd Duke of Buckingham and Chandos
    Diary. 3 vols. 1812
Grenville, Richard, 3rd Duke of Buckingham and Chandos
    Diary. 1847–48
    Memoranda Books. 4 vols. ca.1855
    Appointment diary. 2 vols. 1867–68
    Diary. 1868
    Diary and notebook of journey home from Madras.
        1880–81
Morgan, Elizabeth Lydia Player (Brigstocke)
    Diary. 1884–85
Morgan, George Manners
    Commonplace Book (re birds), 1863
Morgan-Grenville, Mary, Baroness Kinloss Diary. 1874

Also: miscellaneous and unidentified journals and commonplace books; school report books and notebooks for George and Mary Anne Grenville (1799), Lady Anne (Grenville) Hadaway (1861–65), Lady Caroline Jemmia Elizabeth Grenville (1861–65), and Mary Anne (Grenville) Arundell (1800–01); address books; and other miscellaneous volumes.

Household volumes:

1738–77	Wine Book for London and Wotton Underwood, including inventory of plate for 1743–54
1749–54	Wine Book for Stowe
ca.1750?	Household menus book [Stowe?]
1814–21	Cellar Book [Stowe?], 4 vols.
1839–40	Plate Book for Stowe
ca.1845?	Household menus book for Wotton Underwood
1864–67	Cellar Book for Stowe

Additional items of interest or importance:

1562	Articles between William Maitland and Lord William Howard, re a proposed meeting of Queen Elizabeth of England and Queen Mary of Scotland at York
1725	Scheme of articles for the impeachment of Thomas Parker, 1st Earl of Macclesfield
1767	Recommendation for John Stackhouse to be a member of the SPCK
ca.1770	An account of what titles of honor were conferred on the Royal Family since the time of Henry III
1771–77	Grenville, Richard, 2nd Earl Temple. "Account of my nephews and nieces."
1771–84	Extracts from parish registers concerning the Tomkins family
1774–75	Extracts from the parish registers at Wotton Underwood (list of burials)
1779	Post mortem examination of Richard Grenville-Temple, 2nd Earl Temple
ca.1810	Grenville, Richard, 1st Duke of Buckingham and Chandos. History of the War of the Austrian Succession & the Seven Years War. vol. 2 only
1848	Minutes of meetings between the 2nd and 3rd Dukes of Buckingham and Chandos re the bankruptcy of the former and the management of the Grenville estates
1856<	Morgan, George Manners. Account of a voyage from Malta to the Bosporus

VIII. GRENVILLE SPECIAL SUBJECTS

1. *Admiralty Affairs: 9 pieces, 1787–1807*

In addition to Thomas Grenville's letterbooks as First Lord of the Admiralty (1806–07), and over 2,600 letters addressed to him chiefly in that capacity as noted in *Grenville Correspondence*, the collection contains the following separate volumes concerning the British Admiralty:

Abstract of ships registered in Great Britain. 1787
Abstract of ships registered in Ireland. 1788
Navy flag signals. 2 vols., 1803 and ca.1806
Warrant officers applications for promotion. 1806–07
Book of applications for naval employment. 1806–07
Book of applications for naval commissions. 1806–07
Appointments of commissioned officers. 1806–07
Book of recommendations for promotion in the Navy
[Area lists]. 1806–07
Six rolls of "quietus est" acquittances to George Grenville
as Treasurer of the Navy, 1756–62

2. *Buckinghamshire Militia: ca.800 pieces, >1760–1889*
In addition to over 600 letters (chiefly to George Grenville,
1st Marquis of Buckingham and Richard Grenville, 3rd Duke
of Buckingham and Chandos) in the *Grenville Correspondence,* the collection contains numerous records pertaining
to the Buckinghamshire Militia and to the Royal Bucks. Yeomanry Cavalry during the later 18th and 19th centuries. Three
Grenvilles in particular were closely involved with these
county forces: the 1st Marquis of Buckingham as Colonel of
the Bucks. Militia, the 2nd Duke as Lieutenant Colonel of
the 2nd (or Hussar) Regiment of the Royal Bucks. Yeomanry
Cavalry, and the 3rd Duke as Lord Lieutenant of the county.
The papers include commissions to officers, lists and returns
of eligible men, muster rolls and returns of the Bucks. Yeomanry Cavalry (1779–1889, incomplete runs), papers concerning courts martial, accounts (ca.300 pieces), drill and other
regulations, reports and inventories of arms, ordnance, clothing, etc., notices of social events concerning the Militia, and
miscellaneous circulars, speeches, reports, etc. on the subject
of the county's forces.
Of particular interest are the following separate volumes:
orderly books, 1778–1831 (44 vols.); returns of militia 1793–99;
proceedings at courts martial 1797–1812; John Foster's "The
Young Private Soldier's Monitor, or Pocket Companion,"
1799<; quartermaster's returns, 1801–06; officers accounts of
pay and general expenses, 1803–06; records of enlistment and
service bounties, 1803–06; four volumes of returns for meat
and bread drawn by the Royal Bucks. Militia, 1803–10;

paymaster's general abstracts of accounts for militia, 1804–
05; record of absentees 1805–08; weekly state of the Royal
Bucks. regiment, 1806–12; plans for field maneuvres by Richard Grenville, 1st Duke of Buckingham and Chandos, ca.1810;
three volumes of morning state of the Royal Bucks. Militia,
1811–13; return of clothing, 1812–17; account of pay, 1814; regimental order book for the 2nd Bucks. Hussars, 1815–32; and
a list of prize winners, 1825–33.

3. *Elections: ca.3,400 pieces, 1679–1902*
The vast majority of these papers (over 2,700 pieces) consist
of election accounts for the expenses of various members
of the Grenville family, chiefly relating to their standing for
Buckinghamshire shire or borough seats, and in particular
for: William Wyndham Grenville, Baron Grenville, in 1784
and 1790; Thomas Grenville in 1804 and 1806; Richard Grenville, 1st Duke of Buckingham and Chandos, in 1802, 1806,
1807, and 1812–13; Richard Grenville, 2nd Duke of Buckingham and Chandos, in 1818, 1820, 1826, and 1830–38; and
George Nugent Grenville, 2nd Baron Nugent, in 1818 and
1820.

Also included are election canvasses and poll results (chiefly
for Buckinghamshire during the period 1784–1857, but also
for the borough of Winchester in 1831), lists of freeholders
in various Buckinghamshire hundreds (late 18th and early
19th centuries), oaths of allegiance of the Freeholders and
Mayors of St. Mawes, Cornwall (1726–1830), and numerous
printed election broadsides and newspaper clippings concerning elections.

Of individual interest are: a report on the state of elections
in Sussex, including remarks on the constitution, specific political heads, and persons of power, by borough, 1762?; a note
by Thomas Dalby Jago on members of Parliament from the
borough of St. Mawes, 1735–1822.
See also Grenville Parliamentary Affairs; Ireland

4. *Fine Arts: ca.100 pieces, 1798–ca.1910*
Chiefly pencil, pen and ink, and watercolor sketches by various members of the Grenville family, many amateurish. Subjects portrayed include human heads and figures, horses,
buildings, landscapes, etc. Of particular interest are: sketches

of Stowe by Lady Mary Anne (Grenville) Arundell, Baroness Arundell, and of Stowe and Wotton by Mary Elizabeth (Nugent) Grenville, Marchioness of Buckingham; sketches and views made by the 1st Duke of Buckingham and Chandos during his Mediterranean tour, including a volume of scenes in France and Italy, the Farnese Gardens, St. Andrews Church in Rome, Milan, and Mount Etna; a volume of 29 etchings of ?Scotland, by "W. W." and others, ca.1870s; an anonymous volume of garden scenes from Stowe (19th cent.?); and several needlepoint designs.

Music includes: "Lord Breadalbane's March," hymns, folk songs and airs (no lyrics), a small volume of four songs with piano accompaniment, "The Grosvenor Polka" dedicated to the Marquis of Breadalbane by Joseph Czerkaski, and a composition titled "Song of the Siberian Swans on Wotton Lakes" [a transcription of swan sound into musical notation] by Mary (Campbell) Grenville, Duchess of Buckingham and Chandos, in whose handwriting many of the above pieces are written.

5. *Genealogy: ca.200 pieces, 1639–ca.1900*
Pedigrees, extracts from parish registers, genealogical notes, coats of arms, etc., concerning the Grenville and related families, including those of Kinsman, Frogatt, Cavendish, Manners, Tennant, Brigstocke, Chew, Markham, Brill, Morris, Brackley, Hercy, and Parry. Also concerning the baronies of Ferrers of Groby, Beauchamp, and Bourchier. Of particular interest are: a paper titled "Notes of myne ancestors," concerning the Grenville family ca.1160–1585, made in the ?17th century; a large drawing of the Grenville arms, with 81 quarterings, 1784; papers re the claim to the barony of Kinloss by Anna Eliza (Brydges) Grenville, Duchess of Buckingham and Chandos, ca.1823–27; a statement regarding the claim to the English throne of the 3rd Duke of Buckingham and Chandos, ca.1837; newspaper obituaries for various members of the Grenville family (including for Lady Kinloss, 1944).

6. *India: ca.180 pieces, 1858–85*
In addition to the 3rd Duke of Buckingham and Chandos's three-volume letterbook as Governor of Madras (1875–80), and over 400 letters addressed to him as such (many from

native Indian rulers) as noted in the *Grenville Correspon-dence,* the collection contains miscellaneous papers (many very fragmentary and decayed) concerning India and Indian affairs, including: papers re the visit of the Prince of Wales, 1875; a report on a list of vessels lost at Madras harbor, 1857–77; a report on the Buckingham Canal [Kottapatam] Division during the Madras famine, 1877–78; various letters sent during the 3rd Duke's governorship, ca.1880; a report on the Red Hills Reservoir, with plan, by the Madras Public Works Department, 1885; a map of the Indian Districts (19th cent.); numerous programs, guest lists, menus, stationery, etc. concerning the social life of British India.

Also ca.400 newspaper clippings concerning India and the 3rd Duke's governorship, and a scrapbook of newspaper clippings on India kept by Lady Mary Morgan-Grenville (ca.1875–80).
See also: Photographs

7. *Ireland: 15 pieces, 1778–1816*
In addition to the four-volume letterbook of George Grenville, 1st Marquis of Buckingham, as Lord Lieutenant of Ireland (1782–83 and 1787–89) and over 200 letters and other official papers, as noted in the *Grenville Correspondence,* the collection contains the following separate volumes relating to Ireland:

Memoranda relative to the quartering of troops in Ireland, 1778

List of persons recommended to the 1st Marquis of Buckingham as Lord Lieutenant for ecclesiastical preferment in Ireland, 1782

List of persons recommended to the 1st Marquis as Lord Lieutenant for miscellaneous preferment in Ireland, 1782

Contemporary sketches by the 1st Marquis of the Members of the Irish Parliament in 1782. 2 vols. 1782–83?

"A state of the borough interest . . . Of Ireland . . ."[with a political history of the Representatives of 1784] [?by] Charles Manners, 4th Duke of Rutland, continued by the 1st Marquis of Buckingham. 1784–87

A list of persons seeking preferment and the answers

they received from the Duke of Rutland, late Lord
Lieutenant of Ireland. 2 vols. 1787

A list of members of the Irish Parliament, by constituen-
cies, including a list of those who control each seat.
1787

A list of members of the Irish Parliament, arranged by
patrons. 1787

A list of persons recommended to the 1st Marquis as Lord
Lieutenant for preferment in Army, Church, or State
in Ireland. 1787–88

An account by the 1st Marquis of monies expended in
Ireland during his residence as Lord Lieutenant. 1787–
89

A survey by John Pratt of brass and iron ordnance, small
arms, etc., in Ireland. 1788

A record by the Irish Treasury of the civil establishment
in Ireland. 1788

A volume of writings, drafts of speeches, etc. by the 1st
Duke of Buckingham and Chandos, including a project
for the better arrangement of the collection of tithes
in Ireland. 1816

See also: Admiralty affairs

8. *Literature: ca. 200 pieces, 1680–>1914*

Chiefly literary compositions written, copied, or collected by
various members of the Grenville family, and in particular
those written by Richard Grenville, 1st Duke of Buckingham
and Chandos and written or copied by his daughter-in-law,
Mary (Campbell) Grenville, Duchess of Buckingham and
Chandos. Also includes some occasional verse by various authors, many unidentified and fragmentary pieces, and some
political satires. Most of the pieces are undated.

Among the Grenville family compositions are: birthday
poems by George Grenville, 1st Marquis of Buckingham, to
his wife, 1775 and 1779; a prayer based on Bp. Thomas Wilson's
Sacra Privata by [William Wyndham Grenville, Baron?] Grenville; an essay on dueling (composed for the Bachelor's Prize
of the University of Oxford in 1807), an "Ode written in the
little house . . . in Stowe gardens," an "Ode to Christmas,"
and "An Ode of Horace translated" by George Nugent Gren-

ville, 2nd Baron Nugent of Carlanstown; manuscripts of four
novels ("A Tale of the Civil Wars," "The Legend of the House
of Yonne," "A Tale of Sicily," and "The Zitza") written by
Richard Grenville, 1st Duke of Buckingham and Chandos,
with corrected page proofs for the final three, >1830–ca.1832;
poetry (including among others "This is a wondrous age. . .",
"The boast of Waterloo," "The Marquis of Chandos," "View
from the Observatory at Stowe," "Sweet Stowe Farewell!"
and "I watched a bud among the flowers"), an essay (on happi-
ness), a meditation on her 48th birthday, notes on literature
read (including James Fenimore Cooper, Robert Southey's
Life of Wesley, Sir John Malcolm's *Life of Robert, Lord Clive,*
and Nathaniel Hawthorne's *Scarlet Letter*), and a commonplace book, all by Mary (Campbell) Grenville, Duchess of
Buckingham and Chandos; book review, notes on birds, accounts of a military picnic at Valetta, and the loss of the
Monitor and the Battle of Naxiaro by George Manners Morgan.

Among copies (chiefly 19th cent.) of other literature are
versions of: "Sir Richard Grenville's Farewell," Gervase
Markham's "The Most Honorable Tragedie of Sir Richard
Grinvile, Knight," Richard Brinsley Sheridan's "Le Bouquet
d'hiver," Thomas Babington Macaulay's "The Battle of Ivry,"
and a commonplace book [belonging to Robert Christopher
Browne-Lundin?] of "Extracts from Various Authors." Occasional verses include among others: "Verses supposed to be
found on opening a Druid's Barrow in Dorsetshire 1775,"
"Installation Verses for [William Henry Cavendish Bentinck,
3rd] Duke of Portland" upon his election to the Chancellor-
ship of the University of Oxford, by Cyril Jackson, 1793; a
poem in praise of Abp. William Markham, "On the present
Archbishop of York inclosing the tomb of Archbishop Grey,"
by Frederick Howard, 5th Earl of Carlisle; "Lines dropped
on board the 'Venerable' previously to the sailing of the expedition against Flushing, in 1809"; a eulogy for William Wyndham Grenville, Baron Grenville, by Lady Charlotte Proby,
1835; "Lines sent to the noble Author of Childe Harold,"
by Granville Penn; "On seeing the Blind Asylum at Edinburgh," "Upon the death of General Lord Wm. Bentinck,"
a reflective poem upon visiting the Jordan River near Bethel

and Jericho (1840?), and a poem "Written at Rome, on hearing an exaggerated account of the Duke of Wellington's illness," all by Francis Egerton, 1st Earl of Ellesmere; and "A New Year's Carol. Impromptu on seeing an account of the Queen's intended visit to Stowe," 1844, with covering letter addressed to the 2nd Duke of Buckingham and Chandos.

Other pieces of interest include: "The Golden Age Reverst," an anonymous political poem answering William Walsh's *The Golden Age Restor'd* and/or *The Golden Age*, 1703; "Epilogue for the play of the Jealous Wife" (19 couplets on the 1761 play by George Coleman the elder) by Frederick Howard, 5th Earl of Carlisle, 1792; "As I lay musing on my Bed," a political satire on Lord North's election as an M.P. for Banbury; "While honest John Bull . . ." a political satire on the choice of a successor to Pitt the Younger; various unidentified 19th-century poems.

9. *Parliamentary Affairs: ca.100 pieces, 1661–1888*

A miscellaneous collection of material concerning Parliament, including the following items of interest: copy of a speech by Charles II to Parliament, Feb. 18, 1663; copy of a letter from Charles II to the Scottish Parliament, with a speech of the Earl of Lauderdale and the answer of the Scottish Parliament, 1669; a protection issued by Peregrine Osborne, 2nd Duke of Leeds, to Thomas Townshend against a breach of privilege, 1713; instructions issued to the knights of the shire for Buckinghamshire, 1715; several printed copies of late 18th- and 19th-century bills; papers concerning the disputed election for the borough of Aylesbury, July 1802, and charges of bribery against James Dupré and Robert Bent by Thomas Fremantle, the 1st Marquis of Buckingham, the 1st Duke of Buckingham and Chandos, and Sir Scrope Bernard-Morland; a petition by 55 retail brewers of London to the Lords Commissioners of the Treasury for relief from harassment by Common Informer under the Licensing Act, 1829; a report of a Select Committee and other papers concerning the disputed election at St. Mawes, Cornwall, 1830; notes in the handwriting of the 3rd Duke of Buckingham and Chandos concerning discussions in the House of Commons for Free Trade as against the Corn Laws, ca.1853?; a petition by the

3rd Duke claiming the right to vote at elections of the Irish
Parliament, 1861
See also: Elections

10. *Photographs: ca.100 pieces, ca.1865–1916*
Chiefly photographs of India (during the 3rd Duke's stay
there as Governor of Madras, 1875–80), Stowe house and gardens, and various members of the Grenville family. Among
the Indian photographs are those of: Panhalla Hill Fort, Kol-
hapur (including palace, shrines, public buildings, and the
Chief Judge's Court), and unidentified temples, and a roll
photograph panorama of Amravati, Undavalli, and Conda-
philli. Tentatively identified personal photographs include
those of: Caroline (Harvey) Grenville, Duchess of Buckingham and Chandos; Mary (Grenville) Morgan-Grenville, Baroness Kinloss, 1884 and early 20th century; John and George
Dormer?; Cecil Louise (Mackenzie) Maitland; Alice Anne
(Graham-Montgomery) Grenville, Duchess of Buckingham
and Chandos; Thomas Morgan-Grenville, ca.1913?; Col. Hibbert, ca.1913?; Alice Hughes, 1916. Photographs of Stowe include those of the Gothic Temple, the Marble Saloon, and
the Temple of Concord and Victory, all probably late 19th
century. Also unidentified photographs of people, animals,
buildings, and landscapes, chiefly late 19th century.

The Library has also acquired (from Marlborough Rare
Books, Ltd., in 1979) two photograph albums of Stowe,
ca.1872–82. The first includes over 50 photographs of the inte-
rior of Stowe House, taken by J. Mudd and Sons; the second
includes 27 photographs of the exterior of the house and
gardens, taken by L. Varney.

11. *Queen Anne's Bounty Papers: ca.100 pieces, 1878–89*
Chiefly printed minutes, agendas, and reports of the General
Court and Governors concerning the administration of
Queen Anne's Bounty (a fund for the relief of poor clergy
established by Queen Anne from the revenues due to the
Crown from ecclesiastical first fruits and tenths). Included
are: a list of the number and value of benefices, ca.1885; a
list of bad debts on loans made between 1876 and 1885; reports
of the finance committee; and schedules of applications for
grants.

12. *Religious and Ecclesiastical Affairs: ca.60 pieces, 1758–ca.1915*

A very miscellaneous collection of private and public religious and ecclesiastical papers, including: a letter from John Jeffreys Pratt, 1st Marquis Camden, to the 1st Marquis of Buckingham concerning the appointment of French and Irish clergy and the Catholic Education Bill, 1795<; draft of a bill for the better prevention of clandestine marriages among Catholics, n.d. (18th cent.?); a volume sent to the 1st Marquis of Buckingham containing a summary of correspondence 1799–1800, with appendix of supporting documents 1677–1808, re the conditions and rights of Catholic clergy in Ireland (printed); petitions of Roman Catholics to Parliament for relief, with copies of relevant speeches, 1810; an anonymous defense against charges of intolerance in dissenting clergy, 1817<; religious meditations and prayers by Mary (Campbell) Grenville, Duchess of Buckingham and Chandos, n.d.; letters of John Brown of Langton Manse, Berwickshire, to John Campbell, 1st Marquis of Breadalbane, and to Sir Robert Peel, concerning patronage in the Church of Scotland, 1833 and 1837<, with remarks on the claims of the courts of the Church of Scotland, 1843, and his sermon preached upon the death of Mary Turner (Gavin) Campbell, Marchioness of Breadalbane, 1845; two sermons by Thomas Martyn, 1857 and 1863; additional notes for sermons on or other religious themes.

N.B.: Numerous papers concerning presentations to livings and other parish affairs will be found throughout the *Grenville Manorial and Loal Affairs Papers.*

13. *Schools and Education: ca.420 pieces, ?17th cent.–1879*

School exercises, notes, and report books, chiefly of the Grenville family children, including: a school report book (1792–99) for Mary Anne Grenville, later Baroness Arundell, with her transcriptions and translations in French and Italian, some with comments by Charles O'Conor, and other pieces; exercises and instructions for the future 3rd Duke of Buckingham and Chandos; school report books for Lady Caroline Grenville (1861–65) and Lady Anne (Grenville) Hadaway (1861–65). Also a volume titled "Letters on History from a

Father to his Son," 1847, and advice on manners, morals, behavior, etc. from Mary (Campbell) Grenville, Duchess of Buckingham and Chandos, to her daughter.

Also papers concerning Stowe School and Wotton School, accounts for teachers' wages, wool and drapery supplies, children's clothes, food, shoes, etc., for both Stowe (1796–1829) and Wotton (1779–1839) schools.

14. *Transportation (chiefly railroads): ca.2,700 pieces, 1773–1889*

In addition to over 1,000 letters in the *Grenville Correspondence* concerning the 3rd Duke's involvement with railroads, the collection contains a large number of accounts and other papers relating to various railroads in which the 3rd Duke had an interest. In particular there are: monthly accounts of earnings from goods and coaching traffic on the Wotton Tramway (1871–88), together with miscellaneous proposals, schedules, notes, plans, diagrams, and legal, financial, and technical papers concerning the Tramway; miscellaneous accounts and reports and minutes of the Directors of the Aylesbury and Buckingham Railroad; papers concerning the purchase by the Buckingham Railway Co. of lands from the 2nd and 3rd Dukes (1846–53); accounts, reports, memoranda, legal and financial papers, and other miscellaneous material concerning the London and North Western Railway, of which the 3rd Duke was a Director (1847–84); papers concerning the bill for the construction of the Great Western Railway, with maps and legal papers concerning its acquisition of lands from the 2nd and 3rd Dukes (1834–61); miscellaneous papers concerning other railroads, many concerning the legal or Parliamentary aspects of the companies; miscellaneous printed brochures, circulars, reports, etc. concerning various railroads.

Also included are: ca.1,600 accounts of the 1st Marquis of Buckingham with the Grand Junction Canal Company (1797–1812); printed parliamentary bills for making various navigable canals (1792–94); a few papers concerning telegraphs; a printed catalog of Rock & Hawkins, Coach Builders, for 1884; and miscellaneous papers concerning other forms of transportation.

15. *West Indian Estates: ca.310 pieces, 1807–83*
In addition to nearly 400 letters in the *Grenville Correspondence* concerning the Jamacian estates inherited by the Grenvilles from Anne Eliza (Gamon) Elletson Brydges, Duchess of Chandos, through the marriage of her daughter to the 1st Marquis of Buckingham, the collection contains numerous financial and legal papers concerning these properties. Included are: maps and descriptions of the Hope and Middleton Plantations; deeds, abstracts of title, leases, and other papers re conveyancing land in Jamacian estates; legal papers in connection with the administration of the estates after the certified lunacy of the Duchess of Chandos; accounts of sugar sales and of transactions by the dukes of Buckingham and Chandos with various firms, merchants, and other individuals; lists and returns of slaves on the Hope Plantation (1813–32), with a petition from former slaves to the Marquis of Chandos (afterward 3rd Duke of Buckingham and Chandos) against eviction from their property on Hope Plantation, 1854; a few papers concerning a group of immigrants to Jamaica supported by the 1st Duke of Buckingham and Chandos, 1835; a few papers concerning water supplies, 1840–50.
See also Brydges West Indies Estates papers.

16. *Miscellaneous: ca.300 pieces, 1660–1910*
A very miscellaneous collection of material, chiefly of domestic or personal interest but also including a few items of national or political significance.

Among the items of political importance or interest are: a list of the names of the Governors of the Charter House, 1660s; a volume recording Exchequer payments on the Civil List, with a summary of income to be applied to the List, 1761–62; a volume made by (or for) William Wyndham Grenville, Baron Grenville, listing the Colonial officers, their appointments, and salaries, ca.1790; a letter from the Freeholders and Inhabitants of Cornwall, in the hand of Sir Scrope Bernard-Morland, "To the Magistrates who signed the Requisition to call a County Meeting" concerning the Manchester ("Peterloo") riots, 1819; notes by Mary (Campbell) Grenville, Duchess of Buckingham and Chandos, on the national debt and the economic situation, 1846<.

Personal and domestic papers include: directions for the management of servants and for the village sick; lists of servants; household hints and recipes; medical prescriptions, advice, and notes on treatment; menus, recipes, and table arrangements, chiefly at Stowe; and papers concerning public admissions to the gardens at Stowe.

Among the general miscellaneous items are: a dictionary of architectural terms; a plan of an American ice house; proposals for dealing with poachers; "The Guide of Travelers throughout Italy" including advice on transportation, currencies, inns, servants, routes, charges, etc., ca.1782?; 26 documents in Turkish, ca.1681–86.

Temple Papers (ca.23,000 pieces)

The fortunes of the Temples of Stowe began in the mid-16th century when Peter Temple (d. 1578), the younger son of a minor Leicestershire family, began leasing lands in Burton Dassett, Warwickshire and, slightly later (1571), at Stowe and Dadford in Buckinghamshire.* His son John Temple (1542–1603) purchased the manor of Stowe outright in 1590, and continued his father's accumulation of lands in Buckinghamshire and Warwickshire, on which he raised sheep to great profit. He served as a Justice of the Peace, and probably as Sheriff of Buckinghamshire, and by the end of the century the Temples were firmly established as "rising gentry." John Temple married Susan Spencer, daughter of Thomas Spencer of Everton, Northamptonshire; their daughters married well and their eldest son Thomas Temple (1567–1637) was a member of Parliament (1588–89), knighted by 1603, Sheriff of Oxfordshire (1606–07), and able to purchase a baronetcy in 1611. As Sir Thomas Temple, 1st Bart., of Stowe, he served as Sheriff of Buckinghamshire (1616–17) and of Warwickshire (1620–21). He married Hester Sandys (d. 1656), daughter of Miles Sandys;

---

* The following account is much indebted to Edwin F. Gay, "The Rise of an English Country Family: Peter and John Temple, to 1603," *Hunt. Lib. Quarterly* 1,4 (1938): 367–90, and "The Temples of Stowe and Their Debts: Sir Thomas and Sir Petter Temple, 1603–1653," *Hunt. Lib. Quarterly* 2,4 (1939): 399–438, and to Godfrey Davies, "The Political Career of Sir Richard Temple (1634–1697) and Buckinghamshire Politics," *Hunt. Lib. Quarterly* 4,1 (1940): 47–83.

she bore him 15 children, 13 of whom survived, and after his death in 1637 was active in the management of the Stowe estates and in the numerous lawsuits to which the family seemed prone.

Their eldest son Sir Peter Temple, 2nd Bart. (1592–1653), was a Justice of the Peace by 1634 and Sheriff of Buckinhamshire in 1635, in which capacity he was responsible for collecting Ship Money. He was an M.P. in both the Short and Long Parliaments, and a supporter of Parliament in the ensuing Civil War, during which he held a commission under the Earl of Essex. By the 1650s, however, he had fallen into political disfavor and financial trouble; sheep-farming had by now given way to leasing out his estates, but unwise borrowing and extravagant spending left his son Richard with a shaky inheritance.

Sir Richard Temple, 3rd Bart. (1634–97), was the son of Sir Peter's second wife Christian (Leveson) Temple. (His father's first marriage, to Anne Throckmorton, produced no sons). He gradually rebuilt the family fortunes, took an interest in the building and gardens at Stowe, and changed from parliamentary supporter during the Protectorate (when he was an M.P. in 1654 and 1659) to a secret Royalist and eventually an active place seeker under Charles II and James II. At the Restoration he was returned M.P. for Buckingham and retained the seat for the rest of his life (with a brief interruption in 1679). Sir Richard also served as a Justice of the Peace, a Colonel of Foot (1660), and Deputy Lieutenant for Buckinghamshire in 1680. He was on the Council for Foreign Plantations in 1671, and a Commissioner of Customs intermittently from 1672 to 1694, in which capacity in 1684 he undertook an official survey of the customs offices in southern English ports. He married Mary Knapp, daughter of Henry Knapp of Rawlins, Oxfordshire, and at his death in 1697 was succeeded by his eldest son Richard.

Richard Temple, 4th Bart. and later 1st Viscount Cobham (1675–1749), was an M.P. like his father (for Buckingham in 1697–1702 and 1708–13, and for Buckinghamshire 1704–08), but his main calling was military. He fought in Marlborough's Flemish wars, and rose to the rank of Lieutenant General by 1710; he commanded as Colonel, successively from 1710, the 4th Dragoons, the Royal 1st Regiment of Dragoons, the King's Own Horse (1st Dragoon Guards), the 1st Horse Grenadier Guards, the 6th Horse, and the 10th Dragoons. Created Baron Cobham in 1714 and Viscount Cob-

ham in 1718, he served as Governor of Jersey (1723–49), Lord
Lieutenant of Buckinghamshire (1728–38), General in the Army
(1735), and Field Marshal (1742). Cobham's military career had
been interrupted more than once by political reversals; in 1733,
as an opponent of Walpole's Excise Tax, he was dismissed from
his regiment, and thereafter broke with the Walpole Whigs, forming with Pitt, Lyttleton and George Grenville the "Boy Patriots."
Returned to command of a regiment by 1742, he nevertheless
opposed English fighting in support of Hanoverian interests and
in 1744 joined the Pelham-Newcastle coalition. Cobham continued
his father's interest in Stowe, rebuilding the house and laying
out the gardens, and was a notable literary patron and a friend
of Pope.

Cobham married, about 1715, Anne Halsey, the daughter of
the wealthy brewer Edmund Halsey of Southwark, Surrey, and
Stoke Poges, Buckinghamshire. They had no children, and on
his death in 1749 Stowe passed to his sister Hester (Temple) Grenville, *suo jure* Viscountess Cobham and later Countess Temple.

I. TEMPLE ACCOUNTS AND FINANCIAL PAPERS
   ca.15,400 pieces, 1418–1767
Most of the papers in this category are estate and household accounts from the time of Sir Richard Temple, 3rd. Bart., and his
son Richard, Viscount Cobham, although there are approximately
1,000 pieces distributed evenly over the first half of the 17th century and a few scattered items for the 16th century. (The 15th
century is represented by a single piece.)

1. *Estate accounts (ca.8,000 pieces)* pertain predominantly to
Stowe, although there is some scattered material for Burton
Dassett and for other Temple lands. Included are both summary accounts (by estate officials) and individual bills, receipts, pay vouchers, etc. for the goods, labor, and services
connected with the operation of a major estate. There are
accounts for building and repair work at Stowe (particularly
during the rebuilding of the house by Cobham), numerous
garden accounts (again, principally during Cobham's time),
accounts of estate and home farm labor (including reaping,
mowing, digging up stones, weeding, setting out trees, plow-
ing and harrowing, etc.), and accounts of the sale of cattle,
sheep, and wood, dairy and kiln accounts, etc. Also included

are a few receipts and other accounts for tithes, rents, and local taxes and levies.

Separate volumes of accounts include:

> Temple, Peter. A note of reckoning [account of sheep bought and sold, rents, etc.]. 1532–45
>
> Temple, Sir Thomas, 1st Bart. "The booke of the wooll sold" [includes some accounts of John Temple and of Sir Edward Wotton]. 1592–1626
>
> Temple, Sir Thomas, 1st Bart. Notes on reckonings. 1611–22
>
> Temple, Sir Peter, 2nd Bart. Book of accounts and reckonings from Henry Rose . . . [continued by Sir Richard Temple, 3rd Bart.]. 1642–57
>
> Temple, Sir Richard, 3rd Bart. Accounts at Stowe. 1653–57
>
> Temple, Sir Richard, 3rd Bart. "Mr. William Chaplin's Accompts." 1654–59
>
> Darnelly, Richard. Book of Receipts. 1656–66
>
> Knapp, Henry. Accounts of profits and expenses of Rawlins Farm [Oxfordshire]. 1667–72
>
> Temple, Sir Richard, 3rd Bart. Accounts at Stowe. 1668–70
>
> Dodington, George. Account of rents received. 1697
>
> Temple, Richard, 1st Viscount Cobham. Rent book. 1733–34
>
> Temple, Richard, 1st Viscount Cobham. Account of arrears of rent and of arrears of wood sold. 1733–41

2. *Household Accounts (ca.5,000 pieces)* are predominantly for Stowe, and consist chiefly of bills, receipts, and other accounts for food and drink, silver, pewter, cutlery, linen and other cloth, furniture, upholstery, plumbing, laundry, and stables. Also included are housekeeper's lists of provisions consumed. There are some London accounts.

Separate volumes of accounts include:

> Temple, Sir Richard, 3rd Bart. House Book. 1674–76
>
> Temple, Sir Richard, 3rd Bart. Day Book. 1680–84
>
> Temple, Sir Richard, 3rd Bart. London House Book. 1688–91
>
> Temple, Sir Richard, 3rd Bart. "Brotherton's Accompts"

(of wine, ale, etc. consumed in the household). 1689–
90
Temple, Richard, 1st Viscount Cobham. Accounts. 3 vols.
1701/02–1705, 1716–17, and 1718–19.
Temple, Richard, 1st Viscount Cobham. Accounts of
Money Received and Payments Made. 3 vols. 1720–
23, 1713–28, and 1736–41
See also Temple Personal and Family Papers, p. 223 for
related volumes.

3. *Personal Accounts (ca.2,400 pieces)* are unusually rich in
the bonds, acquittances and other financial papers which re-
flect the debts of the first three baronets of Stowe and of
Viscount Cobham. Also included are bills, receipts, vouchers,
etc. for clothing, travel, schooling, gifts, entertainment, books,
etc., as well as accounts of legal expenses, payments on annuities and legacies, and other miscellaneous legal and financial
charges.
Separate volumes of accounts include:
Temple, Sir Richard, 3rd Bart. "Book of Accompts" [in-
cludes notes re juries, lawyers' fees, etc., especially for
the Baltinglass case]. 1654–55
Temple, Sir Richard, 3rd Bart. Ledger Book. 1677–88
Temple, Richard, 1st Viscount Cobham. Account of receipts and payments. 1697–1706

II. TEMPLE CORRESPONDENCE
ca.2,600 pieces, 1500–1757
Personal, political, legal, estate, and financial correspondence of
the Temple and related families.* The correspondence is scanty
for the 16th and 18th centuries, but very full for all of the 17th,
and particularly rich during the 1630s and 1680s.

Subjects covered include: personal and family affairs and news;
management of the Temple estates, and building at Stowe, particularly as seen in full runs of letters to and from William Chaplyn,
the steward of Sir Richard Temple, 3rd Bart.; national and local
(chiefly Buckinghamshire) politics and government, including in-

---

* For a separate collection of the correspondence of Lady Hester (Sandys) Temple,
see below, pp. 357–58.

formation about Parliament, Ship Money, local elections, the official activities of the Temples as sheriffs, justices of the peace, deputy lieutenants, etc., the Customs (the 3rd Bart. was a Commissioner of the Customs, and in 1684 undertook a survey of the southern ports from Portsmouth to Dartmouth); legal and financial affairs of the Temple family, lawsuits, negotiations for marriages, the financial troubles of the 2nd Bart., etc.

Also included is correspondence from or relating to: Sir Anthony Cooke, including his financial dealings with John Temple and his dispute with his father-in-law Sir William Waldegrave; the correspondence of Sir William Andrewes of Lathbury, Bucks., concerning his work as Keeper of the manor of Grafton, Northants., and as Sheriff and Justice of the Peace for Buckinghamshire; letters from John Dodington, secretary to the English ambassador at Venice, 1669–1773, to his brother-in-law the 3rd Bart., relating political and diplomatic gossip, his financial affairs, etc.

Authors represented by five or more letters are listed below:
    Andrewes, Lady Anne (Temple) (8)
    Andrewes, Sir Henry, 1st Bart. (9)
    Binett, Robert (6)
    Broughton, Christopher (20)
    Chaplyn, William [Steward of Sir Thomas Temple, 1st Bart.] (8)
    Chaplyn, William [Steward of Sir Richard Temple, 3rd Bart.] (274)
    Charlton, John (5)
    Cooke, Sir Anthony (8)
    Denton, Sir Thomas (10)
    Denton, William (10)
    Dodington, Hester (Temple) (7)
    Dodington, John (78)
    Egerton, John, 2nd Earl of Bridgwater (13)
    Farmer, John (12)
    Fewtrell, William (10)
    Fortescue, Sir John (6)
    Galloway, James (7)
    Gibbs, Elizabeth (Temple), Lady (7)
    Gifford, Peter (6)
    Goodwyn, Sir John (5)
    Gower, Sir Thomas (6)

Great Britain.
  Commissioners of the Customs (6)
  Privy Council (34)
Grey, Arthur, 14th Baron Grey de Wilton (7)
Grey, Henry, 1st Earl of Stamford (5)
Hamersley, Chamberlaine (5)
Hart, William (11)
Harte, William (9)
Hillesdon, Thomas (7)
Hilyard, George (17)
Holbech, Ambrose [of Mollington, Oxon.] (5)
Holbech, Ambrose [lawyer, of Clements Inn] (39)
Horley, Spencer (8)
Lawley, William (17)
Lenthall, Sir John (114)
Leveson, Sir Richard (17)
Lloyd, Leonard (5)
Longueville, Margaret (Temple), Lady (19)
Martyn, Augustin (7)
Ogle, Thomas (6)
Osney, Ro[bert] (6)
Overton, F[   ] (6)
Palmes, William (8)
Paulet, Lord William (11)
Pollard, John (24)
Poole, Robert (5)
Raynes, Thomas (5)
Ridgeway, Frances (Temple), Countess of Londonderry (7)
Ridgeway, Robert, 4th Earl of Londonderry (15)
Risley, Christian (Temple) (5)
Risley, John (6)
Roper, Anne (Temple), Viscountess Baltinglass (8)
Roper, Thomas, 2nd Viscount Baltinglass (8)
Rose, Henry (7)
Rous, Sir John (7)
Royle, Peter (5)
Sandys, Henry (9)
Sandys, Miles (6)
Stuart, Ludovic, 2nd Duke of Lennox & 1st Duke of Richmond
  (5)
Sybthorpe, Robert (21)

Taylor, J[   ] (6)
Temple, Hester (Sandys), Lady (13)
Temple, John [1542–1603, father of Sir Thomas Temple, 1st
    Bart.] (21)
Temple, John [ca.1635–72<, younger brother of Sir Richard
    Temple, 3rd Bart.] (25)
Temple, Sir John (5)
Temple, Mary (Knapp), Lady (5)
Temple, Miles (19)
Temple, Peter (5)
Temple, Sir Peter, 2nd Bart. (34)
Temple, Sir Purbeck (8)
Temple, Sir Richard, 3rd Bart. (92)
Temple, Richard, 1st Viscount Cobham (17)
Temple, Thomas [b. 1604, son of Sir Thomas Temple, 1st Bart.]
    (32)
Temple, Thomas [fl. 1673–1789, surveyor of port of Wey-
    mouth] (13)
Temple, Sir Thomas (109)
Temple, William (5)
Thornton, Thomas (11)
Tracy, Paule (15)
Turner, John (5)
Tyrrell, Sir Edward, 1st Bart. (10)
Verney, Sir Raphe (9)
Villiers, George, 1st Duke of Buckingham (6)
Waterhouse, Noble (38)
Willes, Edward (6)
Wotton, Edward, 1st Baron Wotton (5)
Wotton, Thomas (9)

III. TEMPLE DEEDS (partial listing)
    ca.400 pieces, 1228–1799
In addition to individual deeds, some of which are listed below,*
this category contains two separate volumes of interest. The first,
made about 1560 by Peter Temple, contains copies of "evidences"
concerning lands in Burton Dassett, Warwickshire. The second,

---

* *See also* Stowe Unsorted Deeds, below, pp. 255–62.

compiled by Sir Thomas Temple, 1st Bart., is "A breviat of leases
made by me . . . to others," 1619–35.

The following places, listed by county with inclusive dates, appear
in five or more deeds:

Buckinghamshire:

Biddlesden (20) 1538–>1749
Bourton (5) 1624–>1749
Buckingham (15) 1588–1718
Calverton (7) 1637–1718
Dadford (32) 1531–>1749
Gorrall (11) 1538–>1749
Heyford (6) 1712–ca.1718
Lamport (alias Langport) (30) 1391–>1749
Leckhampstead (6) 1624–52
Luffield (20) 1550-n.d. (18th cent.)
Maids Moreton (9) 1588–1718
Oldwickc (5) 1570–1647
Padbury (7) 1549–1648
Shalstone (10) 1570–ca.1710
Stowe (56) 1391–>1749
Thornborough (28) 1519–>1749
Thornton (7) 1637<–>1749
Water Stratford (9) 1546–ca.1718
Westbury (31) 1230–1718

Cornwall:

Gwennap (5) 1624–58
Tregavethan (6) 1621–1708

Leicestershire:

Lutterworth (28) 1564–>1749

Northamptonshire:

Astwell with Falcutt (5) 1540–46
Silverstone (5) 1571–>1653
Syresham (16) 1540?–46
Wappenham (5) 1540?–46
Whittlebury (6) 1637<–>1656

Oxfordshire:

Finmere (16) 1614–>1749
Water Eaton (6) 1537?–>1637
Wood Eaton (5) 1588–>1637

Warwickshire:
>   Burton Dassett (83) 1545?->1749
>   Bubbenhall (9) 1628–93
>   Chadshunt (7) 1637<->1749
>   Fenny Compton (5) 1637<->1749
>   Kineton (5) 1637<->1749
>   Knightcote (16) 1554->1749
>   Northend (13) 1559->1749
>   Radway (15) 1554-n.d. (17th cent.)
>   Stretton Dunsmore (9) 1628–93
>   Wappenbury (9) 1628–93
>   Wolston (8) 1628–93

Yorkshire:
>   Byland (5) 1628–85
>   Coxwold (6) 1628–85
>   Oswald Kirk (6) 1628–85
>   Wasse (6) 1628–85

IV. TEMPLE INVENTORIES, LISTS, AND CATALOGS
124 pieces, 1569–1759

Primarily 17th-century inventories of the goods and chattel of
various persons, with lists of plate, linens, and other household
goods (particularly of Lady Hester [Sandys] Temple).

Some of the more interesting items are listed chronologically
below:

1569	Inventory of goods and chattel of Robert Temple, late of Goodwich Castle, dec.
1581	Inventory of the goods and chattel of Anthony Temple of Temple Hall, dec.
1583	Inventory of goods and chattel of Millicent Temple, widow, late of Stowe
16th cent.?	"A schedule indented of the catell, plate and household stuff late Margaret Denton's . . . of Hillesdon, Bucks."
1603	Inventory of the goods of John Temple, late of Stowe (room by room)
1605	Inventory of the goods of Robert Brudenell *alias* Bridewell of Thornborough
1605	Inventory of the goods of Robert Spencer, 1st Baron Spencer (or made by him?), delivered to Thomas and Mary Webb

1609	Inventory of the goods of Giles Spencer, dec., of Northend in Burton Dassett, Warwicks.
1609	Inventory of all the goods of Thomas Spratley, late of Water Eaton, Oxon., with appraisal
1619	Inventory of the goods, chattel, and debts of John Harley, dec.
1624	"A booke of Sundry parcells of household stuff, beddinge, victualls, etc. leaft by Sir Thomas and the Lady Temple at Stow when Sir Peter began housekepeing there . . ."
1625	Inventory of the goods of William Hall, late of [Gottesbatch?], Leics.
1630	Inventory by Henry Rose of the goods and household stuff at [Burton?] Dassett
1653	Inventory of goods sold by Sir Peter and Lady Christian (Leveson) Temple to Lady Hester, with prices
1656	Inventory taken at Stowe of the goods of Lady Hester Temple. 2 pieces
1656–78	List of deeds and mortgages of Sir Richard Temple, 3rd Bart.
1672	Inventory by Thomas Temple of the goods and chattel of Weston Ridgeway, 3rd Earl of Londonderry, dec.
1674	Inventory of goods in Woodcott House of Henry Knapp, dec.
>1697	Catalog of the books of Sir Richard Temple, 3rd Bart., at Stowe, with other notes
1697	General inventory of all the goods of the late Sir Richard Temple, 3rd Bart., with appraisal
18th cent.?	Inventory of part of the goods of Mrs. Elizabeth Temple, dec., of Lathbury, Bucks.

V. TEMPLE LEGAL PAPERS

ca.2,000 pieces, 1542–1738?

The Temples were an unusually litigious family and their legal papers, in contrast to those of the Hastings, Grenville, or Brydges families, are extraordinarily full. There are nearly 250 separate cases, by far the greatest number of which belong to the 17th century. At least half of the cases were heard before the Court of Chancery, although there are several from each of the other major central courts. Predictably, most of the cases are concerned with land and rights over it, including questions of leases and grants, mortgages, marriage settlements, trespass and ejectment, poaching, and questions of common lands and enclosures. There are also numerous cases dealing with the Temple family debts (defaults on personal loans, annuities, etc.) and with nonpayment of tithes to the vicars of various parishes, and further cases dealing with personal charges of libel, perjury, and assault and battery. Also included are numerous miscellaneous legal notes and papers, not immediately identified with any particular case.

The following people appear in five or more cases as either plaintiff or defendant:

Collett, Thomas (6)
Cooke, Sir Anthony (6)
Duffield, Francis (5)
Harris, Peter (6)
Pollard, John (5)
Roper, Anne, Viscountess Baltinglass (17)
Roper, Thomas, 2nd Viscount Baltinglass (13)
Temple, Lady Christian (Leveson) (8)
Temple, Lady Hester (Sandys) (14)
Temple, John (7)
Temple, Sir Peter, 2nd Bart. (35)
Temple, Sir Richard, 3rd Bart. (55)
Temple, Sir Thomas, 1st Bart. (33)
Waller, Elizabeth (Hogan) (6)
Waller, Thomas (6)

Among some of the more interesting or important cases are:

A series of cases involving Sir Anthony Cooke (1504–76), Peter Temple (d.1578), and Thomas Wotton (1521–87) concerning disputed land in Burton Dassett, Warwickshire. 1568–75

Peter Temple (1589–1657), lunatic, by Sir James Ley, afterward 1st Earl of Marlborough *v.* Sir Thomas Temple, 1st Bart., and others re nonpayment of a legacy left to the plaintiff by his father, John Temple (1542–1603). Heard in the Court of Wards and Liveries. 1619–20

Sir Peter Temple, 2nd Bart., *v.* Kenelm Smith for assault and battery. 1639

A series of cases involving, principally, the 2nd and 3rd Barts., Thomas Roper, 2nd Viscount Baltinglass (d. ca.1670) and his wife Anne, Viscountess Baltinglass, daughter of the 2nd Bart., re lands settled on Lady Baltinglass at her marriage or descending to her at the death of her father. 1639–76

John Wyatt *v.* the 2nd Bart. re nonpayment of tithes to the plaintiff, vicar of Stowe parish. 1640–62

Arthur East and Peter Harris *v.* Peter Dayrell and others for assault and battery on the part of the defendants while poaching on the 2nd Bart.'s estate at Dadford, 1641–42

The Lord Protector [Oliver Cromwell] *v.* Edward Browne, re perjury of the defendant in the case of Sir Thomas Gower, 2nd Bart., *v.* Sir Richard Temple, 3rd Bart. Heard in the General Sessions of the Public Peace, London. 1657–58

Crown *v.* Henry Robinson and others, for publishing false, seditious, scandalous, and defamatory libels in print against the Bailiff and Burgesses of the Borough and Parish of Buckingham. 1679?

Among the additional miscellaneous items of general legal interest are: a volume of legal notes, 1607–09?; a summary of court actions involving Sir Thomas Temple, 1st Bart., 1623–25; notes on the trial of Sir Richard Temple, 3rd Bart., by [Ambrose Holbech?], 1669; complaints against John Risley as a J.P. for Buckinghamshire, 1677?.

VI. TEMPLE MANORIAL AND LOCAL AFFAIRS PAPERS
ca.1,600 pieces, 1296?–1746<

Slightly over half of the papers in this category refer to lands in Buckinghamshire, and another third to Temple properties and interests in Oxfordshire and Warwickshire. Later records for many of the places mentioned here will be found in the *Grenville Manorial and Local Affairs Papers*. This category also contains a number of items concerning the county militia (for supplemental material, see *Temple Military Affairs Papers*, below). There are relatively few of the individual receipts for rents, tithes, taxes, and local levies which dominate the Grenville papers.

Listed below by county are: all places represented by five or more pieces, with covering dates and a few selected items of interest; all court rolls; all compotus rolls; rentals; and selected additional miscellaneous items of interest or importance.

    1. *Places represented by five or more pieces:*
      Buckinghamshire:

        Ashendon: 8 pieces, 1296?–1742

          Includes: a list of knights fees, 1296?; an extract from the hundred rolls for Ashendon Hundred, 1316–17; accounts of the Overseers of the Poor for Ashenden with Pollicott, 1727.

        Biddlesden: 156 pieces, >1637–1723

        Boycott: 6 pieces, 1629->1700

        Buckingham: 47 pieces, 1508-n.d. (18th cent.)

        Chetwode: 5 pieces, 1682–84

        Dadford: 120 pieces, 1543–1723

        Gorrall: 7 pieces, ca.1650-n.d. (17th cent.)

        Lamport: 77 pieces, 1543–1740

        Leckhampstead: 35 pieces, 1624–48

          Includes papers of the Committee for "plundered ministers" concerning the advowson and church at Leckhampstead, ca.30 pieces, 1646–48

        Luffield: 68 pieces, 1630-n.d. (18th cent.)

        Maids Moreton: 8 pieces, 1508->1697

        Pollicott (Great & Little): 5 pieces, 1607–1746

        Stowe: ca.290 pieces, 1478–1742

          Includes: parish registers [for Stowe and Burton Dassett, Warws.?] 1568–1656; a list of the Churchwardens at Stowe, 1605–36, by Sir Peter Temple, 2nd Bart.; a volume of "Busynes to be remembered" by Sir Peter Temple, ca.1630, containing memoranda of estate work, etc.; a note of houses "depopulated" by Sir Peter, >1653; miscellaneous instructions and agreements re building at Stowe, 5 pieces, 1677–ca.1686; a small notebook containing a description of "Lord Cobham's gardens," 1738

        Thornborough: 126 pieces, 1621<-n.d. (18th cent.)

        Tingewick: 67 pieces, 1620–1722

        Westbury: 110 pieces, ca.1501-n.d. (18th cent.)

      Gloucestershire:

        Longborough: 32 pieces, ca.1607–59

Leicestershire:
> Lutterworth: 6 pieces, 1595–ca.1696

London: 5 pieces, 1671–ca.1684

Northamptonshire:
> Silverstone: 13 pieces, ca.1714–32?

Oxfordshire:
> Cudlington: 6 pieces, 1545–>1637
> Finmere: 74 pieces, 1474–1648
> Water Eaton: 10 pieces, 1545-n.d. (17th cent.)
> Woodcote (*alias* Rawlins): 6 pieces, 1629<-n.d. (18th cent.)

Warwickshire:
> Bubbenhill: 11 pieces, 1686–93
> Burton Dassett: ca.260 pieces, 1448-n.d. (18th cent.) Includes a copy of the inquisition into what lands and buildings there were in Dassett and what had been enclosed, 1517; appointments of various vicars to the living at Burton Dassett, with related papers, 11 pieces, 1618–34
> Knightcote; 9 pieces, 1517–1700<
> Northend: 7 pieces, 1517–1700<

Yorkshire:
> Malton (Old Malton): 5 pieces, 1685–90

2. *Court Rolls and other court papers:*

Buckinghamshire:
> Ashendon: roll (view of frankpledge only, with Little Pollicott) for 1669
> Buckingham: Borough courtbooks, 1562, 1576; Borough court proceedings, ca.1561
> Dadford: rolls for 1580, 1618–23
> Pollicott (Great and Little): *See* Ashendon
> Stowe: roll for 1597?
> General and unidentified: courtbook for 1615–17

Gloucestershire:
> Bourton-on-the-Water: roll for 1550
> Longborough: copy of court rolls, ca.1607–59, ca.25 pieces

Hampshire:
> Avington: roll (view of frankpledge only) for 1492–93

    Kent:

        Godmersham: rolls for 1418–19, 1424–25

    Oxfordshire:

        Finmere: rolls (most views of frankpledge only) for
            1501, 1562, 1563, 1564, 1565, 1566, 1567 (2), 1569,
            1570, 1571, 1572 (2), 1574 (2), 1575, 1576

    Warwickshire:

        Burton Dassett: rolls for 1606, 1622

3. *Compotus Rolls:*

    Cornwall:

        Tregair: roll for 1403–04

        Liskeard: roll for 1533–35

    Dorsetshire:

        Badbury: roll for 1535–36

    Essex:

        Belchamp: roll for 1513–14

    Kent:

        Godmersham: rolls for 1364–65, >1373

    Worcestershire:

        [Unidentified manor]: roll for ca.1475

4. *Rentals:*

    Buckinghamshire:

1493	Wotton Underwood
1620–22	Dadford
1630	Thornborough and Luffield
1632–33	Stanton [Bury?]
1634	Stowe
1649	Stowe
1658	Thornborough chantry lands
ca.1675	Stowe
ca.1675	Dadford with Gorrall and Westbury (2)
1682	Chetwode
1684	Chetwode and Lenborough
>1697	Stowe, with Dadford and Lamport ("The vicars halfe yeare dues")

    Cornwall:

1655	Treaga [Treagoe?]
1665	Tregavethan

    Oxfordshire:

1627	Finmere

>1637   Finmere with Great Barton
1647–48   Finmere, 10 pieces

Warwickshire:

1527   Burton Dassett (roll)
1572   Stockingford
1607   Burton Dasset with Northend, Knight-
           cote, and Radway
1653–1743   Burton Dassett (6 rolls, 12 other rentals
           and related papers)

Yorkshire:

1593–1608   Bedale with Askew
1687   Old Malton

Land in more than one county:

There are general rentals, chiefly for Temple lands in Buckinghamshire, Leicestershire, Oxfordshire, and Warwickshire, for 1580, 1658, 1675, >1697, 1712, 1715, 1733, and 1736–37.

Other miscellaneous rentals include those for all of the lands of the late Sir Edward Belknap (1540) and for the estates in Bedfordshire and Northampton-shire of Henry Mordaunt, 2nd Earl of Petersborough (ca.1671).

5. *Additional Items of Interest:*

Buckinghamshire:

1660: "The Value of each person's Estate of every Parish"

Channel Islands:

1660–89: Extracts from various documents concerning the government of the island of Jersey.

Somersetshire:

ca.1470–80: "The Antient Laws and Customs of Mendipp and touching the mineries and mineral works thereupon."

1713: A survey book of the lands of George Dodington

VII. Temple Personal and Family Papers
     ca.450 pieces, 1418–1790

The material in this category is fullest for the 17th century; there is surprisingly little from the time of Richard Temple, 1st Viscount Cobham. There are a large number of wills, together with marriage settlements, inquisitions, a few household record books and various agreements concerning the legal and financial affairs of the Temple and related families.

Listed below chronologically are all wills, *inquisitions post mortem,* marriage settlements, household record books, and selected additional items of interest or importance. Many of the documents are copies or drafts.

Wills:

1521	Sir Edward Belknap (3 copies)
1537	Thomas Heritage
1558	George Brooke, 9th Baron Cobham
1559	William Brooke
1568	Robert Temple
1571	Peter Temple (3 copies)
1571	John Alexander (alias Myllward)
1577, 1597	John Temple (d. 1603) (2 copies)
1582	Millicent Temple
1582	Edward Olney
1588	Edmunde Mannynge
1592	Thomas Sondes
1602	Emmanuel Newport
1605	Robert Brudenell
1606	Alice Hayton
1606	Giles Spencer (2 copies)
1611	Susan (Spencer) Temple
1612	Robert Aries
1614	William Gorges
1615	Richard Baker
1616	John Aries
1618	John Horley
1618	Alice Bawden
1620<, >1629	Henry Sandys
1621	William Greene
1623	Sir Arthur Throckmorton
1628	Lady Anne (Lucas) Throckmorton
1628–31	Thomas Petley (with codicil)
1631	Ambrose Warren
1632	John Temple
1633	Sir Thomas Temple, 1st Bart. (2 copies)
1634	Edward Barrett, 1st Baron Barrett

1638	Ralph Adams
1648	Hugh Ethersay
1648<, 1653	Lady Christian (Leveson) Temple (2 wills)
1649, 1653, 1654	Lady Hester (Sandys) Temple (3 wills)
1652	John Jones
>1653	Sir Peter Temple, 2nd Bart. (incomplete copy)
ca.1661	Sir Richard Leveson
1662	[ ] Opie (incomplete copy, father of Richard and Nicholas Opie)
1665	Williams Lambert
1672	Grace Greene
1673	Edward Hill
1675	Thomas Love
1678	Grace (Blake) Perry
1678	Hester (Clarke) Knapp
1679	William Stevens
1683–97	Sir Richard Temple, 3rd Bart. (4 copies, with codicils, and a variant codicil? of 1694)
1706	William Temple
1733	Bartholomew Paxton (2 copies)
1737–48	Richard Temple, 1st Viscount Cobham (4 copies)
1759	Anne (Halsey) Temple, Viscountess Cobham
1790	Elizabeth Irish

Inquisitions Post Mortem:

1488	Henry Belknap
1506	Nicholas Temple
ca.1512	Edward Belknap (Burton Dassett, Warws. only)
1548	John Dockary
1552	John Foxe
1559	Sir Henry Palmer (with writ of *diem clausit extremum*)
1576	Anthony Sondes
1578	Peter Temple (d. 1577)
1597	William Brooke, 10th Baron Cobham
1603	John Temple (d. 1603)

1604	George Brooke
1616	Sir John Leveson
1659	Sir Peter Temple, 2nd Bart.

Marriage settlements:

1547–1607	Marriage covenant for Sir Alexander Temple and Mary Langston
1582	For a marriage between John Croket and Frances Kingesmill (incomplete)
1588	For a marriage (never solemnized?) between Dorthy Temple and Edward Olney
1596	For a marriage between Martin Culpeper and Elizabeth Temple
>1600	For a marriage between George Stratford and Alice Shakerley
>1603	For a marriage (never solemnized?) between Edward Haselwood and Elizabeth Temple
1614	For a marriage between Sir Peter Temple, 2nd Bart., and Anne Throckmorton
1620<	For a marriage (never solemnized) between Sir Peter Temple, 2nd Bart., and Lady Anne (Sackville) Beauchamp
>1632	Part of a settlement between Edward Vaux, 4th Baron Vaux of Harrowden, and Elizabeth (Howard) Knollys, Countess of Banbury
1643<	For a marriage between Nicholas Knollys, 3rd Earl of Banbury, and Isabella Blount, daughter of the 1st Earl of Newport
1650	For a marriage between Weston Ridgeway, 1st Earl of Londonderry, and Frances Temple
1666	For a marriage between Edward Broughton and Martha Temple
1702	For a marriage between Richard West and Maria Temple
1715	For a marriage between Richard Temple, 1st Viscount Cobham, and Anne Halsey
1756	For a marriage between Sir Richard Temple, 7th Bart., and Anne Sophia Temple

Household Record Books:

1674–76 House Book of Sir Richard Temple, 3rd Bart.

1680–84 Day Book for Sir Richard Temple, 3rd Bart.

1688–91 London House Book for Sir Richard Temple, 3rd Bart.

1731–42 Four volumes of House Books for Richard Temple, 1st Viscount Cobham

1742–49 Cellar Book for Richard Temple, 1st Viscount Cobham

Additional items of interest or importance:

1537 Assignment by Thomas Heritage of wardship of Anthony Shyrley to Peter Temple and John Palmer

1604 Inquisition *de lunatico inquirendo* for Lady Margaret Sandys

1626 Draft of a speech by Sir Thomas Temple, 1st Bart., to be given on behalf of the King and the kingdom at Newport

1638 Copy of a welcome speech delivered to the Marquis of Hamilton, as the king's commissioner, by the Clergy of the Church of Scotland

1643 Account by Sir Thomas Hyde, 2nd Bart., of his usage while a prisoner in his journey with "my Lord General"

>1653 Names of the creditors of Sir Peter Temple, 2nd Bart., who have subscribed to an agreement with him re debts, with related papers

1661 Minutes of a Privy Council meeting relating to the marriage of James Duke of York (later James II)

1669 Copy of instructions by Charles II for the funeral of his mother Queen Henrietta Maria

VIII. TEMPLE SPECIAL SUBJECTS

1. *Customs: ca.25 pieces, 1660<–1718*

Papers stemming chiefly from the position of Sir Richard Temple, 3rd Bart., as one of the Commissioners of the Customs, including: his reports on the Customs operations at the ports of Poole and Portsmouth made during a survey of 1684; various petitions and depositions made to the Customs Commissioners; notes relating to the collection of customs, smuggling, imports, etc. Also a volume containing particulars of excise on liquor, etc., by the Commissioners of Excise, 1662–1718.

2. *Elections: ca.40 pieces, 1656?–90*
Chiefly papers concerning disputed elections of members of Parliament from the borough of Buckingham, 1680–90, including certificates, petitions, reports of the Committee of Privileges and Elections of the House of Commons, etc. Also includes: a Warwickshire election poll list for 1656; certificates returning Sir Richard Temple, 3rd Bart., as M.P. (1659, 1661); "A Rareshew or ye Monster of Stowe Wood—described in all his shapes more various than Proteus . . ." [concerning Sir Richard Temple, 3rd Bart., and the election of M.P.s for Buckinghamshire] 1679?; an order from Thomas Edgerley to his bailiffs concerning the meeting of a county court to elect knights of the shire for Buckinghamshire (1679); and a copy of William III's instructions to the Chief Magistrates of Buckinghamshire concerning the return of Members of Parliament.
See also Parliamentary Affairs, below.

3. *Foreign Affairs: 7 pieces, 1635–90 and n.d. (18th cent.)*
A very miscellaneous collection of papers dealing with foreign matters, including: a discussion of the situation in Bohemia, 1635?; a copy of the proceedings of the Council of State concerning the petition of M. de la Tour re Nova Scotia, 1656; a copy of the privileges granted by Louis XIV to the French East India Co., 1661<; a notification re customs in Amsterdam, 1672; a note "About Scots going to France," 1677; an extract from an article of the treaty between England and Savoy, 1690; a paper concerning cutting a canal in France, n.d. (18th cent.?).

4. *Genealogy: ca.50 pieces, ca.16th–19th centuries*
Pedigrees, coats of arms, and other genealogical papers concerning the Temple and related families, including those of Burdett, Lenthall, Belknap, Spencer, Sandys, Chapman, Draper, and Bentinck. Included are: a volume of pedigrees of the Temples of Stowe, with coats of arms in color, made

about 1650; extracts from parish registers; records of births, baptisms, and burials; an incomplete copy of the tomb inscription of Sir Thomas Temple; and a brief history of the Montfort family and title, made in the 18th century.

5. *Literature: 23 pieces, ca.1584–1732?*
A very miscellaneous and largely undated collection including: eulogies and epitaphs for various individuals, including an anagram for "Mistress Cisley Puckering"; fragments of poetry; political and occasional satires and other verse, including "Advice to a Painter" against the Earl of Arlington, "Hodge's Vision," "Dr. Wild's Ghost . . . ," "A Dialonge [sic] between ye K[ing] and Ld. S," a quatrain on the death of Peregrine Osborne, 2nd Duke of Leeds, and the hasty remarriage of his widow, and "An Inscription . . . for Laurence" Hyde, 1st Earl of Rochester; satirical poem of 10 couplets in French titled "Abjuration de L'Electeur de Saxe pour monter sur le Trone de Pologne;" and "The False Patriot unmasked, or a Short History of the Whigs . . ." by Sir Richard Temple, 3rd Bart., ca.1690.

6. *Military Affairs: ca.90 pieces, 1324–1732*
Chiefly 17th-century papers stemming from the position of the three Temple baronets as Sheriffs or Deputy Lieutenants of the county of Buckinghamshire, or from the role of Sir Peter, 2nd Bart., as Colonel of a troop of Parliamentary horse and a member of the Parliamentary Committee for Buckinghamshire during the Civil War. Included are papers concerning: general musters and assizes of arms; copies of letters from James I and Charles I to George Villiers, 1st Duke of Buckingham, re the militia, with his answers; the Parliamentary Committee for Buckinghamshire during the Civil War and the raising of horse; the Committee for Settling the Militia of 1660, with a list of officers' names and of those persons charged with finding foot soldiers and providing horses; various royal instructions re county militia; finances of the Restoration navy.

Of individual interest are: a 17th-century copy of an order of 1324 from Abp. Walter Reynolds to Henry de Cobham and others in Kent to take oaths and superintend the arming of inhabitants; a 1618 muster roll for Buckinghamshire; a petition of the maimed soldiers of Buckinghamshire to James Ley, 1st Earl of Marlborough, for payment of their pensions, 1622; a copy of Charles I's speech to the army, Sep. 19, 1642; a catalog [by Sir Peter Temple, 2nd Bart.?] "of such of their names as went to list themselves for souldiers . . . against the Parliament," 1642; "A List of the Land Forces" by William Blathwayt, 1695; a volume of proposals for the Royal Navy by Charles Cornwallis, 4th Baron Cornwallis, 1705/06; a list of the officers of Viscount Cobham's regiment, 1730–32.

7. Parliamentary Affairs: ca.140 pieces, 1330–1737
The majority of the parliamentary papers fall into the succes-sive periods when Sir Peter Temple, 2nd Bart., and his son Sir Richard, 3rd Bart., sat as Members of Parliament, that is, from 1640 to 1697. Included are: extracts from or notes concerning statutes, Parliamentary Rolls, and the Commons and Lords Journals on various topics; papers concerning the privileges of M.P.s or the House of Commons, *temp.* Charles I; copies of acts, some concerning commerce and customs; speeches or other representations made to Parliament (by John Finch, Baron Finch, in 1628, Charles I in 1628 and 1640, Philip Herbert, 4th Earl of Pembroke, ca.1640, Sir Francis Winnington, 1679, and Sir Richard Temple, 3rd Bart., >1697); a few papers concerning the lawsuits between Sir Peter Tem-ple, 2nd Bart., and his daughter and son-in-law, Viscount and Viscountess Baltinglass; papers concerning the proceedings of the Committee for Plundered Ministers in a dispute over the possession of the rectory of Leckhampstead, Buckingham-shire, 1646–48; petitions to Parliament concerning the debts of Sir Richard Temple, chiefly from his creditors; a few papers concerning the seditious charges brought against the 2nd Bart. by James Bastion in 1652; reports from various commit-tees of which the 3rd Bart. was a member, including those to consider preventing the sale of offices (1663), to inspect the various branches of royal revenues (1663), and to consider a bill for the supression of pedlars, hawkers, and petty chap-men (1685).

Also of individual interest are: an account of Parliament's dealings with Charles I concerning parliamentary privileges, 1641?; a petition to Parliament from Thomas Roper, 2nd Vis-

count Baltinglass, re the illegality of Sir Richard Temple, 3rd Bart., being an M.P. for Warwickshire while still a minor, 1654; the 3rd Bart.'s own account of the several sessions of Parliament, 1661–78; a petition to the House of Lords from George Digby, 2nd Earl of Bristol, against a breach of privilege by Edward Hyde, 1st Earl of Clarendon, 1663?; a report to the House of Lords from the Parliamentary Committee on Trade between England and Scotland, 1668; a list of the names of those members of the House of Commons "as did not sign the Association," 1696.
See also Elections, above

8. *Religious Affairs: 33 pieces, 1591–1713<*
Chiefly undated and anonymous 17th-century religious literature, including prayers, sermons, meditations, etc. Also includes: a warrant from the Court of High Commission authorizing Humphrey Cross to search and seize Papists with their books, letters, etc., 1616; Sir William Waad's "List of names of those who should not be disarmed if they attend divine service," >1623; a petition to Charles I from the Churches of Foreign Nations in London that they be considered free of the "taint of Calumpny," 1634; Abp. Michael Boyle's defense for putting Catholics into Commissions of the Peace in Ireland, >1685; and a copy of James II's speech concerning actions against Roman Catholics, Aug. 21, 1686.
See also Parliamentary Affairs, above, for papers re the proceedings of the Committee for Plundered Ministers in a dispute over the rectory of Leckhampstead, 1646–48.
N.B.: Numerous papers concerning presentations to livings (particularly in vicarages under the patronage of the Temples of Stowe, including Stowe, Thornborough, and Burton Dassett) and parish affairs will be found in the *Temple Manorial and Local Affairs Papers*.

9. *Ship Money Papers: ca.100 pieces, 1634–42*
Private and official papers concerning the collection of Ship Money in Buckinghamshire, for which Sir Peter Temple, 2nd Bart., was responsible in his capacity as sheriff of the county in 1635. Included are: notes and queries on legal matters concerning Ship Money; warrants to constables; abstracts of the King's writ; lists of towns and hundreds assessed, lists

of rates for assessment; returns made by the constables and assessors; receipts for Ship Money collected; and miscellaneous notes and papers concerning the administration of the writ.

10. *Miscellaneous Papers: ca.20 pieces, ca.1583–1810*

A very miscellaneous collection of papers, chiefly of the 17th century, including among other pieces: A "Recipe for a physick," ca.1583; an explanation by the Merchant Adventurers Company of the objections of English merchants in Hamburg to signing the Solemn League and Covenant, 1645; an account of the escape of Charles II from England after the battle of Worcester, ca.1660?; notes on the Navigation Act and on trade between England and Scotland, 1668–72; a proposal made to Charles II re the awarding of places in the government; "Some proposalls to be taken into Consideracion att our meeteinge" [re the Cavalier Club?]; "Directions for setting up ye Aereoscope [Baroscope?] or quicksilver weather glass," 17th cent.?; a description and wax impression of the seal of the Treasurer of the Monastery of St. Augustine, Canterbury [by James Gomme?], 1810.

Brydges Papers (ca.15,800 pieces)

The Brydges papers at the Library span basically only three generations, and in contrast to the Grenville and Temple subcollections the early material here is both the most extensive and the most interesting. The first and most important of the three Brydges dukes of Chandos, James Brydges (1673–1744) was the eldest son of the 8th Baron Chandos of Sudeley. He was an M.P. for Hereford (1698–1714) and a successful trimmer, following the Tories under Anne and the Whigs under the first two Georges. Brydges served as Paymaster General of the Forces Abroad (1705–13), from which he turned a sizeable profit, and held the sinecure post of reversionary Clerk of the Hanaper, 1714, from which he expected but failed to realize still greater benefit. He was Governor of the Turkey Company (1718–36), interested in the Royal African Company, and Lord Lieutenant of Herefordshire and Radnor (1721–42). Created Earl of Carnarvon in 1714 and Marquis of Carnarvon and Duke of Chandos in 1719, he built the fabulous mansion of Canons, in Little Stanmore, Middlesex, and was noted as a patron of literature and the arts. Handel spent two years there (1718–20) composing music for the chapel.

The Duke married three times: his first wife, Mary Lake, died in 1712; his second, Cassandra Willoughby, was a second cousin and died in 1735; his third, the wealthy widow Lydia Catherine (van Hatten) Davall, brought him another fortune and survived him to die in 1750. His son James, styled Marquis of Carnarvon, died in 1727, and the 1st Duke's only surviving son (also by his first wife), Henry Brydges (1708–71), succeeded as 2nd Duke of Chandos in 1744. He was a courtier, and like his father held the Clerkship of the Hanaper, but played little role in politics or in the arts. Canons was sold shortly after the 1st Duke's death to pay off debts caused in part by speculation in stock, and the family took up residence at Avington in Hampshire, inherited from a cousin. The 2nd Duke, like his father, married thrice: in 1728 Mary Bruce (d. 1738), daughter of the 3rd Earl of Ailesbury; in 1744 Anne (Wells) Jefferies (d. 1759), his former mistress; and finally in 1767 Elizabeth Major, daughter of Sir John Major, Bart., who survived him to die in 1813.

James Brydges, 3rd Duke of Chandos (1732–89), the 2nd Duke's only son by his first wife, succeeded his father in 1771 and from his maternal grandfather inherited the title Lord Kinloss. He was a Whig M.P. for Winchester (1754–61) and for Radnor (1761–68) during his father's lifetime, held posts at Court as a Lord of the Bedchamber to George III (1760–64) and Lord Steward of the Household (1783–89), and served as Lord Lieutenant for Hampshire in 1763–64 and 1771–80. The 3rd Duke married first, in 1753, the heiress Margaret Nicol. After her death in 1768, he married in 1777 Anne Eliza (Gamon) Elletson, the daughter of Richard Gamon and widow of Roger Hope Elletson, Governor of Jamaica (1766–69) and owner of the Hope and Middleton plantations there. The 3rd Duke had no male heirs, and at his death in 1789 the dukedom became extinct. The barony of Kinloss, however, descended along with his estates and fortune to his only surviving daughter Anna Elizabeth, who married Richard Grenville, later 1st Duke of Buckingham and Chandos.

I. BRYDGES ACCOUNTS AND FINANCIAL PAPERS
ca.10,300 pieces, 1620–1813

Most of the papers in this category belong to the time of the 2nd and 3rd dukes of Chandos; apart from the individual volumes listed below there is disappointingly little material from the time of the 1st Duke.

1. *Estate Accounts (ca.2,900 pieces)* are strongest for Hampshire (chiefly at Avington), with much additional material for Middlesex (including Canons and Minchenden House) and Somerset (chiefly Keynsham and Rodney Stoke), and some accounts for Brydges' properties in Cheshire, Herefordshire, and Radnorshire. Included are both summary accounts (by estate officials) and individual bills, receipts, pay vouchers, etc., for the multiplicity of goods, labor, and services connected with the operation of a major estate. There are records of building and repair work (masons, bricklayers, carpenters, glaziers, etc.), farm and garden labor, livestock and dairy production, wood sales, milk and brickmaking, blacksmiths, etc. Also included are receipts and accounts for rents, tithes, and local taxes and levies. There are some papers relating to Brydges' mines and mineral interests in Derbyshire (1746–1813), and receivers' accounts for the estates of the Dowager Duchess Anne Eliza, adjudged a lunatic.

Separate volumes of accounts include: 1st Duke's account of workmen employed on new works and in keeping the gardens at Canons (2 vols., 1720–25); 1st Duke's accounts with various tradesmen for work at Canons (1721–23); account of stock and produce for the Brydges family, presented by George Baxter (4 vols., 1726–30); 2nd Duke's farm accounts (1756–64); book of rents, taxes, and general estate and personal accounts kept for the 2nd Duke by Sir William Hillman (1768–72) and a similar volume, also by Hillman, for the 3rd Duke (1772–76).

2. *Household Accounts (ca.6,600 pieces)* pertain chiefly to Avington (with the exception of a few early pieces for Canons) and consist of bills, receipts, summary accounts, etc. for servants' wages and liveries, furniture and other household furnishings, food and drink, entertainment, garden supplies,

general housekeeping expenses, traveling expenses, etc. Most of the accounts for later years are in their original monthly packets.

Separate volumes of accounts include: 1st Duke's stable expenses (2 vols., 1704–14); 1st duke's receipt book for wages paid to employees (1718–20); 1st Duke's account of payments to servants and tradesmen (kept by Walter Fergusson?) (1722–32); 1st Duke's accounts with Walter Fergusson, house steward at Canons (1729–35); house bills for Marquis of Carnarvon (later 3rd Duke of Chandos) (1759–63).
See also Brydges Personal and Family Papers, p. 242, for related volumes.

3. *Personal Accounts (ca.800 pieces)* include 17th-century material for families related to the Brydges (including Keck and Poole family and John Nicolls), but little Brydges material proper until 1720. Included are accounts for clothing, books, newspapers, stationery, schooling, gifts, travel, charities, pictures, feasts given for tenants, etc. Also included are business and legal accounts, chiefly bonds, with additional accounts of debts and investments and some bills for legal services.

Separate volumes include: Margaret Poole's cash book of annuities and other personal accounts and transactions (2 vols., 1708–19); 1st Duke's accounts with brokers, etc. (4 vols., of which the last includes adjusted accounts as Paymaster General, 1711–44); account book of Lydia Catherine, Duchess of Chandos (1736–74); accounts of the 3rd Duke with the firm of Messrs. Hoare (1765–77).

II. BRYDGES CORRESPONDENCE
ca.2,170 pieces, 1670<–1812

The correspondence deals with the full range of family, personal, business, estate, financial, and some political affairs of the 1st, 2nd, and 3rd dukes of Chandos, their family, and associates. Of particular interest are: letters to and from Duchess Cassandra, with her copy letterbook; over 800 letters from the 1st Duke to his principal secretary and steward James Farquharson, 1727–44, and over 70 letters to Farquharson from the 2nd Duke; over 300 business letters addressed to the 3rd Duke, more than half of them by James Coulthard of Lincolns' Inn, dealing with financial, estate, and other business and legal affairs; approximately 200 letters concerning the Jamaican estates of Anne Eliza (Gamon) Elletson Brydges, Duchess of Chandos; and some early correspondence dealing with the Keck and other families.

In addition to the individual letters in this category (the authors of some of which are listed below), there are 57 volumes of out-letterbooks from the 1st Duke, covering the period 1694–1744, and another 14 volumes of in-letterbooks for the shorter period 1700–12; this correspondence is also broad ranging in topic, from personal and business to political, but of particular interest are the letters to and from William Cadogan, Marlborough's quarter-master-general, Adam de Cardonnel, Marlborough's secretary, and Marlborough himself, during the War of the Spanish Succession. There are also 2 volumes of letters of Roger Hope Elletson, to and from Jamaica, covering the years 1769–76.

Persons represented by five or more letters (excluding the separate letterbooks) are listed below:

Alexander, William (12)
Black, W. (13)
Brydges, Cassandra (Willoughby), Duchess of Chandos (25)
Brydges, Henry, 2nd Duke of Chandos (111)
Brydges, James (29)
Brydges, James, 1st Duke of Chandos (816)
Brydges, James, 3rd Duke of Chandos (52)
Brydges, Mary (Bruce), Marchioness of Carnarvon (17)
Chamberlayne, Emma (Brydges) (5)
Cornwallis, Letitia (24)
Coulthard, James (181)
Davison, Jacob (12)
East, Edward (65)
Flood, Henry (6)
Graham, Thomas (40)
Hibbert, Robert (23)
Hibbert, Fuhr & Hibbert (firm) (18)
Hibbert, Purrier & Co. (firm) (28)
Hillman, William (19)
Hume, Sir Abraham, 1st Bart. (8)
Kearney, Lady Augusta Anne (Brydges) (14)
Lee, Robert Cooper (11)
Leigh, Lady Caroline (Brydges) (43)

Leigh, James (65)
Pool, John (26)
Price, Henry (8)
Robinson, Emma (Charlton) Cornwallis (6)
Tomkinson, James (29)
Williams, William Peere (5)

The Library has also acquired (from Mrs. Inez Dacres of Bath in 1958) an additional 49 Brydges letters, chiefly from Francis Brydges to William Brydges, 1719–31.

III. BRYDGES DEEDS (Partial listing)
  794 pieces, 1554–1803
The principal Brydges estates were located in Hampshire and Somersetshire, and the vast majority of deeds belong to the 18th century.* Surprisingly, there are few deeds for either Canons, the 1st Duke's famous mansion in Little Stanmore, Middlesex, or Avington House in Hampshire, which became the family seat after the loss of Canons.

The following places, listed by county with covering dates, appear in five or more deeds:
  Hampshire:
        Abbotts Ann (6) 1768–73
        Andover (49) 1749–75
        Appleshaw (15) 1766–73
        East Wellow (14) 1707–ca.1775?
        Easton (16) 1605–1754
        Martyr Worthy (5) 1605–1723
  London:
        St. Sepulchre's parish (5) 1722–23
  Somerset:
        Bawdrip (18) 1760–1802
        Bridgwater (10) 1726–1802
        Burnham (8) 1760–75
        Catcott (118) 1712–71
        Cheddar (14) 1712–69
        Compton Martin (63) 1672–1776?

---

* *See also* Stowe Unsorted Deeds, below pp. 255–62.

      Crandon cum Puriton (22) 1712–75
      Draycott (13) 1672–1769
      Edington (8) 1760–64
      Huntspill (19) 1712–75
      Keynsham (68) 1554–1786
      Priddy (9) 1753–71
      Puriton (11) 1760–76 (*See also* Crandon cum Puriton)
      Rodney Stoke (37) 1665–1803
      Saltford (21) 1760–84
      Tiverton (29) 1760–84
      Wedmore (132) 1712–74

IV. Brydges Inventories, Lists, and Catalogs

ca.30 pieces, ca.1705–1815

Chiefly lists or schedules of deeds and other papers re Brydges estates or affairs, with a few lists and inventories of household and personal goods. Among the more interesting items are:

1720	Pepusch, John Christopher. "Catalogue of [musical] instruments . . . and anthems . . . belonging to the Duke of Chandos." In the hand of Mr. Noland. 1 vol.
1725	A volume containing floor plans, dimensions, and room-by-room inventories of the 1st Duke of Chandos' seat at Canons and his house in St. James Square, London, made by John Gilbert.
1737	An alphabetical account of the Library at Avington [with other notes, accounts, lists of hounds' names, etc.] 1 vol.
1748	A catalog of the books of John Nicoll at Baddesley.
1753	Inventory of Plate & Jewels delivered by John Vanhattem to James Brydges, 3rd Duke of Chandos, as Marquis of Carnarvon, with valuations.
ca.1753?	List of estates of James Brydges, 3rd Duke of Chandos, as Marquis of Carnarvon.
1766–69	Inventories of pictures at Avington, 3 pieces.
1772	An Inventory of the household furniture of Lady Elizabeth (Bruce) Bathurst, deceased, with appraisals.

1772   An inventory of the goods of Henry, 2nd Duke
        of Chandos.

V. BRYDGES LEGAL PAPERS

ca.215 pieces, 1640–1814

Most of the papers in this category date from the lifetime of
James Brydges, 1st Duke of Chandos, or from the years after the
death of the 3rd Duke and during the lunacy of his last Duchess.
There are very few formal lawsuits (less than 30, chiefly concerning lands, inheritances, and debts), but many legal opinions on
various aspects of the Brydges family affairs, including material
on the York Buildings Company during the 1720s and mines and
mineral rights during the 1730s. No one individual appears in
as many as five separate lawsuits; the 3rd Duke comes closest
with four.

Among the more interesting or important cases and other legal
papers are:

Opinion by Philip Yorke, afterward Lord Chancellor and 1st
Earl of Hardwicke, re the charter of the Royal African
Co. with an extract from a letter of Governor Hereford
and a copy of grant of territories from the Crown to the
Company. 1723

"A copy of ye case propos'd to be sent to ye Solicitor-General
for his opinion relating to ye Contract depending between
ye York Buildings Co. and ye Charitable Corporation." 1725

Opinion by Thomas Lutwycke on the "case of a Minor's sitting
in Parliament." 1728

Opinions of Nicholas Fazakerley and Humphrey Henchman
on "ye University statutes relating to ye time required &
indulg'd to noblemen's sons in taking their degrees," with
copies of the relevant University statutes. 1739

Attorney-General *v.* James Brydges, Marquis of Carnarvon
(afterward the 3rd Duke of Chandos) *et al.* re estates in
Ireland. 1761

Richard Grenville, 1st Duke of Buckingham and Chandos,
and Anna Elizabeth, his wife, *v.* Anne Eliza (Gamon) Elletson Brydges, Duchess of Chandos, a lunatic, re problems
arising from the latter's lunacy. Heard in Chancery. 1794<–
1813

VI. BRYDGES MANORIAL AND LOCAL AFFAIRS PAPERS
   ca.580 pieces, 1382–1863
Although the Brydges family held land in several counties, the vast majority of their holdings were centered in Hampshire (at Avington), Middlesex (at Canons in Little Stanmore) and Somersetshire (chiefly at Keynsham and Rodney Stoke).

   Listed below by county are: all places represented by five or more pieces, with covering dates and selected pieces of interest; all court rolls, rentals, and compotus rolls; selected additional items of interest or significance.

   1. *Places represented by five or more pieces:*
      Berkshire:
         Shaw: 10 pieces, 1722–ca.1750
      Hampshire:
         Avington: 37 pieces, 1382–1789
            Includes: 17th-cent. copy of a document, titled "The Bounedry of ye Manour of Avington made in King Edgars daies anno domini DCCCCLXI"; a list of the inhabitants of Avington parish, 1765; and a list of persons desiring to be inoculated in Avington parish, 1773.
         East Wellow: 11 pieces, 1660–ca.1760 (many with West Wellow in Wiltshire)
         Southhampton: 13 pieces, 1669–1766
         Winchester: 13 pieces, 1753–1825
            Includes: a "General view of the Constitution [of Winchester] and the present situation of the Bow with respect to the Aldermen," 1770; lists of Grand Jurors at the Summer Assizes at Winchester, 1770–76.
      See also Brydges Parliamentary Affairs papers, below, p. 244.
      Middlesex:
         Stanmore (Great and/or Little): 18 pieces, 1738–1863
            Includes sketches, reports, and other papers re Brydges family memorials in the church of St. Lawrence Whitchurch, 8 pieces, ca.1840–63
      Somerset:
         Catcott: 16 pieces, 1698–1776
            Includes homage roll from court records, 1724
         Compton Martin: 10 pieces, 1720-n.d. (18th cent.)

Huntspill: 8 pieces, 1706–75
Keynsham: 15 pieces, 1626–n.d. (18th cent.)
Rodney Stoke: 21 pieces, 1650–1785
Saltford: 6 pieces, 1685–87
Wiltshire:
West Wellow, 11 pieces, 1665–ca.1760 (many with East
Wellow in Hampshire)

2. *Court Rolls:*
Gloucestershire:
Adlestrop & Longborough (1): 1623–36 (a courtbook
of 42 ff.)
Hampshire:
Avington (7): 1382, 1390, 1481, 1509–10, 1524–25, 1566,
1575–76
Middlesex:
Stanmore (Great & Little) (1): courtbook, 1758–82

3. *Compotus Rolls:*
Hampshire:
Avington (5): 1434–35, 1445, 1452–53, 1535–36, 1542.

4. *Rentals:*
Berkshire:
Particular and rental of part of the estate of the late
Viscount Bolingbroke, at Henwick, Thatcham, and
Colthrop, 1721 (printed)
Gloucestershire:
Rental of the manors of Ashton and Grafton, ca.1730?
Hampshire:
Rental of [Keck or Nicoll?] property in Baddesley,
Townhill, Southampton, Ramsey, and the Isle of
Wight, 1735
Rental of Itchen Abbas *et al.,* 1760
Rental & particular of tenants at Avington, 1763
Quit-rent roll for Bighton, 1772–73
Rental for Hants. properties, 1773
Rent-roll of the estate of Henry Grey at Ecchinswell
and Kingsclere, n.d. (18th cent.) (printed)
Lancashire:
Rental of property of Catherine Lawthers in Fur-
ness, 1756
Middlesex:
Quit-rent roll for Middlesex lands, 1713–25

Quit-rent rolls for Great Stanmore, 1741, and for Stanmore, 1749

Radnorshire:

Rental of some lots for sale, 1771

Somerset:

Rental for Somerset lands, 1767

Rental for Draycott, Westbury, Priddy, and Wedmore, arranged alphabetically by tenant's name, ca.1771

Rental for Huntspill, Catcott, and Crandon, ca.1775

Rental of the Somerset estates of Anne Eliza, Duchess of Chandos, 1808<

Ireland:

Rental for Villierstown, Co. Waterford, 1793–97

Rental for Villiers, [i.e., Villars Estate, Co. Leix?], 1792

Lands in More than One County:

Rental of the estates of the Duke of Chandos in Herefs., Middx., Gloucs., Hants., and Radnor, 1719–20

Rental of the estates of George Rodney Brydges, 3 pieces, 1728

Abstract of rentals of lands of Duke of Chandos in various counties, 1728

Rental of East Wellow, Hants., and West Wellow, Wilts., 1751

Rent roll of the London and Middlesex estates of the Marquis of Carnarvon, 1754

Rent roll of the estates of the Marquis of Carnarvon in Radnor, Middx., London, Cheshire, Hants., Lincs., Soms., Sussex, and Worcs., 1754

"Rental of the estates of the Duke of Chandos [in Hants. and Soms.] in the collection of William Hillman," 1777?

Rentals for lands in Hants. and Soms., 2 pieces, 1780, 1786

5. *Additional Items of Interest:*

Hampshire:

List of Deputy Lieutenants for the county, with list of other offices and their values, 2 pieces, 1763

"State of the Hampshire Boroughs," 1763

Lists of Justices of the Peace for Hants., 6 pieces, 1763?

List of the jurors at the March Assizes at Alton, Bishops Sutton, etc., 1771

Somerset:

An account of the estates in Somerset belonging to the Duke of Chandos, with observations, by William Hillman, 1773

Survey of the Manor of Rodney Stoke, 1775

Particular of the Duke of Chandos' estates at Keynsham, Saltford, and Tiverton

Particular of the Duke of Chandos' estate at Batcombe, 1781

Particular of the Duke of Chandos' estate at Keynsham, 1781

List of Grand Jurors for the Assizes [for Soms.?], n.d. (18th cent.)

General:

List of land purchases made for the Duke of Chandos by Francis Peters, 1713–31

Four volumes of "Contract Books" of Henry Brydges, 2nd Duke of Chandos, with James, Marquis of Carnarvon (afterward the 3rd Duke), containing copies of contracts entered into with various people, chiefly for leases on the Brydges estates, 1760–71

See also Stowe Brydges West Indies Estates papers for additional manorial papers concerning the Jamaican estates of Duchess Anne Eliza, inherited from her husband Roger Hope Elletson

VII. BRYDGES PERSONAL AND FAMILY PAPERS
   ca.210 pieces, 1416–1847

The material in this category is strongest for the 18th century, and pertains chiefly to the wills and marriage settlements (with other property settlements) of the three dukes of Chandos and their immediate families. Related families include, among others, those of Leigh, Thistlethwaite, and Bathurst. Also included are diaries and journals of the Brydges family, and a few papers concerning the Brydges households at Canons (Middlesex), and London, including household managements and record books. There are numerous papers concerning the lunacy of the 3rd Duke's wife, Duchess Anne Eliza, and the resulting legal complications. Listed below are all wills and marriage settlements (many copies or drafts), diaries, journals, and commonplace books, household books, and a few additional selected items of interest.

Wills:

1416	Lady Margaret (Reincourt) Cromwell
1573	Edmund Brydges, 2nd Baron Chandos of Sudeley
1659	William Leigh
1691–96	Thomas Preston (with codicils)
1695	Elizabeth Coleman
1705	Sir Thomas Brydges
1705–07	Sir Thomas Brydges (with codicils)
1714–17	Richard Norton (with codicils)
1715–18	George Brydges (with codicils)
1728–47	George Brydges (with codicils)
1735	William Mundy
1739	Thomas Baker, of Easton, Hants.
1742–44	James Brydges, 1st Duke of Chandos (with codicils, probate, summaries, and schedules)
1748	Charles Seymour, 6th Duke of Somerset
1750	George Brydges
1755	Sir William Lowther, 3rd Bart. (abstract only)
1760	Lady Elizabeth (Bruce) Bathurst
1764–71	James Brydges, 3rd Duke of Chandos (with codicils)
1766	George Coningsby
1766	John Brown
1766	Robert Thistlethwayte
1766	Edward Pugh
1766	Ann Froud
1766	Henry Brydges, 2nd Duke of Chandos
1770	James Walter
1770	Jane Bird
1780–82	James Brydges, 3rd Duke of Chandos (with codicil and probate)
1789	Anne Eliza (Gamon) Elletson Brydges, Duchess of Chandos

1818   Gamon, Sir Richard Grace-, 1st Bart. (probate only)

Marriage Settlements:

1661   For the marriage of Sir Francis Holles, later 2nd Baron Holles, and Lucy Carr, da. of Sir Robert Carr

1672   For the marriage of Harry Brydges and Lady Diance Holles

1689   For the marriage of Theophilus Leigh and Lady Mary Brydges

1692   For the marriage of Francis Keck and Jane Dunch

1712   For the marriage of George Brydges and Anne Wolfe

1717   For the marriage of [Harry Brydges?] and Elizabeth Freeman

1717   For the marriage of John Lowther and Jane Jeffreys Lowther

1722   For the marriage of Mary Lord and William Leigh

1722   For the marriage of Cassandra Willoughby and James Brydges, Duke of Chandos (abstract only)

1723   For the marriage of Lady Elizabeth Cavendish and Sir Thomas Lowther, 2nd Bart.

1734   Subsequent to the marriage of Henry Brydges, later 2nd Duke of Chandos, and Lady Mary Bruce

1753?   Proposals for a marriage of Margaret Nicol and James Brydges, 3rd Duke of Chandos

1755?   Memoranda re settlement on marriage of Lady Caroline Brydges and James Leigh

1767   For the marriage of Henry Brydges, 2nd Duke of Chandos, and Elizabeth Major

1777   For the marriage of James Brydges, 3rd Duke of Chandos, and Anne Eliza (Gamon) Elletson

1778   For the marriage of Henry John Kearney and Lady Augusta Ann Brydges

1784   For the marriage of Henry John Kearney and Ann Banks (abstract only)

Diaries, Journals and Commonplace Books:

1697–1702   Brydges, James, 1st Duke of Chandos. Journal of daily actions. 2 vols.

1732–71   Brydges, Henry, 2nd Duke of Chandos. Diary. 10 vols.

1743   [Brydges, George?]. Journal of a voyage from Spain to Flanders. 1 vol.

1751–88   Brydges, James, 3rd Duke of Chandos. Diary. 4 vols.

1757<   Brydges, James, 3rd Duke of Chandos. Memoranda and Commonplace Book, including miscellaneous notes re history, activities, etc.

Household Books:

1718–31   Wine Books for London and Canons. 3 vols.

1721   Brydges, James, 1st Duke of Chandos. Instructions to his servants (including a list of the household at Canons and the steward's recommendations to the Duke at the Audit Board)

1721–22   Book of strangers dining at Canons

1721–38   Minutes of the Audit Board for Canons

Additional items of interest:

1719   Levett, Henry *et al.* Account of the post mortem examination of Elizabeth (Barnard) Brydges, Lady Chandos

1734   Brydges, James, 1st Duke of Chandos. Contract with Howard the gardener "for keeping the gardens & for doing the office of a Bailiff at Cannons."

1755   Oath of a Privy Councillor taken by James Brydges, 3rd Duke of Chandos. (copy)

1791–1813   Legal and other papers concerning the maintenance and estates of Duchess Anne Eliza, a lunatic. 35 pieces

VIII. BRYDGES SPECIAL SUBJECTS

    1. *Genealogy: ca.100 pieces, ca.16th–19th centuries*

Pedigrees and other genealogical material concerning the Brydges and related families, including those of Chandos, Stanley (earls of Derby), Scudamore, Twistleton, Woodville (earls Rivers), Pescod, and Mildmay. Included are notes of burials, tomb inscriptions, a few extracts from parish registers, papers concerning the claims of the Brydges to the barony of Bruce and of other claims to the barony of Kinloss and to the viscountcy of Mayo, and to the claim of the Duke of Atholl to the barony of Strange. Also included is an account by Elizabeth (Barnard) Brydges, Baroness Chandos, of the births, marriages, and deaths of the family, with additional notes by other family members, ca.1668–1768, and an account by Joseph Edmonson of arms belonging to the Duke of Chandos, 1764<.

2. *Hanaper Accounts: ca.1,100 pieces, 1680–1772*
In 1728 the 1st Duke of Chandos became Clerk of the Hanaper of Chancery (the reversionary rights to which office he had obtained in 1714); he was succeeded in office by his son, Henry, the 2nd Duke, who held the post until his own death in 1771. The 1st Duke also obtained the farm of the Six-Penny Writ Office in Chancery about 1729, although neither this nor the Hanaper clerkship brought the profits for which he had hoped.

Included in the Brydges papers are yearly Hanaper account rolls from 1728–29 to 1770–71 (excepting only the years 1747–48, 1753–54, 1755–56, 1756–57, 1757–58, 1759–60, 1767–68, 1768–69, and 1769–70).

Also included are lesser series of accounts, not always consecutive (some copies or drafts), such as: private monthly accounts of the Clerk and Keeper of the Hanaper (1728–36); accounts of casual and dividend fees of the Lord Chancellor (1728–71), the Master of the Rolls (1729–71), the Six Clerks (1738–71), the Clerk Comptroller (1729–61), the Sealer (1728–71), the Chaffwax (1728–71), and the Examiner (1729–71); a few papers related to the Six-Penny Writ Office (1727?–47); receipts for legacies and annuities (1745–72); and other miscellaneous accounts and papers related to the Chancery offices.

3. *Literature: 6 pieces, 1697–1778<*
Commonplace book of James Brydges, 1st Duke of Chandos, containing observations out of the Old and New Testament, also out of Lord Bacon's Essays and Fuller's Holy State. [Also contains lists of English forces 1693, of ships lost or damaged 1688–91, of Secret Service money paid to M.P.s, and a note of Exchequer receipts and payment, 1691]. 1697

Transcript of "verses . . . seal'd . . . to the blank leaf opposite to the title page of Dr. [Edward] Young's *Universal Passion*, Satire the last . . . which seem to be the Dr.'s own hand." Addressed to James Brydges, 1st Duke of Chandos. 1728<

Draft of a memorial ode (?) "Sacred to the Memory . . ." of Anne (Wells) Jeffries Brydges, Duchess of Chandos. 1759

A volume of notes by James Brydges, 3rd Duke of Chandos, on volumes 4 and 5 of Clarendon's *History of the Rebellion*. 1760

Extract from Samuel Johnson and George Steevens' edition of Shakespeare. 2 pieces, 1778<

4. *Military Affairs: 27 pieces, 1763–75*
Papers of the Hampshire Militia. Included are returns of the North and South Battalions and lists of officers during the period 1763 to 1775 (incomplete runs).
See also the 1st Duke's Commonplace Book, described under *Literature* above.

5. *Parliamentary Affairs: 8 pieces, 1660–1783*
Printed copy of the speech of George Digby, 2nd Earl of Bristol, in the House of Lords on the Bill of Indemnity, 1660

Lists of freemen of the Borough of Winchester, Hants., and related papers re elections in Winchester, 6 pieces, 1753–83

Excerpts from [John Church's?] "Memorials of the Method and Manner of Proceedings in Parliament . . ." re privileges granted to servants of M.P.s ca.1766
See also the 1st Duke's Commonplace Book, described under *Literature* above.

6. *Paymaster-General Accounts: 5 vols, 1705–13*
Five volumes of the accounts of James Brydges, 1st Duke of Chandos, as Paymaster-General of the Forces in Flanders, Spain, and Portugal. 1705–13

7. *West Indies Estates: ca.300 pieces, 1689–1816*
In addition to ca.200 letters concerning the Brydges interests in Jamaica, the collection contains legal, financial, and estate

papers (chiefly 1754–88) for the Hope and Middleton Plantations of Roger Hope Elletson, first husband of the future
Duchess of Chandos. Included are: maps, plans, and descriptions of the Hope and Middleton Plantations; accounts of
rum and sugar production, and of other financial matters,
for Roger Hope Elletson's plantations and for other properties
of the Elletson family; lists of slaves; lists of stock and supplies; legal papers concerned with water rights to the Hope
River.

Also a few miscellaneous earlier items, including among
others: a Declaration of Account of Thomas Foxe, late Re-
ceiver-General of H. M. Customs, for Barbados, Nevis, Mont-
ferrat, and St. Christophers, 1689–91; an inventory of the
slaves and stock of William Downing on Weston Hall and
Woodbury plantations, 1724; an address by the Grand Jury
and Council Board of Jamaica to Governor Sir Thomas Robinson in support of his conduct, 1746 (printed); an account of
Jamaican produce exported to Great Britain and North America in 1767.
See also Grenville West Indies Estates papers

8. *Miscellaneous: ca.35 pieces, 1720–1910?*
Notes, papers, volumes, etc., touching on a wide variety of
subjects, the most interesting of which are listed chronologically below.

> Copies of proposals, orders, and other papers concerning
> the South Sea Co., with a list of extra clerks in the
> service of the company. 4 pieces, 1720–21
> A commentary on two ancient shields . . . of Brydges
> and Chandos now affix'd in the . . . chappel at Windsor.
> 1724
> A volume of copies of documents and papers concerning
> the Royal African Company ca.1660–1723, made for the
> 1st Duke of Chandos. ca.1725
> Hill, James. The annals of the most noble families of
> Bruges [i.e., Brydges] and Chandos. <1726
> A volume titled "A Collection of remarkable papers"
> including copies of papers concerning the Royal Afri-
> can Company, Mary Queen of Scots, and estate man-
> agement. ca.1735?

Nugent Papers (ca.2,100 pieces)

Of the four main families at Stowe, the Nugents are the least well represented in the collection. Robert Nugent (ca.1702–88), 1st Earl Nugent, came from an Irish family with lands in Carlanstown, Co. Westmeath. He served as M.P. for St. Mawes (1741–54, 1774–84) and Bristol (1754–74) as a Whig until 1770, and a Tory thereafter, and was appointed a Lord of the Treasury (1754–59), Vice Treasurer of Ireland (1759–65, 1768–82), and First Lord of Trade (1776–68). Nugent married first, in 1730, Emilia Plunkett, who died the following year. His second marriage, in 1737, to Anna (Craggs) Newsham Knight, brought him both wealth and political influence. Her father was John Craggs, one of the Postmasters General, and her second husband, John Knight, of Gosfield Hall in Essex, was a prominent Member of Parliament with considerable interest in the colonial trade, particularly with the West Indies. After Anna's death in 1756 Nugent was married a third time, to Elizabeth (Drax) Berkeley, Dowager Countess of Berkeley. In 1775 Nugent's eldest daughter and co-heiress, Mary Elizabeth, married George Grenville, afterward 1st Marquis of Buckingham; the following year he was created Earl Nugent, with a special remainder to his son-in-law. He died in 1788 at Gosfield Hall, which thus came along with other Knight lands into the Grenville family.

I. NUGENT ACCOUNTS AND FINANCIAL PAPERS

ca.1,100 pieces, 1695–1803

The largest group of papers in this category belongs to the first half of the 18th century and deals with the personal and financial affairs of the Nugent family, consisting of bonds, promissory notes, acquittances, orders to pay, receipts for annuities, bills and receipts concerning legal settlements, and miscellaneous accounts. Included is Lord Clare's receipt book (1768–72).

Also included are some 350 items pertaining to the financial affairs of John Knight, covering the years 1702–42, consisting of bonds, receipts, banking papers, and records of his commercial and investment activities (including South Sea Company material relating to James Craggs). There are also four account rolls of William Knight, as Paymaster, of orders to pay annuities disbursed under an Act of Parliament (1695–97), as well as a cash account book probably belonging to John Knight (1725–33).

Most of the estate and household accounts pertain to Gosfield Hall, Essex, during the middle of the 18th century, and include two volumes of rent accounts (1744–48 and 1767–1803), a cash book (1764–67) and book of disbursements (1763), two journal accounts (1764–65 and 1765–79), and a wood book (1775–98).

II. NUGENT CORRESPONDENCE

317 pieces, 1672<–1784

The correspondence deals chiefly with the family and business affairs of Robert Craggs Nugent, 1st Earl Nugent, and his circle. Of particular interest is a series of 35 letters addressed to John Knight concerning his business, legal, and estate affairs. Those authors represented by five or more letters are listed below.

Baker, John (10)
Chevers, Christopher (6)
Cleeve, Richard (6)
Collier, John (7)
Delamar, Peter (5)
Eliot, Richard (10)
Fetherston, Thomas (7)
Martin, Elizabeth (7)
Montague, Mary (Churchill) (5)
Nugent, James (8)
Nugent, John (6)
Nugent, Mary Ann (10)
Nugent, Robert, of Bobsgrove (8)
Nugent, Robert Craggs, 1st Earl Nugent (6)
Palles, Ignatius (8)

III. NUGENT DEEDS (Partial listing)

57 pieces, 1609–1788

Listed below are the number of deeds concerning land in various counties. *See also* Stowe Unsorted Deeds, below, pp. 255–62

Ireland:

Co. Cavan (3) 1638–1764
Co. Clare (3) 1677–1724
Co. Dublin (2) 1688, 1769
Co. Kildare (1) 1668
Co. Longford (12) 1609–1714
Co. Mayo (1) 1677

       Co. Meath (3) 1668–1724
       Co. West Meath (20) 1637–1734
       Unspecified (2) 1704, 1788
   England:
       Buckinghamshire (1) 1723
       Cornwall (2) 1730, 1788
       Durham (2) 1715–23
       Essex (1) 1721
       Middlesex (1) 1724
       Northumberland (4) 1715–23
       Unspecified (2) 1776<
Also: Copies of some deeds involving Robert Craggs Nugent, 1st Earl Nugent, in a volume of copies of bonds, etc. with Mrs. Elizabeth Eliot, 1746–49

IV. NUGENT INVENTORIES AND LISTS
   8 pieces, 1625–1788
This small category consists of the following items:
   List of papers relating to A[dam] Cusack, father to Clare, wife to Edmond Nugent, in the hands of James Tuite of Cavan. 1625–46. 3 copies
   A schedule of Cornish writings in the custody of Robert Craggs Nugent, 1st Earl Nugent. 1775
   Schedule of deeds and papers belonging to Robert Craggs Nugent. 1762
   Schedule of deeds and papers belonging to Captain [Charles Edmund?] Nugent, for use of Robert [Craggs] Nugent of Gosfield, 1st Earl Nugent. 1764
   List of deeds and other papers in a large iron chest related to the estate of the late Robert Craggs Nugent, 1st Earl Nugent, 1788. 2 variant copies

V. NUGENT LEGAL PAPERS
   ca.340 pieces, 1589–>1788
Virtually all of the papers in this category are copies, either contemporary or later. Most of the papers belong to the 18th century and concern lawsuits or other court actions involving lands or rights over lands. A surprisingly large number of the suits were brought by one member of the Nugent family against another. Most of the records are incomplete.

The following persons appear in five or more cases, as either plaintiff or defendant:

Nugent, Christopher, *styled* Lord Delvin (10)
Nugent, Edmund (8)
Nugent, Laurence (10)
Nugent, Michael (18)
Nugent, Robert [more than one man of this name] (41)

Among the more important, interesting, or complete cases are:

Charles, John, and Edmund Riley *v.* Thomas, Robert, Michael, Laurence, and Garrett Nugent, Thomas Hanly, William Googhegan, and Michael and [Teige] Corkran, heard in the Exchequer, concerning lands at [Aughnegarron?], Co. Longford. With countersuits. 1701–26

John Knight *v.* Henry Hyde, 2nd Earl of Clarendon, re debts. 1701

Robert Nugent *v.* The Forty-Nine Trustees, in a case arising out of the Act of Settlement. 1708

VI. Nugent Manorial and Local Affairs Papers
63 pieces, 1621–1803

The papers in this category are in no sense a full run of estate and manorial papers of the sort found in the Grenville and Temple papers. Here are a few miscellaneous papers pertaining to the estates of the Nugent family, chiefly those in West Meath, Ireland, and few in England (including St. Mawes, Cornwall).

Listed below, by county, are all of the places represented, with the number of pieces, the covering dates, and note of all rentals and surveys. (Aside from a collection of extracts for St. Mawes, there are no court rolls).

Ireland:

Co. Cavan, 3 pieces, 1764–66 (including a rental for 1764)
Co. Clare, 5 pieces, 1662–n.d. (18th cent.)
Co. Dublin, 1 piece, n.d. (18th cent.)
Co. Galway, 1 piece, 1656 (Survey of Robert Nugent's lands)
Co. Kerry, 1 piece, 1677
Co. Longford, 6 pieces, 1641<–n.d. (18th cent.)
Co. Meath, 2 pieces, ca.1662

Co. West Meath, 17 pieces, 1641<–1794< (including a sur-
vey, 1641<, and a list of [Nugent?] tenants, 1701)
Ulster, 1 piece, 1677
General, 14 pieces, 1661–n.d. (18th cent.)

England:
Cornwall, 6 pieces, 1621–n.d. (18th cent.) (including trans-
lations and extracts from St. Mawes Court rolls, 1621–
1726, and an account book of rents collected at Truro,
1734–36).
Essex, 2 pieces, 1744–1803 (rentals for Gosfield, 1744–48
and 1767–1803)
Kent & Sussex, 1 piece, 1773–77 (account of rents re-
ceived for estates belonging to Robert Nugent, 1st Earl
Nugent, and Edward Eliot)
Warwickshire, 9 pieces, ca.1729 (papers of John Knight
re the estate of James Newsham and re enclosures at
Wellesbourne and Mountsfort)
Wiltshire, 1 piece, 1751 (List of rent charges due to Ann
Nugent *et al.*)

VII. NUGENT PERSONAL AND FAMILY PAPERS
ca.90 pieces, 1589–1875

Most of the material in this category falls within the years 1650–
1750 and pertains to the affairs of Robert Nugent of Carlanstown
or to various marriage settlements involving the Nugent family.
Listed below are all of the wills and marriage settlements and
some additional items of interest or significance.

Wills:
1666   Robert Nugent of Ballentullagh
1679   Balthasar Nugent
1679   Robert Nugent of Aughnegarron
1701   Richard Nugent of Aughnegarron
1703   Edmund Nugent
1721   Sir Theobald Butler
1739   Michael Nugent of Carlanstown
1743   Mary Ann Nugent
1811   Sir George Nugent, 1st Bart.

Marriage Settlements:
1661   For the marriage between Edmund Nugent and
Clare, da. of Adam Cusack

1686 Indenture further to the marriage settlement between Robert Barnewall, 9th Baron Trimleston, and Margaret, sister to William Dungan, 1st Earl of Limerick. (later copy)

1690 For the marriage between Garrett Dardis and Alison [Bridget?], da. of Edmund Nugent

1699 For the marriage between Robert, son of Edmund, Nugent and Mary, da. of Sir John Fleming

1715 For the marriage between Edward Dondal and Jane, da. of Andrew Palles

1727 For the marriage between Mary, da. of Ignatius Palles, and John Nugent of Killsona

1730 For the marriage between Robert Nugent and Emilia, da. of Peter Plunkett, 4th Earl of Fingall

Additional interesting or significant items:

An account of a military skirmish at the Battle of Blackwater, 1598?, by "Christopher Nugent, 14th Baron Devlin." 1602

Certificates and other papers affirming service to the English done by Robert Nugent of Carlanstown during the Rebellion. 7 pieces. 1653–56

Marsh, Francis, Bp. of Ardagh and Kilmore. Testimonial to the character of Edmund Nugent (in Latin). 1677

Genealogical account of the Craggs family from 5 Edward VI to 1683, partly in the hand of Sir William Dugdale. >1686

"The humble Petition and Claime of Richard Newgent an Innocent Papist." ca.1708

Newspaper account of the death of Louise Elizabeth (Nugent) Fremantle, Baroness Cottesloe (printed). 1875

VIII. NUGENT SPECIAL SUBJECTS

1. *War of 1689–91: ca.65 pieces, 1689–>1696*

Letters and other papers, chiefly military, concerning the war in Ireland between the forces of the deposed James II (under the command of Richard Talbot, Earl and titular Duke of Tyrconnel) and those of William III. Colonel Edmund Nugent (to whom most of these letters and orders, including many from Ignatius White, Marquis de Albeville, are addressed) commanded a regiment for James II and Thomas

Nugent, afterward 4th Earl of Westmeath, served with James at the Boyne and at Limerick.

2. *West Indian Affairs: ca.70 pieces, 1716–65*
Chiefly correspondence between Lt. Gen. William Matthew (Governor of the British Leeward Islands in 1730) and John Knight of Gosfield Hall, Essex, concerning their mutual personal, family and financial affairs, trade (including sugar and the slave trade), land values, and Island politics. Also a few official papers concerning St. Christopher and Leeward Islands, including: small volume listing the civil and military personnel of St. Christophers, 1717; papers concerning the seizure of the sloops "Relief" and "Pink" by pirates, 1720.

O'Conor Papers (1,439 pieces, 1747–1827)
The O'Conor papers are not, properly speaking, part of the family archives which comprise the Stowe Collection. They are, rather, the correspondence and other papers of Dr. Charles O'Conor (1764–1828), the Irish antiquarian and Roman Catholic priest who served, after 1798, as librarian to the Marquis of Buckingham at Stowe.

O'Conor was the grandson of Charles O'Conor of Belanagare (1710–91), another Irish historian, antiquarian, and collector. The younger O'Conor studied theology at Rome and received an appointment to the parish of Castlerea in 1789, two years after his grandfather had received a pension in recognition of his scholarly achievements from the newly appointed Lord Lieutenant of Ireland, George Grenville, 1st Marquis of Buckingham. In 1798 the Marquis brought O'Conor to Stowe as chaplain for the Marchioness and as librarian for his own growing collection of books and manuscripts. There O'Conor continued to study and write about things Irish, sponsored by the Marquis and later by the 1st Duke. He published *Rerum Hibernicarum Scriptores Veteres* (1814–26) from annals and chronicles in the Stowe Library, and his *Bibliotheca MS. Stowensis* appeared in 1818.

O'Conor was excommunicated by the Church in 1812, and in later years suffered from delusions of persecution and insanity. He died in 1828. Many of the fine early Irish manuscripts collected by his grandfather, which had come to Stowe with the grandson, were sold by the 2nd Duke of Buckingham in 1849 to the Earl of Ashburnham, after whose own death in 1883 they were purchased for the British Museum. Others of the elder O'Conor's manuscripts were deposited with the Royal Irish Academy in Dublin.

Subject matter: Irish literature, language, antiquities, and history, and the Roman Catholic Church, as reflected in the correspondence of Dr. Charles O'Conor with other Irish scholars such as Joseph Bosworth, Sir John Coxe Hippisley, Sir James Mackintosh, and Charles Watkin William Wynn, and in his notebooks and other working papers; drafts of O'Conor's *Rerum Hibernicarum Scriptores Veteres* and the *Memoir* of his grandfather Charles O'Conor of Belangare; the younger O'Conor's disputes with the Roman Catholic Church; also a few letters of the elder O'Conor concerning Irish politics and history, and notes for his "Irish Annals" (published as *Dissertations on the History of Ireland. . .*).

Persons represented by five or more items:
 Archer, James (6)
 Arundell, Mary Anne (Grenville), Baroness Arundell (59)
 Bates, Benjamin (8)
 Bathurst, Henry, Bp. (5)
 Betham, Sir William (6)
 Bonomi, Giovanni Carlo (9)
 Bosworth, Joseph (12)
 Browne, Robert (7)
 Brownrigg, Sir Robert, 1st Bart. (5)
 Butler, Charles (24)
 Caleppi, Lorenzo, Abp. (11)
 Compton, Margaret (Douglas-Macleen-Clephane), Marchioness of Northampton (7)
 Coote, Charles Henry, 2nd Baron Castlecoote (5)
 Devereux, John (10)
 Dibdin, Thomas Frognall (5)
 Ebrington, Thomas (5)
 Fletcher, John (6)
 Fremantle, Sir William Henry (16)

French, Edmund, Bp. (7)

Grady, Patrick (19)

Grenville, Anna Elizabeth, Duchess of Buckingham and Chandos (13)

Grenville, Anne Lucy (Poulett), Baroness Nugent (10)

Grenville, George Nugent, 2nd Baron Nugent (16)

Grenville, Mary Elizabeth (Nugent), Marchioness of Buckingham (22)

Grenville, Richard, 1st Duke of Buckingham and Chandos (72)

Grenville, Thomas (37)

Grenville, William Wyndam, Baron Grenville (13)

Hales, William (14)

Hervey, William (42)

Hippisley, Sir John Coxe, 1st Bart. (9)

Hodson, Frodsham (7)

Hue, François (5)

Kirk, John (7)

McDermot, Hugh (51)

Mackintosh, Sir James (9)

MacNamara, Maria L. (6)

Mason, William Monck (11)

Moore, James Carrick (6)

Morlands, Auriol & Co. (firm) (5)

Moylan, Francis, Bp. (8)

O'Conor, Charles of Belangare (1710–91) (7)

O'Conor, Charles (1764–1828) (189)

O'Conor, Matthew (13)

O'Conor Don, Denis (34)

O'Conor Don, Owen (61)

O'Gorman, Thomas le Chevalier (9)

Payne & Foss (firm) (6)

Petrie, Henry (11)

Plunkett, George Thomas, Bp. (6)

Seeley, John (8)

Troy, John Thomas, Abp. (27)

Vallancey, Charles (16)

Walker, Joseph Cooper (25)

Wilds, William (5)

Wynn, Charles Watkin Williams (5)

Stowe Unsorted Deeds (ca.4,350 pieces, 13th–19th centuries)

The vast majority of the deeds in the Stowe collection have been listed, but not as yet sorted into the various family groups to which they belong. Of these deeds, most are undoubtedly concerned with Grenville estates; most of those remaining belong to the Temples.*

Listed below by county are all places appearing in five or more deeds, with the number of pieces and inclusive dates:

Berkshire:
      Shaw (5) 1737–44
      Speen (6) 1737–51

Buckinghamshire:
      Ashendon (46) 1507/08–1854
      Aston Clinton (15) 1664–1769
      Aylesbury (88) 1672–1832
      Barton Hartshorn (6) 1588/89–1755
      Beachampton (6) 1647–1701
      Biddlesden (123) 1483/84–1856
      Bierton with Broughton (34) 1693–1843
      Boycott (42) 1556/57–1836
      Brill (136) 1639–1854
      Buckingham (277) 1512–1868
      Calverton (31) 1647–1836
      Chearsley (16) 1595–1853
      Chilton (8) 1595–1658
      Dinton (8) 1646/47–1768
      Dorton (8) 1595–1658
      Foscott (34) 1568–1857
      Fulmer (9) 1726/27–1728/29
      Hillesden (14) 1587–1853
      Hughenden (5) 1806–07
      Leckhampstead (7) 1597–1775
      Lillingstone Dayrell & Lovell (26) 1647–1861
      Long Crendon (16) 1715–1854

---

* In addition to the deeds listed here and under the individual family groups, the collection contains approximately 5,000 unsorted related land papers (chiefly abstracts of title, mortgages, notes on leases, etc.) for the Grenville family, most of them for Buckinghamshire and many of them for the middle and later nineteenth century.

Ludgershall (75) 1667–1854
Luffield (65) 1641/42–1842
Maids Moreton (131) 1612–1853
Missenden (Great and Little) (9) 1703–1821
Oakley (51) 1624–1853
Padbury (21) 1508–1843
Preston Bisset (7) 1734–1853
Quainton (5) 1711/12–1871
Radclive (68) 1624–1844
Shalstone (31) 1647–1836
Stantonbury (6) 1600–1614/15
Stoke Mandeville (20) 1668–1807
Stowe (345) 1469–1854
Thornborough (236) 1472/73–1857
Thornton (23) 1472/73–1836
Tingewick (8) 1588–1853
Tyringham with Filgrave (5) 1656/57–1702
Waddesdon (20) 1628/29–1854
Water Stratford (72) 1556/57–1853
Wendover (30) 1601–1807
Westbury (184) 1338–1853
Westcott (189) 1603/04–1859
Weston Turville (94) 1593–1843
Winchendon (22) 1595–1848
Woodham (51) 1616–1854
Wotton Underwood (79) 1595–1854

Cornwall:

Breage (5) 1416–1666
Budock (5) 1339/40–1631
Constantine (25) 1508–1737
Creed (7) 1475–1699
Feock (5) 1576–1737
Germoe (5) 1475–1620/21
Gerrans (6) 1475–1737
Goran (11) 1564–1660
Gwennap (93) 1358–1832
Gwinear (32) 1425–1624
Illogan (6) 1475–1666
Kea (29) 1475–1737
Kenwyn (102) 1579/80–1824
Liskeard (6) 1475–1666

Lostwithiel (7) 1577–1740
Madron (9) 1475–1737
Mevagissey (175) 1380–1824
Paul (15) 1334/35–1666
Penponds (6) 1473–89
Perranzabuloe (22) 1358–1824
Probus (7) 1358–1620/21
St. Agnes (19) 1576/77–1737
St. Austell (15) 1301–1737
St. Cleer (6) 1475–1666
St. Clement (19) 1411–1737
St. Columb Major (9) 1475–1666
St. Erme (8) 1607–1737
St. Erth (9) 1475–1666
St. Ewe (5) 1475–1666
St. Hilary (5) 1579/80–1666
St. Issey (9) 1328–1620
St. Just in Penwith (5) 1475–1666
St. Just in Roseland (9) 1576–1824
St. Keverne (11) 1358–1666
St. Levan (7) 1475–1666
St. Mawes (54) 1606–1824
St. Neot (5) 1475–1601
Sennen (5) 1475–1666
Stithians (29) 1565–1737
Tolcarne (8) 1652–1796
?Treyage (10) 1556
Truro (18) 1579/80–1824
Tywardreath (8) 1358–1824
Veryan (5) 1576–1737
Derbyshire:
Crich (5) 1728/29–1836
Eyam (6) 1728/29–1836
Stony Middleton (5) 1728/29–1836
Durham:
Wolsingham (9) 1282/83–1630
Essex:
Bocking (20) 1712–1824
Braintree (17) 1712–62
Finchingfield (17) 1712–62
Gosfield (23) 1712–1824

  Halstead (19) 1712–96
  Rayne Parva (15) 1712–62
  Shalford (19) 1712–96
  Sible Hedingham (20) 1712–1824
  West Ham (9) 1573–1674
  Wethersfield (18) 1712–1824
Gloucestershire:
  Adlestrop (38) 1613–1763
  Broadwell (11) 1627–1755
  Longborough (32) 1624–1768
Hampshire:
  Avington (106) 961 (copy), 1576/77–1881
  Bighton (46) 1680–1881
  Bishops Waltham (35) 1715–1881
  Cheriton (5) 1658–79
  Easton (114) 1541–1881
  Headbourne Worthy (5) 1658–79
  Hursley (22) 1605
  Itchen Abbas (53) 1728/29–1842
  Itchen Stoke (21) 1688–1836
  Kings Worthy (5) 1658–79
  Martyr Worthy (32) 1541–1725
  Medstead (23) 1541–1700/01
  Ovington (6) 1658–1813
  Romsey (6) 1596–1609/10
  Stoneham (8) 1804–36
  Wellow, East (106) 1577–1829
  Wallop, Nether (19) 1632–1727
  Wonston (26) 1663–1829
Herefordshire:
  Huntington (6) 1722–58
Kent:
  Canterbury (9) 1612–77
  St. Margaret's (5) 1612–46/47
Lancashire:
  Cartmel (14) 1675–1723
Leicestershire:
  Knaptoft (19) 1506/07–1655
  Lutterworth (47) 1557–1719
London: (60) 1558–1857

Middlesex:
 Acton (8) 1777–1829
 Edgware (15) 1713–1829
 Edmonton (11) 1678–1836
 Finchley (8) 1777–1829
 Friern Barnet (11) 1743–1842
 Hendon (5) 1752–1836
 Kingsbury (6) 1720–1842
 Stanmore (Great and/or Little) (28) 1676–1836
 Stepney (9) 1578–1829
 Willesden (14) 1703–1836

Norfolk:
 Fring (5) 1668–69
 Peterston (6) 1668–69
 Thornham (5) 1668/69–1669

Northamptonshire:
 Astwell with Falcutt (9) 1778–1854
 Luffield (17) 1641/42–1735
 Silverstone (24) 1622–1844
 Syresham (13) 1534–1856
 Towcester (11) 1647–77
 Wappenham (38) 1700–1858
 Whittlebury (20) 1647–1833
 Woodend (12) 1713–80

Oxfordshire:
 Barford St. John & St. Michael (16) 1539–1607
 Boycott (41) 1556/57–1842
 Checkendon (5) 1633/34–98
 Finmere (111) 1575–1853
 Gosford with Water Eaton (26) 1537–1624
 Kidlington (28) 1537–1715
 Milton-under-Wychwood (33) 1611–1713
 Mollington (15) 1474–1631
 Sandford St. Martin (30) 1575–1716
 Shipton-under-Wychwood (27) 1589/90–1713
 Steeple Barton (9) 1575–1715
 Stoke, South (5) 1633/34–98
 Tew (Great and/or Little) (25) 1624–1716
 Westcott Barton (5) 1666–1715
 Wood Eaton (24) 1537–1624

Radnorshire:

Beguildy (17) 1722–58
Boughrood (20) 1722–58
Cascob (17) 1722–72
Cefnllys (8) 1668/69–1772
Clyro (18) 1715–58
Cregrina (15) 1722–58
Gladestry (15) 1601/02–84/85
Glasbury (20) 1722–58
Glascwm (12) 1661–84/85
Harpton and Wolfpits (9) 1629–69
Kinnerton, Sallord, and Badland (5) 1668/69–1669
Knighton (31) 1590–1758
Llananno (17) 1722–72
Llanbadarnfawr (7) 1668/69–1772
Llanbister (34) 1667–1758
Llandegley (5) 1668/69–1669
Llandrindod (5) 1668/69–1669
Llanfihangel Nant Melan (33) 1627/28–58
Llanfihangel Rhydithon (34) 1546–1758
Llangunllo (15) 1722–58
Llansantffraid Cwmdeuddwr (16) 1734–58
Llanstephan (19) 1722–58
Nantmel (13) 1668/69–1772
Norton (6) 1676–1684/85
Presteigne (31) 1668/69–1758
Radnor (Old and/or New) (48) 1667–1772
Rhulen (22) 1654–1765
St. Harmon (14) 1734–58
Trewern and Gwaithla (8) 1661/62–69

Somerset:

Banwell (44) 1690–1845
Batcombe (75) 1544–1829
Bath (7) 1728–44
Bawdrip (24) 1703/04–1845
Brent, East (29) 1717–1828
Bridgwater (8) 1719–1831
Brislington (26) 1657–1845
Burnham (15) 1613–1832
Cannington (11) 1600–1831

Catcott (26) 1563/64–1845
Cheddar (132) 1664–1845
Chewton Mendip (31) 1717–1828
Christon (5) 1677–1738
Compton Martin (29) 1690–1845
Cossington (8) 1563/64–1832
Dodington (37) 1563/64–1838
Holford (51) 1563/64–1834
Huntspill (47) 1563/64–1845
Keynsham (97) 1657–1846
Kilton (26) 1639/40–1832
Lilstock (23) 1592–1831
Loxton (33) 1677–1796
Mark (48) 1593–1828
Otterhampton (6) 1796–1831
Pawlett (33) 1548–1832
Petherton, North (8) 1563/64–1831
Priddy (93) 1600–1845
Puriton (17) 1717/18–1845
Rodney Stoke (240) 1605–1845
Saltford (54) 1717/18–1845
Stockland Bristol (11) 1592–1832
Stogursey (41) 1563/64–1834
Stowey (including Over and/or Nether Stowey) (36) 1563/64–1831
Stringston (21) 1585–1831
Tiverton (25) 1717/18–1845
Wedmore (91) 1593–1845
Wells (St. Cuthbert) (43) 1690–1845
Wembdon (9) 1592–1831
Westbury (78) 1600–1845
Wookey (44) 1690–1845

Surrey:
Southwark (5) 1598/99–1637
Sussex:
Falmer (5) 1728/29–1836
Warwickshire:
Burton Dassett (138) 1295–1796
Chadshunt (32) 1564/65–1819
9
Coventry (31) 1410–1648

        Farnborough (11) 1500–1648
        Fenny Compton (7) 1614–1717
        Kineton (11) 1601–1796
        Radway (35) 1542–1796
Wiltshire:
        Blunsdon (10) 1615–1706
        Cricklade (7) 1615–1706
        Wellow, West (54) 1601/02–1829
Worcestershire:
        Bengeworth (5) 1728/29–56
        Feckenham (7) 1728/29–1836
        Ombersley (7) 1728/29–1836
        Rock (5) 1589/90–1756
Yorkshire:
        Bradfield (5) 1728/29–56
        Ecclesfield (5) 1728/29–56
        Handsworth (5) 1630–1756
        Penistone (5) 1728/29–56
Ireland:
        Co. Clare (23) 1680<–1853
        Co. Dublin (7) 1762–69
        Co. Leix (50) 1626/27–1853
        Co. Longford (23) 1697–1853
        Co. Westmeath (61) 1569–1853
West Indies:
        Jamaica (48) 1736/37–1836

Stowe Maps and Plans (ca.800 pieces, 1564<–1913)
    Although many of the maps and plans in this category are fragmentary or unidentified, there are over-200 estate and field plans, chiefly for Grenville properties in Buckinghamshire, and over 300 plans (many of them of small details only) for the house, furnishings, architectural details, and gardens at Stowe. Most of the pieces date from the later 18th and 19th centuries, but there are earlier Temple maps for Stowe. Some of the maps are printed, or partly printed.
    Listed below by county are the identified maps and plans.

Buckinghamshire:
  Akeley:
    Plan of the parish of Akeley cum Stockholt, 1825<
  Ashendon:
    Survey and plan of Little Pollicott . . . ca.1800
    Plan of land around church, ca.1840
    Map of lands in Ashenden cum Pollicott & Ludgers-
      hall, ca.1850
    Plan of lands . . . exchanged by 3rd Duke of Buck-
      ingham and Chandos and 7th Duke of Marlbor-
      ough, 1870
  Aston Clinton:
    Plan of an estate in Aston Clinton. 4 pieces, 1836,
      1847
  Aylesbury:
    Plan of Bridge and Long Meadows, n.d. (18th cent?)
    Ground plan of farm house and three tenements
      of the Marquis of Buckingham, 1804
    Sketch of allotments showing the situation where
      the footpath is claimed by Jenkins & others, 1805
    Plan of land near Aylesbury, 1806
    Plan of an estate belonging to Messrs. Smith & Trin-
      dal as Trustees for the sale thereof, 1818
    Plan of estates at Weedon & Aylesbury, 1849
    Plan of Hayden Hill, 1849
    Plan of Aylesbury Gaol premises, n.d.
  Biddlesden:
    Plan of alterations in the road through Luffield
      Grounds & Wittlebury to Bilston, ca.1800?
  Bierton:
    Plan of estates at Bierton & Hulcott, 1849
  Brill:
    Plan of lands in Brill, ca.1780?
    Plan of the Marquis of Buckingham's estate at Mor-
      leys, ca.1800
    Plan of Closes at Brill exchanged, 1811
    Plan of Brewers Close showing new fence, 1829
    Plan of Pole Trees Farm, Brill & Ludgershall,
      1850

Plan of house and repairs needed at Clearfield Farm, ca.1850?

Plan of meadowland at Brill, "lot 16," n.d. (19th cent.)

Buckingham:

A terrier of Buckingham tithe, 1752

A sketch of several old enclosures in the parish of Buckingham some of which are liable to Impropriate Tithes to the Rt. Hon. Earl Temple, >1784

Estimate and plan of "Marshales House," n.d. (18th cent.?)

Plan of river crossing, ca.1806?

Plan of borough town of Buckingham. Freehold estate, 1822

Map of lands near Chetwode & Buckingham belonging to Mary Holte Bracebridge

Plan for proposed roads and buildings on the Parsonage closes, 1853

Plan of Buckingham town hall, 1857

Plan of White Hart premises, 1869

Part of Buckingham Street made with respect to the situation of the Butchers Shambles, 1808<

Plan of town, 1894

Plan of properties in the town, 1894

Chearsley:

Plan of Chearsley Farm, ca.1800?

Claydon:

Plan and elevation of double cottage at Claydon, ca.1820?

Dadford:

Plot of Dadford Common with two closes adjoining rented by William Jackson and Job Boardman, 1754<

A Plot of Dadford Common surveyed by John King, 1754

Dorton:

Plan of Dorton Park, ca.1820?

Foscott:

Plan of Foscott copied from the survey of 1650, made ca.1800

Gawcott:
>Plan of Gawcott, n.d. (18th cent.?)
>Extract from the plan of the hamlets of Gawcott and Prebend End, n.d.

Hillesden:
>Map of the parish of Hillsden describing the glebe lands belonging to the Dean & Chapter of the Cathedral Church of Christ in Oxford & the ancient demesne & titheable land belonging to the Duke of Buckingham and Chandos, 1847

Horsenden:
>Plan of Meads Farm, 1800<
>Tracing of a plan made to accompany a valuation of the Horsenden estate, 1847
>*See also* Princes Risborough

Hulcott:
>*See* Brierton

Long Crendon:
>Plan of Tetershill Wood, n.d. (17th cent.?)
>Sketch plan of Long Crendon Road, 1824<
>Plan of a piece of land in Long Crendon parish, n.d. (19th cent.)

Ludgershall:
>Plan of Ludgershall Farm, n.d. (18th cent.)
>Plan of lands in the parish, ca.1800?
>Kingswood Farm, ca.1830
>Poltree's Farm, Ludgershall, ca.1840

Maids Moreton:
>Plan of Maids Moreton, 1817
>Plan of estates at Maids Moreton, 1865
>Mr. G. Pilgrim's holding, 1869
>Sketch from the map of Maids Moreton, 1800<?

Oakley:
>Plan of Moor Lays Farm, ca.1800

Padbury:
>Plan of properties belonging to the Marquis of Chandos and the Rev. W. T. Eyre, 1858

Prebend End:
>Plan of estate at Prebend End, 1858

See also Gawcott

Preston Bissett:

Plan of estates of the Marquis of Chandos, 1848

Plan of Donville Estate, 1913

Princes Risborough:

Plan of Princes Risborough and Horsenden estates,
1841

Map of lands in Longwick, part of the estate of Mrs.
Margaret Bird, lately purchased of William
Gomme Sr., 1728

Map of lands in Princes Risborough and Monks Risborough part of the estate of Mrs. Margaret Bird
purchased of William Gomme, 1728

Radclive:

Field plans, ca.1820

Shalstone:

Plan of the park of the Shalstone Estate, n.d. (19th
cent.)

Stoke Mandeville:

Survey and plan of several old enclosures in the parishes of Weston Turville and Stoke Mandeville belonging to the Marquis of Buckingham, 1787

Sketch of the Marquis of Buckingham's land at Stoke
Mandeville, >1822

Plan of estates in the parish of Weston Turville and
Stoke Mandeville, 1849

Stowe:

Plans of house, parterre, forecourt, and gardens. 23
pieces, late 17th cent.?

Plan of estate properties under plough, n.d. (18th
cent.?)

Plan of Eleven-Acre Land at Stowe, n.d. (18th cent.?)

Plan for parish burial ground, n.d. (18th cent.?)

Survey of land about Stowe kiln, 1805<

Plans of Stowe Gardens, 3 pieces, 1820

House, floor, and room plans for Stowe House, with
architectural detail sketches, etc., ca.200 pieces,
ca.1839–45

Plans, elevations, etc. for Stratford Lodge on the
Stowe estate. ca.10 pieces, ca.1839–44

Map of Ford's Farm, ca.1840?

Plan and elevations, with some architectural details, for Lamport Lodge, part of the Stowe estate, 14 pieces, ca.1840–41

Tithe plan of the parish of Stowe, 1843

Plan of the Stowe Estate in the counties of Bucks., Oxon., and Northampton, 1843

Plan of the Stowe Estate in Bucks., 1848

Map of estates in the Stowe division referred to in an annexed indenture [now lost], 1848<

Stowe indemnity map, ca.1850

Plan of "The Buckingham Estates" to be sold, 1854

Map of the Drill ground, 1908

Thornborough:

"The plott and description of the demeasnes in the parish of Thornebourrough in the county of Buck: called the Chauntrie Land: taken for the Right Worll. Sir Peter Temple knight and barronet," 1637

Map of Thornborough, ca.1800

Tingewick:

Plan of lands in Tingewick belonging to the Duke of Buckingham and Chandos, 1845

Waddesdon:

Map of the estate of Bartholomew Paxton at Little Collick in the parish of Waddesdon, 1728

Plan of lands on the boundary of Pitchcott and Waddesdon parish? n.d. (19th cent.)

Plan of Oving Hill farm, n.d. (19th cent.)

Weedon:

Plan of land at Weedon, 1826?

Plan of a farm in the hamlet of Weedon, 1831

See also Aylesbury

Westbury:

Map of Westbury common (woodland) >1784

Map of Westbury, ca.1800?

Westcott:

Plan of proposed house for J. Cannon, 1828

Plans for cottages at Westcott. 2 pieces, 1860

Map for proposed exchange of lands between the

Duke of Buckingham and Chandos and Baron Ferdinand de Rothschild, ca.1860?

Plan of severance lands in the area of Westcott. 4 pieces, 1870

Weston Turville:

See Stoke Mandeville

Winchendon:

Survey of lands in Lower Winchendon held by the Rev. I. Kipling, ca.1830

Woodham:

Plan of the Ovinghill Estate purchased from Lord Chesterfield, 1848

Wotton Underwood:

Map of Wotton Underwood, [1564<>1586]

Map of Tithershall Wood, ca.1780?

Map of Rushbeds and Grenville woods, 1788

"A plan of the Marquiss of Buckingham's seat & pleasure ground at Wotton in the county of Bucks.," 1789

Miscellaneous field plans belonging to Wotton. 9 pieces, 1794<

Map of Tithershall wood and close, ca.1800?

Map of Wotton woods, Rushbeds wood, ca.1812?

Plan of proposed alteration to the Still Room and offices at Wotton House, 1830

Plans of part of Wotton House. 7 pieces, 1842

Plan and elevation of the Turkish Summer House, 1843

Sketch of Ham Green before subdivision, 1846

Plans of a farm at Wotton occupied by John Harper. 2 pieces, 1856, 1858

Plan of catacomb to hold coffin in Wotton Church, 1859

Plan of water supply to moat (at Wotton farm?), 1869

Plan showing water to Church Farm on the Wotton Estate, 1884

Plan of lands in the Wotton-Kingswood area, n.d. (19th cent.)

Plan of lands in Wotton Division, n.d. (19th cent.)

Diagrams of drainage levels. 3 pieces, 1870

Cornwall:
 Kenwyn:
  Map of Creegbroaze, ca.1840?
 Lamburn:
  Plan of Lamburn watercourse, 1770
 Mevagissey:
  Plan of church and poor grounds etc. near Mevagis-
   sey, 1812<
 Perranporth?:
  Tracings of Gear Sands, ca.1850?
 Redruth:
  Plan of cross courses and monopolies of mines &
   water, Redruth, ca.1836
 St. Agnes:
  Sections of East and West Wheal of the mines in
   the parish of St. Agnes, 1836
 St. Mawes:
  Map of St. Mawes, ca.1730?
  Plan of the borough and manor of St. Mawes, ca.1800
  Plans of St. Mawes Chapel. 4 pieces, ca.1805–09
  Map of Penhallow's & Carew's lands, 1821
  Plans of part of the boundary between the borough
   of St. Mawes and the Bogullas & Symons' en-
   croachments. 5 pieces, ca.1825
  Map of the borough and manor of St. Mawes, 1830
  Plan of the St. Mawes estate for sale by auction by
   Francis Fuller & Co., 1842
  Sketch of land around chapel, 1879
 Tolcarne:
  Map of the manor of Tolcarne, ca.1820?
  Map of Lady Caroline Grenville's manor of Tolcarne,
   1888
 Tregavethan:
  Plans of a house and alterations to be done by Wm.
   Bryant, 1827
  Plan of tenements to be leased by Marquis of Chan-
   dos, 1827<
  Plan of part of Tregavethan manor, 1881
 Miscellaneous:
  [Plan of a stable in Cornwall? 1826]

Essex:
    Gosfield
        Floor plan of Gosfield Hall, 1800<?
        Map of road in village, 1800<?
        Rough plan of Gosfield woods, 1814<
        Map of the Gosfield Hall estate. 2 pieces, 1819
           (printed)

Gloucestershire:
    Bristol:
        Ground plan of the asylum for lunatics at Brislington
           House near Bristol, erected 1806 by Dr. Fox,
           1806<

Hampshire:
    Avington:
        Plans of house and gardens at Avington House, in-
           cluding plans for proposed alterations. 7 pieces,
           n.d. (18th cent.)–1826
    Bighton:
        Plan of Bighton rectory and glebe land, 1840
    Itchen Abbas:
        Plans of lands at Itchen Abbas, the property of the
           Duke of Buckingham and Chandos, which the Rev.
           Robert Wright wishes to have enfranchised. 3
           pieces, ca.1839–41
        Plan of lands sold to Lord Ashburton, n.d.
    Itchen Stoke?:
        Plan of an allotment "at Stoke," ca.1820?
    Ryde:
        Plans for the "New Sewer of Western District," with
           notices to owners of properties involved. 2 pieces,
           1883–84
    Miscellaneous:
        Plan of property of the Duke of Buckingham and
           Chandos in Hampshire? n.d. (19th cent.)

Kent:
    Sandgate:
        North and south elevations of the house and offices
           belonging to Henry Dawkins Esq., 1882

London:
        Floor plan and elevation of the United Service Club
           (London?), ca.1825

Plan of a house in John Street, Fitzroy Square (London?)

Plan of Great Exhibition Building, Crystal Palace, ca.1851

See also floor plans for St. James Square House in the Brydges papers, above, p. 234

Middlesex:

Canons:

Plan of Canons and vicinity, 1731<

Miscellaneous plans, possibly for Canons?. 6 pieces, 18–19th cent.

Plans for a dining room at Canons? n.d. (19th cent.)

See also floor plans for Canons in the Brydges papers, above, p. 234

Kensington:

Plan of Kensington Palace gardens, ca.1730

Willesden:

Plan of the farm at Willesden, 1837

Northamptonshire:

Astwell:

Plan of the farm belonging to the Duke of Buckingham and Chandos in the occupation of Nathaniel Stilgoe, 1822<

Plan of farms belonging to the Duke of Buckingham and Chandos, 19th cent.

Silverstone:

Map of exchanges between the Marquis of Buckingham and Thomas Barford and the Duke of Grafton, 1820

Whittlebury:

Plan of enclosure, 1861; plans of Whittlebury Estate in Northampton, Buckingham, and Oxford. 7 pieces, 1872–89

Plan of Shalstone Estate freeboards adjoining the Whittlebury Estate, 1894

Oxfordshire:

Finmere:

Map of Finmere (fragment only), n.d. (17th cent.?)

Plan of Mr. Yates' and part of Mr. Paxton's farm in the parish of Finmere belonging to the Marquis of Buckingham, 1813

Plan of that portion of the Finmere estate sold to
the Duke of Buckingham, 1822<

Map of the Duke of Buckingham's exchange of allotment with Rev. W. J. Turner at Finmere, 1822<

Map of part of Finmere estate? 1825

Sketch of fields in Water Stratford and Finmere
through which the road from Stratford Lodges
would pass, ca.1880

Somerset:

Bath:

Plan of Chandos Buildings, Chapel Court, and Het-
ling Court. 2 pieces, 1885

Plan of St. John's Hospital, Bath, up to 1935, drawn
by Rolfe and Crozier Cole. 2 copies, 1939

Bridgwater:

Plan of intended turnpike road from Nether Stowey
to Bridgwater through Earl Temple's land, >1784

Brislington:

See Keynsham

Bruton:

Plan of Bruton hospital, 1824

Burnham:

Map of Mr. Balch's allotments, 1784<

Plan of Broadwarth and Hook in Burnham parish
and of Cheeseman's in Huntspill parish, 1826

Compton Martin:

Plans of the common upon Mendip taken from an
old survey. 2 pieces, ca.1780?

Crowcombe?:

Plan of "The two Mousneys. . ." 1824

Dodington:

Plan of the parish and manor of Dodington with
its members, 1764

"Plan of such part of the Quantock Hills as belong
to the R. Hon. Earl Temple," 1765

Map of the Marquis of Buckingham's woods on Quan-
tocks, 1784<

"Plan of such parts of Quantock Hills as belong to
. . . the Marquis of Buckingham," 1791

Plan of woods at Dodington. 3 pieces, 1824

Huntspill:

 Map of Earl Temple's tenement and allotment at Hackney Common, Huntspill, 1786

 Plan of an allotment in Huntspill set out to Henry Sutton, held under the Marquis of Buckingham, ca.1820

 See also Burnham

Keynsham:

 Map of the parish or manor, ca.1820

 Map of proposed new road to avoid the hills and dangerous turns on the present road opposite the Lamb and Lark Inn, 1822<

 Plan of alteration in the Bristol turnpike road, 1825–29

 Sketch showing the Duke of Buckingham and Chandos' boundary adjoining the premises of Henry Eden Mynors, Esq., 1832

 Plan of estates for sale at Keynsham and Brislington. 2 pieces, 1841–44

 Plan of property at Keynsham belonging to the Marquis of Chandos, 1849

Kilton:

 Plan of Hisher Woodland in the parish of Kilton and Currill in the parish of Holford, 1784<

Lilstock:

 Plan of the manor and parish of Lilstock belonging to Earl Temple, 1774

 Plan of lands of the Marquis of Buckingham proposed to be exchanged, 1806

Pawlett:

 Plan of lands in the freehold property of the Duke of Buckingham at Pawlett and Wembdon, 1824

Rodney Stoke:

 Field plan, 1665

 Map of the manor of Rodney Stoke, 1820

 Map of the manor of Rodney Stoke, 1858

 Map of the manor as per sales particulars. 2 pieces, 1858

 Plan of lots 1–22 and 48–192 for sale, 1859

 Map of the manor. 2 pieces, ca.1880?

Stogursey:

Map of Stogursey to show a disputed close, 1818

Warwickshire:

Blunsden St. Andrew:

Plan of an estate in Blunsden St. Andrew and Cricklade belonging to the co-heirs of Francis Keck, ca.1770?

Burton Dassett:

Plan of part of the Stowe Estate southwest of Burton Dassett, ca.1760

Sketch of W. Yerrow's Farm, Burton Dassett, 1812<

Moreton Morrell:

Plan and survey of an estate at Moreton Morrell belonging to the Hon. Henry Grenville, >1784

Scotland:

Taymouth:

Sketches of area, houses, etc. around Breadalbane property at Taymouth Castle. 23 pieces, ca.1834

Ireland:

Enniskillen:

Plan of a gallery for soldiers intended for burial at Enniskillen Church, 1789

Italy:

Plans of Pompeii. 5 pieces, 19th cent.

Miscellaneous: Unidentified or only partially identified estate and field plans, sketches of architectural features or details, etc. ca.160 pieces, 18th–19th centuries

See also Grenville and Brydges West Indies Estates papers, pp. 202, 244, and Grenville Transportation Papers, p. 201, for notice of a few additional maps and plans.

OTHER COLLECTIONS AND
INDIVIDUAL ITEMS

ABERCROMBY, JAMES (1706–81)
ca.1,000 pieces, 1674–1787, mostly 1758

James Abercromby, British general, was a native of Banffshire, Scotland. He entered the army as a youth and rose to the rank of major general in 1756. In that year, through the influence of his friend the Earl of Loudoun, Abercromby was made second in command to Loudoun in North America. When Loudoun was recalled in 1758, Abercromby succeeded him. Abercromby's failure to capture Fort Ticonderoga led to his replacement in 1759 by Jeffery Amherst, the conquerer of Louisbourg.

Subject matter: the 1758 campaign of the British army in North America during the Seven Years' War, specifically: the embargo on colonial shipping, the fall of Fort William Henry, the surrender of Louisbourg, the expedition against Fort Ticonderoga, activities on the Mohawk River and at the Oneida Carrying Place, the conquest of Fort Frontenac (Cadaraqui), John Forbes' expedition against Fort Duquesne, British use of and relations with the Indians, the internal affairs of the British army, and the recall of Abercromby; also, the genealogy of Abercromby.

Persons represented by five or more pieces:
    Abercromby, James (448)
    Amherst, Jeffery, 1st Baron Amherst (9)
    Appy, John (29)
    Bradstreet, John (10)
    Burton, Ralph (7)
    Campbell, John, 4th Earl of Loudoun (5)
    De Lancey, James (28)
    Denny, William (18)

Forbes, John (25)
Furnis, James (8)
Hallowell, Benjamin (6)
Hancock, Thomas (17)
Hopson, Peregrine Thomas (10)
Hutchinson, Thomas (6)
Johnson, Sir William (29)
Lawrence, Charles (15)
Loring, Joshua (6)
Lyttelton, William Henry (10)
Moncton, Robert (5)
Montresor, James Gabriel (12)
Napier, James (8)
Pitt, William, 1st Earl of Chatham (20)
Pownall, Thomas (36)
Saul, Thomas (5)
Stanwix, John (22)
Vaudreuil [Cavagnal, Pierre François de Rigaud], Marquis
   de (10)
Wentworth, Benning (5)

Physical description: letters, documents (reports, memorials, returns, etc.); a few manuscripts (e.g., journal of Christian Frederick Post).

Source: purchased from Lathrop C. Harper, 1923.

Bibliography: letters of John Forbes are printed in *Writings of General John Forbes,* ed. Alfred P. James (Menasha, Wis.: The Collegiate Press, 1938).

ADAMS, LADY AGNES ANNE (COOK) (1869–1942)
515 pieces, 1929–44

Lady Agnes A. Adams was born in Aberdeen, Scotland, and educated in Switzerland. In 1893 she married Sir John Adams, a professor at the University of Glasgow. He became the first Professor of Education at the University of London, wrote books, lectured around the world, and finally settled in Los Angeles where he lectured at the University of California at Los Angeles. After his death in 1934, Lady Adams continued to live in Hollywood, and helped organize the Los Angeles chapter of the English-Speaking Union.

Subject matter: personal affairs of Lady Agnes A. Adams; life in London during World War II as reflected in letters of scholars and other friends to Lady Adams when she was living in Hollywood.

Persons represented by five or more pieces:
Adamson, John William (6)
Anderson, Maggie (6)
Ashley Cooper, Kathleen (27)
Ashley Cooper, Patricia (7)
Ashley Cooper, Patrick (19)
Brock, Eircne (10)
Chambers, Gertrude (10)
Cockerell, Theodore Dru Alison (5)
Conway, Margaret M. (6)
Cook, George Stevani Littlejohn (8)
Cook, Robert Haldane (9)
Dykes, Christopher (8)
Fisher, Godfrey (6)
Frankenburg, Charis (9)
Grassam, Elsie (8)
Halliday, Clive (6)
Hay, Silvia (10)
Helm, Ida E. (6)
Isaac, May (6)
Littlejohn-Cook, William (9)
Loring, Theodosia (Thackeray) (5)
Mackesy, Dorothy (35)
Munro, Helen (5)
Newton, Anne (5)
Nosworthy, Lyle (14)
Raton, Agatha (5)
Roscoe, Frank (11)
Roxburgh, Jean (33)

Shepherd, Gertrude M. (9)
Synge, Dinah (13)
Weekes, Rose (12)

Physical description: letters, photographs, clippings.

Source: gift of Mrs. Robert A. Millikan, June, 1946.

ANDRÉ, JOHN (1751–80)
[Journal] (1777–80)
Autograph MS. volume 117 pp.

Relates the operations of British and American armies from June 1777 to November 1778. Contains forty-four ink and color maps. Published as the *Journal of John André,* ed. Henry Cabot Lodge (Boston: Bibliophile Society, 1903).

ANONYMOUS
[List of names and expenses of all those who attended the funeral of Henry VII] 1509
MS. volume 126 pp.

ANONYMOUS
The names of such as came with William the Conqueror (ca.1572)
MS. volume 28 pp.

A baronage from the reign of William I to that of Henry III. Followed by "A Reporte of the valiance of Sir John Hawckwood among the florentynes."

ANONYMOUS
The progenie of yᵉ monarchs of the English men (1595)
MS. volume 187 pp.

A brief history of the kings and queens of England and their ancestors, beginning with "Bedwy," and dedicated to Queen Elizabeth.

ANONYMOUS
The Arraignment, conviction, & condemnation of Rob[ert Devereux, 2nd] Earle of Essex, and Henrie [Wriothesley, 3rd] Earle of Southampton . . . [with an account of the trial of Captain Thomas Lee] (ca.1601)
MS. volume 59 pp.

ANONYMOUS
A generall collection of all the offices of England with their ffees in the Quenes guifte . . . (>1603)
MS. volume 75 pp.

Includes valuations for bishoprics and deaneries, as well as for various legal, military, household, and other administrative offices in the gift of the Queen.

ANONYMOUS
The Order for Swans both by the Statutes, and by the ancient Orders and Customes used within the Realme of England (1617<)
MS. volume 16 pp.

Includes drawings of 22 registered swan beak markings.

ANONYMOUS
[Parliamentary Diary] (1621)
MS. volume 532 pp.

Diary for the House of Commons for the Parliament of 1621, published as "The Belasyze Diary" (after the family in whose posses-

sion the manuscript once was) by Wallace Notestein, Frances
Helen Relf, and Hartley Simpson in *Commons Debates 1621* (New
Haven: Yale University Press, 1935), 5:3–246.

ANONYMOUS
A booke of Sundrie Justices works, what a Justice of the Peace
may do (1627)
MS. volume 392 pp. (many blank)

Discussion of duties, procedures, legal terms, etc. relating to the
work of a Justice of the Peace, arranged by topic in alphabetical
order.

ANONYMOUS
A Breefe Memoriall of the Lyfe & Deathe of Doctor James Spottis-
wood Bishopp of Clogher in Ireland . . . (ca.1630–ca.1640)
MS. volume 30 pp.

Includes a continuation of the biography in another hand.

ANONYMOUS
[Parliamentary Diary] (1640)
MS. volume 184 pp.

A diary of the Short Parliament, with copies of parliamentary
letters and speeches for a few earlier parliaments.

ANONYMOUS
A Discourse of the Privilege and Practice of the high Court of
Parliament in England collected out of the Common Lawes of
this Land (>1660)
MS. volume 37 pp.

Printed in part in William Hakewill's *Modus Tenendi Parliamentum* (1660).

ANONYMOUS
[Newsletters] (1689–1710)
126 Ls.

A set of newsletters from London dealing with political, foreign, and social news, sent to a friend and associate of a Member of Parliament for Tamworth.

ANONYMOUS
[Tracings from the title pages of Emblem Books in the libraries of Thomas Corser, Henry Yates Thompson, and Henry Green] (>1900?)
MS. 3 volumes

With indexes and often extensive bibliographical comments on each volume.

ANONYMOUS
Report of Demonstration at Falkirk . . . in support of Scottish self-government (1926)
Typescript 36 pp.

ASHCOMBE, SIR WILLIAM (fl. 1591–1625)
Diary: Memorable accidents (1591–1625)
MS. 32 pp.

Includes references to Sir Walter Ralegh and to his wife's family, the Temples of Stowe.

BACON, SIR NICHOLAS (1509–79)
[Commonplace Book] (ca.1585)
MS. volume 190 pp.

Copies, not in Bacon's hand, of his speeches in Parliament and Star Chamber, and of his poems (1559–79)

BALFOUR, EUSTACE JAMES ANTHONY (1854–1912)
83 pieces, 1854–1937

E. J. A. Balfour was the son of James M. Balfour and Lady Blanche Balfour, sister of Lord Robert Cecil, 3rd Marquis Salisbury, and the brother of statesman Arthur James Balfour and naturalist Francis Maitland Balfour. He became a painter and architect, and designed the rebuilding of the Crown Court church. Balfour's wife, Lady Frances (Campbell) Balfour (1858–1931), was the daughter of Sir George Campbell, 8th Duke of Argyll. Her brother, John Douglass Campbell, 9th Duke of Argyll, was married to Princess Louise, the daughter of Queen Victoria. Lady Balfour was active as a churchwoman, suffragist, and author.

Subject matter: personal affairs of E. J. A. and Lady Francis (Campbell) Balfour; politics, art, science, etc., as reflected in the letters of prominent Victorians and Edwardians such as Arthur James Balfour, Ford Madox Brown, William Benjamin Carpenter, Joseph Chamberlain, Walter Crane, Sir John Gilbert, William Holman Hunt, Henry James, Rudyard Kipling, Princess Louise Caroline Alberta, Duchess of Argyll, James Russell Lowell, John Morley, Sir Richard Owen, and Henry Charles Keith Petty-FitzMaurice, 5th Marquis of Lansdowne.

Persons represented by five or more pieces:
    Boulanger, Georges Ernest Jean Marie (7)
    Burne-Jones, Sir Edward Coley (7)
    Gascoyne-Cecil, Robert Arthur Talbot, 3rd Marquis of Salisbury (5)

Physical description: letters, 1 pencil sketch.

Source: gift of S. Kerrison Preston, 1971 (purchased from Sotheby's, ca.1945).

BARKER, THOMAS, *ET AL.*
[Household account book] (1626–1636/37)
MS. volume 274 pp.

Accounts kept by Barker and others for the [Townshend?] family at Raynham, Norfolk.

BARTHOLOMEW, A. J. (fl. 1857)
Armour and Military Costumes from William I to Victoria, 1066–1857 (1857)
MS. volume 271 pp.

Profusely illustrated with line drawings, wash, and color, accompanied by written explanations.

BEAUFORT, SIR FRANCIS (1774–1857)
2,143 pieces, 1710–1953

Admiral Sir Francis Beaufort, Hydrographer to the Royal Navy, was the son of an Irish rector of Huguenot descent. He first went to sea in 1789 under the command of Lestock Wilson (whose daughter Alicia Magdalena he married in 1813), and from 1790 to 1800 was active in the naval war with France and Spain, serving successively on the "Latona," the "Aquilon," and the "Phaeton." He was involved with "Cornwallis's retreat" in 1795, promoted lieutenant in 1796, and seriously wounded in 1800, after which he was given the rank of commander and invalided home. In 1809, after four years as commander of the storeship "Woolwich,"

Beaufort was again given active command (of the "Blossom"); the following year he made post rank and was sent out to Malta on the "Frederickssteen," where he was active in conducting geographical and hydrographical surveys of the eastern Mediterranean. Following another serious wound in 1812 Beaufort was again invalided home, this time to write the widely acclaimed *Karamania, or a Brief Description of the South Coast of Asia Minor . . .* (1817), and to become active in the Royal Society. In 1829, after years of petitioning for reactivation in the Navy, Beaufort was named Hydrographer of the Navy and until his retirement in 1854 this position was his constant concern. He expanded the staff and physical facilities of the hydrographical department, established surveys over the entire globe, and served on numerous naval commissions. Beaufort's wife died in 1834; five years later he married Honora Edgeworth, the daughter of his long-time friend Richard Lovell Edgeworth and sister of the novelist Maria Edgeworth. He was promoted to Rear-Admiral (ret.) in 1846, knighted in 1848, and retired in 1854. Beaufort died in 1857.

With the Beaufort papers are two other groups of related Papers: the correspondence and travel diaries of his daughter, Emily Anne (Beaufort) Smythe, Viscountess Strangford (d. 1887), a noted humanitarian and traveler; and the papers of the Larpent family, mainly the correspondence of John James Larpent, 7th Baron de Hochepied, during his tenure as British consul in Antwerp, ca.1825–37.

Subject matter: British naval history, especially during the Napoleonic wars, including Beaufort's journals for 1791–96 (with gaps); geography and hydrography, especially pertaining to the eastern Mediterranean, including Beaufort's journal for the surveying voyage of the H.M.S. "Frederickssteen," the basis for his *Karamania,* and his professional diaries as naval hydrographer, 1840–57; the research and working papers for the *Karamania;* Irish affairs, particularly economic and commercial, together with the diaries of Sir Francis' father, Daniel Augustus Beaufort, 1780–1821; the Royal Society and scientific affairs in England; Maria Edgeworth and the Edgeworth family circle in Ireland; description and travel in England, Ireland, and the Near East, together with Emily Anne (Beaufort) Smythe's journal of her life and travels during the Turko-Bulgarian war; diplomatic relations between England and

Belgium, particularly during the French revolution of 1830, as seen in the Larpent papers.

Persons represented by five or more pieces:
Allott, Richard (8)
Arnold, Thomas (7)
Barow, Sir John (9)
Beaufort, Alicia Magdalena (Wilson) (22)
Beaufort, Daniel Augustus (61)
Beaufort, Sir Francis (867)
Beaufort, Mary (Waller) (14)
Beaufort, William Augustus (13)
Beaufort, William Lewis (22)
Beaufort, William Morris (16)
Bidwell, John (10)
Blackwood, Frederick Temple, 1st Marquis of Dufferin (6)
Blennerhasset, Jeanne (6)
Brinkley, John, Bp. (14)
Canning, Stratford, 1st Viscount Stratford de Redcliffe (7)
Croker, John Wilson (12)
Dalrymple, Alexander (15)
Edgeworth, Maria (6)
Edgeworth, Richard Lovell (7)
Gilbert, Davies (5)
Great Britain. Admiralty. Commissioners (13)
Hall, Basil (9)
Larpent, Catherine Elizabeth (Reeves) (7)
Larpent, John James, 7th Baron de Hochepied (44)
Melvill, Sir Peter Melvill (12)
Palmer, William (8)
Pellew, Edward, 1st Viscount Exmouth (7)
Porter, George Richard (6)
Rennell, James (29)
Smythe, Emily Anne (Beaufort), Viscountess Strangford (7)
Wagner, Henry (5)
Walpole, Robert (7)
Wilson, Lestock (10)
Woods, Albert W. (9)
Zhary, Alexandre (14)

British Historical Manuscripts

Physical description: letters, manuscripts, documents.

Source: purchased from Francis N. Beaufort-Palmer, 1968–73.

BELL, T[HOMAS] (fl. 1750s)
Gen. Wolfe's Evolutions of a Regiment of Cavalry [and] Gen.
Wolfe's Evolutions of a Battalion of Infantry (ca.1759)
MS. two volumes

With 27 ink and color diagrams of various cavalry and infantry
maneuvres, written by General Wolfe's aide-de-camp.

BENSON, FRANCIS (fl. 1670s)
[Newsletters] (1676–80)
Autograph MS.S. 2 volumes

Approximately 235 newsletters written from Whitehall to Sir Leoline Jenkins (1623–85) while the latter was serving as English rep-
resentative at the Hague and Nijmegen.

BLACK FAMILY COLLECTION
103 pieces, 1738–1837

In 1716 John Black (1681–1767), an Irish merchant resident in Bordeaux, married Margaret Gordon; the couple had fifteen children,
twelve of whom survived into adulthood, including their son Joseph Black (1728–99), the prominent Edinburgh chemist and physician. Another son, Alexander, joined his uncle, Robert Black,
in Cadiz where the latter was a merchant and where Robert
and John Black's brother Charles was British consul. While Joseph
Black's career prospered, Robert's business failed; after Robert's
death, ca.1761, Alexander moved to London and established a
commercial glassworks, relying in part on his brother Joseph's
advice and assistance. Their father John Black retired to Blamont,
the family home in Co. Antrim, Ireland, in 1759, and died there
eight years later.

Subject matter: Black family affairs, as seen in the correspondence of John and Margaret Black and their numerous children and grandchildren; trade and mercantile affairs in Bordeaux, Cadiz, and London; some news of European affairs, especially as they are expected to affect trade; Joseph Black's life (with practically nothing about his work, or science in general).

Persons represented by five or more pieces:
    Black, James (9)
    Black, John (d. 1767) (21)
    Black, John (d. 1782) (7)
    Black, Joseph (10)
    Black, Robert (10)

Physical description: letters.

Source: purchased from James B. Pittillo, 1979.

BLATHWAYT, WILLIAM (1649–1717)
461 pieces, 1657–1770

William Blathwayt, politician and colonial administrator, began a distinguished career in the English civil service with a clerkship in the Plantations Office in 1675, a post obtained through the influence of his uncles Thomas and Richard Povey. Advancement came rapidly, and among the offices he held were: clerk of the Privy Council, 1675; secretary to the Lords of Trade, 1679; auditor general of plantation revenues, 1680; secretary at war, 1683; acting secretary of state with William III in Flanders, 1692; member of the Board of Trade, 1696. In 1712 he retired from public life.

Subject matter: administrative operations, taxation, defense, slavery, piracy, trade and shipping, Anglo-French rivalry, Indian affairs, tobacco and politics in the West Indies and North America. Strongest for the period 1680–1709.

Persons represented by five or more pieces:
    Beeston, Sir William (5)
    Berkeley, Sir William (14)

Blathwayt, William (32)
Calvert, Philip (7)
Clarke, George (8)
D'Oyley, Edward (6)
Dudley, Joseph (9)
Hyde, Edward, 3rd Earl of Clarendon (7)
Lowndes, William (9)
Nanfan, John (16)
Penhallow, Samuel (6)
Povey, John (8)
Randolph, Edward (10)

Physical description: letters and documents.

Source: purchased from A. S. W. Rosenbach, 1924.

Bibliography: about forty pieces summarized in *Calendar of State Papers, Colonial Series; America and the West Indies* (London: H.M.S.O.).

BLATHWAYT, WILLIAM (1649–1717)
[Collection of state papers] (1688–90)
MS. 36 pieces bound in one volume

A collection of state papers and letters concerning the siege of Londonderry, annotated by Blathwayt as Secretary at War.

BOTHMER, JOHANN CASPAR VON (1656–1732), *ET AL.*
[Letters] (1713)
Autograph Ls.S. bound in one volume

Fifty-five letters from Bothmer, the Hanoverian courtier and diplomat, at The Hague, to Jean de Robethon at Hanover, bound together with other letters, mostly addressed to Bothmer, from C. F. Krienberg, L. J. Schrader, George Ridpath, John Churchill, 1st Duke of Marlborough, and various other British and European politicians and diplomats.

BRUCE, HENRY AUSTIN, 1ST BARON ABERDARE (1815–95)
537 pieces, 1843–1923

Henry Austin Bruce, 1st Baron Aberdare, barrister and politician, was called to the bar at Lincoln's Inn and served as a Liberal M.P. for Merthyr Tydvil (1852–68) and for Renfrewshire (1869–73). Aberdare was Undersecretary (1862–64) and Secretary of State for Home Affairs (1869–73). He was admitted to the Privy Council in 1864 as Vice President of the Committee of Council on Education, and in the same year was appointed a charity commissioner for England and Wales. In 1873 Aberdare became a peer, and Gladstone appointed him Lord President of the Council. When Gladstone was turned out, Aberdare's political career ended. Always interested in education, he served as the first president (1883–95) and first chancellor (1895) of University College of South Wales. He was also a Fellow of the Royal Society (1876), a member of the Royal Geographical Society (1876), and, from 1886, governor of the Royal Niger Company.

Subject matter: a wide variety of subjects are touched upon, including women in medicine, Scottish commercial fishing, capital punishment, education, patronage in church and state, electioneering, English and Irish politics, the Royal Horticulture Society, the Royal Geographical Society, and the Sanitary Law Commission.

Persons represented by five or more pieces:
Bright, John (9)
Cardwell, Edward (6)
Cooper, Anthony Ashley, 7th Earl of Shaftesbury (10)
Finter, W. E. (6)
Froude, James Anthony (5)
Jowett, Benjamin (6)
Leveson-Gower, Granville George, 5th Earl of Granville (19)
Lowe, Robert (11)
Villiers, George William Frederick, 4th Earl of Clarendon (6)

Physical description: letters.

Source: purchased from Alta California Bookstore in 1970.

BRYDGES, HENRY, 2ND DUKE OF CHANDOS (1708–71)
Journal (1720)
MS. volume 47 pp.

Kept while visiting Oxford and English and Scottish country houses, at the age of 12.

BURTON, WILLIAM (1609–57)
Britanniae Romanorum . . .
MS. 2 volumes

Apparently an unfinished dictionary of persons, places, etc. associated with Roman Britain (entries A through C only), followed by working notes and extracts from other sources; with additional notes, in another hand, on medieval England.

CANADIANA
270 pieces, 1642–1924

The Canadiana collection consists of miscellaneous material (mostly 19th century with a few earlier items) acquired over a number of years. The collection is divided into three sections: I. letters addressed to John Horn, Jr., editor of *Canada First* and autograph collector; II. papers of Henry George Vennor (1840–84), Canadian meteorologist, who was born in Montreal and graduated from McGill University in 1860. Vennor became interested in many of the natural sciences, studying ornithology as an avocation. He joined the staff of the Geological Survey of Canada in 1866, and was elected a member of the Geological Society of London in 1870. Vennor published *Our Birds of Prey* (1876) and the *Vennor Almanac* (1877); III. miscellaneous single items and small groups of letters, many from or addressed to important persons such as Queen Victoria, Benedict Arnold, and Ethan Allen, and prominent figures in Canadian history.

Subject matter: I. (86 pieces, 1859–94), information about various persons requested by John Horn, Jr. for *Canada First,* along with letters of no substantive interest collected for their autographs; II. (33 pieces, 1860–86), Henry George Vennor, chiefly his books and property affairs; the Geological Survey of Canada; III. (151 pieces, 1642–1924), Jesuit missions, Hudson's Bay Company (journals, minutes from council meetings, etc.); other scattered topics in Canadian history including the American revolutionary period, the Seven Years' War (fortifications at Quebec in 1759), and the War of 1812.

Persons represented by five or more pieces:
  Hudson's Bay Company (firm) (8)
  Le Moine, Sir James MacPherson (5)

Physical description: letters, manuscripts, and documents.

Source: Anderson Galleries (1912–19), and others.

CAREW, SIR GEORGE (d. 1612)
Account of the State of France, at his return from thence, where he was sent Ambassader by King James A° 1606 (1609)
MS. volume 72 pp.

CARLILE, RICHARD (1790–1843)
620 pieces, 1819–1900

Richard Carlile, British freethinker and journalist, was born in Ashburton, Devonshire, where he was educated in a village free school. Carlile became a strong advocate of freedom of the press, and was first arrested in 1817 for the illegal distribution of periodicals. Thereafter he was prosecuted several times for publishing the works of Thomas Paine and other blasphemous or radical literature, and altogether spent over nine years in prison as a result. His first wife, Jane, his sister, Mary Ann Carlile, and some of his shop workmen were also prosecuted for assisting him in printing and selling blasphemous or libelous tracts. Foremost among Carlile's publications was the periodical *The Republican*

(1819–26), most of which was written during his six-year confinement in Dorchester Gaol. He also encouraged freedom of speech, and promoted public discussions at the Rotunda in London in 1830. A freethinker in religion as in politics, Carlile was strongly anticlerical and was once imprisoned for resisting the payment of church rates.

Subject matter: the blasphemy and libel trials of Richard Carlile for publishing Paine's *Age of Reason* and Elihu Palmer's *Principles of Nature* in 1819 and for writing an article inciting agricultural workers to riot in 1830, and of Jane Carlile and Mary Ann Carlile for printing various articles; liberty of the press; Carlile's religious views; prison conditions.

Persons represented by five or more pieces:
    Campbell, Theophila (Carlile) (7)
    Carlile, Eliza (Sharples) (43)
    Carlile, Richard (265)
    Farrar, Squire (6)
    Holyoake, George Jacob (7)
    Mitchell, Logan (9)
    Morison, Alexander (6)
    Place, Francis (7)
    Taylor, Robert (40)

Physical description: letters, manuscripts (including 1 volume and 2 volumes of diaries), and documents.

Source: purchased from Mrs. Norman F. Stevens, 1936.

CAVENDISH, GEORGE (1500–61?)
Life of Cardinal Wolsey
MS. volume 246 pp.

A copy made ca.1600. For a detailed description, see *Guide to Medieval and Renaissance Manuscripts in the Huntington Library.*

CLARKSON, THOMAS (1760–1846)
210 pieces, 1787–1847

Thomas Clarkson, English abolitionist, was born at Wisbech, Cambridgeshire, the son of the headmaster of the local free grammar school. Clarkson was awarded grants to study at St. John's College, Cambridge, and graduated with a B.A. in 1783. He became interested in the slavery problem when, in 1785, he entered a Latin essay contest on the question of the slave trade. The next year, the publisher of the prize-winning essay introduced Clarkson to others active in the cause, and they formed a committee for the suppression of the slave trade. He devoted the rest of his life to the movement, traveling extensively, collecting and distributing material on the subject, and bringing this problem to the attention of the public. In 1789 he spent several months in Paris working to persuade the French government to abolish the slave trade. Clarkson was a vice-president of the Anti-Slavery Society formed in 1823 for the abolition of slavery in the West Indies, but poor health prevented his direct participation when the Emancipation Bill was passed in 1833. Clarkson was honored for his abolitionist work by the city of London in 1839.

Subject matter: slavery; the slave trade; the Sierra Leone Colony; activities of the British and Foreign Anti-Slavery Societies; Clarkson's relations with important figures in the British and American abolitionist movement, and with Mirabeau, Alexander I of Russia, and "the clergy and slaveholders of the United States, particularly the Southern." There is also an unpublished manuscript of Clarkson's "History of the African Institution as connected with the Abolition of Slavery and the Foreign Slave Trade"; and drafts and copies of his speeches.

Persons represented by five or more pieces:
    Beaumont, John (8)
    Chapman, Maria Weston (5)
    Clarkson, Thomas (48)
    Smith, Gerrit (6)
    Sturge, Joseph (15)
    Wright, Henry Clarke (8)

Physical description: letters, manuscripts, and documents.

Source: purchased from Eric M. Bonner, 1949, and Maggs Brothers, 1953.

[CLERKE, FRANCIS] (fl. 1594)
De curiis ecclesiasticus que auctoritate Reverendissimi Cantuarensi Archiepiscopi infra civitatem Londoni celebrantur (ca.1610)
MS. volume 332 pp.

The text of this treatise on the Court of Arches was published in 1666 as *Praxis Francisi Clarke.* . . . (Wing C 4440), with a last chapter not present in this manuscript.

[CLOGIE, ALEXANDER] (1614–98)
Speculum Episcoporum, or, The Apostolique Bishop, being a breiff account of the lyfe & death of that Reverend Father in God D. William Bedell Lord Bishop of Kilmore . . . (ca.1675)
Autograph Df. volume 117 pp.

COBBE, FRANCES POWER (1822–1904)
854 pieces, 1855–1902

Frances Power Cobbe, philanthropist, early social worker, journalist, and author, was born in Dublin to a family of Anglo-Irish gentry with strongly evangelical religious beliefs. After education at a select boarding school in Brighton and extensive travel in Europe and throughout the Mediterranean, she settled in Bristol in 1858 and began a career as a social worker at the Red Lodge Reformatory and in numerous schools for poor children. Thereafter, her social work, continuing travels, religious beliefs (which shifted to a more general Theism), and a strong interest in the women's movement and in the Anti-Vivisection League, provided subjects for a steady stream of books, articles, editorials, and lectures. Miss Cobbe was acquainted with many prominent figures of the day, including philosophers and writers such as John Stuart Mill, Charles Lutwidge Dodson, Henry James, and Robert Louis Stevenson, and spent several years in London during the 1860s and 1870s. In 1884 she retired to Hengwrt in Wales, and ten years later published a two-volume autobiography.

Subject matter: women's suffrage and rights; antivivisection; Frances Power Cobbe's social work at Bristol and her moral and religious writings; comments on her books and articles by friends.

Persons represented by five or more pieces:
 Browne, Bp. Edward Harold (8)
 Butler, Frances Anne (Kemble) (5)
 Carpenter, Mary (23)
 Channing, William Henry (5)
 Colenso, John William Bp. (11)
 Cooper, Anthony Ashley, 7th Earl of Shaftesbury (238)
 Darwin, Charles Robert (5)
 Froude, James Anthony (34)
 How, Bishop William Walsham (5)
 Hutton, Richard Holt (8)
 Kesavachandra, Sena (14)
 Lecky, William Edward Hartpole (5)
 Manning, Henry Edward, Cardinal (5)
 Martineau, James (26)
 Morley, John, 1st Viscount Morley of Blackburn (5)
 Parker, Theodore (17)
 Pécaut, Felix (12)
 Spencer, Herbert (5)
 Stanley, Arthur Penryn (10)
 Ward, Mary Augusta (Arnold) (10)
 Wilberforce, Albert Basil Orme (7)

Physical description: letters, manuscripts, and 1 pencil drawing.

Source: purchased from Ifan Kyrle Fletcher, 1949.

COLEMAN, MORGAN (fl. 1621–22)
A Booke wherein is declared sundry orders and duties to be . . . sett downe for the better ordering and direction of the house

of the right Honble Lyonell . . . Cranfield [1st] Earle of Middlesex
. . . (1621–22)
MS. volume 69 pp.

COLLET, JOHN (fl. 1776–79)
209 pieces. 1776–79

John Collet was appointed to the post of British consul in Genoa,
succeeding James Hollford in December, 1776. He was assisted
by Joseph Brame, vice consul. Their correspondent in the series
of letters that constitute this collection was William Deane Poyntz,
British chargé d'affaires in Turin, Italy.

Subject matter: political, commercial, and military news of Europe, including the actions of American privateers in the Mediterranean and the Atlantic; news from America about the War for
Independence.

Persons represented by five or more pieces:
    Brame, Joseph (22)
    Collet, John (170)

Physical description: letters.

Source: purchased from Maggs Bros. of London in 1976.

COMMONPLACE BOOK. ECONOMICS
MS. volume 156 pp.

Copies of treatises and records concerning English currency, the
wool trade, foreign exchange, the Royal Mint, etc. (ca.1550)

COMMONPLACE BOOK. ENGLISH HISTORY
MS. volume 82 pp.

Copies of letters of Sir Walter Ralegh, Robert Devereux (2nd
Earl of Essex), Henry Brooke (8th Baron Cobham), Sir Philip Sid-

ney, William Cecil (Baron Burghley), Thomas Egerton (1st Viscount Brackley), and other prominent persons. 1580–1620

COMMONPLACE BOOK. ENGLISH HISTORY
MS. volume 243 pp.

Includes copies of "Leicester's Commonwealth," "Burghley's Commonwealth," Sir Francis Bacon's "Certain Observations Made Upon a Libel," letters by Sir Walter Ralegh, etc. (ca.1610)

COMMONPLACE BOOK. ENGLISH HISTORY
MS. volume 88 pp.

Accounts of foreign and domestic affairs *temp.* Charles I, including the English landing on the Isle of Ré, the Seige of La Rochelle, Privy Council proceedings involving Sir John Corryton, and a description of "the Late deceased Prince of Bohemia." (ca.1627–29)

COMMONPLACE BOOK. ENGLISH HISTORY
MS. volume 258 pp.

Extracts from medieval records about defense, including information about general musters, the provision of ships for defense, the defense of the sea coast, and the use of beacons. (ca.1630)

COMMONPLACE BOOK. ENGLISH HISTORY
MS. volume 287 pp.

Copies of letters, treatises, and accounts of legal proceedings, chiefly in England, in the late 16th and early 17th centuries, including accounts of the rebellion, trial, and execution of the Earl of

Essex, a copy of the "Liber Intrationem [in Camera Stellata tempore Regis Henr. Septimi]", other proceedings in Star Chamber, Sir Henry Wotton on George Villiers, Duke of Buckingham, etc. (1633<)

COMMONPLACE BOOK. ENGLISH HISTORY
MS. volume 124 pp.

Extracts from the works of Francis Bacon, maxims of state, notes on a book of ancient history, etc. (ca.1660)

COMMONPLACE BOOK. ENGLISH LAW
MS. volume 212 pp.

Extracts from Year Books, abridgements of cases and decisions, law reports, precedents and formularies, notes on the Assize of Forests and other legal matters. Owned by [and partly in the hand of?] Sir John Port. (ca.1480–ca.1540)

COMMONPLACE BOOK. ENGLISH LAW
MS. volume 371 pp.

A "book of entries," or collection of precedents of pleading. (ca.1550)

COMMONPLACE BOOK. PARLIAMENT
MS. volume 302 pp.

Copies of speeches in Parliament, 1623–28, preceded by a roll of knights created 1603–24. (ca.1630)

COMMONPLACE BOOK. PARLIAMENT
A Booke Conteyning the whole Passages of the last Parliament ended the 10th daie of March 1628 Wth other materiall passages that happened from the yeare 1623 untill the end of the Parliament in the Yeare 1628[/29]. (ca.1629)
MS. volume 529 pp.

COMMONPLACE BOOK. POETICAL AND LEGAL
MS. volume 182 pp.

Contains poems by Ben Jonson, John Donne, Richard Corbett, and others, with (in a different hand) instructions for Justices of the Peace, arranged by topic in alphabetical order. ca.1623–40

COMMONPLACE BOOK. RELIGIOUS
MS. volume 84 pp.

Contains copy of Abp. Tillotson's letter to a friend, Abp. Ussher's "Last Prediction," a sermon on the death of Lady Elizabeth Hastings, etc. Owned by Selina (Shirley) Hastings, Countess of Huntingdon. (ca.1740)

COMMONPLACE BOOK. ROYAL HOUSEHOLD
MS. volume 438 pp.

Copies of regulations, ordinances, and tracts concerning the operation and expenses of Yorkist and Tudor royal households. (1572◁)

COMMONPLACE BOOK. SERMONS AND TRAVEL
MS. volume ca.300 pp.

A collection of sermons, notes for sermons, and notes on travel in Africa and Persia, by an unknown Englishman. ca.1680–1700

CORNWALL. STANNARY PARLIAMENT
Proceedings of the 24 stannators or parliament of tinners . . .
1635 & 1662 . . . vera copia. (ca.1670)
MS. volume 100 pp.

CORNWALLIS, SIR WILLIAM (d. 1631?)
A Brife discourse in praise of kinge Richard the Third . . . (ca.1600)
MS. volume 41 pp.

COTTON, SIR ROBERT BRUCE (1571–1631)
[Records collected by Sir Robert Cotton concerning impositions
and defense] (ca.1605)
MS. volume 135 pp.

COWARD, MAGDALEN (fl. 1695)
Booke of Receipts (1695)
Autograph MS. volume 169 pp.

Contains medical and culinary recipes.

DERING, SIR EDWARD (fl. 1650s)
Ephemeris [Diary and Commonplace Book] (1656–62)
Autograph MS.S. volume 376 pp.

DOUGLAS, SAMUEL (fl. 1780s)
Letterbook. (1782–88)
MS. volume 93 pp.

Business and family correspondence of a British merchant living
in New York and traveling between New York and London.

DUNDAS, ROBERT SAUNDERS, 2ND VISCOUNT MELVILLE
(1771–1851)
42 pieces, 1812–14

Robert Saunders Dundas, British statesman, entered politics as a Member of Parliament in 1794, succeeded his father as 2nd Viscount Melville in 1811, and was appointed First Lord of the Admiralty the following year. He occupied this post during the War of 1812 and throughout the long Tory ministry of Lord Liverpool, returned briefly in 1828 under Wellington, and retired from active political life in 1830.

Subject matter: the War of 1812 between Great Britain and the United States as reflected in Admiralty reports and memoranda, particularly concerning: strategy and ship deployment of British Admirals Cochrane, Schanck, and others on the American and West Indian stations; the superiority of American over British frigates and attempts to remedy the situation; a little information about the American navy and American military preparedness.

Physical description: letters and documents.

Source: acquired from Maggs Bros. of London in 1923.

DYMOCKE, JAMES (d. 1718?)
Dictionary of Memorable Things in Nature, Arts & Sciences. (1700?)
Autograph MS.S. volume 776 pp.

[FILMER, SIR ROBERT] (d. 1653)
[Quaestio Quodlibetica, or a Discourse Whether it may bee Lawfull to take Use for Money] (1626<>1635)
Autograph MS. volume 119 pp.

FISHER, EDWARD
[Journal of voyage up the Elbe on the frigate "Proserpine" accompanying Thomas Grenville to Berlin as British Ambassador] (1799)
MS. 27 pp.

[GEORGE, DUKE OF CLARENCE (1447–78)]
The Stablishements and Ordinances made at Waltham abbey the xth daye of December the yere of oure Lord God MCCCCLXVIII and the viii yere of King Edward the Fowrth for the Rule ordinance and guiding of the houshoulde of the Right high and mightye prince the Duke of Clarence. (1500<)
MS. volume 120 pp.

A 16th-century copy, followed by "The Order of a Nobleman's House as Duke, Marques, Earle," by ?Robert Boys.

GIBSON, EDMUND (1669–1748)
76 pieces, 1694–1767

Edmund Gibson, Bishop of London, was born at Knipe, Westmoreland, and educated at Bampton Grammar School, and at Queens College, Oxford, where he received a B.A. in 1691 and an M.A. in 1694. Gibson began to publish books dealing with Anglo-Saxon studies and general antiquarian interests, and in 1692 published a catalog of the manuscripts in the library founded by Thomas Tenison at St. Martins-in-the-Fields. Gibson was ordained priest in 1697, and owed much of his subsequent ecclesiastical preferment to Tenison, now Archbishop of Canterbury, who appointed him domestic chaplain and librarian at Lambeth. In 1713 he published his most important work, the *Codex Juris Ecclesiae Anglicanae,* a comprehensive compilation of the laws of the Church of England, which became the standard authority on church law and of which an abstract was published by Richard Grey in 1730. Gibson was created Bishop of Lincoln in 1716 and translated to London in 1723, where he continued his literary activities and instituted campaigns for theological orthodoxy and against contemporary immorality. A High Church Whig, Gibson was an influential advisor to Sir Robert Walpole until the two fell out over Gibson's strenuous and successful opposition to the Quaker's Relief Bill of 1736. In 1737 Gibson, long recognized as a candidate for the Archbishopric of Canterbury, was passed over in favor of John Potter. At the latter's death in 1747 Gibson was at last offered the appointment, but declined on the grounds of age and ill health, and died in Bath the following year.

Subject matter: 18th-century English religious affairs and ecclesiastical patronage, as reflected in the correspondence of Bishop Edmund Gibson with important religious and political figures such as the Archbishop of Canterbury, the Bishops of Worcester, Chichester, Salisbury, Derry, and Lincoln, the Duke of Newcastle, the 3rd Earl of Burlington, the 1st Earl Hardwicke, and 5th Baron of Baltimore; some material concerning the publication of the *Codex Juris Ecclesiae Anglicanae* after Gibson's death; and some personal and financial affairs.

Persons represented by five or more pieces:
    Gibson, Edmund, Bp. (18)
    Herring, Thomas, Abp. (6)
    Hough, John, Bp. (5)

Physical description: letters, manuscripts, and documents.

Source: gift of Frank Marcham, 1940.

GORDON, FREDERICK (fl. 1807)
[Pocket-book containing Exercises and Maneuvres for Light 6-pounders, as devised for the use of the Royal Regiment of Artillery by William Congreve in 1778, and Alexander Young Spearman in 1796] (1807)
Autograph MS.S. volume 143 pp.

Includes pen drawings and diagrams.

GRANVILLE, SIR BEVIL (fl. 1690s)
[Accounts as Colonel of the Earl of Bath's Regiment of Foot]
(1692–98)
MS. volume 212 pp.

Includes service in Flanders and England.

GREAT BRITAIN. ARMY. ENGINEER CORPS
[Orderly Book] (1776)
MS. volume 96 pp.

Contains General Orders given by Matthew Dixon, Chief Engineer, on Long Island, August 14–September 20, 1776.

GREAT BRITAIN. ARMY. 71ST REGIMENT. 2ND BATTALION.
[Orderly Book] (1778)
MS. volume 222 pp.

For Brigadier General Sir Archibald Campbell's command, Staten Island and New York City, April 21–September 9, 1778.

GREAT BRITAIN. ARMY. PROVINCIAL FORCES OF NEW YORK. KING'S ROYAL REGIMENT OF NEW YORK.
[Orderly Book] (1776–77)
MS. volume 145 pp.

For Lieutenant Colonel Sir John Johnson's company, at La Praire, La Chine, and Buck's Island, November 5, 1776–July 19, 1777.

GREAT BRITAIN. ARMY. PROVINCIAL FORCES OF PENNSYLVANIA.
Col. Bouquet's Orders. (1758)
MS. volume 68 pp.

An orderly book of the 3rd Battalion of the Pennsylvania Regiment, containing the orders of Col. Henry Bouquet in connection with Gen. John Forbes's assault on Fort Duquesne. Also pertains to Forts Raystown and Lyttleton, Pa. Covers June 17 to Sept. 14, 1758. Published in *The Papers of Henry Bouquet*, ed. S. K. Stevens, Donald Kent, and Louis Waddell (Harrisburg: The Pennsylvania Historical Museum Commission, 1951–), 2:656–90.

An Orderly Book of Samuel Grubb's Company. (1759)
MS. volume 99 pp.

Covers June 18 to July 24, 1759. Concerns the activities of the British army around Ford Bedford (Raystown) and Carlisle, Pa. The volume also contains commercial accounts by William Worrall, 1771–92.

GREAT BRITAIN. ATTORNEY AND SOLICITOR GENERAL
General Reports. (1763–67)
MS. volume 176 pp.

Copies of official papers on various American colonial subjects, including Newfoundland fisheries, admiralty courts, the northern boundary of West Florida, and inventions.

GREAT BRITAIN. BOARD OF TRADE
To the Right Hon[ora]ble Lords Spiritual and Temporal in Parliament Assembled: [A Representation of the State of the Trade of This Kingdom] (1707)
MS. volume 199 pp.

Published in Historical Manuscripts Commission, *The Manuscripts of the House of Lords, 1706–1708* (London: His Majesty's Stationery Office, 1921), n.s., 7:232–309.

GREAT BRITAIN. BOARD OF TRADE
[Report of conditions in America] (1721)
MS. volume 129 pp. (Contemporary copy)

GREAT BRITAIN. COURTS. COURT OF EXCHEQUER CHAM-
BER
[Transcript of the Ship Money Case] (ca.1638)
MS. volume 512 pp. (Contemporary copy)

[GREAT BRITAIN. COURTS. COURT OF STAR CHAMBER]
The proceedinges in the Starrchamber against Mr. Prinn for Writ-
ting a Booke intituled Histrio Mastix. (1633)
MS. volume 111 pp.

GREAT BRITAIN. CUSTOMS COMMISSIONERS
The Establishment of the Officers of the Customs. (1702)
MS. volume 36 pp.

Contains names and salaries of Customs Commissioners, deputies,
and other Customs officials at individual English ports.

GREAT BRITAIN. EXCHEQUER
[Names of all] the Lordes . . . and gentilmen of the [several coun-
ties] . . . and also the certificate of all them that shalbe made
Knightes of the Bath anno sextodecimo. (1500–01)
MS. volume 110 pp.

[GREAT BRITAIN. EXCHEQUER?]
Booke of Ayds for Knightinge the King's eldest sonne & for mar-
riage of his eldest daughter. 1609
MS. volume 145 pp.

GREAT BRITAIN. NAVY
[Book of Signals] (1779)
MS. volume 104 pp.

This volume formerly belonged to Sir William Chaloner Burnaby,
Bart.

[Book of Signals] (ca.1780)
MS. volume 100 pp.

[GREAT BRITAIN. PARLIAMENT]
[Names of members of the Convention Parliament] (1688)
MS. volume 50 pp.

GREAT BRITAIN. PARLIAMENT. HOUSE OF COMMONS
[Returns for the Westminster election of 1784]
MS. volume 45 pp.

Alphabetically arranged, giving the name, residence, and occupation of the electors.

GREAT BRITAIN. PARLIAMENT. HOUSE OF LORDS
[Journal] (1701)
MS. volume 486 pp.

A contemporary copy of the House of Lords Journal from February 10, 1700/01 through June 24, 1701.

GREAT BRITAIN. PARLIAMENT. HOUSE OF LORDS
Remembrances for order and decency to be kept in the Upper House of Parliament . . . (ca.1710)
MS. volume 94 pp.

A copy of the "Lords Standing Orders."

[Another copy] (ca.1711)
MS. volume 102 pp.

[Another copy] (ca.1728)
MS. volume 100 pp.

GREAT BRITAIN. PAYMASTER GENERAL
184 pieces, 1766–1827

The official under whose authority the papers in this collection
were created was the Receiver and Paymaster General of the
Forces until 1835, when his office was combined with others to
form H. M. Paymaster General Office. The Paymaster General
of the Forces was responsible for preparing payrolls, requisition-
ing funds from the Treasury, and paying the army. Sometimes
colonial civil government was funded through his office because
the colonial governors were also commanders of the armed forces
in their respective colonies. During the period encompassed by
this collection, the operations of the office were reformed to end
abuses.

Subject matter: military pay warrants, receipts, and estimates for
British forces in the Mediterranean and North America, particularly Nova Scotia, Upper and Lower Canada, and Quebec; pay
warrants for the colonial governments of Canada; miscellaneous
documents such as returns of provisions and assignments of off-
reckoning.

Persons represented by five or more pieces:
    Milnes, Sir Robert Shore (11)
    Prevost, Sir George (56)
    Sherbrooke, Sir John (9)

Physical description: documents.

Source: unknown.

GREAT BRITAIN. PRIVY COUNCIL
Copies and Extracts of All Such Papers and Letters Transmitted
to the Councill Office as Relate to the Riots . . . in America in

Opposition to the Putting in Execution the Stamp Act . . . Likewise Copies of All Orders &c Issued from the Councill. (1765)
MS. volume 148 pp.

———————

Copies of Papers Transmitted to the Council Office re: the Assemblys of Massachusetts Bay and New York Previous to the Passage of the [Stamp Act] (1764–65)
MS. volume 47 pp.

[GREW, NEHEMIAH (1641–1712)?]
The Meanes of a most Ample Encrease of The Wealth & Strength of England In a few years. (ca.1707–08)
Autograph MS.S. volume 207 pp.

A comprehensive program of suggestions for dealing with the land, agriculture, minerals, enclosures, stock, manufacturing, trade, roads and rivers, etc.

[GREY, HENRY, *ET AL.?*]
[A volume of charters, laws, ceremonies, and notes of meetings of "the most Ancient & Honourable Order of the Gregoreans"]
(1747–1804)
MS. volume 173 pp.

GROVE, HENRY (1684–1738)
A System of Pneumatology in a Series of Lectures . . . (ca.1740)
MS. volume 327 pp.

HACK, WILLIAM (fl. 1681–1710)
A Description of the Sea Coasts in the South Sea of America from the Port of Acapulco to the Straights of Lemaire. (ca.1684)
MS. volume Atlas of 130 charts

An English copy of the Spanish atlas "Derrotero general del Mar del Sur" of 1669, taken from Captain Bartholomew Sharp's *South Sea Waggoner.*

HAMILTON-GREVILLE COLLECTION
87 pieces, 1769–1801

Sir William Hamilton (1730–1803), diplomat and archaeologist, served as British ambassador to the court of Naples from 1764 to 1800. During this period he studied volcanoes and earthquakes and collected Greek and Roman artifacts. In 1791 he was made a Privy Councillor. In 1769 he began a regular correspondence with his nephew, Charles Francis Greville (1749–1809), with whom he shared numerous interests and tastes.

Subject matter: gossip about various persons in English and Neapolitan ruling and cultural circles of the day; political observations and opinions; diplomacy; volcanism and earthquakes; the collecting of Greek and Roman artifacts.

Persons represented by five or more pieces:
    Greville, Charles Francis (50)
    Hamilton, Sir William (37)

Physical description: letters.

Source: unknown.

Bibliography: the entire collection is published in Alfred Morrison, comp., *The Hamilton-Greville Papers,* 2 vols. (n.p., 1893–94).

HASTINGS, ELIZABETH (STANLEY), COUNTESS OF HUNTINGDON
Certaine Collections of the right Honble Elizabeth late Countess of Huntingdon for her own private use. (1633)
MS. volume 57 pp. (Contemporary copy)

A commonplace book of prayers, meditations, etc.

HASTINGS, HENRY, 3RD EARL OF HUNTINGDON (1535-95)
[Letterbook] (1580-90)
MS. volume 406 pp.

Copies of official correspondence concerning the military defense
of the North, written in the Earl's official capacities as Lord President of the North and Lord Lieutenant of several northern counties.

HASTINGS, THEOPHILUS, 7TH EARL OF HUNTINGDON
(1650-1701)
[Receipt Book] (1687-96)
MS. volume 268 pp.

Signed receipts from tradesmen, laborers, etc. for personal and
estate expenditures by or on behalf of the 7th Earl.

HERBERT FAMILY COLLECTION
419 pieces, 1667-1780

Thomas Herbert (d. 1712) of Whittlebury, Northamptonshire,
served from 1672 until his death as bailiff on the estates near
Whittlebury of Henry Bennet, 1st Earl of Arlington, which passed
in turn to the Earl's daughter Isabella (Bennet) Fitzroy Hanmer,
Duchess of Grafton, and at her death to her son Charles Fitzroy,
2nd Duke of Grafton. Of Herbert's two sons one, Thomas, remained in Whittlebury and succeeded his father as bailiff of the
Grafton estates. Thomas Herbert the younger died in 1728, leaving
as survivors his widow, Alice, and at least one daughter who married Thomas Cooke about 1772. The elder Herbert's other son,
Edmund, left Whittlebury, took part (1709-10) in an expedition
to the Scilly Isles to recover sunken treasure, and finally settled
in London, where he entered Gray's Inn in 1725 and worked in
the Treasury or Pay Office of the Marines as first clerk and later
as deputy to Arthur Swift. Edmund Herbert was an active student
of foreign languages (sixteen of them), and an avid book collector.

He died unmarried and his estates Shrob Walk and Stocking House, near Whittlebury, were inherited by his niece.

Subject matter: Thomas Herbert and his estate accounts as bailiff, including wood books and other papers relating to Whittlebury Forest; Edmund Herbert's personal life (including copious expense and memoranda notebooks, covering almost daily expenses for the years 1708–34 and 1739–68), residence at Gray's Inn, correspondence with his sister and nieces, and work in the Marine Pay Office (including accounts and memoranda, drafts of memorials addressed to the Treasury Commissioners, and correspondence regarding payment to marines).

Persons represented by five or more pieces:
    Cooke, Agnes (Herbert) (19)
    Herbert, Edmund (ca.150)
    Herbert, Thomas (35)
    Leighton, John (8)
    Scrope, John (11)
    Williams, Sir Charles Hanbury (6)

Physical description: letters, documents (including many accounts), and manuscripts.

Source: Purchased from H. M. Fletcher in 1954.

HERBERT, SIDNEY, 1ST BARON HERBERT OF LEA (1810–61)
96 pieces, 1849

Sidney Herbert, British statesman and military reformer, was born at Richmond, Surrey, and educated at Harrow and at Oriel College, Oxford, where he was president of the Oxford Union Society. He was elected Conservative M.P. for Wiltshire in the Parliament of 1834, and appointed Secretary of the Board of Control by Sir Robert Peel. Thereafter Herbert held office in several administrations (first as a Conservative, then a Peelite, and finally as a Liberal after 1858), including the posts of Secretary to the Admiralty, Secretary at War, and Colonial Secretary. He was created 1st

Baron Herbert of Lea in 1860, but ill health forced his resignation from office and he returned to a private life devoted to extensive charitable concerns.

Subject matter: reaction to and discussion of Sir Sidney Herbert's "Proposals for the Better Application of Cathedral Institutions to their Intended Uses" (a pamphlet printed privately in 1849 in the form of a letter to Edward Denison, then Dean of Salisbury), as seen in lengthy letters to Herbert from leading lay and clerical figures (including many associated with the Oxford Movement) such as: Archbishop of Canterbury Charles Thomas Longley, bishops Richard Bagot of Salisbury, Christopher Bethell of Exeter, Edward Denison of Salisbury, John Kaye of Lincoln, Alfred Ollivant of Llandoff, and Samuel Wilberforce of Oxford, Dean of Canterbury William Rowe Lyall, Archdeacon of East Riding Robert Isaac Wilberforce, Sir Thomas Dyke Acland, William Ewart Gladstone, John Keble, George William Lyttleton, 4th Baron Lyttleton of Frankton, Charles Marriott, and Lord Chancellor William Page Wood, Baron Hatherley.

Physical description: letters.

Source: purchased from Dawson's Book Shop, 1952, for the Huntington Library as a gift of A. B. Ruddock through the Friends of the Library.

HISTORIANS' FILE

The Historians' File is an artificial collection consisting of the research notes and working papers of various historians of English history and society, donated to the Huntington over the years for the benefit of future scholars.

Among the papers are those of the following scholars:
1) *C. H. Collins Baker.* Research notes, indexes, and some preliminary drafts for his biography *The Life and Circumstances of James Brydges, 1st Duke of Chandos* (Oxford University Press, 1949). Included are extensive extracts

    from, and indexes to, the 71 volumes of Brydges letterbooks and to the Duke's two-volume Journal. (3 boxes, 12 notebooks, and 3 index card files)

2) *Godfrey Davies.* Professional correspondence, research notes, transcripts of original documents, lecture notes, and other papers concerning, among other topics, England in the 17th century, British foreign policy, and some contemporary events and issues (World War II, English and Irish life, etc.). (Approximately 4,500 pieces)

3) *Guernsey Jones.* Notes, transcripts, etc. from manuscripts in London and on the Continent (chiefly at Simancas) dealing with Anglo-Spanish and Anglo-Portuguese relations in the 17th century. (2 boxes.)

4) *Richard Ager Newhall.* Notes from, and many full transcripts of, over 9,000 documents in English and French archives dealing with the military, financial, and administrative aspects of English government in Normandy, ca.1416–49. (9 boxes)

5) *Charles William Wallace.* Personal and professional papers pertaining to his research on the English drama and English theaters in the 16th and 17th centuries, including extensive transcripts of source material dealing with plays presented at Court, personalities in the theater, individual theaters, and numerous legal cases and proceedings involving the theater and theatrical personalities. (15 boxes and 2 index files)

Physical description: notebooks, loose papers, note- and index-cards, draft manuscripts, photostats, etc.

Source: gifts of various scholars or their families or estates over many years.

HOWARD, HENRIETTA (HOBART), COUNTESS OF SUFFOLK (1688?–1767)
40 pieces, 1715–1824

Henrietta Hobart, daughter of Sir Henry Hobart, 4th Bart., married in 1706 Charles Howard, afterward 9th Earl of Suffolk (1675–1733). She was the acknowledged mistress of the Prince of Wales (afterward George II), and a Lady of the Bedchamber to his wife, Princess (later Queen) Caroline. As such, the Countess was much courted for favor and patronage, and was also well known in literary circles of the time. She retired from Court in 1734, and the following year married, for a second husband, the Hon. George Berkeley (d. 1746). She died in 1767 at the age of 86. A selection of her letters, edited by John Wilson Croker, was published in 1824.

Subject matter: activities and social life of the Countess of Suffolk and her circle; requests for favor and thanks for past assistance; family matters. Included are an anonymous but purportedly first-hand account of the alleged murder of Samuel Molyneux by the physician Nathaniel St. Andre, and Sir Walter Scott's autograph review of the 1824 edition of the Countess's letters. There is little concerning George II or Court politics.

Persons represented by five or more pieces:
     Howard, Henrietta (Hobart), Countess of Suffolk (5)

Source: purchased through George D. Smith (from a larger collection owned variously by Thomas Phillipps, Hoe, and Robinson) in the ?1920s.

HOWE, RICHARD, EARL HOWE (1726–99)
408 pieces, 1776–99

Richard Howe, Admiral of the Fleet and Earl Howe, entered the Royal Havy in 1739 and was promoted to Captain in 1748, Rear Admiral in 1770, and Vice-Admiral in 1776, when he was sent to the American Colonies as Commander of the North American Station. Although waging a successful defensive campaign there, Howe resigned in 1778 out of discontent with the current ministry. He returned to duty four years later as Commander of the Channel Fleet with the rank of Admiral, and served as First Lord of the Admiralty from 1783 to 1788, when he was created Earl Howe. As a naval administrator Howe instituted dockyard reforms, improved the signaling system, and maintained an interest in the lot of the common seaman and in ship design and construction. In 1793 he took command of the Channel Fleet, but opposed a close blockade of French ports and was criticized for not engaging the enemy fleet. In the following year he inflicted a major defeat on the French in the battle of "The Glorious First of June," but his active fighting career ended shortly therafter. Although still nominal Commander-in-Chief of the Channel Fleet, Howe spent increasing time ashore. He presided at the courtmartial of Vice-Admiral Cornwallis in 1796, and in the following year was instrumental in ending the naval mutiny at Spithead. This was his last official work, and he died in 1799.

Subject matter: British naval operations, chiefly in the Channel during the wars of the First and Second Coalitions; the preparation of the Channel Fleet; naval administration and personnel; ships and their design, construction, repair, and equipment; signaling and signal books, some personal affairs of Earl Howe. There is a very little on the navy during the American war, and only passing references to the "Glorious First of June." The collection consists almost entirely of Howe's letters to Admiral Sir Roger Curtis.

Persons represented by five or more pieces:
    Howe, Richard, Earl Howe (402)

Physical description: letters.

Source: purchased from Maggs Bros. of London in 1927.

IRELAND
[Copies of ancient charters, deeds, etc. concerning Ireland]
(ca.1816)
MS. volume 352 pp.

Copies of ancient charters, treaties, grants, extracts from Parliament Rolls, etc. concerning Ireland, and particularly Co. Galway, during the years 1170–1320.

JORDAN, DOROTHY (1761–1816)
approximately 550 pieces, 1796–1852

Dorothy Jordan (nee Bland), actress and mistress of William IV, was born in London but lived in Ireland as a young girl. Her stage career began in Dublin in 1779 but after bearing a child to her stage manager there she returned to England, and by 1785 was acting in London, where she had two additional children by Richard Ford, a share-holder and actor at the Drury Lane Theater. In 1790 she attracted the attention of the Duke of Clarence (afterward William IV), and following a financial settlement with Ford for the care of her children she moved into William's apartments at St. James and Clarence Lodge, following him to Bushby Park when he was appointed Ranger of Bushby in 1797. Mrs. Jordan continued her career on the stage but also managed to bear five sons and five daughters to William between 1794 and 1810. At his wish they separated in 1811, after which she moved to France, where she died destitute in 1816.

Subject matter: personal affairs of Dorothy Jordan and William IV; the British theater (1800–11); some political commentary. The bulk of the collection falls within the period 1800–11.

Persons represented by five or more pieces:
Jordan, Dorothy (529)

Physical description: letters, a few documents, and ephemera.

Source: purchased from William K. Bixby, 1918.

Bibliography: many of the letters have been published in *Mrs. Jordan and Her Family, Being the Unpublished Correspondence of Mrs. Jordan and the Duke of Clarence, Later William IV,* Arthur Aspinall, ed. (London: Arthur Barker Ltd., 1951).

KEENE, JOSHUA (fl. 1813)
[Notebook] (1813)
Autograph MS.S. volume 93 pp.

Records concerning H.M.S. "Peacock," including the engagement with the U.S. sloop-of-war "Hornet," with tabulated lists, etc.

KEITH, SIR ROBERT MURRAY (1730–95)
[Letterbook] (1776–92)
Autograph MS. volume 401 pp.

Volume consists of 99 letters written by Keith, British ambassador to the court of Vienna (1772–87), to his cousin Frances Maria Murray, daughter of Lt. Gen. Thomas Murray. Contains gossip about Keith's and Frances Murray's circles of friends, relatives, and acquaintances, personal news, and remarks on international affairs, especially the British conflicts with France and the American colonies.

KIDD, WILLIAM LODGE (fl. 1800–18)
Journal (1806–18)
Autograph MS.S. 14 volumes

Journal of a British naval surgeon on H.M. ships "Bacchante," "Tromp," "Peloris," and "Raleigh."

———

Sundays [Records of Sermons heard] (1805–15)
Autograph MS. volume 71 pp.

———

A Concise Account of the Typhus Fever at present prevalent in Ireland . . . (1817)
Autograph MS.S. volume 34 pp.

Written for the Royal Physical Society of Edinburgh, of which Kidd was President.

KNOLLYS, SIR FRANCIS (1514?–96)
A Booke of exchange of merchants (ca.1590)
MS. volume 46 pp.

A discussion of the principles of mercantile exchanges of weights and currencies, with examples, followed by a brief treatise on the Mint and coinage.

LARKIN, THOMAS OLIVER (fl. 1856)
Names of the British Subjects & Citizens of the United States who resided in Alta California prior to 1840, with their place of residence, profession, & the year of their arrival . . . (1856)

D. 14 pp.

Contains 249 names, alphabetized.

LARPENT, ANNA MARGARETTA (PORTER)
[Diaries] (1790–1830)
Autograph MS. 16 volumes

Accounts of domestic and theatrical events kept by the wife of John Larpent (1741–1824), Examiner of Plays. (A large collection of plays presented for Larpent's approval during his tenure as Examiner is described in *Guide to Literary Manuscripts in the Huntington Library*.) Lacks entries for the years 1801, 1819, 1822–23, and 1825.

A Methodized Journal (1773–87)
Autograph MS.S. volume

"LEICESTER'S COMMONWEALTH"
MS. volume 165 pp.

A contemporary attack on Robert Dudley, Earl of Leicester, formerly attributed to the Jesuit Robert Parsons. More properly titled

"The Copy of a Letter written by a master of Art of Cambridge . . . concerning . . . some proceedings of the Earl of Leicester and his friends in England." (ca.1590)

LLOYD, ABRAHAM (fl. 1674–86)
Journal of . . . [a] voyage in ship Katherine of Bristoll . . . unto the iland of Barbados [and of other journeys in the same and other ships] (1674–86)
Autograph MS.S. volume 150 pp.

Other ships include the "Friendship" and the "Michael," both of Bristol; other destinations include Goteburg (Sweden), Boston, Antigua, and the Cape Verde Islands.

LOK, MICHAEL (fl. 1570s)
Thaccount gyven by Michael Lok of the third voiage of Martin furbusher for the discourye of Cathaj &c by the Northwest partes. (1578)
MS. volume 54 pp.

An account prepared for the Privy Council hearings into the failure of Frobisher's voyage, including lists of the original shareholders in the Cathay Company.

LONDON. (INHABITANTS OF)
[Petition to Charles II asking that Parliament protect King and country from the "Popish Plot."] (1679)
MS.S. 169 ff.

Original signatures of approximately 20,000 citizens, merchants, and other inhabitants of the City of London.

LONDON. TOWN CLERK

Town Clerk's journal of bussiness done by himself in office (1758)
MS. volume 276 pp.

Daily journal of transactions kept by Sir James Hodges as Town
Clerk of the City of London.

LOUDOUN COLLECTION—SCOTTISH

ca.6,000 pieces, 1510–1839

The papers of the Campbell family, earls of Loudoun, comprise
some 16,000 pieces, more than half of which relate to the 3rd
Earl's military role in American affairs and are described in the
*Guide to American Historical Manuscripts in the Huntington Li-
brary.* The remainder of the collection is the subject of the following entry.

The vast majority of the Loudoun Scottish Collection consists
of the political and military correspondence, memoranda, and
other papers of Hugh Campbell, 3rd Earl of Loudoun (ca.1668–
1731) and his son John Campbell, the 4th Earl (1705–82). There
are a few earlier pieces, pertaining chiefly to the Mure family,
Lairds of Rowallan, who are connected to the Campbells through
the marriage about 1720 of Lady Jean Boyle, heiress of Sir William
Mure of Rowallan, to Sir James Campbell of Lawers, father of
James Mure Campbell, 5th Earl of Loudoun (1726–86).

Hugh Campbell, 3rd Earl of Loudoun, began a national political
career with an appointment to the Scottish Privy Council in 1697.
He also served as an extraordinary Lord of Session (1699–1731),
joint Secretary of State for Scotland (1704), and Keeper of the
Great Seal of Scotland (1708–13). A strong supporter of the Union,
he was appointed to the English Privy Council in 1708, and in
the Jacobite Rebellion of 1715, in his capacity as Lord-Lieutenant
of Ayrshire, assisted the Duke of Argyll in suppressing the revolt.
In 1700 the 3rd Earl married his cousin, Margaret Dalrymple.

Their son John, the 4th Earl, was born in 1705 and entered
the army in 1727, four years before succeeding to his father's
title. He was a captain in the Queen's Own Regiment of Dragoons
by 1734, Governor of Stirling Castle in 1741, and Lieutenant-Colo-
nel and Aide-de-Camp to George II with the Allied army in

Germany in 1743. Loudoun was then ordered to raise a new High-land regiment for service in America, but his work was inter-rupted by the Rebellion of 1745. A Loyalist like his father, the Earl took his untried regiment into battle, and after Prestonpans he was sent North to organize other independent militia compa-nies among the Highlanders. He remained in Invernesshire after Culloden, hunting the Prince and other rebels, and did not leave Scotland until 1747, when he and his regiment were sent to Hol-land. At their return in December, 1748 the regiment was dis-banded, and the Earl entered semiretirement until again taking up command in 1755 with a commission as Major-General. The following year he replaced Braddock as Commander-in-Chief of British Forces in America during the French and Indian War, and was appointed titular governor of Virginia. After an unsuc-cessful two years he was recalled to England in 1758, served in Portugal in 1762, was promoted to General in 1770, and died in 1782 in Loudoun Castle, the family seat in Ayrshire. The Earl never married.

Subject matter:

(1) The Jacobite Rebellions of 1715 and 1745; for the '15, mate-rial concerning the movements of the Jacobite and English armies, the defense of Glasgow, and the financing, supply, ordnance, and activities of a troop of Ayrshire dragoons commanded by Major James Cathcart and Captain "Black" John Campbell; for the '45, material concerning the landing of Prince Charles Edwart Stuart in Scotland and his progress through Scotland and England, the re-cruiting and equipment of Loudoun's Highland Regiment and of the independent Highland companies under his command; commissioning of officers and the provision of quarters, clothing, arms, and pay for Loudoun's troops; the operations of the Earl's regiment in and around Inver-ness, the relief of Fort Augustus, and the retreat to Ros-shire, Sutherland, and Skye; the intrigues of Simon Fraser, 11th Baron Lovat; the Battles of Prestonpans, Falkirk, and Culloden; movements of French privateers; the examina-tions of prisoners; and the disarming of the Highlands.

(2) Other military affairs, including: requests to both the 3rd and 4th Earls for military preferment and patronage;

forces under the 4th Earl's command, including the 3rd
Foot Guards, of which he commanded a company in 1741
(with a few muster rolls, casualty lists, and contingent
and subsistence accounts), the Highland regiment he was
raising for American service prior to the rising of 1745
(records of recruitment, supply, pay, etc.), and the 30th
Regiment of Foot which he commanded after 1758 (recruitment, clothing and arms returns, etc.); European military affairs, particularly the English campaigns in Flanders in 1747 and in Portugal in 1762.

(3) National and local (chiefly Ayrshire) politics, including material concerning: comments on Scottish politics in correspondence; requests to both the 3rd and 4th Earls for
patronage and preferment in the government (many of
which were channeled, for the 3rd Earl, through his Edinburgh agent George Dalrymple, Baron Dalrymple of Dalmahoy); the Lord-Lieutenancy of Ayrshire; Ayrshire politics in general (including Ayrshire election lists, 1727–53);
a few instructions to the 3rd Earl as commissioner to the
General Assembly; and a few papers concerning the election of Scottish peers to the House of Lords (requests for
votes) principally during the period 1770–80. There is disappointingly little on the Union of Scotland and England.

(4) Family and personal affairs of the 3rd and 4th Earls of
Loudoun, with a few early papers relating to Sir William
Mure, Laird of Rowallan.

(5) Estate management and finances, mainly as seen in correspondence with the chief Loudoun factors: Robert Campbell, James Arnot, and George Douglass; includes a little
material re the discovery of coal on the Loudoun estates;
also material concerning the 4th Earl's interest in planting
trees on his Loudoun estate. There are few manorial papers, deeds, or other legal or financial papers. Of individual interest are: a household inventory of Sorn Castle,
1761, two volumes of Loudoun household accounts for 1771,
and accounts of work done on the Sorn estate 1742–72.

Persons represented by five or more pieces:
Adams, John (55)
Aird, John (6)

Alston, James (8)

Anne, Queen of Great Britain (17)

Arnot, James (50)

Ayr (Scotland). Provost and Magistrates (6)

Ayrshire Company. Loudoun Castle (18)

Baillie, James (8)

Barbour, Elizabeth (6)

Barrington, William Wildman, 2nd Viscount Barrington (8)

Blair, William (5)

Boswell, Alexander, Lord Auchinleck (5)

Bowie, George (12)

Boyd, William, 3rd Earl of Kilmarnock (18)

Boyd, William, 4th Earl of Kilmarnock (6)

Boyle, David, 1st Earl of Glasgow (9)

Brodie, Alexander (16)

Brodie, Alexander, Lord Lyon (7)

Bruce, Christian Leslie Graham, Marchioness of Montrose (5)

Bruce, Thomas (6)

Cameron, Donald (5)

Campbell, Alexander. [Captain; Governor of Fort William, Scotland] (10)

Campbell, Alexander. [Lieutenant in the Earl of Seaforth's . . . Company, Scotland] (9)

Campbell, Alexander. [Of Delnies, Scotland; factor to John Campbell of Cawdor] (8)

Campbell, Archibald, 3rd Duke of Argyll (20)

Campbell, Archibald, 1st Marquis of Argyll (5)

Campbell, Colin (7)

Campbell, Daniel (6)

Campbell, David (5)

Campbell, Duncan (6)

Campbell, Hugh, 3rd Earl of Loudoun (79)

Campbell, James. [son of James Campbell of Lawers, Scotland, d. 1723] (14)

Campbell, James. [Lieutenant at Annapolis Royal, Scotland] (5)

Campbell, Sir James (78)

Campbell, Sir James, 2nd Bart. of Aberuchill (49)

Campbell, James Mure, 5th Earl of Loudoun (15)

Campbell, Lady Jean Campbell (19)

Campbell, John. [Of Shankstoun, Scotland; 2nd son of the 2nd Earl of Loudoun (8)

Campbell, John. [Of Wallwood, Scotland; "Black Captain Campbell"] (11)

Campbell, John. [Of Shawfield, Scotland; son-in-law of 3rd Earl of Loudoun] (6)

Campbell, John, 2nd Duke of Argyll and Duke of Greenwich (17)

Campbell, John, 4th Duke of Argyll (11)

Campbell, John, 5th Duke of Argyll (30)

Campbell, John, 1st Earl of Breadalbane and Holland (9)

Campbell, John, 3rd Earl of Breadalbane and Holland (7)

Campbell, John, 4th Earl of Loudoun (419)

Campbell, Josiah (5)

Campbell, Margaret (Dalrymple), Countess of Loudoun (126)

Campbell, Mungo (5)

Campbell, Patrick (31)

Campbell, Robert (93)

Carmichael, John, 3rd Earl of Hyndford (7)

Carnegie, David, 4th Earl of Northesk (5)

Cathcart, Alan, 7th Baron Cathcart (9)

Cathcart, Charles, 8th Baron Cathcart (82)

Cathcart, Charles Schaw, 9th Baron Cathcart (23)

Cathcart, James (9)

Cathcart, M. (17)

Chalmer, John (21)

Cope, Sir John (29)

Craig, James (18)

Cunningham, Sir William, 3rd Bart. (20)

Cunningham, David (7)

Dallas, Alexander (8)

Dalrymple, Charles. [4th son of William Dalrymple, d. 1729] (6)

Dalrymple, Charles. [Ayr, Scotland (fl. 1756–75)] (5)

Dalrymple, Sir David, 1st Bart. of Hailes (46)

Dalrymple, Eleanor (Campbell) Primrose, Countess of Stair (6)

Dalrymple, George, Baron Dalrymple of Dalmahoy (107)

Dalrymple, Sir Hew, Lord Drummore (19)

Dalrymple, Hew, 1st Bart. and Lord North Berwick (28)
Dalrymple, John (6)
Dalrymple, Sir John, 2nd Bart. (6)
Dalrymple, John, 1st Earl of Stair (7)
Dalrymple, John, 2nd Earl of Stair (96)
Dalrymple, John, 5th Earl of Stair (10)
Dalrymple, Robert (6)
Dalrymple, William (15)
Dalrymple-Chrichton, William, 5th Earl of Dumfries and 4th
    Earl of Stair (30)
Douglas, James, 2nd Duke of Queensberry and 1st Duke of
    Dover (6)
Douglass, George (66)
Drummond, George (5)
Elphinstone, John, 4th Baron Balmerino and 3rd Baron Cou-
    par (14)
Erskine, James, Lord Grange (27)
Erskine, John, 6th or 11th Earl of Mar (17)
Fergusson, James, 2nd Bart. and Lord Kilkerran (12)
Fergusson, William (7)
Fielding, Basil, 6th Earl of Denbigh (5)
Fletcher, Andrew, Lord Milton (7)
Folliott, Fraser (11)
Forbes, Duncan (68)
Fox, Henry, 1st Baron Holland (20)
Franklin, John (5)
Fraser, James (31)
Fraser, Simon, Master of Lovat (17)
Fraser, Simon, 11th Lord Lovat (9)
Frederick, Mariscoe (5)
George I (6)
George II (24)
Germain, George Sackville, 1st Viscount Sackville (5)
Godde, B. (5)
Gordon, Adam (10)
Gordon, Lord Charles (8)
Gordon, Cosmo George, 3rd Duke of Gordon (7)
Graham, James, 1st Duke of Montrose (15)
Grant, Alexander (6)
Grant, Ludovick (16)

Grant, Patrick (9)
Grant, Sueton (5)
Gray, James (13)
Great Britain.
    Army. Earl of Loudoun's Highland Regiment (206)
        Foot Guards (20)
        Foot Guards. 3rd Regiment (44)
        30th Regiment (18)
    Parliament (6)
Gun, Alexander (33)
Halkett, Sir Peter, 2nd Bart. (12)
Hamilton, George, 1st Earl of Orkney (7)
Hamilton, John [of Bargeny Ayrshire, d. 1781] (8)
Hamilton, John [of Ayrshire, Scotland; clerk and factor. (fl. 1737–71)] (5)
Home, William, 8th Earl of Home (23)
Huck-Saunders, Richard (6)
Hudson, M. (6)
Hunter, Andrew (6)
Hunter, James (9)
Huske, John (8)
Inglis, Hugh (11)
Innes, Sir Harie, 5th Bart. (7)
Jones, Daniel (17)
Kennedy, David, 10th Earl of Cassillis (10)
Keppel, William Anne, 2nd Earl of Albemarle (27)
Knevit, C. (12)
Lindsay, Alexander, 4th Earl of Balcarres (20)
Lindsay, Colin, 3rd Earl of Balcarres (55)
Lindsay, James, 5th Earl of Balcarres (13)
Lindsay, Margaret (Campbell) 3rd Countess of Balcarres (37)
McBeth, William (5)
McDonald, Alexander (6)
MacDonald, Sir Alexander, 7th Bart. (7)
McDonald, Donald (13)
MacDonald, James (5)
MacDonnell, Coll. (9)
MacDowall-Crichton, Patrick, 6th Earl of Dumfries (8)
Mackay, Alexander (52)
Mackay, George (24)

Mackay, George, 3rd Baron Reay (12)

Mackay, Hugh. [Of Bighouse, Scotland; 2nd son of the 3rd Baron Reay, d. 1770] (11)

Mackay, Hugh. [Major in British Army during the rebellion in Scotland (fl. 1745)] (8)

MacKenzie, Alexander (7)

MacKenzie, Kenneth, *styled* Lord Fortrose (10)

MacKenzie, William (24)

McKersie, Andrew (32)

MacIntosh, Æneas (6)

MacIntosh, William (7)

MacLeod, Hugh (10)

MacLeod, John (19)

MacLeod, Norman (43)

MacNab, Archibald (17)

MacPherson, James (8)

Maitland, James (5)

Maitland, James, 7th Earl of Lauderdale (7)

Mann, Galfridus and James (firm) (17)

Melville, David, 3rd Earl of Leven and 2nd Earl of Melville (19)

Menzies, Neill (5)

Merchant, Roderick (7)

Middleton, Christopher (7)

Mitchelson, James (7)

Montagu, John, 4th Earl of Sandwich (6)

Montgomerie, Alexander, 9th Earl of Eglinton (7)

Montgomerie, John (6)

Moor, William (7)

Morgan, Thomas (8)

Munro, George (44)

Munro, Sir Harry, 7th Bart. (19)

Mure, Sir William, Laird of Rowallan (7)

Murray, James, 2nd Duke of Atholl (5)

Nairne, Sir David (20)

Ogilvy, James, (6)

Ogilvy, James, 4th Earl of Findlater and 1st Earl of Seafield (13)

Ogilvy, James 5th Earl of Findlater and 2nd Earl of Seafield (9)

O'Hara, James, Baron Kilmaine and 2nd Baron Tyrawley (7)

Pelham-Holles, Thomas, 1st Duke of Newcastle-upon-Tyne and of Newcastle-under-Lyme (12)

Pombal, Sebastian Jose de Carvalho y Mello, Conde D'Oeyras, Marquez de (23)

Powell, Cranfield Spencer (8)

Primerose, Hugh, 3rd Viscount Primerose (7)

Ramsay, George, 8th Earl of Dalhousie (5)

Reeve, Richard (9)

Ritchmont, Duncan (11)

Robertson, John (28)

Ross, George. [Of Galstoun, Scotland] (14)

Ross, George. [Agent for the independent companies in Scotland] (11)

Ross, James. [Of Portavoe, County Down, Ireland; nephew of the 3rd Earl of Loudoun; Colonel in the British Army] (12)

Rosse, William, 12th Baron Rosse (5)

Schevez, Robert (6)

Scotland. Privy Council (13)

Seton, James (29)

Smith, Adam (7)

Smith, William (134)

Sorn Castle (11)

Stevenson, John (11)

Stewart, Sir William James (7)

Stuart, John (27)

Stuart, John, 3rd Earl of Bute (19)

Sutherland, John (14)

Sutherland, Patrick (11)

Sutherland, William, 17th Earl of Sutherland (27)

Townshend, George, 4th Viscount and 1st Marquis of Townshend (7)

Veaitch, Charles (21)

Wade, George (5)

Walker, Catherine (5)

Welsh, Jean (5)

Wentworth, Hugh (5)

Whitefoord, Allan (26)

Whitefoord, Sir John, 2nd Bart. (5)
Wilkenson, William (37)
William Augustus, Duke of Cumberland (12)
Wilson, Edward (7)
Wyndham, Charles, 2nd Earl of Egremont (10)
Wynyard, William (15)
Yonge, William (6)
Young, John (8)

Physical description: letters and documents.

Source: purchased from the Campbell family through the agency of Sotheby's and Sir Joseph Duveen, in 1923, and from Edith Maud Abney-Hastings, Countess of Loudoun, with the Hastings Collection, through the agency of Maggs Brothers, in 1926.

Bibliography: Thomas I. Rae, "The Loudoun Scottish Papers in the Huntington Library," *Scottish Historical Review* 2, 148 (October, 1970): 227–31 (to which the present description is much indebted).

MACARTNEY, GEORGE, 1ST EARL MACARTNEY (1737–1806)
[Commonplace Book] (ca.1767–78)
Autograph MS. volume 452 pp.

Includes accounts of or treatises on Russia, Canada, Trinidad, and Scotland.

MACAULAY, ZACHARY (1768–1838)
1,014 pieces, 1793–1888

Zachary Macaulay, the English philanthropist who devoted most of his life to the antislavery movement, was born in Scotland in 1768, the son of a minister. At the age of sixteen he was sent to Jamaica, where he eventually became a plantation manager, but his unhappiness with the treatment of slaves brought about his return to England in 1792. He then obtained an appointment to the council of the new African colony of Sierra Leone, founded by William Wilberforce and other abolitionists as a settlement for liberated slaves, and became governor after his arrival there in 1793. His accomplishments in the colony were many, but difficulties finally forced him to resign his post in 1799, and from 1799 to 1808 he was secretary of the Sierra Leone Company in England. From 1802 until 1816 Macaulay edited *The Christian Observer,* an antislavery publication and oracle of the "Clapham sect" in London, and in 1823 he helped form the Anti-Slavery Society. Macaulay was a close friend of the religious writer Hannah More and of many prominent abolitionist leaders, and his acquaintances included numerous political and literary figures in both England and Europe.

Subject matter: family matters; the antislavery movement, including the Sierra Leone Colony, the Anti-Slavery Society, and the activities of Zachary Macaulay, William Wilberforce, Thomas Clarkson, and other abolitionists; Macaulay's friendship with Hannah More and references to her business affairs; social life in Calcutta in 1863 (as represented in the papers of Macaulay's son-in-law Sir Charles Edward Trevelyan, governor of Madras [1859–60] and finance minister of India [1862–65], his wife Hannah More [Macaulay] Trevelyan, and their children).

Persons represented by five or more pieces:
  Babington, Thomas (33)
  Babington, Thomas Gisborne (37)
  Brougham, Henry Peter, 1st Baron Brougham & Vaux (32)
  Clarkson, Thomas (27)
  Cropper, Margaret (Macaulay) (62)
  Drummond, Henry (5)
  Dugdale, Alice Frances (Trevelyan) (17)
  Dumont, Louis (47)
  Evans, William (6)
  Macaulay, Frances (86)
  Macaulay, Henry William (6)
  Macaulay, Selina (Mills) (34)
  Macaulay, Thomas Babington, 1st Baron Macaulay (11)
  Macaulay, Zachary (229)

Milner, Isaac (9)
More, Hannah (58)
More, Martha (8)
Stael-Holstein, Baron Auguste Louis (44)
Stephen, James (22)
Stephen, Sir James (16)
Trevelyan, Lady Hannah More (Macaulay) (35)
Wilberforce, William (47)

Physical description: letters, manuscripts, and documents.

Source: purchased from Maggs Bros. of London 1952.

MATHEWS, R. (fl. 1780s?)
[Commonplace Book] (1782)
MS. volume 280 pp.

Contains accounts of America and the war, observations on the history of England and on current events, lists of English ships, recipes, and other miscellaneous material. Written in London.

MAYNWARING, GEORGE
A Catalogue of the Nobilitie of England, and a Collection as well of his Maties Courtes of Record . . . (1617)
MS. volume 92 pp.

MILLAR, SAMUEL (1762–1819<)
Memores and Vicissitudes (ca.1819)
Autograph MS. volume 285 pp.

A journal covering the years 1775–1819 in the life of a Scottish merchant sailor and eventual shipowner, including three ink and watercolor drawings of ships.

MOFFETT, THOMAS (1553–1604)
Nobilis: sive Vitae Mortisque Syndiadis . . . [a biography of Sir Philip Sidney] (ca.1594)
Autograph MS. volume 75 pp. (in Latin)

Edited with an introduction and notes by V. G. Heltzel and H. H. Hudson as *Nobilis: or, a View of the Life and Death of a Sydney and Lessus Lugubris* (San Marino: Huntington Library, 1940).

MOLYNEUX, SIR THOMAS, 5th BART. (d. 1841)
Autobiography (1820–21)
MS. volume 127 pp.

Chiefly an account of General Molyneux's military career, beginning with peacetime service in Canada in 1786, continuing with active service in the West Indies with General Sir Charles (later Earl) Grey, eventually service in Ireland, and concluding with retirement in Wales.

MONTAGU, ELIZABETH (ROBINSON) (1720–1800)
6,923 pieces, ca.1620–1923

Elizabeth Robinson Montagu, socially prominent "bluestocking," author, and indefatigable correspondent, was married in 1742 to Edward Montagu, a grandson of the 1st Earl of Sandwich and a Whig Member of Parliament for Huntingdonshire who owned estates in Berkshire and Yorkshire as well as coal mines in Northumberland. The Montagus spent the early years of their marriage at Allerthorpe in Yorkshire and Sandleford Priory in Berkshire, or in visits to Bath and Tunbridge Wells, but after 1750 Mrs. Montegu was firmly estalished in Hill Street, London, where her "bluestocking assemblies" were both famous and fashionable as a gathering place for the literary and intellectual elite. To these salons came Dr. Johnson, Horace Walpole, Edmund Burke, Hannah More, David Garrick, Sir Joshua Reynolds, and her long-time

333

friend George Lyttleton, 1st Baron Lyttleton, while other acquaintances (and sometimes rivals) included Hester Thrale Piozzi, Frances Boscawen, Elizabeth Carter, and Hester Chapone. In 1760
Mrs. Montagu contributed three dialogues to Lyttleton's *Dialogues of the Dead*, and in 1769 responded to Voltaire's criticism
of Shakespeare with *An Essay on the Writings and Genius of
Shakespear Compared with the Greek and French Dramatic Poets,
with some Remarks Upon the Misrepresentations of Mons. de Voltaire.* Following the death of her husband in 1775, she assumed
the management of his estate and colliery affairs, traveled, enter-
tained lavishly at new mansions at Sandleford and in Portman
Square, London, and continued a voluminous correspondence
with many friends. After her death in 1800, her nephew and executor Matthew Montagu, 4th Baron Rokeby, published four volumes
of her letters.

Subject matter: literary affairs, personalities, and gossip, including
references to current books and plays; social and everyday life
of Elizabeth Robinson Montagu at Sandleford Priory, London,
Bath, and Tunbridge Wells; description and travel in the course
of Mrs. Montagu's visits to Newcastle-upon-Tyne, Sandleford,
Tunbridge Wells, Bath, Spa (in 1763), Paris (1776), and Scotland
(1766 and 1770), as well as to numberous cathedrals, castles, the
university towns, and country homes and parks; current political
events, including the Jacobite Rebellion of 1745, the Seven Years
War, the coronation of George III, the John Wilkes affair, and
the trial of Warren Hastings; coal mines and mining in Northumberland.

Persons represented by five or more pieces:
    Alison, Dorothea (Gregory) (90)
    Anstey, Mary (7)
    Archdeacon, William (22)
    Beattie, James (7)
    Bentinck, Margaret Cavendish (Harley), Duchess of Portland
        (62)
    Bentinck, William 2nd Duke of Portland (5)
    Blagden, Sir Charles (30)
    Blair, Hugh (7)
    Boscawen, Frances Evelyn (Glanville) (73)

Botham, Lydia (Lumley) (29)
Bower, Archibald (11)
Burrows, John (8)
Chapone, Hester (Mulso) (5)
De la Coliniere, [   ] (5)
De Medalle, Lydia (Sterne) (7)
De Messine, [   ] (5)
Donnellan, Anne (64)
Dromgold, Jean (21)
Drummond, Robert Hay (12)
DuBoccage, Marie Anne (Le Page) Fiquet (11)
Durey de Meinieres, Octavie Belot (Guichard) (18)
Ellis, Anne (Stanley), Baroness Mendip (6)
Freind, Grace (Robinson) (6)
Freind, William (25)
Garrick, David (6)
Garrick, Eva Marie (Veigel) (7)
Gregory, John (30)
Harcourt, Elizabeth (Venables-Vernon), Countess Harcourt
    (17)
Harcourt, George, 2nd Earl Harcourt (7)
Harris, James (7)
Hervey, Elizabeth (7)
Home, Henry, Lord Kames (12)
Hood, Mary (West) (6)
Howard, Mary (Finch), Viscountess Andover (7)
Johnstone, James (6)
Knollys, Mary (Law), Viscountess Wallingford (8)
Le Courayer, Pierre François (7)
Lyttelton, Charles, Bishop of Carlisle (16)
Lyttelton, George, 1st Baron Lyttelton of Frankley (116)
Lyttelton, Thomas, 2nd Baron Lyttelton of Frankley (6)
Medows, Jemima (Montague), Lady (26)
Monpellier, [   ] (13)
Monsey, Messenger (71)
Montagu, Dorothy (Fane), Countess of Sandwich (50)
Montagu, Edward (439)
Montagu, Edward Wortley (19)
Montagu, Elizabeth (Charlton) (104)
Montagu, Elizabeth (Robinson) (3,500)

Montagu, John, 4th Earl of Sandwich (7)
Montagu, Matthew, 4th Baron Rokeby (129)
More, Hannah (22)
Pepys, Sir William Weller, Bart. (13)
Petty, Sophia (Carteret), Countess of Shelburne (13)
Petty, William, 1st Marquis of Lansdowne (11)
Pitt, Anne (19)
Pitt, Hester (Grenville), Countess of Chatham & *suo jure* Baroness Chatham (7)
Pitt, Mary (5)
Potter, Robert (26)
Pratt, Samuel Jackson (6)
Pulteney, Frances, Lady Pulteney (7)
Pulteney, Harry (12)
Pulteney, William, Earl of Bath (283)
Remona [   ] (5)
Robinson, Charles (12)
Robinson, Elizabeth (Drake) (40)
Robinson, Mary (Richardson) (7)
Robinson, Matthew (6)
Robinson, Morris (19)
Robinson, Richard, 1st Baron Rokeby (42)
Robinson, Robert (7)
Robinson, Thomas (7)
Robinson, Sir William, Bart. (20)
Robinson-Morris, Matthew, 2nd Baron Rokeby (57)
Scott, Sarah (Robinson) (367)
Somerset, Elizabeth (Berkeley), Duchess of Beaufort & *suo jure* Baroness Botetourt (25)
Smelt, Leonard (9)
Stanley, Sarah (Sloane) (13)
Stillingfleet, Benjamin (11)
Talbot, Mary (de Cardonnel), Countess Talbot (6)
Vesey, Elizabeth (Vesey) Handcock (96)
West, Catherine (Bartlett) (6)
West, Gilbert (54)
Wilberforce, William (26)
Williams, Lady Frances (Coningsby) (12)
Woodhouse, James (14)

Wright, John (7)
Yorke, Philip, 2nd Earl of Hardwicke (5)

Physical description: primarily letters, with some manuscripts.

Source: purchased from A. S. W. Rosenbach, 1925.

Bibliography: many of the letters were edited and published by her nephew, Matthew Montagu, as *The Letters of Mrs. E. Montagu, with some of the letters of her correspondents* (London: 1880–1913).

MONTAGU, RICHARD (1577–1641)
A Meditation . . . upon occasion of our . . . deliverance from the more than Popish designs of the 5th of November, 1605 (1605?) Autograph MS.S. volume 128 pp.

MORT, THOMAS (fl. 1703–25)
[Account book] (1703–25)
MS. volume 364 pp.

Detailed daily personal and estate accounts of a gentleman farmer.

MYNGS, CHRISTOPHER (d. 1725?)
[Register] (1702–04)
MS. volume 332 pp.

Contains copies of dispatches, orders, sailing instructions, correspondence, etc. between the Admiralty and Captain Christopher Myngs while the latter was in command of, successively, the "St. Michael," "Victory," and "Lancaster."

NELSON, HORATIO, VISCOUNT NELSON (1758–1805)
291 pieces, 1777–1925

Horatio Nelson, British admiral, entered naval service as a midshipman on the "Raisonnable" in 1771. He joined an expedition toward the North Pole in 1773 and two years later went to the East Indies on the "Seahorse," during which voyage he contracted a fever that plagued him the remainder of his life. In 1777 he went to Jamaica as a lieutenant on the "Lowestoft." With war came rapid promotion, first to commander in 1778 and then Post-Captain in 1779. In 1780 he commanded the "Hinchingbrooke" in an expedition against San Juan. Although serving on the American station in 1781 in the "Albemarle," he took no part in major fleet actions. From 1784 to 1787 he enforced the Navigation Acts against the Americans. Marrying in 1787, Nelson retired for five years. In 1793 he gained command of the "Agamemnon," blockaded Corsica, reduced Bastia and Calvi, and captured the "Ça Ira" (1795). As commodore in the "Captain" he made a national reputation with his victory at the Battle of Cape St. Vincent in 1797, whereupon he was promoted to Rear Admiral and awarded the Order of the Bath. In the same year he beat the French at Aboukir Bay in the "Vanguard" and began his famous affair with Lady Hamilton. In 1801 he took part in the Baltic Expedition and won the Battle of Copenhagen Harbor, leading to his being created Viscount. With the renewal of war in 1793 Nelson returned to the Mediterranean in the "Victory" to blockade the French coast. He was killed in action during his greatest victory, when the French fleet was engaged and destroyed off Cape Trafalgar in 1805.

Subject matter: Nelson's career from 1777, particularly the Baltic Expedition, the Battle of Copenhagen, and the Battle of Trafalgar; various minor encounters between British and enemy warships; Prince William Henry, later King William IV, and his naval activities; routine naval operations; domestic and personal news, especially in connection with Lady Hamilton.

Persons represented by five or more pieces:
Nelson, Horatio, Viscount Nelson (221)

Physical description: letters and documents.

Source: various manuscript dealers before 1927.

Bibliography: Nicholas Harris Nicolas, ed., *The Dispatches and Letters of Nelson,* 7 vols. (London: Henry Colburn, 1845–46); John K. Laughton, ed., *The Naval Miscellany,* vol. 1, in *Publications of the Navy Records Society,* vol. 20 (1901); *The Nelson and Hamilton Papers,* 2 vols., in *The Collection of Autograph Letters . . . Formed by Alfred Morrison,* 7 vols. (1893–97); George Naish, ed., *Nelson's Letters to His Wife,* in *Publications of the Navy Records Society,* vol. 100 (1958).

NORFOLK. BLICKLING
[Extracts from manorial records] (1575)
MS. volume 230 pp.

Extracts from the court roll of the manor of Blickling and from deeds, made in a dispute between Edward Clere and his tenants.

NORTH, FRANCIS, 1ST BARON GUILFORD (1637–85)
98 pieces, 1617–1737

Francis North, 1st Baron Guilford, Lord Keeper of the Great Seal, was born at Kirtling, Cambridgeshire, the third son of Dudley North, 4th Baron North. He was educated at St. John's College, Cambridge, entered the Middle Temple in 1655, and was admitted to the bar in 1661. His accomplishments as a barrister led to his appointment as Solicitor-General in 1671, in which year he was knighted. In 1668, North had helped with the settlement of the estate of Sir Thomas Pope, 3rd Earl Downe, upon the death without heirs of Downe's son, the 4th Earl, a few months later. North subsequently married Frances, the 3rd Earl's daughter, in 1671, and succeeded to the estates at Wroxton, Oxfordshire. Following the marriage, they lived in a large home in Chancery Lane, London, where artists, musicians, and people of letters often gathered. Sir Francis advanced to Attorney-General in 1673, to Chief Justice in 1675, and finally to keeper of the Great Seal in 1682, and was created Baron Guilford the following year. Continued ill health forced his retirement to Wroxton shortly after James II's accession, although North retained the Great Seal until his death.

Subject matter: family and household matters of Francis North, 1st Baron Guilford (mainly personal concerns dealing with the upbringing of his children, at first by his mother-in-law, Lady Beata Pope and then, after his wife's death, by his own mother, Lady Anne North) and his father Dudley North, 4th Baron North; estate affairs of Sir Thomas Pope, 3rd Earl Downe, at Wroxton, Oxfordshire, from 1631 to 1633 (letters from his steward regarding timber, animals, buildings, tenants, neighbors, etc.).

Persons represented by five or more pieces:
  Lichfield, Anthony (30)
  North, Anne (Montagu), Baroness North (14)
  Pope, Beata (Poole), Countess of Downe (24)

Physical description: letters and documents.

Source: purchased from Hofman and Freeman, 1968.

ORDE, JAMES P.
84 pieces, 1823–42; 1740, 1801

James P. Orde, of Edge Hill, commissioned the artist George Perfect Harding (d. 1853) to copy portraits in various English country houses for use in a projected illustrated work on John Evelyn. Harding, who learned painting from his father, worked chiefly in making watercolor copies of portraits but also exhibited miniatures at the Royal Academy during the years 1802–40.

Subject matter: artist George Perfect Harding and his commission for copying portraits in English country houses; information on the location of many pictures in private ownership during the early 19th century.

Persons represented by five or more pieces:
  Orde, James P. (84)

Physical description: letters.

Source: purchased from Winifred Myers, 1972.

PERY, EDMOND SEXTON, VISCOUNT PERY (1719–1806)
347 pieces, 1759–90

Edmond Sexton Pery, Irish M.P. and Speaker of the House of Commons of the Irish Parliament, belonged to a long-established and influential family owning property in and around the city of Limerick. He was called to the Irish bar in 1745, elected M.P. for Wicklow (1751–60) and later for Limerick (1760–85), and elected Speaker of the House in 1771, at which post he served until his retirement from politics in 1785. Although frequently opposed to English policies in Ireland, Pery as Speaker was an effective mediator between Government and Opposition. He supported free trade, opposed the Union, and was jealous in upholding the privileges and authority of the Irish House of Commons. Pery married, first, in 1756, Patty Martin and second, in 1762, Elizabeth Vesey, daughter of John Denny Vesey, 1st Baron Knapton. At Pery's retirement he was created Viscount Pery of Newtown-Pery.

Subject matter: the vast majority of the letters in the collection are addressed to Pery and deal with: Irish politics and parliamentary affairs, particularly during Pery's speakership; English policies toward Ireland, particularly concerning revenue and trade; Pery's relation with Viscount (afterward 1st Marquis) Townshend and successive Lords Lieutenant of Ireland; political and ecclesiastical patronage; a little information on Pery's financial and business affairs, chiefly in Limerick.

Persons represented by five or more pieces:
    Andrews, Francis (18)
    Bingham, Charles, 1st Earl of Lucan (18)
    Eden, William, 1st Baron Auckland (9)
    Ellis, Welbore, 1st Baron Mendip (14)
    Germain, George Sackville, 1st Viscount Sackville (11)

Hamilton, Sackville (5)
Hamilton, William Gerard (32)
Henley, Robert, 2nd Earl of Northington (5)
Hobart, John, 2nd Earl of Buckinghamshire (11)
Jenkinson, Charles, 1st Earl of Liverpool (12)
Orde-Powlett, Thomas, 1st Baron Bolton (13)
Townshend, George, 1st Marquis of Townshend (12)

Physical description: letters.

Source: formerly the property of Lord Emly of Tervoe, Co. Limerick, a descendant of Pery's sister. Purchased by Mr. Huntington from Sotheran & Co. in 1926.

Bibliography: many but by no means all of the letters (which comprise Pery's political correspondence, as opposed to his estate and family papers, now in the National Library of Ireland) were calendared in the Historical Manuscripts Commission's *Eighth Report, Appendix,* pp. 174–208, and *Fourteenth Report, Appendix,* pp. 155–99. See also A. P. W. Malcomson, "Speaker Pery and the Pery Papers," *North Munster Antiquarian Journal* 16 (1973–74): 33–60.

POCOCK, SIR GEORGE (1706–92)
1,170 pieces, 1733/34–93

Sir George Pocock, English admiral, entered the navy in 1718. From 1726 to 1728 he was a lieutenant on the "Burford," then moved successively to the "Romney," the "Canterbury," and the "Namur." On February 26, 1733/34, he became commander of the fireship "Bridgewater." In August 1738 he took over the "Aldborough" frigate, attached to the Mediterranean fleet of Rear-Admiral Nicholas Haddock. In 1741 he commanded the "Woolwich" in the Channel, then was transferred to the "Shrewsbury" in 1742. The same year he moved to the "Sutherland" and cruised in the Bay of Biscay and on the north coast of Spain. In 1744 Pocock convoyed the African and East Indian trade. He joined Commodore Fritzroy Henry Lee in 1745 in the West Indies and afterward Commodore Edward Legge. Upon Legge's death in 1747 he took over the chief command, soon capturing a French convoy. From 1748 to 1752 he lived in England, and then was appointed to the "Cumberland" in home waters. In 1755 Pocock was promoted to Rear-Admiral of the White, then Vice-Admiral in 1756. In 1757 he succeeded to the chief command of the East Indian squadron and engaged the French several times. Promoted to Admiral of the Blue in 1761, in 1762 Pocock was made commander-in-chief of a successful expedition against Havana, Cuba. This was the crowning achievement of his career and he retired from the service in 1766.

Subject matter: administration of the British admiralty; the management of various vessels under Pocock's command; naval activities in the English channel, the Mediterranean, and the West Indies, 1733–48; intelligence concerning the French conquest of St. Johns, Newfoundland, 1762; the British expedition against Havana, 1762; the administration of Dawson Drake as governor of Manila during the brief British occupation of the city; social life and politics during Drake's residence at Fort George, Madras.

Persons represented by five or more pieces:
  Amherst, Jeffrey, 1st Baron Amherst (13)
  Balchen, Sir John (17)
  Barlow, Nathaniel (14)
  Brome, J. (5)
  Cavendish, Philip (12)
  Collins, James (5)
  Drake, Dawson (61)
  Haddock, Nicholas (62)
  Hardy, Sir Charles (26)
  Howe, William, 5th Viscount Howe (15)
  Keppel, Augustus, Viscount Keppel (66)
  Keppel, George, 3rd Earl of Albemarle (46)
  Lee, Fitzroy Henry (14)
  Martin, William (6)
  Medley, Henry (6)
  Norris, Sir John (7)
  O'Hara, Patrick (10)
  Pitchford, Samuel (5)

Pocock, Sir George (227)
Vanbrugh, Philip (10)
Wager, Sir Charles (7)
Walton, Sir George (19)
Wasey, William George (9)

Physical description: letters and documents.

Source: purchased from the Museum Book Store in 1925.

POCOCK, SIR GEORGE (1706–92)
[Letterbook] (1757–65)

MS. volume 270 pp.

Kept during his commands in the East and West Indies.

POPE, RICHARD (fl. 1770s)
[Military journal and commonplace book](1775–77)
MS. volume 218 pp.

Kept by a British soldier in the 47th Regiment at Boston, Ticonderoga, and Saratoga.

PORTER, SIR ROBERT KER (1777–1842)
372 pieces, 1794–1842

The correspondence of Sir Robert Ker Porter, artist, traveler,
and sometime diplomat, forms a small subcollection of the papers
of Jane and Anna Maria Porter.* Sir Robert, born in 1777, grew

---

* The Porter Family Collection of ca.3,400 pieces was acquired too late for inclu-
sion in the *Guide to Literary Manuscripts in the Huntington Library.*

up in Edinburgh and London and studied at Somerset House, achieving early recognition for his paintings of battles and other military scenes. He was appointed historical painter to the Czar of Russia in 1804 and thereafter spent much time at St. Petersburg (where he married Princess Mary Scherbatoff in 1812) and traveling throughout Europe gathering impressions for his work. He accompanied Sir John Moore during the Corunna campaign. Porter was knighted in 1813, but increasing debts and the enmity between his novelist sisters and his wife prompted his return to Russia, which then became his base for subsequent travels in Persia and the Middle East. Porter was appointed British consul to Venezuela in 1826, and lived in Caracas for the following fifteen years (with lengthy leaves in England), returning to England in 1841 and thence to Russia, where he died, the following year.

Subject matter: Porter's life and experiences, as described in letters to his sister Jane, his mother, his wife, his brother William Ogilvie Porter, and a few others, including information about: his paintings and family; travel in England, Ireland, Europe, Russia, and the Middle East; European affairs; the Napoleonic wars; Porter's book *A Narrative of the Campaign in Russia during 1812.* There is little information on Venezuela.

Persons represented by five or more pieces:
  Porter, Sir Robert Ker (371)

Physical description: letters, with manuscript drafts for Porter's *Narrative.*

Source: purchased from Sotheby's, 1977, and H. P. Kraus, 1979.

PULTENEY, SIR WILLIAM, BART. (1729–1805)
2,087 pieces, 1750–1818

William Johnstone, afterward Sir William Pulteney, Bart., M.P., was the son of Sir James Johnstone, Bart., of Westerhall, Co. Dumfries. In 1760 he married Frances Pulteney, daughter and sole heir of Daniel Pulteney. The latter had inherited the large estate and fortune of William Pulteney, Earl of Bath (d. 1764) from Bath's only surviving brother, General Harry Pulteney, who died in 1767. Johnstone, who assumed the name Pulteney on his wife's succession, was M.P. for Cromartyshire, 1768–74, and for Shrewsbury, 1775–1805. Frances died in 1782, after which he married, secondly, Margaret, the widow of Andrew Stewart of Castlemilk. Sir William was the author of several political pamphlets, including *Plan of re-union between Great Britain and her colonies* (1778) and *Thoughts on the present state of affairs with America, and the means of Conciliation* (1778).

The Pulteney fortune next passed to Henrietta Laura Pulteney, only daughter and heir of Sir William and Frances, who in 1794 married her cousin, Sir James Murray, Bart. (ca.1755–1811) of Hillhead, Co. Midlothian; he also in turn assumed the name Pulteney. Sir James had served in America in 1775, was adjutant-general to the troops in Flanders, 1793–94, Secretary at War, 1807–09, and served as M.P. for Weymouth 1790–1811.

Subject matter: the Johnstone family, including numerous letters from Sir William Pulteney's brothers, sister, and father relating to family affairs; the administration of Sir William Pulteney's properties in Scotland, including detailed letters from several agents on topics such as crops, fertilization and drainage of farm lands, sheep and cattle, limestone quarries, coal mines and mining, and hiring and firing of farm personnel; political affairs in Great Britain, including material concerning Shropshire elections and politics, electioneering in general, and the American Revolution (including 34 letters from William Alexander, written from Paris and Dijon, 1777–78, on American and European affairs); the East India Company; liquor smuggling; Pulteney Bridge at Bath; the Birmingham canal; road conditions in Scotland; Tobago under George Ferguson as Governor; and the organization of local militia, ca.1800–10.

Persons represented by five or more pieces:
    Alexander, William (34)
    Alison, Archibald (9)
    Cochrane, Jean (Stuart), Countess of Dundonald (9)
    Corbet, John (5)
    Crawford, James (5)

Dempster, George (47)
Douglas, John, Bp. of Salisbury (5)
Ferguson, George (42)
Harcourt, Mary (Danby) Lockhart, Countess Harcourt (21)
Harrison, John (11)
Hepburn, William (27)
Hepburne, R. (10)
Johnstone, Betty (52)
Johnstone, Charlotte (Dee) (9)
Johnstone, George (22)
Johnstone, Gideon (8)
Johnstone, James (31)
Johnstone, Sir James, 3rd Bart. (65)
Johnstone, Sir James, 4th Bart. (28)
Johnstone, John (47)
Johnstone, Sir John Lowther (37)
Johnstone, Walter (33)
Kinckel, Hendrik August, Baron van (8)
Kinnaird, Charles, 6th Baron Kinnaird (14)
Kinnaird, George, 7th Baron Kinnaird (11)
Laurie, Sir Robert, 5th Bart. (33)
Littleton, Sir Edward, 4th Bart. (11)
Mackenzie, Sir Alexander Muir, 1st Bart. (90)
Malcolm, George (240)
Malet, Sir Charles Warre, 1st Bart. (6)
Maxwell, John (321)
Mitchelson, Samuel (10)
Molesworth, William (16)
Murray, Alexander, 7th Baron Elibank (5)
Murray, Patrick, 5th Baron Elibank (11)
Murray-Pulteney, Henrietta Laura (Pulteney), Countess of
    Bath (34)
Murray-Pulteney, Sir James, Bart. (6)
Pulteney, Sir William, Bart. (109)
Scott, Richard (5)
Sinclair, Sir John, 1st Bart. (6)
Stuart, Andrew (115)
Thorne, Peregrine Francis (15)
Tourville, — (6)
Ure, Masterton (11)

Vane, Henry, 2nd Earl of Darlington (10)
Wedderburn, Sir John, 6th Bart. (12)
Young, Alexander (12)

Physical description: letters

Source: purchased from Maggs Brothers in 1952.

RAILROAD (INTERNATIONAL) COLLECTION
17 volumes, 1812–84

This collection consists of material pertaining to various railroads, especially Australian and British.

Subject matter: the formation and/or operation of the Victorian Railways (Australian), the Midland Great Western Company (Irish), the Norwich and Spalding Railway (English), the Southampton, Manchester, and Oxford Junction Railway (English), the Edinburgh, Glasgow, and Leith Railway and other Scottish railroads, the Fond Du Lac of Lake Superior Railway (American), and the Baltimore and Port Deposit Railroad (American); the activities of the civil engineer Isambard Kingdom Brunel from 1842 to 1851; the work of Sir John Rennie on the projected Northern Railway; the work of John Duncan, Superintendent of Works, for the East India Railroad Company, 1845–47; the civil engineer Thomas Sopwith's work on railroads from about 1835 to about 1870; bridges and other structures planned for the London and Birmingham Railway as drawn in watercolor by the civil engineer Robert Stephenson; the building of a bridge over the Seine at Maisons for the Paris and Rouen Railway; a right-of-way dispute between a property owner in Leeds and the Leeds and Bradford Railway.

Persons represented by five or more pieces:
    Stephenson, Robert (34)

Physical description: letters and documents, including drawings and schematic diagrams; and Thomas Sopwith's journal.

Source: purchased from Anderson Galleries in 1919.

"RED DRAGON" (SHIP)
Log-book (1586–87)
MS. volume 144 pp.

Log of the voyage of the "Red Dragon" from England to Africa and South America, Captain Robert Widdrington in command, kept by Thomas Hood.

REPTON, HUMPHRY (1752–1818)
ca.250 pieces, 1746–1818

Humphry Repton, landscape gardener, was born at Bury St. Edmunds in 1752. At the age of twelve he was sent to Holland to be educated for a commercial life, and returned after four years in order to be trained for the textile trade. Following marriage in 1773, and an attempt at merchandising which failed, he went to live with his sister and her solicitor husband, John Adey, in Sustead, Norfolk. While there, he was encouraged by a former school friend to study botany and gardening. After a brief stay in Ireland in 1783 as deputy to William Windham, Repton returned to Romford, Essex, and began a career as a professional "landscape gardener" (a term which he coined). He was at first influenced by Lancelot Brown, but gradually developed his own more formal style, and as England's leading landscape gardener during the next three decades he planned gardens for many English noblemen, was responsible for the design of Russell Square, made alterations in Kensington Gardens, and wrote several books on landscape gardening. He was the father of sixteen children, of whom two, John Adey Repton (1775–1860) and George Stanley Repton (d. 1858) became architects.

Subject matter: personal and legal affairs of Humphry Repton and his family, landscape gardening.

Persons represented by five or more pieces:
   Adey, Dorothy (Repton) (44)
   Repton, George Stanley (16)
   Repton, Humphry (50)

Repton, John Adey (10)
Repton, William (45)

Physical description: letters, documents.

Source: purchased from Sotheby's, 1974.

RICRAFT, JOSIAH (fl. 1645–79)
A survey of England's champions (ca.1647)
MS. volume 137 pp.

Followed by a later index of men killed in the Civil War, 1642–46.

[RISDON, TRISTRAM] (1580?–1640)
A Chorographical and historical description of the County of Devon & City of Exon. . . .
MS. volume 121 pp.

A copy made ca.1659.

ROSS, SIR JOHN (1777–1856)
An Account of the Natives of The Track of land forming the N.E. point of North America Discovered in 1829 . . . (1830)
Autograph MS. volume 34 pp.

———

[Journal of the voyage of the "Isabella" to the Arctic regions] (1818)
Autograph MS. volume 113 pp.

Narrative of the Discovery Ship "Victory" . . . (ca.1829–33?)
Autograph MS.S. 3 volumes

Covers the period 1829–33, chiefly during a voyage from England
to the Gulf of Boothia with meteorological observations; also some
later papers concerning Sir John Franklin's expedition of 1845.

SARDI, ALESSANDRO (ca.1520–88)
Liber de Nummis
MS. volume 32 pp.

A 17th-century copy, wrongly attributed to John Selden, and possibly related to the 1675 printed edition *Johannis Seldeni Angli
Liber de Nummis in quo Antiqua pecunia Romana & Graeca
metitur precio ejus, quae nunc est in usu* (Wing S 688).

SCOTT, SIR WALTER (1771–1832)
The History of Scotland (1828–29)
Partly autograph MS. 3 volumes

Written for the *Cabinet Cyclopedia*, edited by Dr. Lardner.

SERLE, AMBROSE (1742–1812)
[Military Journal] (1776–78)
Autograph MS. volume 360 pp.

Kept while Serle was secretary to General Lord William Howe,
May 2, 1776–July 22, 1778. Published in *The American Journal
of Ambrose Serle, Secretary to Lord Howe, 1776–1778*, ed. Edward
H. Tatum (San Marino: Huntington Library, 1940).

SHACKLETON, RICHARD (1728–92)
401 pieces, 1658–1808

Richard Shackleton, Quaker schoolmaster, was born at Ballitore, Co. Kildare, Ireland. He was educated at the Quaker school at Ballitore, founded by his father Abraham (1697–1771), and at Trinity College, Dublin. In 1756, he succeeded his father as master of the school, where he remained until replaced by his son Abraham in 1779. Shackleton's first wife, Elizabeth (Fuller) Shackleton, died in 1754; he later married Elizabeth (Carleton) Shackleton, who was active in local charitable concerns.

Subject matter: the Society of Friends in Ireland (visiting preachers and prominent Friends, accounts of quarterly and yearly meetings), some information regarding activities of Friends in England and America; the Quaker school at Ballitore (daily life at the school, inquiries from parents concerning the education of their children, and comments on university life by former students). The collection is strongest for the period 1750–95.

Persons represented by five or more pieces:
   Archbold, Thomas (5)
   Beauchamp, Richard (11)
   Cambridge, Peter (7)
   Forster, William (6)
   Grubb, Margaret (Shackleton) (8)
   Hutchinson, Elizabeth (7)
   Jones, Rebecca (11)
   Pemberton, John (6)
   Shackleton, Abraham (14)
   Shackleton, Elizabeth (Carleton) (140)
   Shackleton, Richard (67)
   Stuberg, Svend Peter (13)

Physical description: letters, 1 manuscript, and documents.

Source: purchased from Sotheby's, 1953.

SHANNON, CHARLES HASELWOOD (1863–1937)
41 pieces, 1898–1904

Charles H. Shannon, lithographer and painter, was born in Quar-
rington, Lincolnshire, the son of a rector. After attending St. John's
school, he was apprenticed to a wood engraver, in whose work-
shop he met another future artist, Charles Ricketts. The two attended the Lambeth School of Art, became close friends, and
lived and worked together until the death of Ricketts in 1931.
When photoengraving replaced their special skill, they turned
to making drawings, and illustrated Oscar Wilde's *A House of
Pomegranates* in 1891. They then became active in all aspects of
book production, and contributed lithographs (a field in which
Shannon became recognized as one of Britain's major artists),
for *The Dial* from 1889 to 1897. Shannon also made many large
oil paintings, and of his numerous portraits one of the best known
was of Mrs. Chaloner Dowdall.

Subject matter: mainly the arrangements between artist Charles
H. Shannon and Harold Chaloner Dowdall (judge and mayor of
Liverpool), his wife, Mary Frances (Borthwick) Dowdall (a writer),
and his mother, concerning portrait sittings and exhibitions of
their portraits.

Persons represented by five or more pieces:
    Shannon, Charles Haselwood (40)

Physical description: letters, 2 pencil sketches.

Source: purchased from Sotheby's, July, 1973.

SHARPE, J. C. (fl. 1840)
Journal of a Balloon Ascent (1840)
Autograph MS. volume 42 pp.

SHOVELL-ROOKE COLLECTION
88 pieces, 1673–1792

Sir Clowdisley Shovell (1650–1707) and Sir George Rooke (1650–1709), British admirals, spent their naval careers in Channel and Mediterranean duties. Shovell served with Rooke on occasion, as in the 1696 attack on Calais, the aborted 1702 expedition to Cadiz, and, most notably, the 1704 capture of Gibraltar.

Subject matter: instructions from the Admiralty to Shovell when he commanded the Channel Fleet in 1696; reports by Rooke of his preparations for the expedition to Cadiz; miscellaneous routine naval business.

Persons represented by five or more pieces:
    Bridgeman, Sir William (8)
    Burchett, Josiah (7)
    Rooke, Sir George (24)
    Shovell, Sir Clowdisley (7)

Physical description: letters and documents.

Source: purchased from William K. Bixby in 1918.

SHREWSBURY (SHROPSHIRE). SADLERS COMPANY
[Register of admissions] (1739–1854)
MS. volume 360 pp.

Also contains list of Freemen of the Company since 1685, minutes of meetings, correspondence, etc.

SIMCOE, JOHN GRAVES (1752–1806)
[Journal of operations of the Queen's Rangers] (1777–83)
Autograph MS. volume 55 pp.

Comprises the introduction to and a variant part of the text printed in John Graves Simcoe, *Journal of the Operation of the Queen's Rangers* (Exeter, England, [1787]).

[Letterbook] (1791–93)
MS. volume 283 pp.

Kept while Simcoe was Lieutenant Governor of Upper Canada.

[SLINGSBY, SIR HENRY] (1602–58)
An Introduction to ye Christian Faith (>1659)
MS. volume 117 pp.

A personal catechism, transcribed in the hand of and with a pre-
face by Lady Barbara (Slingsby) Talbot, the author's daughter,
in 1687.

SMITH, SIR WILLIAM SIDNEY (1764–1840)
63 pieces, ca.1745–1832

Sir William Sidney Smith, admiral, entered the navy in 1777, first
serving on a storeship. By 1780 he had been promoted to second
lieutenant. Peace interrupted his naval career in 1784, but with
the start of the long Anglo-French conflict in 1793 Smith was
recalled to service. In the siege of Acre (1799) he achieved fame
for the way in which he held back French forces. From 1803 to
1807 he was assigned to duty in the northern Mediterranean,
where he harrassed the French in numerous engagements. After
a year at the South American station, he had a final tour in the
Mediterranean. Poor health put an end to his career in 1814.

Subject matter: claims of the British captors of Cayenne against
the French; the capture of the French ship "Fortune" by the
English ships "Tigre" and "Theseus" (1799); Barbary affairs; a little
on the siege of Acre and on Smith family affairs.

Persons represented by five or more pieces:
    Smith, John Spencer (7)
    Smith, Sir William Sidney (9)

Physical description: letters and documents, many in French.

Source: gift of Mrs. Hardin Craig, Jr., in 1972.

STAFFORD, HENRY, 1ST BARON STAFFORD (1501–63)
[Commonplace Book] (ca.1560–62)
Autograph MS.S. volume 73 pp.

Includes extracts from chronicles, lists of noblemen, extracts from or notes on parliamentary statutes, etc.

STANHOPE, SIR HENRY EDWYN (fl. 1783–1814)
[Diary] (1783–1814)
Autograph MS. 26 volumes

———————

[Copybook of General Orders, and directions to officers of H. M. Squadron under the command of the Vice Admiral of the Blue] (1807)
MS. volume 553 pp.

Written between March 18 and December 31, 1807, at Woolwich and Copenhagen.

STANHOPE, PHILIP DORMER, 4TH EARL OF CHESTER-FIELD (1694–1773)
Account Book (1729–32)
Autograph? MS. volume 44 pp.

Sporadic accounts of expenses while in Rome, Milan, Florence, Venice, and London.

STEVENS, WILLIAM BAGSHAW (ca.1756–1800)
Diary (1792–1800)
Autograph MS. 6 volumes

Kept by Dr. Stevens while he was master at Repton School, Derbyshire.

STOW, JOHN (1525?–1605)
[Survey of London (incomplete)]
MS. volume 444 pp.

A transcript of portions from the 1633 edition, with some additional original pieces.

TALBOT, FRANCIS, 5th EARL OF SHREWSBURY (1500–60)
TALBOT, GEORGE, 6TH EARL OF SHREWSBURY (1528–90)
[Letterbook of official correspondence] (1550–90)
MS. volume 354 pp.

Copies of official correspondence transcribed by John Hopkinson in 1676.

TEMPLE FAMILY ADDENDA
187 pieces, >1600–>1697

The Temple Family (Addenda) Papers, which are separate from the STOWE COLLECTION (q.v.), deal chiefly with the affairs of Lady Hester (Sandys) Temple (d. 1656) and her husband Sir Thomas Temple, 1st Bart. of Stowe (1567–1637). Sir Thomas, the son of John Temple, studied at Lincoln's Inn, served as a Member of Parliament (1588–89), succeeded to his father's estates in 1603, and was knighted in the same year. He purchased a baronetcy and served as Sheriff of Oxfordshire (1606–07), Buckinghamshire (1616–17), and Warwickshire (1620–21). About 1595, Sir Thomas married Hester, the daughter of Miles Sandys of Buckinghamshire. She was active in the management of the Temple estates, in numerous lawsuits, and in the care of their fifteen children.

Subject matter: the Temple family, mainly during the period preceding and including the Civil War: family affairs (domestic quarrels, lawsuits, marriage arrangements); the management of the household and estates, chiefly at Stowe, Burton Dassett, Padbury and Finmere; relations with servants, tenants, and tradesmen regarding rents, the procuring of provisions, clothing and materials, and the landscaping of Stowe; and occasional reports on the current political situation.

Persons represented by five or more pieces:
    Chaplyn, William (fl. 1612–33) (10)
    Harte, William (10)
    Horley, Spencer (5)
    Osney, Robert (6)
    Risley, William (fl.1631–36) (6)
    Rogers, Bridgett (5)
    Rose, Henry (12)
    Temple, Hester (Sandys), Lady (16)
    Temple, Katherine (Kendall) (9)

Physical description: letters and documents.

Source: purchased from Sotheby's, 1973.

THICKNESSE, PHILIP (1719–92)
218 pieces, ca.1770–ca.1785

Philip Thicknesse, soldier and author, traveled to Georgia with Oglethorpe, served in Jamaica and the Mediterranean, and purchased in 1753 the lieutenant-governorship of Landguard Fort, Suffolk. A patron of Gainsborough and the author of numerous pamphlets, guides, letters, and other tracts, Thicknesse spent much time in travel (principally in France and Spain), and lived in Monmouthshire and at Bath. He married three times: first, in 1742,

Maria Lanove (whose large family fortune he unsuccessfully claimed, in a notorious lawsuit, after her death in 1749); second, in 1749, Elizabeth Touchet, eldest daughter of the Earl of Castlehaven; and third, in 1762, Ann Ford, the authoress and musician.

Subject matter: Thicknesse's family life and relations with his wives and children; business and estate affairs, including his lawsuits, the management of his Monmouthshire farm at Quoitca, and his houses at Bath; life and society in Bath; travel on the Continent, particularly in France and Spain, 1775–77, and in Belgium, 1782; there are a few references to his own writings, and to Gainsborough. The collection consists almost entirely of letters from Thicknesse to his friend John Cooke of Monmouthshire.

Persons represented by five or more pieces:
    Thicknesse, Philip (211)

Source: purchased from Ifan Kyrle Fletcher, 1949.

Bibliography: some of the letters in this collection have been printed in the biography by Philip Gosse, *Dr. Viper, the querulous life of Philip Thicknesse* (London: Cassell, 1952).

TOWNSHEND, THOMAS, 1ST VISCOUNT SYDNEY (1733–1800)
47 pieces, 1765–87

Thomas Townshend, 1st Viscount Sydney, Secretary of State for the Home Department, succeeded to that office in 1782. Prior to that time he had served as a Lord of the Treasury (1765), Speaker of the House of Commons (1766), and member of the Privy Council (1767). He joined the opposition in 1768, remaining there until 1782. In his capacity as Home Secretary Townshend guided the negotiations for the Treaty of 1783 between Britain and the United States.

Subject matter: primarily Anglo-American negotiations in 1782; political observations by William Pitt, 1st Earl of Chatham.

Persons represented by five or more pieces:
  George III, King of Great Britain (24)
  Pitt, William, 1st Earl of Chatham (6)
  Townshend, Thomas, 1st Viscount Sydney (3)

Physical description: letters, notably one from George III to Townshend agreeing to the "Seperation" [sic] of the colonies from Britain, and documents, including cabinet minutes for July 25 to November 19, 1782.

Source: purchased from Charles J. Sawyer, Ltd., in 1917.

Bibliography: the letter from George III to Townshend is printed in James Thorpe, ed., *Letters in Manuscript* (San Marino: Huntington Library, 1971).

VICTORIA, QUEEN OF GREAT BRITAIN (1819–1901)
55 pieces, 1812–83

Victoria, Queen of Great Britain and Empress of India, granddaughter of George III and daughter of Edward Augustus, Duke of Kent, and Mary Louise Victoria, youngest child of the Duke of Saxe-Coburg-Saalfeld, was born at Kensington Palace, May 24, 1819. After the death of her father in 1820, Victoria's life was dominated by her mother, with whom she lived at Kensington Palace, and by her governess and tutor, Baroness Lehzen. Upon the death of William IV and Victoria's accession to the throne in June, 1837, she moved into Buckingham Palace, and took an active interest in government affairs under the close supervision of Lord Melbourne. Following the visits of her first cousin, Albert, son of the Duke of Saxe-Coburg-Gotha, in May 1836, and again in October, 1839, Victoria offered marriage, and the wedding took place in February, 1840. Victoria and Albert and their family of nine children resided intermittently at Buckingham Palace, Windsor Castle, Osborne (on the Isle of Wight), and Balmoral in Scotland. Victoria often depended upon Albert's advice in government affairs, and his death in 1861 was a great shock to the

Queen; her popularity declined when she thereafter retired into seclusion, but in time she resumed her public role. Victoria died in 1901 at the age of 81.

Subject matter: personal and family affairs of Queen Victoria and Prince Albert; the Court; included are some routine royal letters and single letters from various members of Albert's family.

Persons represented by five or more pieces:
Princess Mary Louise Victoria, Duchess of Kent (10)
Victoria, Queen of Great Britain (39)

Physical description: letters, documents, 1 printed item. (In English, German, and French.)

Source: purchased from William K. Bixby, 1918.

[VILLIERS, GEORGE, 1ST DUKE OF BUCKINGHAM] (1592–1628)
The Spanish Labarinth or A true Relation of that Narrative made by the Duke of Buckingham . . . [to Parliament on the subject of the negotiations for the marriage of Prince Charles, afterwards Charles I, to the Spanish Infanta] (ca.1624?)
MS. volume 65 pp.

With copies of supplemental documents concerning the negotiations.

WALKER, SIR EDWARD (1612–77)
Historical Discourses
Autograph MS.S. volume 564 pp.

Historical accounts of various aspects of Charles I's life and the Civil Wars, by the King's secretary.

WALSINGHAM, SIR FRANCIS (1530–90)
[Letterbook] (1570–72)
MS. volume 446 pp.

Copies of Walsingham's official correspondence during his embassy to France, later published by Sir Dudley Digges as *The Compleat Ambassador.*

WARWICK, SIR PHILIP (1609–83)
Memoirs or Reflections upon the Reigne of King Charles the First (1679)
MS. volume 194 pp.

Followed by a discourse "of Government" (ca.1678). The whole possibly copied after publication in 1701.

WELLESLEY, ARTHUR, 1ST DUKE OF WELLINGTON (1769–1852)
273 pieces, 1827–48; 1949

Arthur Wellesley, 1st Duke of Wellington, was appointed Constable of the Tower of London by George IV in 1827. A sinecure of high honor, the post of constable was also very lucrative. The constable was not required to reside in the Tower, and the actual administration of it was traditionally carried out by a staff officer, the Tower Major. Wellington, however, took his responsibilities seriously and closely supervised Tower Major J. H. Erlington.

Subject matter: the operations of the Tower of London from 1827 to 1848.

Persons represented by five or more pieces:
    Wellesley, Arthur, 1st Duke of Wellington (207)

Physical description: mostly letters from Wellington to Erlington, with some by the Duke's secretaries; a few documents and manuscripts, including Frank B. Maggs's "The Duke, The Tower, and the Beefeaters" and Ralph Partridge's "The Duke and the Beefeaters."

Source: purchased from Maggs Bros. of London, 1973.

WELLESLEY-BERESFORD COLLECTION
67 pieces, 1809–12; 1823

Arthur Wellesley, 1st Duke of Wellington, commanded the allied armies of Britain, Spain, and Portugal in the Iberian Peninsula from 1809 through 1813 against the forces of Napoleon. A key general under him was William Carr Beresford, Viscount Beresford (1768–1854), who from 1809 through 1810 concentrated on reorganizing the Portuguese Army.

Subject matter: the training and equipping of Portuguese troops during the Peninsular War; acquisition of supplies; troop movements during the war; routine administrative matters.

Persons represented by five or more pieces:
    Jenkinson, Robert Banks, 2nd Earl of Liverpool (12)
    Wellesley, Arthur, 1st Duke of Wellington (39)

Physical description: mostly dispatches from Wellesley to Beresford giving instructions; map of a "Plan of the Attack Upon the French on the Heights of Rolica."

Source: purchased from William K. Bixby, >1924.

Bibliography: some of the letters are published in *The Dispatches of Field Marshal the Duke of Wellington,* ed. John Gurwood, 8 vols. (London: Parker, Furnivall, and Parker, 1844–47).

WELLESLEY, RICHARD COLLEY, MARQUIS WELLESLEY
OF NORRAGH (1760–1842)
[Letterbooks] (1809–11)
MS. 5 volumes

Kept in Wellesley's capacity as Foreign Secretary; vols. 1–3 concern Turkey, vols. 4–5 concern Persia.

WILLIAM IV, KING OF GREAT BRITAIN (1765–1837)
Remarks on Countries, Harbours, Towns &c &c (1780–82)
Autograph MS.S. volume 56 pp.

A commonplace book and diary kept by the future king while serving as a midshipman on the "Prince George," including an account of the siege and relief of Gibraltar and his service in North America.

WILLSON, ALEC J. (fl. 1905–06)
Journal of H.M.S. Renown from the time of T.R.H.ˢ the Prince and Princess of Wales' joining her at Genoa to their return to England. (1905–06)
Autograph MS. volume 124 pp.

Confidential journal kept by a "sub-lieutenant" on the "Renown" during the voyage to India of the future George V and Queen Mary. Breaks off at Port Said, April 5, 1906. With many photographs of India, Suez, etc.

[WITHER, GEORGE (1588–1667)]?
[Legal commonplace book] (1650–60)
[Autograph?] MS. volume 126 pp.

Includes notes on cases, legal opinions, etc.

WOOD, JOHN (fl. 1798)
[Law book] (ca.1798)
Autograph MS. volume 127 pp.

Contains notes on precedents and rules for 18th-century elections, with returns for the Radnorshire election of May 30, 1780.

YONGE, SIR GEORGE, 5TH BART. (1731–1812)
850 pieces, 1750–1814

Sir George Yonge, 5th Bart. and son of the Whig politician Sir William Yonge, served as a Lord of the Admiralty (1766–70), Vice-Treasurer for Ireland (1782), and Secretary for War (1782–94). During his tenure of the latter office he accumulated papers not only for his own term but for those of his predecessors and, later, his successors. Yonge was then appointed Master of the Mint (1794–99) and finished his public career as Governor of the Cape of Good Hope (1799–1801).

Subject matter: chiefly questions of rank, promotions, commissions, and retirement as seen in letters written to Yonge as Secretary at War; also some information about troop movements, desertions, pay, and allowances.

Persons represented by five or more pieces:
  Adair, Robert (5)
  Anstruther, William (6)
  Boyd, Sir Robert (6)
  Callender, Sir John, Bart. (6)
  Craig, Francis (12)
  Crosbie, William (5)
  Edgcumbe, Richard, 2nd Baron Edgcumbe (5)
  Elphinstone, John, 11th Baron Elphinstone (5)
  Ferguson, Sir Adam, 3rd Bart. (7)
  Fitzroy, George Henry, 4th Duke of Grafton (11)
  Herbert, Henry, 10th Earl of Pembroke (6)
  Howard, Thomas, 2nd Earl of Effingham (7)
  Lennox, Lord George Henry (14)

Lindsay, Sir Davis, 4th Bart. (18)
Lyon, William (5)
Osborn, Sir George, 4th Bart. (14)
Parslow, John (5)
Picton, William (14)
Poulett, John, 4th Earl Poulett (5)
Pringle, Henry (6)
Richardson, William Madox (5)
Tonyn, Patrick (6)
Townsend, Samuell (8)

Physical description: letters

Source: purchased from G. Michelmore & Co., 1922.

INDEX

Abbot, George, Abp., 70
Abbot, John A., 157
Abbots Ann (Hants.), 233
Abenbury (Denbigh.), 75
Abercorn, Earl of. *See* Hamilton, James
Abercromby, James, 275–76
Aberdare, Baron. *See* Bruce, Henry Austin
Abergavenny, barony of, 43
Abney, Sir Edward, 84
Abney-Hastings [*formerly* Clifton], Charles Frederick, 1st Baron Donington, 84
Abney-Hastings [*formerly* Clifton], Edith Maud (Rawdon-Hastings), *suo jure* Countess of Loudoun, 80–81, 85, 330
Abney-Hastings [*formerly* Huddleston], Edith Maud (Rawdon-Hastings), *suo jure* Countess of Loudoun, 81
Abolitionist movement, 293, 331
Academy of Science (French), 144
Accounts:
—official: churchwardens, 109; customs, 245; Hanaper, 243; military, 304, 308; militia, 136, 192–93; Overseers of the Poor, 109; Paymaster of Annuities disbursed by Parliament, 246; Paymaster-General of the Forces, 244; Ship Money, 228; tithes, 152, 230
—private: building, 46, 82, 151, 205, 230; elections (Parliamentary), 193; estate, 4, 10, 27, 33, 46, 59, 60, 65, 67, 68, 82, 118, 151–53, 205–06, 230, 247, 311, 312, 323, 337; garden, 82, 153, 205, 230; household, 10, 26, 47, 59, 65, 66, 82–83, 153–54, 206, 230–31, 247, 283, 323; insurance, 154, 155; legal expenses, 83, 154, 207, 231, 246; medical and veterinary care, 154; monastic, 3; personal, 10, 13, 14, 47, 53, 54, 59, 64, 65, 68, 70, 83, 154, 207, 231, 246–47, 311, 312, 337, 356; rents, 152, 206, 230, 247. *See* rentals & rent rolls. *See also under:* art & art objects; books; charity; clothing; furniture; kilns
Acland, Sir Thomas Dyke, 313
Acott, William, 157
Acton, William, 70
Acton (Middlesex), 68, 259
Actresses, 317
Adair, Robert, 365
Adam, William, 85
Adams, Lady Agnes Anne (Cook), 276–78
Adams, John, 323
Adams, Paul, 10
Adams, Ralph, 221
Adamson, John William, 277
Adcock, Mary, 126
Adderley, J., 85
Addison, John C., 157
Adey, Dorothy (Repton), 349
Adelstrop (Gloucs.), 237, 258
Admiralty, 34, 50, 57, 60–61, 72, 149, 155, 162, 191, 285, 301, 312, 316, 337, 343, 354. *See also under* Courts; Navy
Advowsons, 108
Aegidius Romanus, 29
Aelius Lampridius, 55
Africa: British Trading Co. in, 235, 245; English travellers in, 299; Sierra Leone Colony, 293, 331

Agmerhurst (Sussex), 16, 17
Agriculturalist Cattle Insurance Co., 157
Aids (feudal), 306
Aird, John, 323
Akeley-cum-Stockholt (Bucks.), 263
Alan, son of Sigar, 7
Albemarle, Duke of. *See* Monck, George
Albert, Prince-Consort of Victoria, 361
Albeville, Marquis de. *See* White, Ignatius
Alchorne, T., 18
Alciston (Sussex), 1
Aldbrough (Yorks.), 101
Aldermen, of Leicester, 111
Alderney, island of, 36
Alderson, Edward S., 157
Alexander I of Russia, 293
Alexander, H., 85
Alexander, John [*alias* Myllward], 220
Alexander, William, 232, 346
Alexander & Co., 85
Aliens: in London, 38; charity for, 65
Alington, Hildebrand, 5th Baron of Killard, 85
Alison, Archibald, 346
Alison, Dorothea (Gregory), 334
Allan, Robert & Son, 85
Allen, Ethan, 290
Allen, Francis, 70
Aller (Somerset), 100, 115
Aller Moor (Somerset), 115
Allerston (Yorks.), 101
Allerton (Yorks.), 117
Allot, Richard, 285
Alseley (Bucks.), 183
Alstanton (Cheshire), 76
Alston, James, 324
Alta California Bookstore, 289
Altham, Edward, 70
Alton (Hants.), 239
Alton (Leics.), 97, 108
Ambrose, Sir Richard, 12

Amherst, Jeffrey, 1st Baron Amherst, 275, 343
Amsterdam, 224
Anderchurch (Leics.), 97
Anderson, Sir Edmund, 70
Anderson, Maggie, 277
Anderson Galleries, 291, 348
Anderson, J. & F., 85
Andover, Viscountess. *See* Howard, Mary (Finch)
Andover (Hants.), 179, 233
André, John, 278
Andrew, William, 142
Andrewes, Lady Anne (Temple), 208
Andrewes, Elizabeth, 188
Andrewes, Sir Henry, 1st Bart., 208
Andrewes, Margaret, 188
Andrewes, William, 186
Andrewes, Sir William, 208
Andrews, Francis, 341
Andrews, William, 157
Anglesey, 46, 60
Anglo-Dutch wars, 56–57, 136
Angouleme, Louis Antoine, Duc de, 85
Annapolis Royal, British forces at, 65
Anne, Queen of England, 70, 324
Anstey, Mary, 334
Anstey (Leics.), 97, 108
Anstruther, William, 365
Antigua, 320
Antiquities (Greek & Roman), collection of, 310
Anti-Slavery Society, 293, 331
Anti-vivisection movement, 295
Antonelli, Battista, 34
Antrim, Co. (Ireland), 119
Antrobus, Thomas, 188
Antwerp, British consul at, 284
Appleby Magna (Leics.), 97
Appledram (Sussex), 1
Appleshaw (Hants.), 233
Appy, John, 275
Arbor (James) & Son, 157
Archbold, Thomas, 352
Archdeacon, William, 334

Archer, James, 253
Archery, 39
Arches, Court of. *See under* Courts
Architects & architecture, 178, 203, 349
Architectural drawings. *See* maps & plans
Arctic, voyage to, 350
Ardrossan (Scotland), 122
Argyll, Duchess of. *See* Louise Caroline Alberta
Argyll, dukes of. *See* Campbell, Archibald; Campbell, John
Argyll, Marquis of. *See* Campbell, Archibald
Aries, John, 220
Aries, Robert, 220
Arkwright, Richard, 187
Arlington, Earl of. *See* Bennet, Henry
Armagh, Co. (Ireland), 119
Armour, 102, 283
Arms (heraldic): of Cheshire gentry, 28; of Duke of Chandos, 243; of English corporations, 144; of English peers, 28, 56; of Italy, 69; of Spencer family, 28; treatise on, 69
Armstrong, Thomas, 85
Army (British):
—by place: in Flanders, 323; in Ireland, 333; in Mediterranean, 308; in North America, 84, 132, 275, 278, 304–05, 308, 321, 333, 351, 354; in Peninsular Campaign, 84, 363; in Portugal, 323; in Scotland, 322–23; in West Indies, 333. *See also* Ireland, military affairs in.
—by subject: commissions in, 322; Engineer Corps in, 304; individual regiments in, 66, 83, 136, 304, 322–23, 327; levying and transportation of troops, 84, 322–23; lists and schedules of forces, 65, 226, 243; orderly books, 304–05; Paymaster General of the Forces, 231, 244, 308; strategy

and tactics in, 286, 303; uniforms of, 283; volunteer regiments in, 66. *See also:* Accounts, military; Militia; Napoleonic Wars
Arnold, Benedict, 290
Arnold, Thomas, 285
Arnold (Notts.), 114
Arnot, James, 323, 324
Array, commissions of, 10, 44
Arrow (Warwicks.), 116
Art. *See* paintings; drawings and sketches; statues
Art and art objects, accounts of purchase of, 154
Artists, 340, 344–45, 353
Arundel, John, 43
Arundel, Sir John, 43
Arundel, earls of, 43. *See also* Howard, Thomas
Arundel Castle (Sussex), 43
Arundell, James Everard, 189
Arundell, Mary Anne (Grenville), Baroness Arundell, 157, 187, 189, 190, 194, 200, 253
Asgill, John, 65
Ashburnham, Bertram, 5th Earl of Ashburnham, 147
Ashburnham, John, 1st Earl of Ashburnham, 19
Ashburnham, Thomas, 12
Ashburton, Baron, 270. See also Baring, Alexander
Ashby Baths (Leics.), 109
Ashby Castle (Leics.), 102
Ashby Church (Leics.), 109
Ashby de la Zouche (Leics.), 78, 82, 97, 103, 108–09, 118, 120–21
Ashby Woulds (Leics.), 109
Ashcombe, Sir William, 281
Ashenden, James, 11
Ashendon (Bucks.), 176–77, 180, 216, 217, 255, 263
Ashendon Hundred (Bucks.), 181, 216
Ashley, Robert, 30
Ashley (Northants.), 99
Ashley Cooper, Kathleen, 277

Ashley Cooper, Patricia, 277
Ashley Cooper, Patrick, 277
Ashridge (Bucks.), 54, 55
Ashridge, College of the Boni Homines at, 29, 69
Ashton (Gloucs.), 237
Asiatic Society, 143
Askew (Yorks.), 219
Aslackby (Lincs.), 113
Assize of Arms, in Buckinghamshire, 225
Assizes. *See under* Courts
Association for the defense of Queen Elizabeth, 32
Association in support of William III, 227
Astle, Thomas, 157
Astley (Warwicks.), 77
Aston (Bucks.), 106
Aston Abbots (Bucks.), 177, 180
Aston Clinton (Bucks.), 177, 180, 255, 263
Astronomy, list of books *re*, 140
Astwell (Northants.), 114, 179, 211, 271, 259
Atcheson, Henry, 157
Atholl, Duke of, 243. *See also* Murray, James
Atkinson, Charles, 85
Atkinson, John, 85
Atkinson, Joseph, 85
Atkinson, Joseph & John, 85
Atlases, 309–10
Attorney General, 21, 305
Auchinleck, Lord. *See* Boswell, Alexander
Auckland, Baron. *See* Eden, William
Audley, barons, 132
Aughnegarron (Co. Longford), 249
Augustus Caesar, pedigree for, 132
Augustus Frederick, Duke of Sussex, 85
Australia, railroads in, 348
Austrian Succession, war of the, 191
Authorpe (Lincs.), 113
Autobiographies, 133, 333

Avington (Hants.), 154, 174, 175, 179, 217, 229, 230, 234, 236, 237, 258, 270
Aylesbury (Bucks.), 177, 180, 182, 198, 255, 263
Aylesbury and Buckinghamshire Railway, 156
Aylestone (Leics.), 97
Ayleway, Robert, 85
Ayr (Scotland), Provost and Magistrates of, 324
Ayrshire, 323
Ayshire Company [of dragoons], 322, 324

B., T., 29
Babington, Thomas, 331
Babington, Thomas Gisborne, 331
Bache, Thomas, 85
Bacon, Francis, 1st Viscount St. Albans, 34, 35, 53, 70, 137, 297, 298
Bacon, James, 157
Bacon, Nathaniel, 186
Bacon, Sir Nicholas, 40, 282
Bacon, Thomas, 185
Badbury (Dorset.), 218
Baddesley (Hants.), 237
Badland (Radnor.), 260
Baggrave (Leics.), 97
Bagnold, John, 85
Bagot, Richard, Bp., 313
Bagworth (Leics.), 97, 109
Baillie, James, 324
Baily, William, 129
Baker, Arthur Octavius, 157
Baker, C. H. Collins, 313
Baker, George, 129
Baker, John, 247
Baker, Richard, 220
Baker, Thomas [fl. >1739], 240
Baker, Thomas [fl. >1854–66], 157
Baker & Sons, 157
Balcarres, Countess of. *See* Lindsay, Margaret
Balcarres, earls of. See Lindsay, Colin; Lindsay, Alexander; Lindsay, James
Balch, Mr., 272

Balchen, Sir John, 343
Baldwin, Thomas, 157
Balfour, Arthur James, 282
Balfour, Eustace James Anthony, 282–83
Balfour, Lady Francis (Campbell), 282
Ball, Ambrose Edward, 157
Ballitore (Ireland), Quaker School at, 352
Balloon ascensions, 353
Balmerino, Baron. *See* Elphinstone, John
Baltimore, Baron. *See* Calvert, Charles
Baltimore and Port Deposit Railroad, 348
Baltinglass, Viscount. *See* Roper, Thomas
Baltinglass, Viscountess. *See* Roper, Anne (Temple)
Baltinglass family, 207
Bamford, Patrick, 59
Banbury, Countess. *See* Knollys, Elizabeth (Howard)
Banbury, Earl of. *See* Knollys, Nicholas
Bangor, Viscount. *See* Ward, Nicholas
Bankes, Henry, 31
Bankes, Sir John, 140
Bankruptcy: of Fowke & Burrell, founders, 14; of 2nd Duke of Buckingham & Chandos, 156
Banks, Ann, 241
Banwell (Somerset.), 260
Barbados, 155, 320
Barbour, Elizabeth, 324
Barchard, Francis, 188
Barckman, P., 85
Barehurst (Sussex), 6
Barford, Thomas, 271
Barford St. John (Oxon.), 259
Barford St. Michael (Oxon.), 259
Baring, Alexander, 1st Baron Ashburton, 187
Barker, George, 157
Barker, Thomas, 283

Barker & Bowker, 157
Barker, Bowker, & Peake, 157
Barlestone (Leics.), 97
Barlow, Nathaniel, 343
Barlow, R., 31
Barlow, William, Bp., 85, 137
Barnetts Hoare Company, 85
Barnewall, Robert, 9th Baron Trimleston, 251
Barnewell, Peter, 127
Barnhorn (Sussex), 1–18 *passim.*
Baron, Charlotte Anne, 157
Baron, John S., 157
Baronage, post-Conquest, 278. *See also* Peerage
Baronets, creation of rank of, 142
Barow, Sir John, 285
Barradall, Edward, 85
Barratt Mill, 121
Barrett, Edward, 1st Baron Barrett, 220
Barrett, Richard, 157
Barretto, Joseph, 85
Barrington, Percy, 8th Viscount Barrington, 157
Barrington, William Wildman, 2nd Viscount Barrington, 85, 324
Barrodale, Thomas, 85
Barrow-upon-Soar (Leics.), 97, 109
Barrowcoate (Leics.), 109
Bartholomew, A. J., 283
Bartholomew, Mr., 15
Bartlett, Eliza H., 158
Barton (Lancs.), 76
Barton Hartshorn (Bucks.), 255
Bartrum, Thomas, 85
Barwell, Henry, 85
Baskoe, Robert de, 7
Bastion, James, 226
Batcombe (Somers.), 180, 239, 260
Bates, Benjamin, 253
Bath, Countess of. *See* Murray-Pulteney, Henrietta Laura (Pulteney)
Bath, Earl of. *See* Pulteney, William
Bath (Somers.), 260, 272, 334, 359
Baths, public, 109

Bathurst, Lady Elizabeth (Bruce), 234, 240
Bathurst, Henry, Bp., 253
Bathurst family, 239
Battle (Sussex), 1–19 *passim.*
Battle Abbey (Benedictine Abbey of St. Martin at Battle): 1–10 *passim.*, 138
Battles: Blackwater, 251; Bunker Hill, 132; Copenhagen, 338; Culloden, 322; Falkirk, 322; Kip's Bay, 132; Long Island, 132; Naxiaro, 197; Prestonpans, 322; Scanderoon, 48; Trafalgar, 338; White Plains, 132; Worcester, 228; other, 62, 136, 142
Baugham, William, 158
Bawden, Alice, 220
Bawdrip (Somers.), 233, 260
Baxter, George, 230
Bayly, Thomas E., 85
Baynes, Edward Robert, 158
Beachampton (Bucks.), 255
Beachendon (Bucks.), 96
Beacons, 297
Beaconsfield, Earl of. *See* Disraeli, Benjamin
Bearcroft, Henry, 158
Beards, John Thomas, 158
Beards, Thomas [fl. 17th cent.], 55
Beards, Thomas [fl. 19th cent.], 153, 156 *(bis)*, 158
Beattie, James, 334
Beauchamp, Lady Anne (Sackville), 222
Beauchamp, Richard, 352
Beauchamp, barony of, 194
Beaufort, Alicia Magdalena (Wilson), 283, 285
Beaufort, Daniel Augustus, 284, 285
Beaufort, Sir Francis, 283–86
Beaufort, Honora (Edgeworth), 284
Beaufort, Mary (Waller), 285
Beaufort, William Augustus, 285
Beaufort, William Lewis, 285
Beaufort, William Morris, 285

Beaufort, Duchess of. *See* Somerset, Elizabeth (Berkeley)
Beaufort-Palmer, Francis N., 286
Beaumont, George, 129
Beaumont, Sir Henry, 2nd Bart., 85
Beaumont, John, 293
Beche, John A., 9
Beck, John, 188
Beck, Peter, 185
Beck, Thomas, 188
Becke, Edward, 185
Bedale (Yorks.), 219
Bedell, William, Bp., 294
Bedford, dukes of. *See* Russell, Wriothesley; Russell, John
Beech (Sussex). See Battle (Sussex)
Beer, William Jones, 158
Beeston, Sir William, 287
Beguildy (Radnor.), 260
Beigham (Kent), 17
Belasyse, John, 1st Baron Belasyse of Worlaby, 133
Belchamp (Essex), 218
Belgium, 284
Belknap, Edward, 221
Belknap, Sir Edward, 219, 220
Belknap, Henry, 221
Belknap family, 224
Bell, Thomas, 286
Bellamont, Earl of. *See* Coote, Richard
Bellarmine, Robert, Cardinal, 31, 48
Belton (Leics.), 97, 109
Belton (Rutland), 115
Belvoir (Leics.), 97
Bengeworth (Worcs.), 262
Bennet, Henry, 1st Earl of Arlington, 311
Bennett, G. C., 158
Bennett, George, 158
Bennys, John, 9
Benson, Francis, 286
Benson, Martin, 85
Bent, Robert, 198
Bentinck, Margaret Cavendish (Harley), Duchess of Portland, 334

Bentinck, William, 2nd Duke of Portland, 334
Bentinck family, 224
Beresford, William Carr, Viscount Beresford, 363
Berkeley, Elizabeth (Drax). *See* Nugent, Elizabeth (Drax) Berkeley
Berkeley, Sir George Cranfield, 158
Berkeley, Sir William, 287
Berkshire, Earl of. *See* Norreys, Francis
Berkshire: concealed lands in, 68; deeds for lands in, 95, 255; other, 68, 106, 236, 237
Bernard, James, 187
Bernard-Morland, Sir Scrope, 158, 187, 198, 202
Berry, Thomas, 186
Berwick-on-Tweed (Northumb.), 36, 114
Betham, Sir William, 253
Bethell, Christopher, Bp., 313
Bett, Thomas, 186
Betts, George, 70
Bewick (Yorks.), 101
Bexhill (Sussex), 6, 8
Bibles, 29
Biddlesden (Bucks.), 174, 177, 211, 216, 255, 263
Bidwell, John, 285
Bierton (Bucks.), 177, 180, 255, 263
Bighton (Hants.), 237, 258, 270
Bigland, Ed., 85
Bildwas (Salop), 77
Bilsdale (Yorks.), 117
Binett, Robert, 208
Bing, Thomas, 30
Bingham, Charles, 1st Earl of Lucan, 341
Biographies, 280, 292, 294, 333. *See also* autobiographies
Bircham & Co., 158
Bird, Jane, 240
Bird, Margaret, 266 *(bis)*
Birds, treatise by Edward Topsell on, 31
Birt, J., 158

Biscoe, Elisha, 15
Biscoe, Joseph, 15
Bishop, William, 58
Bishops Sutton (Hants.), 239
Bishops Waltham (Hants.), 258
Bittleston, Thomas, 85
Bixby, William K., 317, 354, 361, 363
Black, James, 287
Black, John [d. 1767], 287
Black, John [d. 1782], 287
Black, Joseph, 287
Black, Robert, 287
Black, W., 232
Black family, 286–87
Blackfordby (Leics.), 97, 109
Blackgreff, John, 124
Blackwater, battle of, 251
Blackwood, Adam, 39
Blackwood, Frederick Temple, 1st Marquis of Dufferin, 285
Blagden, Sir Charles, 334
Blagrave, Henry, 125
Blair, Hd., 50
Blair, Hugh, 334
Blair, William, 324
Blake, John, 85
Blake, Thomas John, 85
Blakiston, Nathaniel, 62
Blathwayt, William, 85, 226, 287–88
Blencowe, B. R., 158
Blennerhassett, Eliza, 85
Blennerhassett, Jeanne, 285
Blewett, Benjamin, 131
Blewitt, Thomas, 69
Blickling (Norf.), 339
Blood, Thomas, 128
Bloomfield, Benjamin, 1st Baron Bloomfield, 85
Blount, Isabella, 222
Blount, James, 6th Baron Mountjoy, 118
Blount, W., 13
"Bluestockings," 333–34
Blundell, Anne, 186

Blunsden St. Andrew (Warwicks.), 274
Blunsdon (Wilts.), 262
Board of Control, 157, 162
Board of Trade, 56, 61–62, 72, 287, 305
Boardman, Job, 264
Bocking (Essex), 179, 257
Bodiam (Sussex), 1, 6, 13, 17, 18 *(ter)*
Bodley, Sir Josiah, 129
Bodley, Sir Thomas, 34
Bodmin (Cornwall), 106
Boehm, Sir Joseph Edgar, 1st Bart., 158
Boethius, 29 *(ter)*, 48
Bohemia, 224, 297
Bold, Peter, 85
Bolingbroke, Viscount. *See* St. John, Henry
Bolton, Baron. *See* Orde-Powlett, Thomas
Bolton, dukes of. *See* Paulet, Charles
Bolton Estate Trust, 64
Bolton Percy (Yorks.), 101, 117
Bonham, James, 158
Bonner, Eric M., 294
Bonneville, Marie de, 85
Bonnington (Notts.), 99
Bonomi, Giovanni Carlo, 253
Bonville, Lord, 9
Boodle & Partington, 158
Book of Common Prayer, 63
Books: accounts of purchases of, 83, 154, 207, 231; catalogues of, 47, 103, 174, 213, 234
Boothia, Gulf of, 351
Boothorpe (Leics.), 97, 109
Bordeaux (France), 287
Boscastle [Botreaux Castle] (Cornwall), 96, 106
Boscawen, Frances Evelyn (Glanville), 334
Boscombe (Wilts.), 116
Boston (Mass.), 320, 344
Bosville, Sir Ralph, 18
Boswell, Alexander, Lord Auchinleck, 324

Bosworth, Joseph, 253
Botcheston (Leics.), 97
Botetourt, Baroness. *See* Somerset, Elizabeth
Botham, Lydia (Lumley), 335
Bothe, John [d. >1530], 127
Bothe, John [d. 1542<], 27
Bothmer, Johann Caspar von, 288
Botreaux, Elizabeth, 126
Botreaux, William, 126
Botreaux, William de, Baron Botreaux, 108, 118, 124
Botreaux, barons, 78
Botreaux Castle [Boscastle] (Cornwall), 96, 106
Bottesford (Leics.), 97
Bottley (Cornwall), 96, 106
Boucher, James, 158
Bouchier, barony of, 194
Boughrood (Radnor.), 260
Boughton, Robert, 186
Boughton, Thomas Rutland, 158
Boulanger, Georges Ernest Jean Marie, 282
Bouquet, Henry, 304
Bourton (Bucks.), 13, 211
Bourton-on-the-Water (Gloucs.), 217
Bower, Archibald, 335
Bowes, Ralph, 39
Bowes, Robert, 86
Bowie, George, 324
Box, Philip, 158
Boycott (Bucks. & Oxon.), 216, 255, 259
Boyd, Sir Robert, 365
Boyd, William, 3rd Earl of Kilmarnock, 324
Boyd, William, 4th Earl of Kilmarnock, 324
Boydell, John, 69
Boyle, David, 1st Earl of Glasgow, 324
Boyle, Lady Jean. *See* Campbell, Lady Jean (Boyle)
Boyle, Michael, Abp., 129, 227
Boyle, Richard, 2nd Earl of Cork, 129

Boyle, Richard, 3rd Earl of Burlington, 303
Boyle, Roger, 1st Earl of Orrery, 69, 129
Boylston, Elizabeth (Whistler), 14
Boys, Robert, 302
Boys & Tweedie, 158
Bracebridge, Mary Holte, 264
Bracker, J., 18
Brackley, Viscount. *See* Egerton, Thomas
Brackley, Viscountess. *See* Egerton, Alice (Spencer) Stanley
Brackley family, 194
Brackley (Northants.), 77
Bradbury, Silas, 135
Bradfield (Yorks.), 262
Bradford, George, 187
Bradford (Wilts.), 116
Bradstreet, John, 275
Braham [Brantham] (Suffolk), 9
Braintree (Essex), 257
Brame, Joseph, 296
Bramhall, John, Abp., 102, 128, 129
Bramhall, Sir Thomas, 129
Bramhall family, 128
Bramston, John, 18
Brascote (Leics.), 97
Braunstone (Leics.), 97, 109
Bray (Berks.), 106
Braybrooke, Baron. *See* Griffin, Richard
Breadalbane, marchionesses of. *See* Campbell, Eliza (Baillie); Campbell, Mary Turner (Gavin)
Breadalbane, Marquis of. *See* Campbell, John
Breadalbane family, lawsuits involving, 176
Breadalbane & Holland, Earl of. *See* Campbell, John
Breage (Cornwall), 256
Breedon (Leics.), 97, 109
Brent, East (Somerset), 260
Brereton, Jane, 42
Brereton, Richard, 42
Brereton, Sir William, 42
Brereton family, 42

Bret, Daniel, 86
Brett, Richard, 30, 31
Breval, D., 86
Brewers (of London), petition of, 198
Bricklayers, 19, 152, 230
Bridgeman, William, 63
Bridgeman, Sir William, 354
Bridges: plans for, 121; for railroads, 348
Bridgewater, countesses of. *See* Egerton, Frances (Stanley); Egerton, Elizabeth (Cavendish); Egerton, Jane (Paulet)
Bridgewater, Duchess of. *See* Egerton, Rachel (Russell)
Bridgewater, dukes of. *See* Egerton, Scroop; Egerton, John; Egerton, Francis
Bridgewater, earls of. *See* Egerton, John; Egerton, Scroop [*aftw.* 1st Duke]; Egerton, John William; Egerton, Francis Henry
Bridgwater (Somerset), 233, 260, 272
Bright, John, 289
Brightwalton (Berks.), 1
Brigstocke, George, 188
Brigstocke, Mary Harriette Player, 190
Brigstocke family, 194
Brill family, 194
Brill (Bucks.), 96, 106, 152, 177, 255, 263
Brinkley, John, Bp., 285
Brisbourne, Isaac, 86
Brise, Joseph, 158
Brislington (Somerset), 260, 273
Brislington House, 270
Bristol, Earl of. *See* Digby, George
Bristol (Gloucs.), 183, 184, 270, 295
British Library: Egerton papers in, 24; Stowe papers in, 147, 253
Britton, Thomas, 158
Broadwell (Gloucs.), 258
Brock, Eirene, 277
Brodie, Alexander, 324
Brokesby (Leics.), 109

Brome, J., 343
Brome, James, 86
Bromfield & Yale, lordship of (Denbigh & Flint.), 33, 59, 75
Bromham (Wilts.), 1, 8
Bromley, Sir John, 68
Bromley, Thomas, 158
Brooke, George, 222
Brooke, George, 9th Baron Cobham, 220
Brooke, Henry, 8th Baron Cobham, 296
Brooke, Henry, 11th Baron Cobham, 45
Brooke, Sir Richard, 66
Brooke, Samuel, 30
Brooke, William, 220
Brooke, William, 10th Baron Cobham, 222
Brooke (Norf.), 114
Brookes, Job, 86
Brookes, Joseph, 186
Brookes, Theophilus, 86
Brookes, William, 186
Brookes & Beal, 158
Broom Hall (Cheshire), 76
Broomhall (Sussex), 6
Brotherhulme (Cheshire), 76
Brotherton, ____, 206
Brougham, Henry Peter, 1st Baron Brougham & Vaux, 331
Broughton, Christopher, 208
Broughton, Edward, 222
Broughton (Bucks.), 180, 255
Brounton, Robert, 158
Brown, Ford Maddox, 282
Brown, John [fl. >1766], 240
Brown, John [fl. 1833–37], 200
Brown, Mary, 185
Browne, Sir Anthony, 2, 12
Browne, Anthony, 1st Viscount Montague, 2
Browne, Edward, 215
Browne, Edward Harold, Bp., 295
Browne, Francis, 3rd Viscount Montague, 10, 17, 18, 19
Browne, Robert, 158, 253
Browne, Thomas, 12

Browne-Lundin, Robert Christopher, 197
Brownrigg, Sir Robert, 1st Bart., 253
Broxton hundred (Cheshire), 38
Bruce, Christian Leslie Graham, Marchioness of Montrose, 324
Bruce, Henry Austin, 1st Baron Aberdare, 289
Bruce, Lady Mary. *See* Brydges, Mary (Bruce)
Bruce, Thomas, 324
Bruce, Thomas, 7th Earl of Elgin & 11th Earl of Kincardine, 158
Bruce, barony of, 243
Brudenell, Robert, 220
Brudenell [Bridewell], Robert, 212
Brunel, Isambard Kingdom, 348
Bruton (Somerset), 272
Bryant, William, 269
Brydgeman, Sir John, 70
Brydges, Anna Elizabeth. *See* Grenville, Anna Eliza (Brydges)
Brydges, Anne (Wells) Jeffries, Duchess of Chandos, 229
Brydges, Anne Eliza (Gamon) Elletson, Duchess of Chandos, 229, 235, 238, 240, 241, 242
Brydges, Lady Augusta Ann, 241
Brydges, Lady Caroline, 241
Brydges, Cassandra (Willoughby), Duchess of Chandos, 229, 232, 241
Brydges, Edmund, 2nd Baron Chandos of Sudeley, 240
Brydges, Elizabeth (Barnard), Baroness Chandos, 242, 243
Brydges, Elizabeth (Major), Duchess of Chandos, 229, 241
Brydges, Francis, 233
Brydges, George, 240, 241, 242
Brydges, George Rodney, 238
Brydges, Grey, 5th Baron Chandos of Sudeley, 70
Brydges, Harry, 241
Brydges, Henry, 2nd Duke of Chandos, 229, 230, 231, 232, 235, 240, 241, 242, 243, 290

Brydges, James, 232

Brydges, James, 1st Duke of Chandos, 228, 230, 231, 232, 240, 241, 242, 243, 245, 313

Brydges, James, 3rd Duke of Chandos, 149, 229, 231, 232, 234, 240, 241, 242

Brydges, James, *styled* Marquis of Carnarvon, 229

Brydges, Lydia Catherine (Van Hatten) Davall, Duchess of Chandos, 229, 231

Brydges, Margaret (Nicol), Duchess of Chandos, 229, 241

Brydges, Lady Mary, 241

Brydges, Mary (Bruce), Marchioness of Carnarvon, 229, 232, 241

Brydges, Mary (Lake), Duchess of Chandos, 229

Brydges, Sir Thomas, 240

Brydges, William, 233

Bryon, William, 158

Bubbenhall (Warwicks.), 212, 217

Buckholt (Sussex), 6

Buckhurst, Baron. *See* Sackville, Thomas

Buckingham, dukes of. *See* Stafford, Henry; Villiers, George. *See also* Buckingham & Chandos, dukes of; Buckingham and Normanby, Duke of

Buckingham, Marchioness of. *See* Grenville, Mary Elizabeth (Nugent)

Buckingham, Marquis of. *See* Grenville, George Temple-Nugent-

Buckingham & Chandos, duchesses of. *See* Grenville, Anna Elizabeth (Brydges); Grenville, Mary (Campbell); Grenville, Caroline (Harvey); Grenville, Alice Anne (Graham-Montgomery)

Buckingham & Chandos, dukes of. *See* Grenville, Richard

Buckingham & Normanby, Duke of. *See* Sheffield, John

Buckingham (Bucks.), 177, 211, 215, 216, 217, 224, 255, 264

Buckingham Cattle Assurance Association, 158

Buckinghamshire, earls of. *See* Hobart, John; Hobart, Robert

Buckinghamshire: accounts for estates in, 151–52, 205; assize jurors for, 183; concealed lands in, 68; deeds for lands in, 13, 68, 75, 96, 173, 211, 248, 255–56; deputy lieutenants of, 57, 61, 64, 65, 183, 208, 225; elections in, 59, 65, 68, 193, 208, 224; Jacobite invasion preparations in, 64–65; justices of the peace in, 64, 65, 182, 208; Lords Lieutenant of, 57, 61, 64, 65, 192; maps of estates in, 263–68; Militia in, 57, 61, 65, 70, 155, 192, 193, 225, 226; Parliamentary Committee for, in Civil War, 225; Quarter Sessions in, 68, 183; recusants in, 61; sheriffs of, 208, 225, 227; Ship Money collected in, 227; towns in, listed, 58–59; other, 68, 106, 176–78, 180–81, 182–83, 216, 217, 218, 219

Buckinghamshire Record Office, Stowe manuscripts in, 147

Budd, Thomas William, 158

Budock (Cornwall), 256

Buersall, Edward, 125

Building accounts. *See under* accounts

Bulfett, W. W., 158

Bulkeley, Thomas James Warren, 7th Viscount Bulkeley of Cashel, 158

Bull, H., 158

Bull, Humphrey, 158

Bulwick (Northants.), 114

Bunce, William, 158

Bunche, T., 19

Bunker Hill, battle of, 132

Burbidge, William, 187

Burchett, Josiah, 354

Burdett family, 224

Burdon, Geoffrey, 48

Burge, William, 158
Burgh, Thomas, 127
Burghley, Baron. *See* Cecil, William
"Burghleys Commonwealth," 30, 297
Burgridge, Thomas, 86
Burgundy, heraldry of, 69
Burhope, George, 55, 59
Burhope, Marie, 55
Burke, Sir Henry Franham, 158
Burlington, Earl of. *See* Boyle, Richard
Burnaby, Sir William Chaloner, 306
Burne-Jones, Sir Edward Coley, 282
Burnet, Gilbert, Bp., 105
Burnham (Somerset), 233, 260, 272
Burrard, Alice (Herbert), 59
Burrard, John, 59
Burrell, T., 14
Burrows, John, 335
Burton, Edward, 70
Burton, Francis, 53
Burton, John, 159
Burton, Ralph, 275
Burton, William, 290
Burton (Denbigh.), 75
Burton Dassett (Warwicks.), 152, 153, 180, 203, 205, 212, 214, 217, 218, 219, 261, 274, 358
Burton Hastings (Warwicks.), 100
Burton [on Stather (Lincs.)?], 122
Burton Overy (Leics.), 109
Butcher, William, 187
Bute, Earl of. *See* Stuart, John
Bute, Marchioness of. *See* Stuart, Sophia Frederica Christina (Rawdon-Hastings)
Bute, Marquis of. *See* Crichton-Stuart, John Patrick
Butler, Charles, 253
Butler, Frances Anne (Kemble), 295
Butler, James, 1st Duke of Ormonde, 129
Butler, Sir Theobald, 250

Bygeneure, John de, 7
Byland (Yorks.), 212
Byrkenhead, Dame Margery, 29
Byrne, Robert, 186
Byron, Richard, 2nd Baron Byron of Rochdale, 86

Cabinet minutes, 360
Cadbury (Somerset), 115
Cadbury, North (Somerset), 100
Cadbury, South (Somerset), 100, 115
Cadiz (Spain), 123, 287, 354
Cadogan, William, 232
Caerleon (Monmouth.), 77
Caernarvonshire, 60
Caesar, Sir Julius, 42
Cage, Edward, 43
Calais (France), 102
Calcutta, British social life in, 331
Caleppi, Lorenzo, Abp., 253
California, British subjects in before 1840, 319
Call, Sir John, 126
Callender, Sir John, Bart., 365
Calvert, Charles, 5th Baron Baltimore, 303
Calvert, Philip, 288
Calvert, Reginald, 159
Calverton (Bucks.), 211, 255
Calvins Case, 36
Cambridge, Peter, 352
Cambridge University, 31, 50, 81, 84
Cambridgeshire, deeds for lands in, 96
Camden, Marquis. *See* Pratt, John Jeffreys
Cameron, Donald, 324
Campbell, Alexander [Captain; governor of Ft. William], 324
Campbell, Alexander [of Delnies; factor of John Campbell of Cawdor], 324
Campbell, Alexander [Lieutenant in Earl of Seaforth's Company], 324
Campbell, Sir Archibald, 304

Campbell, Archibald, 3rd Duke of Argyll, 324
Campbell, Archibald, 1st Marquis of Agryll, 324
Campbell, Arthur, 86
Campbell, Colin, 324
Campbell, Daniel, 324
Campbell, David, 324
Campbell, Duncan, 324
Campbell, Eliza (Baillie), Marchioness of Breadalbane, 159
Campbell, Hugh, 3rd Earl of Loudoun, 321, 322, 323, 324
Campbell, James [Lieutenant at Annapolis Royal], 324
Campbell, James [son of James Campbell of Lawers, d. 1723], 324
Campbell, Sir James, 324
Campbell, Sir James, of Aberuchill, 324
Campbell, Sir James, of Inverneil, 159
Campbell, Sir James, of Lawers, 321
Campbell, James Mure, 5th Earl of Loudoun, 321, 324
Campbell, Lady Jean (Boyle), 321
Campbell, Lady Jean Campbell, 325
Campbell, John [physician], 144
Campbell, John [of Shankstoun, 2nd son of the 2nd Earl of Loudoun], 325
Campbell, John [of Shawfield, son-in-law of 3rd Earl of Loudoun], 325
Campbell, John [of Wallwood, "Black Captain Campbell"], 322, 325
Campbell John, 2nd Duke of Argyll and Duke of Greenwich, 325
Campbell, John, 4th Duke of Argyll, 325
Campbell, John, 5th Duke of Argyll, 325
Campbell, John, 1st Earl of Breadalbane and Holland, 325

Campbell, John, 3rd Earl of Breadalbane and Holland, 325
Campbell, John, 4th Earl of Loudoun, 275, 321, 322, 323, 324, 325
Campbell, John, 1st Marquis of Breadalbane, 200
Campbell, John, 2nd Marquis of Breadalbane, 156, 159, 174, 175, 187
Campbell, Josiah, 325
Campbell, Margaret (Dalrymple), Countess of Loudoun, 325
Campbell, Mary, 189
Campbell, Mary Turner (Gavin), Marchioness of Breadalbane, 159, 187, 200
Campbell, Mungo, 325
Campbell, Patrick, 325
Campbell, Robert, 323, 325
Campbell, Theophila (Carlile), 292
Campbell family, 155
Campion, Edmund, 41
Canada: British forces and government in, 308, 333, 355; treatise on, 330; voyages to Northwest Territory, 350; other, 290–91
Canada First, 290
Canals: in France, 224; maps and plans of, 120, 121, 122, 123; other, 66, 141, 201, 346
Canckwell, Bell, 49
Canford Magna (Dorset), 97
Canning, Stratford, 1st Viscount Stratford de Redcliffe, 285
Cannington (Somerset), 260
Cannon, J., 267
Cannon, Thomas, 187
Canons (Middlesex): building and repairs at, 230; gardens at, 230, 242; household at, 242; inventory of, 234; maps and plans of, 234, 271; other, 229, 230
Canterbury, recusants in archbishopric of, 37
Canterbury (Kent), 258; St. Augustines monastery in, 228
Canute, 30
Cape Verde Islands, 320

Capital punishment, 289

Carbery, Earl of. *See* Vaughan, Richard

Cardonnel, Adam de, 232

Cardwell, Edward, 289

Cardwell, Edward, Viscount Cardwell, 159

Carew, Sir George, 291

Carey, Henry, 1st Baron Hunsdon, 84, 86

Carleton, Thomas, 86

Carlile, Eliza (Sharples), 292

Carlile, Jane, 292

Carlile, Mary Anne, 292

Carlile, Richard, 291–92

Carlile, T., 70

Carlisle, Earl of. *See* Howard, Frederick

Carlisle, Bp. of, 39

Carlton Curlieu (Leics.), 97

Carmarthen, Marquis of. *See* Osborne, Peregrine

Carmichael, David Fremantle, 159

Carmichael, John, 3rd Earl of Hyndford, 325

Carnarvon, Marquis of. *See* Brydges, James

Carne, Charles, 159

Carnegie, David, 4th Earl of Northesk, 325

Carpenter, Mary, 295

Carpenter, William Banjamin, 282

Carpenters, 19

Carpimall Co., 159

Carr, Lucy, 241

Carr, Robert, Earl of Somerset, 45

Carswell (Devon.), 107

Carte, Samuel, 86

Carte, Thomas, 86

Carter, John, 49, 70

Carter, Lawrence, 86

Cartmel (Lancs.), 258

Cartularies, 5, 10, 77, 96, 173, 210–11

Cartwright, Richard, 70

Cartwright, Thomas, 138

Carver, Christopher, 86

Cary, Sir George, 129, 130

Cary, Henry, 1st Viscount Falkland, 105

Cary, Lucius, 2nd Viscount Falkland, 105, 137

Carysfort, Earl of. *See* Proby, John Joshua

Cascob (Radnor.), 260

Casley, David, 10

Casolette, plans for a, 123

Cassillis, earls of. *See* Kennedy, Archibald; Kennedy, David

Castle, John ("de Sacro Bosco"), 52, 70

Castle Donington (Leics.), 82, 97, 109–10, 118, 121. *See also* Donington (Leics.)

Castlecoote, Baron. *See* Coote, Charles Henry

Castles, lists of, 44

Castletowne (Ireland), 122

Casus, George, 30

Catcott (Somerset), 233, 236, 238, 261

Cathay Co., 320

Cathcart, Alan, 7th Baron Cathcart, 325

Cathcart, Charles, 8th Baron Cathcart, 325

Cathcart, Charles Schaw, 9th Baron Cathcart, 325

Cathcart, James, 322, 325

Cathcart, M., 325

Cathedrals, list of, 139

Catholic Church, attack on doctrine and practices of, 31, 139

Catholics: in England, 37, 61, 64, 65, 139; in Ireland, 200, 227. *See also* recusants.

Catsfield (Sussex), 6

Cattle: imported from Ireland, 58; Plague, 183, 184

Cause lists (Star Chamber), 41

Cavalier Club, 228

Cavan, Co. (Ireland), 247, 249

Cavendish, Lady Elizabeth, 241

Cavendish, Elizabeth. *See* Egerton, Elizabeth (Cavendish)

Cavendish, George, 292
Cavendish, Jane, 68
Cavendish, Philip, 343
Cavendish, William, 1st Duke of Newcastle, 22
Cavendish family, 194
Cavendish-Bentinck, William Henry, 3rd Duke of Portland, 175
Caverswall (Staffs.), 100
Cawode, Agatha, 127
Cawode, James, 127
Cayenne (Fr. Guiana), capture of by British, 355
Cecil, David, 3rd Earl of Exeter, 46, 71
Cecil, Elizabeth (Egerton), Countess of Exeter, 46, 71
Cecil, Sir Richard, 71
Cecil, Sir Robert, 46
Cecil, Robert, 1st Earl of Salisbury, 33, 35, 71
Cecil, Robert Arthur Talbot Gascoyne, 3rd Marquis of Salisbury, 159, 282
Cecil, William, Baron Burghley, 27, 33 *(bis)*, 39, 44, 45, 71, 297
Cecily, Duchess of York, 9
Cefnllys (Radnor.), 260
Census (religious), for Ireland, 120
Chabot, Louis William de Rohan Chabot, Vicomte de Rohan, 159
Chadshunt (Warwicks.), 212, 261
Chalfont St. Peter (Bucks.), 183
Chalmer, John, 325
Chaloner, Sir Thomas, 38
Chamberlain, Joseph, 282
Chamberlain, Sir Neville Bowles, 159
Chamberlayne, Emma (Brydges), 232
Chambers, Abraham, 125
Chambers, Anne. *See* Grenville-Temple, Anne (Chambers)
Chambers, Gertrude, 277
Champion, Lawrence, 10

Chancellor, Lord: Thomas Egerton as, 21, 32–45 *passim.;* treatise on office of, 29; other, 14, 15
Chancery, 41–42, 72, 142, 243. *See also under* Courts
Chandos, barons. *See* Brydges, Edmund; Brydges, Grey
Chandos, Baroness. *See* Brydges, Elizabeth (Barnard)
Chandos, duchesses of. *See* Brydges, Cassandra (Willoughby); Brydges, Lydia Catherine (Van Hatten); Brydges, Anne (Wells) Jeffries; Brydges, Elizabeth (Major); Brydges, Anne Eliza (Gamon) Elletson
Chandos, dukes of. *See* Brydges, James; Brydges, Henry
Chandos family, 242
Chandos House (London), accounts of, 152
Channel Islands. *See* Alderney; Guernsey, Jersey, Sark
Channing, William Henry, 295
Chantries, 9
Chaplin, Acton, 159
Chaplin, Robert, 86
Chaplyn, William [steward of Sir Thomas Temple, 1st Bart.], 207, 208, 358
Chaplyn, William [steward of Sir Richard Temple, 3rd Bart.], 206, 208
Chapman, John, 186
Chapman, Maria Weston, 293
Chapman, Robert, 71
Chapman, T. S., 159
Chapman, Thomas, 71
Chapman family, 224
Chapone, Hester (Mulso), 335
Charities: accounts of contributions to, 154, 231; other, 11, 65, 84, 139, 144. *See also* Philanthropists
Charles I, King of England, 18, 49, 52, 53, 71, 86, 128, 137, 140–41, 225, 226, 361, 362

Charles II, King of England, 52, 58, 71, 86, 129, 139, 142, 143, 198, 223, 228, 320
Charles Edward Stuart, Prince ("The Young Pretender"), 322
Charleston (S.C.), 132
Charleston Expedition (1776), 132
Charley Chase (Leics.), 97
Charlton, John, 208
Charlton (Berks.), 95
Charnock, Sir George, 58
Charnwood Forest (Leics.), 97, 110, 121
Chartley (Staffs.), 181
Chatham, Countess of. *See* Pitt, Hester (Grenville)
Chatham, Earl of. *See* Pitt, William
Chaucer, Geoffrey, 28, 30
Chaure, John, 8
Cheadle (Staffs.), 116
Chearsley (Bucks.), 96, 177, 255, 264
Checkendon (Oxon.), 259
Cheddar (Somerset.), 180, 233, 261
Cheddington (Bucks.), 177
Cheek, Edward, 20
Cheke family, 19
Chelsea (Middlesex), 68, 77
Chelsea Hospital, 68
Cheltenham (Gloucs.), 120
Cheriton (Hants.), 258
Cherry, Francis, 34
Chertsey (Surrey), 66
Cheshire, George, 186
Cheshire: accounts of estates in, 230; deeds for lands in, 76; other, 54, 68, 106, 238
Cheshunt [formerly Trevecka] College, Cambridge, 81
Chester, Charles Montagu, 159
Chester (Cheshire), 76
Chesterfield, earls of. *See* Stanhope, Philip; Stanhope, George
Chesterman, H., 159
Chetwode (Bucks.), 216, 218
Cheverell, Great (Wilts.), 100
Cheverell, Little (Wilts.), 100
Chevers, Christopher, 247

Chew family, 194
Chewton Mendip (Somerset.), 261
Cheyne, George, 86
Cheyne, Gertrude (Pierrepont), Viscountess Newhaven, 71
Cheyne, Francis, 68
Cheyne, Lady, 64
Cheyne, Sir Thomas, 68
Cheyne, William, 2nd Viscount Newhaven, 67, 71
Cheyne family, 67
Chichele, Henry, Abp., 9
Chichester, Arthur, 1st Baron Chichester, 129, 130
Chichester, recusants in bishopric of, 37
Chilcott, Charles, 159
Chiltington (Sussex), 100
Chilton (Bucks.), 255
Chippenham (Wilts.), 100
Cholesbury (Bucks.), 183
Cholmondeston (Cheshire), 75, 76
Christchurch (Hants.), 97, 108
Christon (Somerset), 261
Church, John, 244
Church of England: *Book of Common Prayer*, 63; Court of Arches, 294; dissent from, 37, 44, 57, 138–39, 200 (*see also* recusants); grants to crown by, 51; Ecclesiastical Commissioners, 57, 139; High Commission, 37, 227; proposals for reform of, 138, 313; valuation of bishoprics and deaneries of, 279; other, 37, 50, 57, 63, 303. *See also* Clergy
Churchill, Elizabeth. *See* Egerton, Elizabeth (Churchill)
Churchill, J., 19
Churchill, John, 12
Churchill, John, 1st Duke of Marlborough, 22, 232, 288
Churchwardens: accounts of, 109; list of, at Stowe, 216
Cippenham (Bucks.), 96, 106
Civil List, 202
Civil Wars, 48, 52, 84, 350, 361; in Ireland, 129

Clapton (Somerset.), 100
Clare, Co. (Ireland), 180, 247, 249, 262
Clare, de, family, 132
Clarence, George, Duke of, 127
Clarendon, earls of. *See* Hyde, Edward; Hyde, Henry; Villiers, George William Frederick
Clarges, Sir Thomas, 129
Clark, W. C., 159
Clark, William, 187
Clarke, George, 288
Clarke, Sir Gilbert, 86
Clarke, R., 159
Clarke & Medcalf, 159
Clarkson, Thomas, 293–94, 331
Claydon (Bucks.), 264
Cleeve, Richard, 247
Clere, Edward, 339
Clergy: dissenting, 200; in Ireland, 200; relief of poor among, 199; taxation of, 113; tenths of, 139
Clerke, Beatrix, 86
Clerke, Francis, 294
Clerks of the Peace, for Buckinghamshire, 177
Clevancy (Wilts.), 100
Clifton, Alice, 125
Clifton, Lady Alice Hastings, 86
Clifton, Augustus Wykeham, 86
Clifton, Charles Frederick. *See* Abney-Hastings [formerly Clifton], Charles Frederick
Clifton, Hetty (Treves), 86
Clifton, Sir Gervase, 1st Bart., 86
Clifton, Sir Richard, 129
Clifton (Warwicks.?), 122
Clifton Reynes (Bucks.), 183
Clinton, Sir Henry, 132
Clinton [or Fiennes], Henry, 2nd Earl of Lincoln, 41
Clogie, Alexander, 294
Clothing, accounts of purchase of, 47, 83, 154, 207, 231
Clutton (Cheshire), 76
Clyro (Radnor.), 260
Clyst Gerred (Devon), 96
Coal. *See* Mines & mining (coal)

Coates, John, 159
Coats of arms. *See* Arms (heraldic)
Cobbe, Lady Elizabeth Beresford, 86
Cobbe, Frances Power, 294–95
Cobham, Henry de, 225
Cobham, barons. *See* Brooke, Henry; Brooke, George; Brooke, William
Cobham, Viscount. *See* Temple, Richard
Cobham, viscountesses. *See* Grenville, Hester (Temple); Temple, Anne (Halsey)
Cocchi, Antonio, 86
Cochrane, Sir Alexander Forrester Inglis, 159, 301
Cochrane, Jean (Stuart), Countess of Dundonald, 346
Cockerell, Theodore Dru Alison, 277
Cockerill, Henry, 186, 187
Codd, Thomas Hudson, 159
Coddiford Farleigh (Cornwall), 106
Codrington, Richard, 159
Codrington, Robert, 47
Coghill, Sir John, 129
Coinage & currency, 37, 38, 50, 58, 63, 296, 318–19, 351. *See also* Mint, Royal
Coke, Sir Edward, 35, 41, 43, 71
Coke-Ash Murder case, 105
Coker, J., 159
Cokesfield (county?), 18
Colcell, John, 9
Colchester, Viscount. *See* Savage, Thomas
Cold Newton (Leics.), 110
Colden (Yorks.), 101
Cole, Crozier, 272
Cole, G., 18
Cole, Rolfe, 272
Coleman, Elizabeth, 240
Coleman, Morgan, 295–96
Colenso, John William, Bp., 295
Coleorton (Leics.), 110
Coles, George, 159

Coleshill (Flint.), 76
Colledge, Stephen, 143
Collegiate churches, list of, 139
Colles, F., 86
Collet, John, 296
Collett, Thomas, 214
Collier, John, 247
Collier, John Payne, 23, 71
Collieries. *See* Mines & Mining (coal)
Collingham (Yorks.), 117
Collingwood, Cuthbert, Baron Collingwood, 159
Collins, Arthur, 12
Collins, James, 343
Collins, William, 186
Collumpton (Devon), 1
Colonial Office, 155, 157, 202
Colonial Secretary, Richard Grenville as, 150, 155, 157
Colthrop (Berks.), 237
Commissions (military & naval), 20, 192, 322, 365
Commissions & Commissioners: of Array, 10, 44; for Charitable Uses, 72; of the Customs, 68, 208, 209, 223, 306; for Defective Titles (Ireland), 129; on Enclosures (1517), 217; of Excise, 224; for Increasing the King's yearly revenue (1626), 142; for the Sale of Crown Lands, 72; for Sewers, 45; for the Subsidy, 72, 88; for Tithes, 163
Committee for Plundered Ministers, 226
Commonplace books: historical, 28, 296–97; legal, 28, 30, 298, 364; mathematical, 140; military, 344; poetical, 48, 59, 282; political, 34, 53, 282, 298, 332, 356; religious, 243, 299, 310; travel, 189, 299, 330, 364; of William IV, 364; other, 31, 43, 70, 189, 190, 197, 296, 299, 300
Commonwealth [Interregnum]: lawsuits during, 215; Parliamentary Committee for Buckingham, 225. *See also* Civil Wars
Compotus rolls, 106, 108, 109, 111–17 *passim.*, 218, 237
Compton, Henry, Bp., 57
Compton, Margaret (Douglas-Macleen-Clephane), Marchioness of Northampton, 253
Compton Martin (Somerset), 180, 233, 236, 261, 272
Concealed lands: in England, 33, 68; in Ireland, 129
Congreve, William, 303
Congreve, Sir William, 2nd Bart., 159
Coningsby, George, 240
Constables, list of (Leics.), 113
Constantine (Cornwall), 256
Contagious Diseases Act, 183
Control, Board of. *See* Board of Control
Convention Parliament, 63
Conway, Edward, 1st Earl of Conway, 104, 128, 129
Conway, Edward, 2nd Viscount Conway, 129
Conway, Francis, 129
Conway, Margaret M., 277
Coo, Thomas, 43, 71
Cook, George Stevani Littlejohn, 277
Cook, Robert Haldane, 277
Cooke, Agnes (Herbert), 312
Cooke, Sir Anthony, 208, 214 *(bis)*
Cooke, John, 359
Cooke, Sir Miles, 86
Cookman, John, 71
Coolstock, Thomas, 11
Cooper, Anthony Ashley, 7th Earl of Shaftesbury, 289, 295
Cooper [Coprario], John, 49
Coote, Charles Henry, 2nd Baron Castlecoote, 253
Coote, Richard, 1st Baron Coote of Coloony, 86
Coote, Richard, 1st Earl of Bellamont, 62, 71
Cope, Sir John, 325

Copenhagen, battle of, 338
Copley, Anne, 14
Copley, Mary, 14
Coprario, Giovanni [John Cooper], 49
Copthall (Essex), 2, 13, 19
Corbet, James, 63
Corbet, John, 346
Corbett, Jasper, 186
Corbett, Sir John, 52
Corbett, Joseph, 185
Corbett, Richard, 299
Corbett, William, 186
Cork, Earl of. *See* Boyle, Richard
Cork, Co. (Ireland), 119
Cork Harbour, 61
Corkran, Michael, 249
Corkran, Teige, 249
Corn Laws, 198
Cornwall: accounts for estates in, 152; deeds for lands in, 96, 211, 248, 256–57; Freeholders of, 202; maps of estates in, 269; Stannary Parliament, 300; other, 60, 106–07, 179, 181, 183, 218, 248, 250
Cornwallis, Charles, 4th Baron Cornwallis, 226
Cornwallis, Letitia, 232
Cornwallis, Sir William, 300
Coronation proceedings, 32
Corporations: coat of arms of, 144; regulation of, 58
Corry, Isaac, 159
Corryton, Sir John, 297
Corser, Thomas, 281
Cory, Henry, 159
Cossington (Leics.), 97, 110
Cossington (Somerset), 261
Cotterill & Sons, 159
Cottesloe, Baron. *See* Fremantle, Thomas Francis
Cottesloe, Baroness. *See* Fremantle, Louise Elizabeth (Nugent)
Cottisford (Bucks.), 173
Cotton, Sir Robert Bruce, 136, 300
Cotton, Rowland, 86
Coulthard, James, 231, 232

Council (King's), registers of, 41. *See also* Privy Council
Council in the Marches of Wales, 35, 51, 69, 72, 115
Council of the North, 36, 82, 84, 311
"Countess of Huntingdon's Connection," 80
Coupar, Baron. *See* Elphinstone, John
Court (Royal), 53, 143, 299, 314, 361. *See also* Household (Royal)
Court books, 5, 16, 75, 108, 111, 115, 116, 181, 217, 237
Court registers, 16, 17
Court rolls, 4–5, 15–17, 33, 46, 47, 54, 59, 68, 74–75, 105–17 *passim.*, 180, 181, 217, 237, 250, 339
Courtenay, Thomas de, 5th Earl of Devon, 9
Courteney, Peter, 126
Courteney, Richard, 185
Courteney, Thomas, 126
Courts: of Admiralty, 33, 34, 50, 72, 305; of Arches, 294; of Assize, 183, 239; of Chancery, 27, 33, 41–42, 72, 176, 214, 235 (*see also* Chancery); of Council in the Marches of Wales, 35, 51, 72, 115; of Duchy of Lancaster, 42, 70, 72; of Exchequer, 27, 52, 72, 249, 306; of High Commission, 37, 227; of Kings Bench, 9, 43, 52, 72, 176; of Requests, 42; of Star Chamber, 40–41, 42, 47, 52, 53, 70, 72, 105, 282, 298, 306; of Wards & Liveries, 14, 27, 72, 214; other and unspecified, 9, 41–42, 58, 62, 72, 104, 214, 215, 249
Coutts, Thomas, 86
Coutts & Co., 86, 154, 159
Coventry, Thomas, 1st Baron Coventry, 53, 137
Coventry (Warwicks.), 261
Coventry & Lichfield, recusants in bishopric of, 37
Coward, Magdalen, 300
Cowley, J. W., 159

Coxe & Chambers, 159
Coxwold (Yorks.), 212
Cradock, John, 86
Cradock, Norrice, 86
Cradock, John & Thomas, 86
Cradock & Son, 86
Craggs, James, 246
Craggs, John, 246
Craggs family, 251
Craig, Francis, 365
Craig, Mrs. Hardin, 356
Craig, James, 325
Cranbrook, Earl of. *See* Gathorne-
  Hardy, Gathorne
Cranbrook (Kent), 20
Crandon (Somerset), 238
Crandon cum Puriton (Somerset),
  234
Crane, Ralph, 48, 54
Crane, Walter, 282
Cranfield, Lady Elizabeth. *See* Eg-
  erton, Elizabeth (Cranfield)
Cranfield, James, 2nd Earl of Mid-
  dlesex, 22, 54
Cranfield, Lionel, 1st Earl of Mid-
  dlesex, 54, 296
Cranfield, Lionel, 3rd Earl of Mid-
  dlesex, 53–54
Cranmer, Thomas, Abp., 144
Craufurd, Sir James Gregan, 2nd
  Bart., 159
Crawford, James, 346
Crawfurd, Thomas, 156, 159
Crawter, Henry [fl. 1843–54, land
  agent for Mercers Co.], 160
Crawter, Henry [fl. 1853–73,
  nephew of above], 160
Crawter, John, 160
Creed (Cornwall), 256
Cregrina (Radnor.), 260
Crendon, Long. *See* Long Crendon
Crewe, Sir Thomas, 137
Cribbs, Letitia Sarah, 187
Crich (Derbys.), 257
Crichton-Stuart, John Patrick, 3rd
  Marquis of Bute, 104
Cricklade (Wilts.), 262, 274

Crime & criminals: measures
  against, 182; Coke-Ash murder
  case, 105
Cripps, Francis, 160
Cripps, Frederick, 160
Cripps, James, 86
Cripps, John, 160
Crocker, Sir Gerard, 185
Croft, Bridgett, 86
Croke, Sir John, 39
Croker, John Wilson, 285
Croket, John, 222
Cromp, Thomas, 71
Crompton, ____, 51
Cromwell, Lady Margaret (Rein-
  court), 240
Cromwell, Oliver, 215
Crook, Charles, 160
Crook, E., 160
Crooke, Sir George, 141
Cropper, Margaret (Macaulay), 331
Crosbie, William, 365
Cross, Humphrey, 227
Cross, William, 160
Crowcombe (Somerset), 272
Crowle, William, 87
Crowley, Theodosia, 87
Crowmarsh (Oxon.), 1
Crown: lands of, 33, 51; relations
  with Parliament, 39–40, 52, 137,
  226; revenues of, 29, 33, 50, 142;
  rights & prerogatives of, 29, 30,
  40
Crownett, Anthony, 12
Crozier, George, 87
Crudeli, Tommaso, 134
Crystal Palace, plan for, 271
Cuddington (Cheshire), 76
Cudlington (Oxon.), 217
Culloden, battle of, 322
Culpeper, Martin, 222
Cumberland, dukes of. *See* Ernest
  Augustus; William Augustus
Cumberland, 107
Cunningham, David, 325
Cunningham, Sir William, 3rd
  Bart., 325
Cunninghame, James, 87

Currency. *See* Coinage & currency
Currey Rivel (Somerset), 77
Currie & Williams, 154, 156, 160
Curtis, Sir Roger, 316
Curzon, Lady Mary Assheton, 87
Curzon, Richard William Penn, 87
Cusack, Adam, 248
Cusack, Clare, 250
Customal rolls, 107
Customs, 68, 208, 209, 223, 245, 306. *See also under* Commissions & Commissioners; Excise
Cutleston (Staffs.), 66
Czerkaski, Joseph, 194

Dacre, Lady Anne, 43
Dacre, William, 3rd Baron Dacre of the North, 43
Dacres, Mrs. Inez, 233
Dacres, James Richard, 160
Dadford (Bucks.), 173, 177, 180, 203, 211, 216, 217, 218 *(ter)*, 264
Dalby, Henry, 87
Dalby, Thomas, 87
Dalby (Leics.), 97
Dale, Hugh, 71
Dale Abbey (Derbys.), 96
Dalhousie, Earl of. *See* Ramsay, George
Dallas, Alexander, 325
Dallow, Edward, 19
Dallway, Alexander, 188
Dalrymple, Alexander, 285
Dalrymple, Charles [d. 1729], 325
Dalrymple, Charles [fl. 1756–75], 325
Dalrymple, Sir David, 1st Bart., 325
Dalrymple, Eleanor (Campbell) Primrose, Countess of Stair, 325
Dalrymple, George, Baron Dalrymple, 323, 325
Dalrymple, Hew, 1st Bart. and Lord North Berwick, 326
Dalrymple, Sir Hew, Lord Drummore, 325
Dalrymple, John, 326
Dalrymple, Sir John, 2nd Bart., 326

Dalrymple, John, 1st Earl of Stair, 326
Dalrymple, John, 2nd Earl of Stair, 326
Dalrymple, John, 5th Earl of Stair, 326
Dalrymple, Robert, 326
Dalrymple, William, 326
Dalrymple-Crichton, William, 5th Earl of Dumfries and 4th Earl of Stair, 326
Dalziel, George, 160
Danby, Earl of. *See* Osborne, Thomas
Dance, Thomas, 129
Daniel, John, 160
Daniell, Richard, 34, 71
Darcy, Robert, 4th Earl of Holderness, 67
Dardis, Garrett, 251
Dardis, William, 160
Darling, James Stermonth, 160
Darlington, Earl of. *See* Vane, Henry
Darnelly, Richard, 206
Dartmouth, Richard, 9
Dartmouth, Earl of. *See* Legge, William
Dartmouth (Devon), 208
Darwin, Charles Robert, 295
Datchet (Bucks.), 96
Davall, J. B., 87
Davenport, Sir Humphrey, 141
Davids, C. H., 160
Davidson & Syme, 160
Davies, Godfrey, 314
Davies, Sir John, 58, 79, 87, 104, 125, 128 *(bis)*, 129, 133
Davies, Lucy. *See* Hastings, Lucy (Davies)
Davies family, 132
Davis, Hewitt, 160
Davison, Francis, 54
Davison, Jacob, 232
Davison, Noll, Templer & Co., 87
Davys, Ferdinando, 87
Davys, John [fl. 1645–70, of Leicestershire], 87

Davys, John [fl. 1670–80, son of the above], 87
Davys, Matthew, 87
Davys, Tristram, 87
Davys, William, 87, 131
Dawes & Sons, 160
Dawkins, Henry, 270
Dawson, Edward, 87, 141
Dawson's Book Shop, 313
Day, John, 71
Daye, Richard, 50
Daylesford (Worcs.), 116
Dayrell, Edmund, 160
Dayrell, Peter, 215
Dayrell, Richard, 186
Dean (Dorset.), 179
Deane, George, 160
Declaration of Right, 63
Defense, notes on, 297, 300
De la Coliniere, ——, 335
Delamaine, Richard, 49, 71
Delamar, Peter, 247
De Lancey, James, 275
De la Palue[?], ——, 160
De la Pole, William. *See* Pole, William de la
De Ligondez, Frances (Fowler) Needham Hastings. *See* Hastings [aftw. De Ligondez], Frances (Fowler) Needham
Delvin, Lord. *See* Nugent, Christopher
De Medalle, Lydia (Sterne), 335
De Messine, ——, 335
Dempster, George, 347
Denbigh, Earl of. *See* Fielding, Basil
Denbigh, lordship of, 59
Denbighshire: deeds for land in, 76; other, 35, 46
Denham, Sir John, 141
Denison, Edward, Bp., 313
Denmark, 49, 156
Denny, William, 275
Denshall, John, 26
Denton, Sir Edmond, 65
Denton, Margaret, 212
Denton, Sir Thomas, 208

Denton, William, 208
Deputy Lieutenants (of counties): in Buckinghamshire, 57, 61, 64, 65, 183, 208, 225; in Hampshire, 238; in Leicestershire, 84, 91, 136; in Rutland, 84, 93; other, 34. *See also* Lord Lieutenants
Derby, countesses of. *See* Egerton, Alice (Spencer) Stanley; Stanley, Anne (Hastings)
Derby, earls of. *See* Stanley, Thomas; Stanley, Edward; Stanley, Henry; Stanley, Ferdinando; Stanley, William
Derby (Derbys.), 107
Derbyshire: accounts for estates in, 152; deeds for land in, 96, 257; map of lands in, 107; Militia in, 136; other, 107
Dering, Sir Edward, 300
Derroteros, 310
Derry, lands of archbishopric of, 119
Desford (Leics.), 97
De Vere. *See* Vere, de
Deverell, Thomas, 160
Devereux, John, 253
Devereux, Robert, 2nd Earl of Essex, 32, 71, 279, 296, 297
Devereux, Robert, 3rd Earl of Essex, 102
Devon, Earl of. *See* Courtenay, Thomas de
Devonshire: concealed lands in, 68; deeds for lands in, 96–97; description of, 350; other, 60, 107, 118
Devotional literature, 48, 55, 134, 138, 200, 227, 310, 355. *See also* Religious tracts & treatises; Sermons
Dewes, W., 87
"Dialogus de Scaccario," 40
Diaries & journals:
—by date: 16th century, 26, 281; 17th century, 46, 48, 241, 279, 280, 281, 300, 320; 18th century, 241–42, 276, 278, 290, 302, 319, 321, 332, 344, 351, 354, 356, 357,

364; 19th century, 189–90, 284, 292, 318, 319, 332, 348, 350, 353, 356, 357; 20th century, 364
—by subject: military, 278, 344, 351, 354; naval & maritime, 48, 189, 302, 318, 332, 350, 364 *(bis)*; Parliamentary, 279, 280; personal, 189, 190, 241–42, 290, 319, 332, 356, 357; political, 189, 190, 321; religious, 26, 319; travel, 189, 190, 242, 284, 302, 320, 350, 364; other, 46, 189–90, 241–42, 276, 281, 292, 300, 348, 353
Dibdin, Thomas Frognal, 253
Dickinson, Robert, 87
Dictionaries, 290, 301
Digby, Sir Everard, 142
Digby, George, 2nd Earl of Bristol, 227, 244
Digby, Sir Kenelm, 48
Dighton, Christopher, 87
Dilhorne (Staffs.), 68, 77, 116
Dilhorne School, 84, 116, 140
Dinton (Bucks.), 255
Diplomatic missions: of 1570–72, 362; of 1598, 34; of 1606, 291; of 1794, 155; of 1799, 155
Diplomats (British): in Austria, 318; in Denmark, 156; in France, 291, 362; in Italy, 67, 296, 310; in Netherlands, 156; in Portugal, 67; in Prussia, 156; in Russia, 34; other, 288
Diplomats (Hanoverian), 288
Diptford (Devon), 96, 107
Diseases: of cattle, 183–84; of horses, 69. *See also* Medicine
Disraeli, Benjamin, 1st Earl of Beaconsfield, 160
Dissenters. *See* Religious dissent
Ditton (Bucks.), 96, 106
Dixie, Wolston, 87
Dixon, John, 187
Dixon, Matthew, 304
Dockary, John, 221
Dockyards, sketch of, 123
Doddington (Cheshire), 66
Dodington, George, 206, 219

Dodington, Hester (Temple), 208
Dodington, John, 208 *(bis)*
Dodington (Somerset), 152, 180, 261, 272
Dodwell, Joseph, 160
Dogered, Thomas, 10
Doggett, William, 160
Doig, R., 160
Dondal, Edward, 251
Donington, barons. *See* Abney-Hastings [formerly Clifton], Charles Frederick; Rawdon-Hastings [formerly Abney-Hastings], Charles Edward
Donington (Leics.), 79, 82, 102, 103, 110. *See also* Castle Donington
Donisthorpe (Leics.), 97, 110
Donne, John, 48, 299
Donnellan, Anne, 335
Donovan, Jeremiah, 87
Dorchester Gaol, 292
Dormer, Anthony, 14
Dormer, Lady Elizabeth, 14
Dormer, George, 199
Dormer, John, 199
Dormer, Robert, 14
Dorset, Earl of. *See* Sackville, Thomas.
Dorset: accounts for estates in, 152; deeds for lands in, 97; other, 108, 179, 218
Dorton (Bucks.), 177, 255, 264
Douglas, Sir Archibald, 104
Douglas, Lady Eleanor (Tuchet) Davies, 87, 104, 138
Douglas, James, 2nd Duke of Queensberry & 1st Duke of Dover, 326
Douglas, John, Bp., 347
Douglas, Samuel, 300
Douglass, George, 323, 326
Dover, Duke of. *See* Douglas, James
Dowdall, Harold Chaloner, 353
Dowdall, Mary Frances (Borthwick), 353
Down, Co. (Ireland), 102, 119
Downe, Earl of. *See* Pope, Thomas

Downes, John, 70
Downes, Roger, 70
Downes family, 69–70
Downing, William, 245
Dowsby (Lincs.), 113
Doyle, Sir Francis Hastings, 87
D'Oyley, Edward, 288
Drake, Dawson, 343 *(bis)*
Drake, Sir Francis, 45
Drake, John, 71
Drakenage (Warwicks.), 100
Drama, in England, 314. *See also*
   Literature & literary papers
Draper family, 224
Drawings & sketches, 31, 69, 193,
   194, 279, 283, 286, 295, 303, 332,
   348, 353
Draycott (Somerset), 234, 238
Drayton, David, 19
Drayton, Margaret, 19
Drayton, Richard, 19
Drayton, Silas, 20
Drayton Beauchamp (Bucks.), 68,
   74, 75
Drelincourt, Charles, 139
Dromgold, Jean, 335
Drummond, George, 326
Drummond, Henry, 331
Drummond, Robert Hay, 335
Drummore, Lord. *See* Dalrymple,
   Sir Hew
Drypool (Yorks.), 101
Dublin, 119, 122
Dublin Castle, 128, 175
Dublin, Co. (Ireland), 102, 119, 247,
   249, 262
DuBoccage, Maria Anne (Le Page)
   Fiquet, 335
Ducali, Venetian, 29
Duckworth, Sir John Thomas, 1st
   Bart., 160
Dudley, Ambrose, 1st Earl of War-
   wick, 27
Dudley, Edmund, 33
Dudley, John, 160
Dudley, Joseph, 288
Dudley, Sir Robert, 136

Dudley, Robert, Earl of Leicester,
   87, 319
Dudley, Samuel B., 160
Dufferin, Marquis of. See Black-
   wood, Frederick Temple
Duffield, Francis, 214
Dugdale, Alice Frances (Trevel-
   yan), 331
Dugdale, Sir William, 87, 133, 173,
   251
Dumaresq, Charles, 63
Dumfries, earls of. *See* Dalrymple-
   Crichton, William; MacDowall-
   Chrichton, Patrick
Dumont, Louis, 331
Dun, Alice de, 7
Dun, Hugh de, 7
Duncan, Jonathan, 160
Duncan, John, 348
Dunch, Jane, 241
Duncomb, Francis, 13
Duncombe, Alexander, 66
Duncombe, Sir Charles, 63
Dundas, Robert Saunders, 2nd Vis-
   count Melville, 301
Dundonald, Countess of. *See* Co-
   chrane, Jean (Stuart)
Dungan, Margaret, 251
Dunkirk, 136
Dunnett, D., 160
Dupré, James, 198
Durant, Nicholas, 12
Durey de Meinieres, Octavie Belot
   (Guichard), 335
Durham, house of Bp. of, 45
Durham, 248, 257
Durley, John, 160
Duveen, Sir Joseph, 330
Dyers, 15
Dykes, Christopher, 277
Dymock, Edward, 41
Dymocke, James, 301

E., J., 52
Eales, John, 160
Eames, John, 87
Earleshall [*alias* Frampton]
   (Lincs.), 75, 77

Earthquakes, 310
East, Arthur, 215
East, Edward, 232
East, Sir Edward Hyde, 1st Bart., 160
East, Sir James Buller, 2nd Bart., 160
East India Co. (English), 143, 346
East India Co. (French), 224
East Indies, British naval forces in, 344
East Marden (Sussex), 116
East Sussex Record Office, 3
East Thorpe (Essex), 18
Easton (Hants.), 179, 181, 233, 258
Eastwood (Notts.), 99
Eatington [Ettington] (Warwicks.), 116
Ebrington, Thomas, 253
Ecchinswell (Hants.), 237
Ecclesfield (Yorks.), 262
Ecclesiastical Commissioners, 57, 139
Ecclestone, Henry, 71
Echingham [Etchingham] (Sussex), 6, 7
Eden, Morton, 1st Baron Henley, 160
Eden, William, 1st Baron Auckland, 160, 341
Edgcumbe, Richard, 2nd Baron Edgcumbe, 365
Edgerley, Thomas, 224
Edgeworth, Maria, 284, 285
Edgeworth, Richard Lovell, 284, 285
Edgware (Middlesex), 259
Edinburgh, plans for Register Office in, 123
Edington (Somerset), 234
Edmonds, Lady Sarah (Harington) Hastings Kingsmill Zouche, 87
Edmonson, Joseph, 243
Edmonton (Middlesex), 99, 259
Education. *See* Schools & education
Edward III, King of England, 8, 71
Edward IV, King of England, 9

Edward VI, King of England, 32, 71
Edward VII, King of England, 195
Edward 'Plantagenet,' 2nd Duke of York, 28
Edward Augustus, Duke of Kent & Strathern, 87
Edwards, Elizabeth, 87
Edwards, R. F., 160
Edwards, Templer & Co., 87
Effingham, Earl of. *See* Howard, Thomas
Egerton, Alice (Spencer) Stanley, Countess of Derby & Viscountess Brackley, 21, 26, 27, 46, 54, 83, 87
Egerton, Bridget, 42
Egerton, Edward, 42
Egerton, Elizabeth (Cavendish), Countess of Bridgewater, 22, 55
Egerton, Elizabeth (Cranfield), Lady Brackley, 22, 54, 59
Egerton, Elizabeth (More) Polsted Wolley, 21
Egerton, Elizabeth (Ravenscroft), 21
Egerton, Elizabeth. *See* Cecil, Elizabeth (Egerton)
Egerton, Frances (Stanley), Countess of Bridgewater, 21, 46, 47, 49, 71
Egerton, Francis, 3rd Duke of Bridgewater, 23, 66, 71
Egerton, Francis Henry, 8th Earl of Bridgewater, 23
Egerton, Francis Leveson-Gower, 1st Earl of Ellesmere, 23, 69, 198
Egerton, George Granville Francis, 2nd Earl of Ellesmere, 23
Egerton, Harriet Catherine, Countess of Ellesmere, 23
Egerton, Hubert D., 161
Egerton, Jane (Paulet), Countess of Bridgewater, 22, 64, 65, 71
Egerton, John [d. 1611], 26
Egerton, John, 2nd Duke of Bridgewater, 23, 66

Egerton, John, 1st Earl of Bridge-water, 21–22, 26, 34 (bis), 46–53 *passim.*, 69, 71, 79

Egerton, John, 2nd Earl of Bridge-water, 22, 53–59 *passim.*, 71, 208

Egerton, John, 3rd Earl of Bridge-water, 22, 59–64 *passim.*, 71

Egerton, John Francis Granville Scrope, 3rd Earl of Ellesmere, 23

Egerton, John William, 7th Earl of Bridgewater, 23

Egerton, Lady Mary, 27

Egerton, Rachel (Russell), Duchess of Bridgewater, 22

Egerton, Roland, 42

Egerton Scroop, 4th Earl & 1st Duke of Bridgewater, 22–23, 60, 64–66, 71

Egerton, Thomas [d. 1599], 21, 28

Egerton, Thomas [fl. 1670s], 71

Egerton, Thomas, Lord Chancel-lor, Baron Ellesmere, & 1st Vis-count Brackley, 21, 26–45 *passim.*, 68, 71, 87, 297

Egerton, Countess of. *See* Gren-ville, Alice Anne (Graham-Mont-gomery)

Eggar, Thomas, 161

Egginton (Derbys.), 96, 107

Eglington Iron Co., 87

Eglinton, Earl of. *See* Montgom-erie, Alexander

Egremont, Earl of. *See* Wyndham, Charles

Egypt, map of Nile R. in, 123

Eighthundred Fen, 47, 65

Elbe River, journal of a voyage on, 302

Elections. *See under* Parliament

Elgin, Earl of. *See* Bruce, Thomas

Elibank, barons. *See* Murray, Alex-ander; Murray, Patrick

Eliot, Edward, 250

Eliot, Mrs. Elizabeth, 248

Eliot, Richard, 247

Elizabeth I, Queen of England, 32, 35, 36, 39, 71, 87, 138, 191

Elizabeth of York, Queen of Henry VII, 33

Ellenbrook Chapel (Lancs.), 42

Ellesmere, Lord Chancellor. *See* Egerton, Thomas

Ellesmere, earls of. *See* Egerton, Francis Leveson-Gower; Eger-ton, George Granville Francis; Egerton, John Francis Granville Scrope

"Ellesmere Chaucer," 28

Ellesmere (Salop.), 47

Elletson, Roger Hope, 229, 232, 245

Elliott, John, 126

Elliott, Joseph, 161

Ellis, Anne (Stanley), Baroness Mendip, 335

Ellis, Edmond, 129

Ellis, Edward, 87

Ellis, H. Leslie, 161

Ellis, J. H., 161

Ellis, S., 135

Ellis, Welbore, 1st Baron Mendip, 341

Elphinstone, George Keith, Vis-count Keith, 161

Elphinstone, John, 4th Baron Bal-merino and 3rd Baron Coupar, 326

Elphinstone, John, 11th Baron El-phinstone, 365

Elsyng, Henry, 49

Ely, Marchioness of. *See* Loftus, Anna Maria (Dashwood)

Ely, recusants in bishopric of, 37

Emblem books, 281

Emden (Germany), Lord of, 34

Emly, Lord, 342

Enclosure Commission (1517), re-turns of, 217

Enclosures, 65, 109, 110, 111, 114, 120, 217, 250, 264, 309

Enderby (Leics.), 97, 110

Enfield (Middlesex), 114, 179

Engineering (railroad & railroad bridges), 348

Englefield (Berks.), 95, 106

Engravings, 69

Enniskillen (Ireland), 274
Epitaphs, 47, 55, 134, 225
Erdington, Henry de, 126
Erlington, J. H., 362
Ernest Augustus, Duke of Cumberland, 87
Erskine, James, Lord Grange, 326
Erskine, John, 6th or 11th Earl of Mar, 326
Esbury Hundred, 38
Escheators, in Welsh Marches, 51
Eske (Yorks.), 117
Essex, earls of. *See* Devereux, Robert
Essex: accounts for estates in, 152, 247; deeds for lands in, 13, 248, 257–58; maps of land in, 270; sheriff of, 20; other, 7, 17–18, 108, 179, 218, 250
Etchings, 194
Ethersay, Hugh, 221
Eton (Bucks.), 96
Ettington (Warwicks.). *See* Eatington
Etwall Hospital (Derbys.), 84, 139–40
Eu, Count of. *See* Henry, Count of Eu
Eure, Ralph, 3rd Baron Eure, 36
Evans, David, 46
Evans, Elizabeth, 71
Evans, John, 88
Evans, Margery, 51
Evans, William, 331
Everard, Robert, 88
Evington (Leics.), 110
Ewelme (Bucks.), 177
Ewhurst (Sussex), 11, 17, 18
Exchequer: appointments to office in, 40; fees and duties of officials in, 63; fraud by clerks of, 53; payments on Civil List by, 202; Pipe Office, 67–68, 72; Pipe Roll, extracts from, 9; other, 40, 306. *See also under* Courts; Treasury
Excise: commissioners of, 224; on liquor, 224. *See also* Customs
Exeter, Earl of. *See* Cecil, David

Exeter (Devon), 1, 350
Exmouth, Viscount. *See* Pellew, Edward
Exploration & discovery, voyages of, 320, 349, 350–51
Eyam (Derbys.), 257
Eyre, W. T., 265
Eyre, William Thomas, 161

F., T., 49
Faculties, accounts of fees for, 26
Faden, W., 123
Fagel, Baron Jacob, 161
Fairbarne, Mary (Norrington), 72
Fairborne, Sir Palmer, 56, 72
Fairlight (Sussex), 18
Falcutt (Northants.), 211, 259
Falkirk (Stirlingshire), 281
Falkirk, battle of, 322
Falkland, viscounts. *See* Cary, Henry; Cary, Lucius
Falmer (Sussex), 261
Farewell, Thomas, 129
Farmanby (Yorks.), 101
Farmer, John, 208
Farnborough (Warwicks.), 262
Farndon, East (Northants.), 99
Farnecombe, Maline, 9
Farquhar, Robert Townsend, 161
Farquharson, James, 231
Farrar, Squire, 292
Farrers & Co., 161
Fasbrooke, Leona, 126
Faulkner, E., 88
Faye, Thomas, 134
Fazakerley, Nicholas, 235
Feckenham (Worcs.), 262
Fellowe, Paul, 186
Fellowe, Rice, 186
Fellowe, Thomas, 185
Fellowes, John, 161
Felstead (Essex), 108
Feltham (Somerset.), 100
Fen Ditton (Cambs.), 96
Fenesham, Stephen, 8
Fenny Compton (Warwicks.), 212, 262
Fens, 39, 58

Fenton, Roger, 31 *(ter)*
Feock (Cornwall), 256
Ferguson, Sir Adam, 3rd Bart., 365
Ferguson, D., 161
Ferguson, George, 346, 347
Fergusson, James, 2nd Bart. & Lord Kilkerran, 326
Fergusson, Walter, 231
Fergusson, William, 326
Fermanagh, Co. (Ireland), 102, 119
Fermor, James, 188
Ferrers, Countess. *See* Shirley, Mary (Levinge)
Ferrers, earls, 132. *See also* Shirley, Robert; Shirley, Washington
Ferrers family, 84
Ferrers of Groby, barony of, 194
Fessey, John, 161
Fetherston, Thomas, 247
Fewtrell, William, 208
Field, Edward, 161
Field, Francis, 161
Field, William, 161
Field & Bignold, 161
Fielding, Basil, 6th Earl of Denbigh, 326
Fiennes, Henry. *See* Clinton [or Fiennes], Henry
Figg, Joseph, 161
Filgrave (Bucks.), 256
Filmer, Sir Robert, 301
Finch, Daniel, 2nd Earl of Nottingham, 62
Finch, Daniel, 7th Earl of Winchelsea, 188
Finch, Heneage, 1st Earl of Nottingham, 88
Finch, John, Baron Finch, 226
Finche, Vincent, 8, 9 *(bis)*
Finchingfield (Essex), 257
Finchley (Middlesex), 99, 259
Findlater, earls of. *See* Ogilvy, James
Finlay, Alexander, 161
Finmere (Oxon.), 179, 211, 217, 218 *(bis)*, 219 *(bis)*, 259, 271, 358
Finter, W. E., 289
Fishbourne, Joseph, 161

Fishbourne, William, 161
Fisher, Edward, 302
Fisher, Godfrey, 277
Fisher, James Hurtle, 88
Fishing & fisheries, 12, 61, 289, 305
Fitch, Joseph, 161
Fitch, Matthew, 161
Fitzgerald, Lady Charlotte Adelaide Constantia (Rawdon), 88
Fitzgerald, Hamilton, 88
Fitzgerald, Richard Purefoy, 161
Fitz-Neale, Richard, Bp., 7
Fitzroy, Charles, 2nd Duke of Grafton, 311
Fitzroy, George Henry, 4th Duke of Grafton, 271, 365
Flanders, British forces in, 244, 323
Flaxfleet (Yorks.), 77
Fleetwood, Gerard Dutton, 186
Fleming, Mary, 251
Flemyng, George, 188
Fletcher, Andrew, Lord Milton, 326
Fletcher, George, 88
Fletcher, H. M., 312
Fletcher, Ifan Kyrle, 359
Fletcher, John, 253
Flick, Nathaniel, 48
Flintshire: concealed lands in, 68; deeds for land in, 76; other, 35, 46, 54, 108
Flood, Henry, 232
Florence, English mercenary in, 278
Florida, 122, 131–32, 305
Folliott, Fraser, 326
Fond Du Lac of Lake Superior Railway, 348
Fooks, Chadwick, Arnold & Chadwick, 161
Forbes, Arthur, 1st Earl of Granard, 88, 130
Forbes, Duncan, 326
Forbes, John, 275, 276, 305
Forbes, Selina Frances (Rawdon), Countess of Granard, 88
Foreign relations. *See under* Great Britain

Foreign Secretary: William Wyndham Grenville as, 149; Richard Wellesley as, 364. *See also:* Secretary of State
Forest law, 39
Forgers & forgeries, 23
Forman, John N., 161
Forster, William, 352
Fortescue, Francis, 88
Fortescue, Hugh, 1st Earl Fortescue, 188
Fortescue, Hugh, 2nd Earl Fortescue, 161
Fortescue, Sir John, 29, 208
Fortescue, Matthew, 2nd Baron Fortescue, 186
Fortrose, Lord. *See* MacKenzie, Kenneth
Forts: Augustus, 322; Bedford, 305; Duquesne, 275, 305; Frontenac (Cadaraqui), 275; George (Madras), 343; Lyttleton, 305; Raystown, 305; Ticonderoga, 275, 344; William Henry, 275; list of in England, 44
Forty-Nine Trustees, the, 249
Forward, John, 130
Foscott (Bucks.), 177, 192, 255, 264
Fossbrook (Staffs.), 68, 77
Foulis, Robert, 130
Fowke, J., 14
Fowler, ——, 55
Fowler, John Kersley, 161
Fowler & Co., 161
Fowler, Harris & Taylor, 161
Fox, Dr., 270
Fox, George Frederick, 161
Fox, Henry, 1st Baron Holland, 326
Foxe, John, 37, 221
Foxe, Thomas, 245
Framland Hundred (Leics.), 98, 110
Frampton [*alias* Earleshall] (Lincs.), 75, 77
France: Academy of Science in, 144; Anglo-Dutch war with, 62; description of, 291; drawings & sketches of, 194; East India Co. of, 224; English administration of (Normandy), 314; in North America, 62, 343; relations with England, 33–34, 62, 155, 287, 318, 362; travel in, 189; in West Indies, 155, 287; other, 102
Frankenburg, Charis, 277
Franklin, John, 326
Franklin, Sir John, 351
Frankpledge, views of. *See* Court rolls
Frankton, John, 161
Fraser, Alex, 161
Fraser, Charles, 161
Fraser, James, 326
Fraser, Simon, 11th Baron Lovat, 322, 326
Fraser, Simon, Master of Lovat, 326
Frecheville, John, 88
Frederick, Mariscoe, 326
Frederick Augustus, Duke of York, 88
Freeman, Edward, 161
Freeman, Elizabeth, 241
Freeman, Thomas, 161
Freer, Blunt & Co., 161
Freind, Grace (Robinson), 335
Freind, William, 335
Fremantle, John, 161
Fremantle, Louise Elizabeth (Nugent), Baroness Cottesloe, 161, 251
Fremantle, Thomas, 198
Fremantle, Sir Thomas Francis, 161
Fremantle, Thomas Francis, 1st Baron Cottesloe, 162
Fremantle, Sir William Henry, 155, 162, 253
French, Edmund, Bp., 254
French, M. H., 162
French, Samuel, 162
French, William Henry, 162
Freshfield & Sons, 162
Friends, Society of, 352
Friern Barnet (Middlesex), 259
Fring (Norfolk), 259
Frobisher, Sir Martin, 320
Frogatt, William, 162
Frogatt family, 194

Frome (Somerset), 100
Froud, Ann, 240
Froude, James Anthony, 289, 295
Fulbourn (Cambs.), 96
Fuller, John, 162
Fuller, William, 130
Fulmer (Bucks.), 96, 255
Fulwar, Thomas, Abp., 130
Furness (Lancs.), 237
Furnis, James, 276
Furniture: accounts of purchase & repair of, 66, 82, 153, 206, 230; other, 102–03, 175, 234

Gailhard, Jean, 88
Gainsborough, Thomas, 358, 359
Gainsford, Thomas, 48
Galloway, James, 208
Galway, Co. (Ireland), 119, 249, 316
Gamekeepers, guide for, 59
Gamon, Anne Eliza. *See* Brydges, Anne Eliza (Gamon) Elletson
Gamon, Sir Richard Grace-, 1st Bart., 241
Gaol delivery, 5, 8, 129
Gardens: at Avington, 270; at Canons, 242; at Donington Park, 110; at Kensington Palace, 271; at Newton Corner, 121; at Stowe, 266, 358; landscape gardening, 349, 358. *See also under* Accounts
Gardiner, William, 88
Gardner, Phoebe Sophia, 162
Gardner, T. W., 162
Garlike, Benjamin, 162
Garrett, Richard, 162
Garrick, David, 335
Garrick, Eva Marie (Viegel), 335
Garth, James, 14
Gathorne-Hardy, Gathorne, 1st Earl of Cranbrook, 162
Gautier de Metz, 29
Gawcott (Bucks.), 177, 265
Gay, George, 162
Geddes, George H., 88
Geneva, travels of Duchess of Buckingham & Chandos in, 189

Genoa, British consul at, 296
Gentlemen Pensioners, 133
Geoffrey of Monmouth, 28
Geography: of Eastern Mediterranean, 284; of Bay of Naples, 190
Geological Survey of Canada, 291
Geology, notes on, 190
Geometry, commonplace book re, 140
George I, King of England, 65, 182 *(bis)*, 326
George II, King of England, 65, 326
George III, King of England, 162, 334, 360
George IV, King of England, 88
George V, King of England, 364
George, Duke of Clarence, 127, 302
George, Prince of Denmark & Consort of Queen Anne, 65
George, Sir Rupert, Bart., 162
George, Thomas, 162
Germain, George Sackville, 1st Viscount Sackville, 326, 341
German, G., 88
German, William, 88
Germany: English merchants in, 228; Protestant refugees from, 65. *See also* Hamburg; Hanover
Germoe (Cornwall), 256
Gerrans (Cornwall), 256
Gervase of Tilbury, 40
Gery, John, 88
Gibbons, William Edward, 162
Gibbs, Elizabeth (Temple), Lady, 208
Gibraltar: British forces at, 65; siege of, 364
Gibson, Edmund, Bp., 302–03
Gibson, James, 88
Gibson-Graig, Dalziel & Brodie, 162
Gifford, Marie, 188
Gifford, Peter, 208
Gilberde, Ambrose, 26
Gilbert, Davies, 285
Gilbert, John, 234
Gilbert, Sir John, 282
Gilbert, Thomas, 67, 72

Gill, Thomas W., 162
Gillett, F. C., 88
Girdwood, James, 162
Girdwood, John, 162
Gissing (Norfolk), 99
Gladestry (Radnor.), 260
Gladstone, William Ewart, 313
Glanville, Sir John, 137
Glasbury (Radnor.), 260
Glascwm (Radnor.), 260
Glasgow, Earl of. *See* Boyle, David
Glasgow (Scotland), 122, 322
Glass, Elliot & Co., 162
Glasse, George Henry, 88
Gloucester, recusants in bishopric of, 37
Gloucester & Edinburgh, Duke of. *See* William Frederick
Gloucestershire: concealed lands in, 68; deeds for lands in, 258; maps for lands in, 120, 270; other, 183–84, 216, 217, 237, 238
Gobions (Essex), 13, 17
Godde, B., 326
Godmersham (Kent), 218 *(bis)*
Golbourne David (Cheshire), 76
Goldsmiths Company, 50
Gomme, James, 228
Gomme, William, 266 *(bis)*
Goodall, John, 162
Goodall, Samuel, 162
Goode, John, 37
Goodwin, George, 30
Goodwyn, Sir John, 208
Googhegan, William, 249
Goold, William, 162
Goran (Cornwall), 256
Gordon, Adam, 326
Gordon, Lord Chalres, 326
Gordon, Cosmo George, 3rd Duke of Gordon, 326
Gordon, Frederick, 303
Gordon, Joseph, 162
Gore-Langton, Lady Anne Elizabeth Mary (Grenville), 162
Gore-Langton, William Henry Powell, 162
Gorges, Sir Arthur, 30

Gorges, William, 220
Gorrall (Bucks.), 211, 216, 218
Gosfield (Essex), 152, 175, 179, 246, 247, 250, 257, 270
Gosford (Oxon.), 259
Goss, Thomas G., 162
Goteburg (Sweden), 320
Gough, Drope, 186
Gough, Richard Drope, 188
Gower, John, 28
Gower, Sir Thomas, 208, 215
Gower, Baron. *See* Leveson-Gower, John
Gower, Earl. *See* Leveson-Gower, George Granville; Leveson-Gower, John
Gower, Lady, 64
Grace-Gamon, Sir Richard, 1st Bart. *See* Gamon, Sir Richard Grace-
Graduals, 29
Grady, Patrick, 254
Grafton, Duchess of. *See* Hanmer, Isabella (Bennet) Fitzroy
Grafton, dukes of. *See* Fitzroy, Charles; Fitzroy, George Henry
Grafton (Gloucs.), 237
Graham, Agnes, 130
Graham, Lady Isabella, 130
Graham, J., 130
Graham, Sir James, 130
Graham, James, 1st Duke of Montrose, 326
Graham, John, 125
Graham, Joghery, 130
Graham, Thomas, 232
Graham, William, 8th Earl of Menteith, 130
Graham family, 128
Graham & Son, 162
Granard, Countess of. *See* Forbes, Selina Frances (Rawdon)
Granard, Earl of. *See* Forbes, Arthur
Grand Jury, in Shropshire, 74
Grand Remonstrance, 52
Grandison, Viscount. *See* St. John, Oliver

Grange, Lord. *See* Erskine, James
Grant, Alexander, 326
Grant, James, 132
Grant, Ludovick, 326
Grant, Patrick, 327
Grant, Sueton, 327
Granville, Sir Bevil, 304
Granville, Earl of. *See* Leveson-Gower, Granville George
Grassam, Elsie, 277
Gray, C. E., 162
Gray, James, 327
Gray, Sir James, 67
Grays Inn (London), 312
Great Britain:
—agencies of. *See* names of individual institutions or officials, e.g. Army; Board of Control; Courts; Parliament; Secretary of State
—foreign relations of: with Belgium, 284; with Bohemia, 224; with Denmark, 49, 156; with France, 33–34, 62, 155, 283, 287, 318, 362; with the Hague, 156; with Hamburg, 156; with Naples, 310; with the Netherlands, 33–34, 49, 56, 62; with Portugal, 67, 314; with Prussia, 156; with Savoy, 224; with Spain, 33–34, 41, 56, 314, 361; with Venice, 67, 208. *See also* Foreign Secretary
—trade and commerce in, 38, 50, 56, 61, 62, 228, 245, 287, 296, 305, 309
Great Exhibition of 1851, 183
Great Western Railway, 163
Greek coinage, 351
Green, Francis, 163
Green, Henry, 281
Green, Richard, 186
Green, William, 163
Greene, Grace, 221
Greene, John, 185
Greene, William, 220
Greenwich, Duke of. *See* Campbell, John
Greenwood, Cox & Co., 88

Gregoreans, Ancient and Honourable Order of the, 309
Gregory, John, 335
Grenville, Alice Anne (Graham-Montgomery) Temple-Nugent-Brydges-Chandos-, Duchess of Buckingham & Chandos [*aftw.* Countess of Egerton], 150, 199
Grenville, Anna Elizabeth (Brydges) Temple-Nugent-Brydges-Chandos-, Duchess of Buckingham & Chandos, 149, 155, 163, 187, 189, 229, 235, 254
Grenville, Lady Anne, 189
Grenville, Anne (Chambers). *See* Grenville-Temple, Anne (Chambers)
Grenville, Anne (Pitt), Baroness Grenville, 149, 189
Grenville, Anne Lucy (Poulett), Baroness Nugent, 254
Grenville, Audrey (Duncombe), 185
Grenville, Sir Bevil, 163
Grenville, Caroline (Harvey) Temple-Nugent-Brydges-Chandos-, Duchess of Buckingham & Chandos, 150, 163, 189, 199
Grenville, Lady Caroline Jemima Elizabeth, 163, 190, 200, 269
Grenville, Christiana (Launceline), 185
Grenville, Edward, 175, 185
Grenville, Elizabeth (Wyndham), 149
Grenville, George [fl. >1553], 185
Grenville, George [Prime Minister], 149, 155, 156, 163, 182, 186, 192
Grenville, George Nugent, 2nd Baron Nugent, 163, 189, 190, 193, 196, 197, 254
Grenville, George Nugent-Temple-, 1st Marquis of Buckingham, 149, 155 *(bis)*, 156, 163, 175, 187, 188, 192, 195, 196, 198, 266, 268, 273

Grenville, Harriet, 189
Grenville, Henry, 148, 155, 163, 274
Grenville, Lady Hester. *See* Pitt, Hester (Grenville)
Grenville, Hester (Temple), *suo jure* Viscountess Cobham and Countess Temple, 148, 205
Grenville, James, 1st Baron Glastonbury, 187
Grenville, Mary. *See* Morgan-Grenville, Mary (Grenville)
Grenville, Mary (Campbell) Temple-Nugent-Brydges-Chandos-, Duchess of Buckingham & Chandos, 150, 155, 156, 163, 188, 189, 196, 197, 200, 201, 202
Grenville, Mary Anne. *See* Arundell, Mary Anne (Grenville)
Grenville, Mary Elizabeth (Nugent) Nugent-Temple-, Marchioness of Buckingham, 149, 163, 188, 194, 246, 254
Grenville, Richard [fl. >1419], 185
Grenville, Richard [fl. 1559], 188
Grenville, Richard [c.1567–1618], 185
Grenville, Richard [1611?–1665], 148, 173
Grenville, Richard [1677–1727], 148
Grenville, Richard [fl. >1813, of Bruton St., Middlesex], 187
Grenville, Richard Temple-Nugent-Brydges-Chandos-, 1st Duke of Buckingham & Chandos, 149, 155, 156, 163, 174 *(bis)*, 175, 187, 189 *(bis)*, 193, 194, 196 *(bis)*, 197, 198, 235, 254, 271, 273 *(bis)*
Grenville, Richard Plantagenet . . . , 2nd Duke of Buckingham & Chandos, 150, 155, 156, 163, 175, 176, 188–93 *passim.*, 265–73 *passim.*
Grenville, Richard Plantagenet Campbell . . . , 3rd Duke of Buckingham & Chandos, 146, 150, 155 *(bis)*, 157, 163, 174, 175 *(bis)*, 176, 187, 190, 192, 194, 195,

198, 200, 265 [as Marquis of Chandos], 273
Grenville, Richard, 2nd Earl Temple. *See* Grenville-Temple, Richard
Grenville, Susanne, 185
Grenville, Thomas [1755–1846], 149, 155, 157, 163, 187, 191, 193, 254, 302
Grenville, William Falke, 187
Grenville, William Wyndham, Baron Grenville, 149, 155, 163, 189, 193, 196, 202, 254
"Grenville Evidences," 173
Grenville-Temple, Anne (Chambers), Countess Temple, 148, 186, 188
Grenville-Temple [*formerly* Grenville], Richard, 2nd Earl Temple, 148, 155, 163, 186, 188, 191, 264, 273
Gresford (Denbigh), 35, 76
Gresley (Derbys.), 107
Greville, Arthur E., 163
Greville, Charles Francis, 310
Greville-Nugent, Rosa Emily Mary Anne (Nugent), Baroness Greville, 163
Grew, Nehemiah, 309
Grey, Arthur, 14th Baron Grey of Wilton, 209
Grey, Charles, 1st Earl Grey, 333
Grey, Charles, 2nd Earl Grey, 163
Grey, Henry, 237, 309
Grey, Henry, 1st Baron Grey of Groby, 88
Grey, Henry, 1st Earl of Stamford, 209
Grey, Thomas, 15th Baron Grey of Wilton, 45
Grey de Ruthyn, barons, 132
Griffin, Anne, 188
Griffin, Edward, 163
Griffin, James, 163
Griffin, John [agent for Grenville family], 163
Griffin, John [of Brillsbury Hall], 163

Griffin, Richard, 2nd Baron Bray-
brooke, 164
Griffith, Edmund, Bp., 50
Griffith, Matthew, 49
Griffiths, Sylvanus, 72
Grimsteed, James, 164
Grimston, Sir Harbottle, 137
Grindal, Edmund, Abp., 138
Grinstead, East (Sussex), 18
Groom, James, 164
Grose, Matthew, 164
Grove, George, 15
Grove, Henry, 309
Grove (Bucks.), 106
Grubb, Margaret (Shackleton), 352
Grubb, Samuel, 305
Gruffyn, Maurice, 37
Guernsey, Island of, 36, 63–64
Guestling (Sussex), 6, 8
Guilford, Baron. *See* North, Fran-
cis, 1st Baron Guilford
Gun, Alexander, 327
Gunpowder Plot, 142, 337
Gurden, William, 164
Gurney, Avis, 188
Gurney, Henry, 164
Gustavus Adolphus, King of Swe-
den, 132
Gutteridge, Daniel, 164
Gutteridge, Joseph, 164
Gwaithla (Radnor.), 260
Gwennap (Cornwall), 211, 256
Gwinear (Cornwall), 256

Hack, William, 309–310
Hackstall, Thomas, 125
Hadaway, Lady Anne (Grenville),
164, 190, 200
Hadaway, George, 189
Haddiloe, T., 14
Haddock, Nicholas, 343
Haiden, Robert, 164
Hakewill, William, 281
Hale, William, 187
Hales, William, 254
Halifax, Marquis of. *See* Savile,
George
Halifax Groving Deck Co., 164

Halkett, Sir Peter, 2nd Bart., 327
Hall, Arthur, 43, 72
Hall, Basil, 285
Hall, Frederick, 164
Hall, Laurence, 164
Hall, Robert [of Avington, Hants.],
164
Hall, Robert [of Easton Lodge,
?Hants.], 164
Hall, Samuel, 187
Hall, William, 213
Halliday, Clive, 277
Hallmoot records. *See* Court rolls
Hallowell, Benjamin, 276
Hallowes, R., 164
Halse (Northants.), 77
Halsey, Anne, 222
Halsey, Edmund, 205
Halsham (Yorks.), 101
Halstead (Essex), 258
Ham (Bucks.), 177
Hamburg, English merchants in,
228
Hamden, ——, 65
Hamersley, Chamberlaine, 209
Hamilton, Emma (Lyon), Lady,
338
Hamilton, Sir Francis, 1st Bart., 88
Hamilton, George, 1st Earl of Ork-
ney, 327
Hamilton, James, 1st Duke of Ham-
ilton [as Marquis of Hamilton],
223
Hamilton, James, 62
Hamilton, John [fl. 1737–71, of
Ayrshire], 327
Hamilton, John [d. 1781, of Bar-
geny, Ayrshire], 327
Hamilton, Mary Gavin (Pringle),
Baillie, 164
Hamilton, Sackville, 342
Hamilton, Sir William, 310
Hamilton, William Gerard, 342
Hampden's Case, 50. *See also* Ship
Money
Hampshire: accounts of estates in,
152, 230; Assizes in, 239; bor-
oughs of, 239; deeds for land in,

97, 233, 258; Deputy Lieutenant of, 238; justices of the peace for, 239; maps of land in, 270; Militia in, 244; other, 108, 179, 181, 184, 217, 236, 237, 238–39
Hampton, Baron. *See* Pakington, John Somerset
Hance, William, 139
Hancock, Thomas, 276
Handel, George Frederick, 229
Handley & Durant (firm), 88
Handsworth (Yorks.), 262
Hankin, Philip James, 164
Hanly, Thomas, 249
Hanmer, Isabella (Bennet) Fitzroy, Duchess of Grafton, 311
Hanover, 288
Hanson, John, 164
Hapton (Bucks.), 106
Harbours, plans for, 122
Harcourt, Elizabeth (Venables-Vernon), Countess Harcourt, 335
Harcourt, George, 2nd Earl Harcourt, 335
Harcourt, Mary (Danby) Lockhart, Countess Harcourt, 347
Harding, Caleb, 135
Harding, G. R., 164
Harding, George Perfect, 340
Hardum, James, 164
Hardwick, earls of. *See* Yorke, Philip
Hardwick (Bucks.), 180
Hardy, Sir Charles, 343
Harefield (Middlesex), household expenses at, 83
Harley, John, 213
Harley, Thomas, 125
Harper, Edward [of Ashendon, Bucks.], 164
Harper, Edward [of Wotton, Bucks.], 164
Harper, John, 268
Harper, J. T., 164
Harper, Lathrop C., 276
Harpton (Radnor.), 260
Harpur, Sir John, 139
Harries, Richard, 50

Harriot, George, 164
Harris, James [1709–80], 335
Harris, James [fl. 1820–24], 164
Harris, James, 1st Earl of Malmesbury, 164
Harris, Nathaniel, 28
Harris, Peter, 214, 215
Harrison, J., 164
Harrison, James, 164
Harrison, John, 347
Harrison, Richard, 46, 72
Harrison & Son, 164
Harrowby, Baron. *See* Ryder, Nathaniel
Hart, William [fl. 1623, professor of rhetoric], 48
Hart, William [fl. 1625/26–>1656, agent of Temple family], 209, 358
Hart, William [fl. 1653–55, of Bucks.], 209
Hartwell St. Marys (Bucks.), 182
Harvey, Anne (Hotham), 164
Harvey, Lady Magdalen Breadalbane (Pringle) Anderson, 164
Harvey, Robert [1791–1863, father of Caroline, Duchess of Buckingham & Chandos], 188
Harvey, Robert [fl. 1820–23, of Bath], 164
Harvey, Sir Robert, 1st Bart., 164
Harvey, Sir Robert Grenville, 2nd Bart., 164
Harvey, Sir Robert John, 188
Harvey, Thomas, 83
Harvey, William, 56
Harwood (Yorks.), 117
Harwood, Little (Bucks.), 183
Haselwood, Edward, 222
Hastings, Lady Alice, 53, 72
Hastings, Lady Alicia, 58
Hastings, Anne (Stafford), Herbert, Countess of Huntingdon, 78
Hastings, Catherine (Pole), Countess of Huntingdon, 78
Hastings, Sir Charles, Bart., 121
Hastings, Sir Charles Abney, 126
Hastings, Lady Christiana, 88, 134

Hastings, Dorothy (Port), Countess of Huntingdon, 79, 125

Hastings, Lady Edith Maud, 110

Hastings, Sir Edward, 128

Hastings, Edward, Baron Hastings of Loughborough, 124

Hastings, Edward, 2nd Baron Hastings of Hungerford, 78, 124, 127

Hastings, Elizabeth [fl. >1739], 125

Hastings, Lady Elizabeth, 88, 114, 139, 299

Hastings, Elizabeth (Lewis), Countess of Huntingdon, 80, 88

Hastings, Elizabeth (Stanley), Countess of Huntingdon, 48, 79, 88, 134, 310

Hastings, Ferdinando, 6th Earl of Huntingdon, 79, 88, 104, 119, 125, 133

Hastings, Flora (Mure-Campbell) Rawdon-, Marchioness of Hastings & *suo jure* Countess of Loudoun. *See* Rawdon-Hastings, Flora (Mure-Campbell)

Hastings, Lady Flora Elizabeth Rawdon-. *See* Rawdon-Hastings, Lady Flora Elizabeth

Hastings, Lady Frances, 89

Hastings [*aftw.* De Ligondez], Frances (Fowler) Needham, Countess of Huntingdon, 80, 91

Hastings, Sir Francis, 79, 81, 89, 125

Hastings, Francis, 2nd Earl of Huntingdon, 78, 118, 124, 127 *(bis)*, 128

Hastings, Francis, 10th Earl of Huntingdon, 80, 89, 103, 126, 127, 132, 135, 140, 141, 144

Hastings, Francis Rawdon-, 2nd Earl of Moira & 1st Marquis of Hastings. *See* Rawdon-Hastings.

Hastings, Gabriel, 89, 125

Hastings, George [fl. 1729–43, son of 9th Earl of Huntingdon], 89, 103

Hastings, George [fl. 1818, claimant to earldom of Huntingdon], 89

Hastings, Sir George, 10, 89

Hastings, George, 1st Earl of Huntingdon, 78, 124, 127 *(bis)*

Hastings, George, 4th Earl of Huntingdon, 79, 83, 89, 120, 127 *(bis)*

Hastings, George, 8th Earl of Huntingdon, 80, 89, 125, 127

Hastings, George Augustus Francis Rawdon-, 2nd Marquis of Hastings. *See* Rawdon-Hastings, George Augustus Francis

Hastings, Hans Francis, 12th Earl of Huntingdon, 81

Hastings, Henry [b. ca.1644, son of Henry Hastings of Humbertson, Leics.], 89

Hastings, Henry [fl. 1684–88, captain in 7th Earl's regiment], 89

Hastings, Henry [fl. 1686], 89

Hastings, Henry [fl. 1733–46, of Newhall & Ledstone?], 89

Hastings, Henry [fl. 1754–87, Customs official], 89

Hastings, Henry, 1st Baron Loughborough, 79, 84, 89, 125

Hastings, Henry, 3rd Earl of Huntingdon, 79, 82, 83, 84, 89, 102, 118, 127, 311

Hastings, Henry, 5th Earl of Huntingdon, 79, 83, 89, 102, 104, 113, 127, 131, 138, 139, 140

Hastings, Sir Hugh de, 124

Hastings, Hugh, 15th Baron Hastings, 133

Hastings, J., 89

Hastings, Katherine, Baroness Hastings, 124

Hastings, Knyvett, 89

Hastings, Sir Leonard, 124

Hastings, Lucy (Davies), Countess of Huntingdon, 79, 89, 103, 119, 125, 128, 134, 138

Hastings, Lady Mary, 89

Hastings, Mary (Hungerford), Baroness Hastings and *suo jure* Baroness Hungerford, Botreaux, and Moleyns, 78, 118

Hastings, Sir Ralph, 124

Hastings, Richard, Lord Willoughby, 118
Hastings, Selina (Shirley), Countess of Huntingdon, 80, 81, 89, 126, 299
Hastings, Theophilus, 7th Earl of Huntingdon, 79–80, 83, 84, 89, 103, 104, 125, 127, 128, 133–40 *passim.*, 311
Hastings, Theophilus, 9th Earl of Huntingdon, 80, 89, 103, 104, 125, 127
Hastings, Sir Thomas, 124
Hastings, Warren, 89, 334
Hastings, Sir William, 78, 114, 117, 118, 124, 127, 133
Hastings, barons, 10, 78
Hastings, Marchioness of. *See* Rawdon-Hastings, Flora (Mure-Campbell)
Hastings, marquessate of, 132
Hastings, Marquis of. *See* Rawdon-Hastings, Francis; Rawdon-Hastings, George Augustus Francis; Rawdon-Hastings, Paulyn Reginald Serlo; Rawdon-Hastings, Henry Weysford Charles Plantagenet
Hastings College, 17
Hastings (Sussex), 12, 100
Hastings, Rape of (Sussex), 116
Hatch, Thomas, 164
Hatherleigh (Somerset), 100
Hatherley, Baron. *See* Wood, William Page
Hathern (Leics.), 98, 110
Hatton, C., 89
Hatton, Sir Christopher, 45
Haughton (Cheshire), 76
Havana, British expedition against, 343
Havers, Richard, 164
Hawker, Robert Stephen, 135
Hawkwood [Hackwood], Sir John, 278
Hay, Richard, 19
Hay, Silvia, 277
Haylesham (Sussex), 6

Hayton, Alice, 220
Hayward, William, 164
Hazel, E. W., 164
Headbourne Worthy (Hants.), 258
Heale, John, 72
Heare, Charles & Co., 165
Hearn, Henry, 164
Hearn & Nelson, 165
Heath, Robert, 89
Heather (Leics.), 110
Heckstall, John, 125
Heckstall, Thomas, 125
Hedger, Joseph, 165
Hedgerly (Bucks.), 183
Hedon (Yorks.), 101, 117
Hele, John, 41
Helm, Ida E., 277
Helmystrowe Hundred, 8
Hem and Hewlington (Denbigh.), 76
Hemington, Robert, 89
Henchman, Humphrey, 235
Hendon (Middlesex), 259
Hendra (Cornwall), 106
Hendrie, Robert, 90
Henherst Hundred, 8
Henley, Baron. *See* Eden, Morton
Henley, Robert, 2nd Earl of Northington, 342
Henley-on-Thames (Oxon.), 100
Henrietta Maria, Queen of Charles I, 223
Henry VI, King of England, 35, 72
Henry VII, King of England, 72, 278
Henry VIII, King of England, 18, 72
Henry, Prince of Wales [son of James I], 32
Henry, Count of Eu, 7
Henshawe, William, 90
Henwick (Berks.), 237
Hepburn, William, 347
Hepburne, R., 347
Heraldry. *See* Arms (heraldic)
Herault, John, 36
Herbert, Anne (Stafford). *See* Hastings, Anne (Stafford) Herbert

Herbert, C., 56, 72
Herbert, Edmund, 311, 312
Herbert, Henry, 4th Baron Herbert of Cherbury, 59
Herbert, Henry, 10th Earl of Pembroke & 7th Earl of Montgomery, 90, 365
Herbert, Mary (Egerton), Baroness Herbert of Cherbury, 46
Herbert, Philip, 4th Earl of Pembroke, 226
Herbert, Richard, 2nd Baron Herbert of Cherbury, 46, 72
Herbert, Sidney, 1st Baron Herbert of Lea, 312–13
Herbert, Thomas [d. 1712], 311, 312
Herbert, Thomas [d. 1728], 311
Herbert, Sir Thomas, 55
Herbert family, 46, 59–60, 311–12
Hercy family, 194
Hereford, recusants in bishopric of, 37
Hereford Cathedral, 37
Herefordshire: accounts of estates in, 230; concealed lands in, 68; deeds for lands in, 258; other, 238
Heritage, Thomas, 220, 223
Herring, Thomas, Abp., 303
Hertfordshire: deeds for land in, 97; Lord Lieutenant of, 57; Militia in, 57; other, 68, 108
Hervey, Elizabeth, 335
Hervey, Mary (Lepell), Lady Hervey, 126
Hervey, William, 254
Hesilrige, Sir Arthur, 105
Hewlington (Denbigh), 76
Heyford (Bucks.), 211
Heyley, William, 124
Heytesbury (Wilts.), 100, 116
Hibbert, Col., 199
Hibbert, Frederick Drummond, 165
Hibbert, Robert, 232
Hibbert, Fuhr & Hibbert, 232
Hibbert, Purrier & Co., 232
Hiccock, Bridget, 185
Hiccock, Thomas, 185

Hickes, Sir Baptist, 142
Hickman, N., 73
Higgs, Dan, 73
High Commission (Ecclesiastical), Court of. *See under* Courts
High Legh (Cheshire), 46
High Ongar (Essex), 14, 17, 18
High Peak (Derbys.), 107
Higham, John, 165
Highland regiments, 323
Hill, Anthony, 14
Hill, Edward, 221
Hill, James, 245
Hill, Joseph, 90
Hill, Robert, 90
Hill, Thomas, 90
Hill (Berks.), 95
Hillesden (Bucks.), 255, 265
Hillesdon, Thomas, 209
Hillman, William, 232, 238
Hillman, Sir William, 230
Hillmorton, 122
Hills, Francis, 185
Hilton (Dorset), 108
Hilton (Warwicks.), 68
Hillyard, George, 209
Hindes, Richard, 165
Hinsby, Maria, 165
Hinton (Somerset), 115
Hippisley, Sir John Coxe, 1st Bart., 253, 254
Histories & historians, 30, 48, 140, 183, 279, 292, 298, 300, 313–14, 351, 361, 362
Hitckcock, Robert, 54
Hitchcock, Thomas, 55
Hoare, Benjamin, 90
Hoare, Messrs., 231
Hobart, George Bertie Benjamin, 165
Hobart, John, 2nd Earl of Buckinghamshire, 342
Hobart, Robert, 4th Earl of Buckinghamshire, 165
Hobley, Richard, 165
Hochepied, Baron. *See* Larpent, John James
Hodges, Sir James, 321

Hodgeson, Thomas, 105
Hodgkins, William, 165
Hodson, Frodsham, 254
Hoe, ——, 315
Hoffman, Francis, 38
Hofman & Freeman, 340
Holbech, Ambrose [lawyer, of Clements Inn], 209, 215
Holbech, Ambrose [of Mollington, Oxon.], 209
Holden, Robert, 90
Holderness, Earl of. *See* Darcy, Robert
Holford (Cheshire), 76
Holford (Somerset), 261, 273
Holland, Baron. *See* Fox, Henry
Holland, Roger, 52, 73
Holland, treatise on, 29. *See also* Netherlands
Holles, Lady Diance, 241
Holles, Sir Francis [*aftw.* 2nd Baron Holles], 241
Holles, John, 1st Duke of Newcastle, 65
Hollier, John, 165
Hollington (Sussex), 6
Hollingworth, Robert, 10
Holte (Denbigh), 76
Holton (Somerset), 100, 115, 183
Holwell (Leics.), 110
Holycake, George Jacob, 292
Homage roll, 236
Home, Henry, Lord Kames, 335
Home, Thomas, 165
Home, William, 8th Earl of Home, 327
Home Secretary, William Wyndham Grenville as, 149. *See also* Secretary of State
Homet, barons, 132
Honors & peerages, creation of, 33
Hoo [Hou, Hoton] (Essex), 1, 6, 7, 8
Hood, Mary (West), 335
Hood, Thomas, 349
Hood, William, 165
Hooker, ——, 54
Hoole (Cheshire), 76

Hooten, Henry, 90
Hope, J., 90
Hope Plantation (Jamaica), 202, 245
Hopkins, J., 11, 19
Hopkinson, John, 357
Hopson, Peregrine Thomas, 276
Hopton, Robert, 90
Hordley (Salop), 47
Horley, John, 220
Horley, Spencer, 209, 358
Horn, John, Jr., 290
Hornby, Charles, 73
Horne, George de, 19
Horningsham (Wilts.), 116
Hornsey (Middlesex), 114
Horsenden (Bucks.), 265, 266
Horses: diseases of, 69; equipment for, 31
Horwood, Edward, 165
Horwood, Thomas, 165
Hoskyns, J., 73
Hospitals, 15, 66, 68, 84, 106, 139–40, 184, 272
Hotham, Sir Charles, 6th Bart., 90
Hotham, John William, 165
Hotham, William, 1st Baron Hotham, 90
Hoton (Leics.), 110
Hough, John, Bp., 303
Hours, Books of, 29
Household (Royal), 42, 62, 299. *See also* Court (Royal)
Households (private): accounts for, 26, 47, 59, 65, 66, 82–83, 153–54, 206–07, 230–31, 247, 283, 323; checkrolls of servants in, 26, 59, 66, 242; instructions for servants, 242; inventories of goods in, 26, 54, 64, 102–04, 175, 212, 213, 234, 323; management & operation of, 26, 32, 46, 53–54, 59, 82–83, 153, 154, 203, 206, 223, 230, 231, 242, 295–96, 302, 358; record books for, 82–83, 190, 223, 242
Houshton, James, 165
How, William Walsham, Bp., 295

Howard, Charles, Baron Howard of Effingham [*aftw.* 1st Earl of Nottingham], 34
Howard, Craven, 63
Howard, Frederick, 5th Earl of Carlisle, 197, 198
Howard, Henrietta (Hobart), Countess of Suffolk, 314–15
Howard, Henry [fl. 1683, of London], 165
Howard, Henry [fl. 1821–26, employed at Avington], 165
Howard, Henry [fl. 1841–48, surveyor & auctioneer], 165
Howard, Henry [fl. 1848–55, son of surveyor], 165
Howard, Henry, Earl of Surrey, 144
Howard, Joseph, 165
Howard, Mary (Finch), Viscountess Andover, 335
Howard, Thomas, 2nd Earl of Arundel, 137
Howard, Thomas, 2nd Earl of Effingham, 365
Howard, Lord William, 191
Howe, Mary Sophia Charlotte (Kilmansegge), Viscountess Howe, 90
Howe, Richard, Earl Howe, 315–16
Howe, William, 5th Viscount Howe, 343, 351
Howe (Norfolk), 114
Howes, Percival & Ellen, 165
Hubbard, J. G., 165
Hubbard, Margaret, 124
Hubbard, William, 124
Hubbard, barons, 132
Huck-Saunders, Richard, 327
Huddleston (Yorks.), 101
Huddleston, William, 165
Hudson, Charles, 123
Hudson, Edward, 185
Hudson, M., 327
Hudson, William, 52
Hudson's Bay, 62
Hudson's Bay Company, 291
Hue, Francois, 254
Hugglescote (Leics.), 110

Hughenden (Bucks.), 255
Hughes, Alice, 199
Hulcott (Bucks.), 263
Hull, Christopher, 165
Hume, Sir Abraham, 1st Bart., 232
Humfrey, F., 165
Humphreys, Ambrose, 165
Hungerford, Margaret (de Botreaux), Baroness Hungerford & Botreaux, 104, 124
Hungerford, Mary. *See* Hastings, Mary (Hungerford)
Hungerford, Robert, 2nd Baron Hungerford, 124, 127
Hungerford, Walter, 127
Hungerford, barons, 78
Hungerford (Berks.), 95
Hunlatt, Thomas, 12
Hunnis, William, 69
Hunsdon, Baron. *See* Carey, Henry
Hunt, William Holman, 282
Hunter, Andrew, 327
Hunter, James, 327
Huntingdon, countesses of. *See* Hastings, Anne (Stafford) Herbert; Hastings, Catherine (Pole); Hastings, Dorothy (Port); Hastings, Elizabeth (Stanley); Hastings, Lucy (Davies); Hastings, Elizabeth (Lewis); Hastings [*aftw.* De Ligondez], Frances (Fowler) Needham; Hastings, Selina (Shirley)
Huntingdon, earls of. *See* Hastings, George; Hastings, Francis; Hastings, Henry; Hastings, Ferdinando; Hastings, Theophilus; Hastings, Hans Francis
Huntingdon (Hunts.), 120
Huntingdonshire, map of land in, 120
Huntington (Herefs.), 258
Huntspill (Somerset), 234, 237, 238, 261, 273
Hursley (Hants.), 258
Huske, John, 327
Hutchins, Ralph, 31
Hutchins, Samuel, 15

Hutchinson, Elizabeth, 352
Hutchinson, Thomas, 276
Hutt, Robert, 165
Hutton, Richard Holt, 295
Hutton, Sir Richard, 141
Hyde, Edward, 1st Earl of Clarendon, 56, 137, 227, 244
Hyde, Edward, 3rd Earl of Clarendon, 288
Hyde, Henry, 2nd Earl of Clarendon, 249
Hyde, Laurence, 1st Earl of Rochester, 225
Hyde, Sir Thomas, 2nd Bart., 223
Hydrography, 283–86
Hyndford, Earl of. *See* Carmichael, John

Ibbetson, James, 90
Icklesham (East Sussex), 1, 4, 6
Idsall [*alias* Snufnall] (Salop), 46, 75
Ilford (Sussex), 18
Illogan (Cornwall), 256
Ilmer (Bucks.), 96, 106
Impeachment. *See under* Parliament.
Impositions, 300
Impressed seamen. *See under* Navy (Royal)
Indentured retainers (Lord Hastings'), 133
India: British administration of, 155, 157, 194, 195; British social life in, 195, 331, 343; Edward VII visits, 195; French in, 224; George V visits, 364; photographs of, 199; railroads in, 348; other, 143–44, 194–95
Indians (of North America), 275, 287
Industries. *See* Iron foundries; Mines & Mining; Railroads
Ingham, B., 90
Ingham, Robert, 90
Inglewood Forest (Cambs.), 107
Inglis, Hugh, 327
Inglis & Leslie, 165

Inkpen (Berks.), 95
Inland Revenue Department, 162
Innes, Sir Harie, 5th Bart., 327
Inns, P., 165
Inquisitions, escheators, 9
Inquisitions *post mortem*, 10, 26–27, 28, 35, 68, 126–27, 188, 221
Insane, institutions for, 184, 270. *See also* Lunatics
Insurance companies, 154, 155, 165
Interregnum. *See* Commonwealth
Inventions, 305
Ipstones (Staffs.), 77
Ireland: antiquities of, 253; Civil Wars in, 128, 129; coinage of, 38; description & travel, 284; English government of, 35, 50–51, 57–58, 62, 128–29, 155, 156, 195–96, 333, 341–42; George Grenville as Lord Lieutenant of, 149, 155, 156, 195–96; historians of, 253; language & literature of, 253; medieval records concerning, 316; military & naval affairs in, 128, 192, 195–96, 333; Parliament of, 128, 130, 196, 199, 341; railroads in, 348; religion & churches in, 120, 129, 196, 200, 253, 352; typhus fever in, 318; War of 1689–91 in, 251
Irish, Elizabeth, 221
Irish, Robert, 185
"Irish Concealed Lands" papers, 129
Iron foundries, 2, 11, 12, 14, 19
Isaac, May, 277
Iscoyd Morton (Flint), 75
Isley Walton (Leics.), 98
Italy: drawings & sketches of, 194; English diplomats in, 34, 67, 296, 310; English mercenary in, 278; English travellers in, 189, 203; heraldry of, 69; plans of Pompeii, 274. *See also* Venice
Itchen Abbas (Hants.), 179, 237, 258, 270
Itchen Stoke (Hants.), 258, 270
Ivanhoe Baths (Leics.), 109, 121

Iveson, John, 90
Ivingho (Bucks.), 74
Ixnyng (Suffolk), 9

Jackson, Charles, 90
Jackson, Cyril, 197
Jackson, John, 90
Jackson, William, 186, 264
Jacob, J., 15
Jacob, Sir John, 3rd Bart., 90
Jacob, Sir Robert, 130
Jacobites, 64, 322, 334
Jacobus de Cessolis, 29
Jacques, Anne, 90
Jacques, Gervase, 90
Jago, George William Stephen, 165
Jago, Robert, 165
Jago, Thomas Dalby, 165, 193
Jamaica, 229, 232, 244–45, 262. *See
also* West Indies
James I, King of England, 32, 35,
36, 39, 49, 73, 90, 130, 137, 225
James II, King of England, 57, 62,
73, 84, 223, 227
James, son of William of Northey,
7
James, Charles, 90
James, Dorothy, 185
James, Henry, 282
James, John [fl. >1716], 185
James, John [fl. 1834–37], 165
James, Mary, 126
James, Thomas, 165
James, William, 126
James, William Smith, 174
Jamestown (Va.), description of, 34
J'Anson, Brian, 90
J'Anson, John, 90
Jean de Meun, 29
Jeffes, John, 185
Jeffes, William, 185
Jenkin, Alfred, 166
Jenkin, Pearse, 166
Jenkin, William, 166
Jenkins, Sir Leoline, 56, 286
Jenkinson, Charles, 1st Earl of Liv-
erpool, 342

Jenkinson, Robert Banks, 2nd Earl
of Liverpool, 363
Jennings, Nicholas, 179
Jersey, Earl of. *See* Villiers, William
Jersey, Island of, 36, 63–64, 219
Jervis, Sir Humphrey, 130
Jervis, John, Earl of St. Vincent, 166
Jesuits, in Canada, 291
Jewelry, inventory of, 66
Jews, ancient customs & institu-
tions of, 30, 31
Joddrell, Paul, 12
Johannes Hispanus, 29
Johnson, Sir John, 304
Johnson, Richard, 90
Johnson, Thomas, 166
Johnson, Sir William, 276
Johnson Brothers, 166
Johnston, Nathaniel, 90
Johnston, Farquhar & Leech, 166
Johnstone, Betty, 347
Johnstone, Charlotte (Dee), 347
Johnstone, George, 347
Johnstone, Gideon, 347
Johnstone, James, 335, 347
Johnstone, Sir James, 3rd Bart., 347
Johnstone, Sir James, 4th Bart., 347
Johnstone, John, 347
Johnstone, Sir John Lowther, 347
Johnstone, Walter, 347
Johnstone, William. *See* Pulteney
[*formerly* Johnstone], Sir Wil-
liam
Johnstone family, 346
Jolley, barons, 132
Jolliffe, Lady Mary (Hastings), 90
Jolliffe, Sir William, 90
Jones, Alexander, 90
Jones, Daniel, 327
Jones, Guernsey, 314
Jones, Henry, 130
Jones, James, 90
Jones, John [fl. >1652], 221
Jones, John [fl. 1849–58], 166
Jones, Ralph A., 166
Jones, Rebecca, 352
Jones, Thomas, 31
Jones, Sir Thomas, 141

Jones, W., 166
Jonson, Ben, 299
Jordan, Dorothy (Bland), 317
Jorden, Katherine, 20
Jorden, Thomas, 13, 14, 20
Jorden, W., 18
Journals. *See* Diaries & journals
Jowctt, Benjamin, 289
Joyce, Medbury, 166
Joyce, William, 73
Joynes, John, 90
Juke, William, 12
Justices, itinerant, 8
Justices of the Forest, 39
Justices of the Peace: in Buckinghamshire, 64, 65, 182, 183, 208; in Hampshire, 239; in Ireland, 128; George I's precepts for, 182; instructions for, 142, 182; treatise on, 280, 299; other, 208
Juvenal, 29
Juyn, J., 8

Kames, Lord. *See* Home, Henry
Karnes, Susanna, 90
Karslake, Crealock & Karslake, 166
Kay, James, 166
Kaye, John, Bp., 313
Kea (Cornwall), 256
Kearney, Lady Augusta Anne (Brydges), 232
Kearney, Henry John, 241 *(bis)*
Keble, John, 313
Keck, Francis, 241, 274
Keck family, 231, 232
Keene, Sir Benjamin, 67
Keene, Ed., 73
Keene, Joshua, 317
Kegsworth (Leics.), 111
Keilway, Robert, 43
Keith, Sir Robert Murray, 318
Keith, Viscount. *See* Elphinstone, George Keith
Kelly, Roger, 104
Kendall, John, 90
Kennedy, Archibald, 2nd Earl of Cassillis, 126

Kennedy, David, 10th Earl of Cassillis, 327
Kennedy, M., 130
Kensington Palace, 271
Kent, Duke of. *See* Edward Augustus
Kent, William, 90
Kent: deeds for lands in, 13, 173, 258; other, 17, 18, 218, 250
Kenwyn (Cornwall), 256, 269
Keppel, Augustus, Viscount Keppel, 343
Keppel, George, 3rd Earl of Albemarle, 343
Keppel, William Anne, 2nd Earl of Albemarle, 327
Kerry, Co. (Ireland), 119, 249
Kesavachandra, Sena, 295
Kettleby (Leics.), 111
Keynsham (Somerset), 152, 180, 230, 234, 237, 239, 261, 273
Kibworth (Leics.), 111
Kidd, William Lodge, 318
Kidlington (Oxon.), 259
Kilby (Leics.), 98
Kildare, Co. (Ireland), 247
Kilkenny, Co. (Ireland), 119
Kilkerran, Lord. *See* Fergusson, James, 2nd Bart.
Killard, Baron. *See* Alington, Hildebrand, 5th Baron Killard.
Killeshin (Co. Leix), 77
Kilmaine, Baron. *See* O'Hara, James
Kilmarnock, earls of. *See* Boyd, William
Kilmersdon (Somerset), 100
Killmoon (Ireland), 119
Kilmorey, Viscount. *See* Needham, Thomas
Kilmorey, Viscountess. *See* Needham, Mary (Shirley)
Kilns, accounts of, 152, 153, 205
Kilton (Somerset), 261, 273
Kilwardby (Leics.), 98
Kilworth (Leics.), 98
Kincardine, Earl of. *See* Bruce, Thomas

Kinckel, Hendrik August, Baron von, 347
Kinder, Philip, 134
Kineton (Warwicks.), 212, 262
King, D. P., 166
King, George, 188
King, Henry, 20
King, James, 166
King, John, 186, 264
King, John, Bp., 31
King, Robert, 130
King, Samuel, 185
King, Thomas, 50
Kinge, T., 55
Kingesmill, Frances, 222
Kings Bench, Court of. *See under* Courts
Kings Mills, dam at, 141
Kings Newton (Derbys.), 96
Kings Norton (Leics.), 110
Kings Worthy (Hants.), 258
Kingsbury (Middlesex), 179, 259
Kingsclere (Hants.), 237
Kingston, dukes of. *See* Pierrepont, Evelyn
Kingston-on-Soar (Notts.), 99
Kinloss, Baroness. *See* Morgan-Grenville, Mary (Grenville)
Kinloss, barony of, 194, 229, 243
Kinloss, Master of. *See* Morgan-Grenville, Richard George Grenville
Kinnaird, Charles, 6th Baron Kinnaird, 347
Kinnaird, George, 7th Baron Kinnaird, 347
Kinnerton (Radnor.), 260
Kinnerton, Lower (Cheshire), 76
Kinsale Harbour, 61
Kinsman family, 194
Kipling, I., 268
Kipling, Rudyard, 282
Kip's Bay, battle of, 132
Kirby, John Malsbury, 187
Kirby, West (Cheshire), 76
Kirby Bellars (Leics.), 98
Kirby Muxloe (Leics.), 98
Kirk, John, 254

Kirkby Mallory (Leics.), 98, 111
Kirke, Lewis, 133
Kirkharle (Northumb.), 99
Kirwan, Lady Victoria Mary Louisa (Rawdon-Hastings), 90
Knapp, Hester (Clarke), 221
Knapp, Henry, 204, 206, 213
Knaptoft (Leics.), 258
Knaresborough (Yorks.), 117
Knevit, C., 327
Knight, Anna (Craggs) Nugent. *See* Nugent, Anna (Craggs) Newsham Knight
Knight, Godwin, 91
Knight, John, 246 *(ter)*, 247, 249, 250, 252
Knight, Richard, 173
Knight, William, 246
Knightcote (Warwicks.), 180, 212, 217, 219
Knighthood: compounding for, 70, 84; list of creations, 298; treatise concerning, 29. *See also* Knights
Knighton (Leics.), 98
Knighton (Radnor.), 260
Knights: of the Bath, 58, 306; Templar, 113. *See also* Knighthood
Knights Fees, inquisition into the holders of, 107
Knightthorpe (Leics.), 98
Knollys, Elizabeth (Howard), Countess of Banbury, 222
Knollys, Sir Francis, 318
Knollys, Mary (Law), Viscountess Wallingford, 335
Knollys, Nicholas, 3rd Earl of Banbury, 222
Kraus, H. P., 345
Krienberg, C. F., 288
Kynaston, Sir Edward, 47

L., G., 34
L., T., 49
Lacey, Charles, 91
Lacey, William, 166
Lake, Sir Edward, Bart., 130
Lalor, Robert, 37

Lalton Farm (Worcs.), 116
Lambarde, William, 40, 73
Lambert, Nathaniel G., 166
Lambert, William, 221
Lamburn (Cornwall), 269
Lamport [Langport] (Bucks.), 211, 216, 218, 267
Lampridius, Aelius, 55
Lancashire: deeds for lands in, 76–77, 258; raising troops in, 45; other, 70, 108, 237
Lancaster, E., 166
Lancaster, Duchy of. *See under* Courts
Land Credit, Office of, 63
Land tax. *See under* Taxes
Landor, Henry Eyres, 166
Lands Improvement Company, 166
Landscape gardening. *See* Gardens
Lane, George, 130
Langford (Devon), 96
Langham, Sir James, 91
Langham, Thomas, 118
Langham, W., 18
Langston, Mary, 222
Langton (Thomas) & Sons, 166
Lansdowne, marquises of. *See* Petty, William; Petty-Fitzmaurice, Henry Charles Keith
Lanteglos (Cornwall), 107
Laplace, C., 91
Lardner, Edmund, 166
Larkin, Thomas Oliver, 319
La Rochelle, Siege of, 297
Larpent, Anna Margaretta (Porter), 319
Larpent, Catherine Elizabeth (Reeves), 285
Larpent, John, 23, 319
Larpent, John James, 7th Baron de Hochepied, 284, 285
Larpent family, 284
Lascelles, Talbot, 91
Latham, John, 91
La Tour, ____ de, 224
Laud, William, Abp., 49, 50, 130

Lauderdale, earls of. *See* Maitland, John; Maitland, James
Laughton (Lincs.), 113, 114
Laurie, Sir Robert, 5th Bart., 347
Laurie & Whittle, 123
Law, Tindal & Hussey, 166
Lawford, E. J. H. & J., 166
Lawford & Houghton, 166
Lawley, William, 209
Lawrence, Charles, 276
Lawrence, Charles William, 166
Lawrence, John, 133
Law: canon, 29; civil, 29; on forests, 39; Entry Book, 298; of manorial courts (*see* Court rolls); Readings, 26, 39; Reports, 43, 70, 298; statute books, 29, 30, 113; tracts & treatises on, 30, 40, 49; Year Books, 43, 298; other, 26, 30, 42–43, 104, 109, 298. *See also* Courts
Lawsuits: accounts of expenses of, 154; appealed from North American colonies, 62; of individuals & families, 27, 42–43, 46, 51, 53, 54, 60, 68, 70, 104, 139, 176, 213–15, 235, 248–49, 358, 359; in Wales, 51. *See also under* Courts
Lawthers, Catherine, 237
Lawyers, lists of, 42
Lea (Wilts.), 100, 116
Leake, William, 91
Leake (Lincs.), 75
Leake (Yorks.), 117
Leake, East (Notts.), 99, 114
Leake, West (Notts.), 99, 114
Leckhampstead (Bucks.), 183, 211, 216, 226, 255
Lecky, William Edward Hartpole, 295
Le Courayer, Pierre Francois, 335
Ledbrooke, Tobias, 166
Ledsham (Yorks.), 101, 117, 122
Ledstone (Yorks.), 117, 122
Lee, Fitzroy Henry, 343
Lee, Robert Cooper, 232
Lee, Thomas, 279
Lee Lodge (Rutland), 115
Leedham, Thomas, 91

Leeds, dukes of. *See* Osborne, Thomas; Osborne, Peregrine
Leeman & Clark, 166
Leer, William, 166
Leeward Islands, government & politics of, 252
Legge, William, 4th Earl of Dartmouth, 132
Legh, Dorothy, 73
Leicester, Earl of. *See* Dudley, Robert
Leicester (Leics.), 91, 98, 111
Leicester, Honour of, 111
Leicester Castle (Leics.), 110
Leicester Forest (Leics.), 98, 111, 121
Leicester Navigation (canal), 122
"Leicesters Commonwealth," 30, 297, 319–20
Leicestershire: constables of hundreds in, 113; deeds for lands in, 97–99, 211, 258; Deputy Lieutenants in, 84, 91, 136; elections in, 84; Lord Lieutenants of, 83–84, 113; maps for lands in, 120–21; muster rolls for, 136; other, 47, 108–13, 118, 217, 219, 238
Leigh, Lady Caroline (Brydges), 166, 232
Leigh, Chandos, 1st Baron Leigh, 187
Leigh, Humphrey, 73
Leigh, James, 233, 241
Leigh, Julia Judith (Twisleton), 166
Leigh, Theophilus, 241
Leigh, William [fl. >1659], 240
Leigh, William [fl. 1722], 241
Leigh family, 239
Leighfield (Surrey), 18
Leighfield Forest (Notts.), 115
Leighton, John, 312
Leix, Co. (Ireland), 119, 180, 262
Leke, Mary Lewis, Countess of Scarsdale, 91
Leke, Robert, 3rd Earl of Scarsdale, 91
Leman, J. Curtis, 91
Le Moine, Sir James MacPherson, 291

Lenborough (Bucks.), 218
Lenham (Kent), 13, 19
Lennox, Duke of. *See* Stuart, Ludovic
Lennox, Lord George Henry, 365
Lenthall, Sir John, 209
Lenthall family, 224
Lenton, Francis, 48
Leppington (Yorks.), 101
Leslie, John, 130
Leslie, Robert, 130
Letterbooks, 67, 113, 156–57, 232, 300, 311, 318, 344, 355, 357, 362, 364
Leukenor, Sir Roger, 18
Leven, Earl of. *See* Melville, David
Leveson, Anne Venables, 91
Leveson, Sir John, 222
Leveson, Sir Richard, 209, 221
Leveson-Gower [*aftw.* Egerton], Francis, 1st Earl of Ellesmere. *See* Egerton, Francis Leveson-Gower
Leveson-Gower, George Granville, 1st Duke of Sutherland, 23, 66, 67, 69
Leveson-Gower, Granville, 1st Marquis of Stafford, 66, 67
Leveson-Gower, Granville George, 5th Earl of Granville, 289
Leveson-Gower, John, 1st Baron Gower, 64
Leveson-Gower, John, 1st Earl Gower, 64
Levett, Henry, 242
Levinge, Sir Richard, 1st Bart., 91
Levinge, Samuel, 91
Levinge, barons, 132
Levy (Charles) & Co., 166
Lewes, Winifred, 188
Lewes (Sussex), 8
Lewis, Elizabeth. *See* Hastings, Elizabeth (Lewis)
Lewis, Sir John, 103, 125
Ley, James, 1st Earl of Marlborough, 214, 226
Ley, Richard, 166

Library, plans for a, 123. *See also under* Books
Licensed houses, returns of in Bucks., 183
Lichfield, Anthony, 340
Lightfoot & Co. *See* Robson, Lightfoot & Robson.
Liguire, Mary, 91
Lilford, Baron. *See* Powys, Thomas Littleton
Lillings Ambo (Yorks.), 101
Lillingstone Dayrell (Bucks.), 255
Lilstock (Somerset), 180, 261, 273
Limerick, surrender of, 62
Limerick, Co. (Ireland), 119
Limpsfield (Surrey), 1, 7
Lincoln, Earl of. *See* Clinton [or Fiennes], Henry
Lincoln, recusants in bishopric of, 37
Lincolns Inn (London), 32
Lincolnshire: deeds for lands in, 77, 99; petitions to Parliament re, 58; other, 47, 238
Lindsay, Alexander, 4th Earl of Balcarres, 327
Lindsay, Colin, 3rd Earl of Balcarres, 327
Lindsay, Sir Davis, 4th Bart., 366
Lindsay, James, 5th Earl of Balcarres, 327
Lindsay, Margaret (Campbell), 3rd Countess of Balcarres, 327
Lindsey, Theophilus, 91
Linnacombe (Devon.), 96
Linslade (Bucks.), 106
Lipscomb, Lawrence, 166
Liquor, excise on, 224
Lisgoole (Ireland), 119
Liskeard (Cornwall), 218, 256
Lister, Nicholas, 91
Literature & literary papers, 28–32, 47–49, 55–56, 59, 69, 134–35, 196–98, 225, 243–44
Little, Jeffrey, 14
Little Cheverell (Wilts.). *See* Cheverell, Little
Little Stanmore (Middlesex), 152

Little Weighton (Yorks.), 101
Littlejohn-Cook, William, 277
Littleton, Sir Edward, 4th Bart., 347
Littleton, Edward, 1st Baron Littleton, 140
Littleton, Sir Thomas, 29
Littlewood, Thomas Y., 166
Liverpool, earls of. *See* Jenkinson, Charles; Jenkinson, Robert Banks
Liverpool, corporation of, 105
Llananno (Radnor.), 260
Llanbadarnfawr (Radnor.), 260
Llanbister (Radnor.), 260
Llandegley (Radnor.), 260
Llandfihangel Nant Melan (Radnor.), 260
Llandfihangel Rhydithon (Radnor.), 260
Llandrindod (Radnor.), 260
Llangunllo (Radnor.), 260
Llansantffraid Cwmdeuddwr (Radnor.), 260
Llanstephan (Radnor.), 260
Lloyd, Abraham, 320
Lloyd, John, 91
Lloyd, Leonard, 152, 209
Lloyd, Sir Marmaduke, 73
Lloyd, Sir Robert, 52
Lock, Matthew, 130
Loder, Sir Edmund Giles, 2nd Bart., 166
Loder, Sir Robert, 1st Bart., 188
Loftus, Anne Maria (Dashwood), Marchioness of Ely, 166
Loftus, Lady Anna Maria Ellen, 166
Lok, Michael, 320
Lollards, 44
Lonceford, William, 9
London:
—by place: Bridgewater House, 59, 64, 77; Christs Hospital, 15; Hartshorne Lane, 15; St. Benet's, 99; St. Giles without Cripplegate, 53; St. James Square house of Duke of Chandos, 234; St. Mary of Bethleham Hospital [Bethlam,

"Bedlam"], 184; St. Mary Overies, 8; St. Mary Woolchurch [Haw], 99; St. Pauls Cathedral, 51, 170; St. Sepulchre's, 233; Whitefriars, 44
—by subject: accounts for property in, 152; Customs accounts for, 68; deeds for property in, 13, 59, 64, 77, 99, 233, 258; inhabitants of, 320; International Health Exhibition in (1884), 167; maps & plans re, 121, 270–71; mercantile affairs in, 287; Plans of buildings in, 270–71; Port of, Select Committee for Improvement of the, 121; porters of, 57; social life in, 277, 281, 334; Stow's survey of, 357; Tower of, 44, 362; Town Clerk's Journal, 321; waterworks in, 63; other, 44, 114, 184, 217, 238. *See also* Middlesex
London (Kent), 13
London & County Bank, 166
London & County Joint Stock Bank, 166
Londonderry, Countess of. *See* Ridgeway, Frances (Temple)
Londonderry, earls of. *See* Ridgeway, Weston; Ridgeway, Robert
Londonderry, Marquis of. *See* Vane, Charles William
Londonderry, Co. (Ireland), 50, 119, 288
Long Crendon (Bucks.), 173, 177, 183, 255, 265
Long Island, battle of, 132
Long Whatton (Leics.), 98
Longborough (Gloucs.), 216, 217, 237, 258
Longford, Co. (Ireland), 180, 247, 249, 262
Longley, Charles Thomas, Abp., 313
Longueville, Margaret (Temple), Lady, 209
Longwick (Bucks.), 266
Lord, Mary, 241

Lord Chancellor. *See* Chancellor, Lord
Lord Steward's Department, 88
Lord Lieutenants (of counties): in Ayrshire, 323; in Buckinghamshire, 57, 61, 64, 65, 192; in Hertfordshire, 57; in Leicestershire, 83–84, 113; in Rutland, 83–84, 136; other, 34, 136, 142. *See also* Deputy Lieutenants
"Lords Standing Orders" [Remembrances for Order and Decency to be kept in the Upper House of Parliament], 56, 63, 138
Loring, Joshua, 276
Loring, Theodosia (Thackeray), 277
Losse, Sir Hugh, 125
Lostwithiel (Cornwall), 183, 257
Loudoun, countesses of. *See* Abney-Hastings [formerly Clifton], Edith Maud Rawdon-Hastings; Abney-Hastings [formerly Huddleston], Edith Maud; Campbell, Margaret (Dalrymple); Rawdon-Hastings, Flora (Mure-Campbell)
Loudoun, earls of. *See* Campbell, Hugh; Campbell, John; Campbell, James Mure
Loudoun Castle, 103
Loughborough, Baron. *See* Hastings, Henry
Loughborough, barons, 78
Loughborough (Leics.), 82, 98, 103, 104, 109, 111, 118, 121
Louis XIV, King of France, 224
Louis Phillippe I, King of France, 91
Louisbourg (Canada), 275
Louise Caroline Alberta, Princess, Duchess of Argyll, 282
Louth, Co. (Ireland), 102, 119, 122
Lovat, Lord. *See* Fraser, Simon
Love, Thomas, 221
Lovell, Ann, 186
Lovell (Bucks.), 255
Loveridge, William, 167

Low, Richard, 187
Low Countries, treatise on, 29. *See also* Belgium; Flanders; Netherlands
Lowe, Robert, 289
Lowell, James Russell, 282
Lower Kinnerton (Cheshire), 76
Lowndes, William, 288
Lowther, Sir Gerard, 129
Lowther, Jane Jeffreys, 241
Lowther, John, 241
Lowther, Sir Thomas, 2nd Bart., 241
Lowther, Sir William, 3rd Bart., 240
Loxton (Somerset), 261
Lubbesthorpe (Leics.), 98, 111
Lucan, Earl of. *See* Bingham, Charles
Ludgershall (Bucks.), 96, 177, 256, 263 *(bis)*, 265
Ludlow (Salop), 58, 115
Ludlow Castle, 51
Luffield (Bucks.), 211, 216, 218, 256
Luffield (Northants.), 259
Lummis, J., 73
Lunatic asylums: admission to "Bethlam," 184; plan for a, 270
Lunatics, 105, 214, 223, 230, 235, 240
Lutterworth (Leics.), 98, 211, 217, 258
Lutwycke, Thomas, 235
Luxembourg, 62
Lyall, William Rowe, 313
Lydgate, John, 28
Lyme (Cheshire), 76
Lyndon, Ann, 188
Lyon, Lord. [Alexander Brodie], 324
Lyon, William, 366
Lytham (Lancs.), 108, 120
Lyttleton, Charles, Bp., 335
Lyttleton, George, 1st Baron Lyttleton, 335
Lyttleton, Thomas, 2nd Baron Lyttleton of Frankley, 335
Lyttleton, William Henry, 276

Macartney, George, 1st Earl Macartney, 330
Macaulay, Frances, 331
Macaulay, Henry William, 331
Macaulay, Selina (Mills), 331
Macaulay, Thomas Babington, 1st Baron Macaulay, 197, 331
Macaulay, Zachary, 330–32
McBeth, William 327
McCarthy, Felix, 91
Macclesfield, Earl of. *See* Parker, Thomas
McClintock, Robert, 91
MacCulloh, Elizabeth, 91
McDermot, Hugh, 254
MacDonald, ———, 167
McDonald, Alexander, 327
MacDonald, Sir Alexander, 7th Bart., 327
McDonald, Donald, 327
MacDonald, James, 327
MacDonald, Thomas, 91
McDonall, W., 91
MacDonnell, Coll. 327
MacDonnell, Rose, 130
MacDowall-Crichton, Patrick, 6th Earl of Dumfries, 327
MacFarlan, ———, 91
McFarland, Lady Maria Gertrude (Van Kemple), 167
McHugh, Dominick, 91
MacIntosh, Aeneas, 328
MacIntosh, William, 328
Mackay, Alexander, 327
Mackay, George, 327
Mackay, George, 3rd Baron Reay, 328
Mackay, Hugh [fl. 1745, major in British Army], 328
Mackay, Hugh [d. 1770, 2nd son of 3rd Baron Reay], 328
MacKenzie, Alexander, 328
MacKenzie, Sir Alexander Muir, 1st Bart., 347
MacKenzie, Kenneth. *Styled* Lord Fortrose, 328
MacKenzie, William, 328
McKersie, Andrew, 328

Mackesy, Dorothy, 277
Mackie, Robert, 91
Mackintosh, Sir James, 253, 254
Maclaren, Lady Edith, 81
MacLeod, Hugh, 328
MacLeod, John, 328
MacLeod, Norman, 328
McMahon, Sir John, 1st Bart., 91
MacNab, Archibald, 328
MacNamara, Maria L., 254
MacPherson, James, 328
Madras (India), 143, 155, 167, 194–95, 343
Madrigals, 32
Madron (Cornwall), 257
Maggs Brothers of London, 81, 294, 296, 301, 316, 330, 332, 348, 363
Maiden Bradley (Wilts.), 100
Maids Moreton (Bucks.), 177, 181, 211, 216, 256, 265
Maitland, Cecil Louise (Mackenzie), 199
Maitland, James, 328
Maitland, James, 7th Earl of Lauderdale, 328
Maitland, John, 2nd Earl & 1st Duke of Lauderdale, 198
Maitland, William, 191
Major, Elizabeth. *See* Brydges, Elizabeth (Major)
Makin, Bathsua, 134
Malcolm, George, 347
Malet, Sir Charles Warre, 1st Bart., 347
Malins, J. B., 167
Malmesbury, Earl of. *See* Harris, James
Malpas (Cheshire), 76
Malton [Old Malton] (Yorks.), 117, 217
Malvern, Little (Worcs.), 101
Malynes, Gerard de, 37, 73
Mammatt, Edward, 91
Mammatt, Edward F., 91
Mammatt, John, 91, 122
Man, Edward, 91
Man, Isle of, 27
Mancetter (Warwicks.), 116

Manila, British occupation of, 343
Mann, Galfridus & James, 328
Mann, Sir Horace, 1st Bart., 91
Manners, Charles, 4th Duke of Rutland, 195
Manners, Edward, 3rd Earl of Rutland, 27
Manners family, 194
Manners & morals, education regarding, 201
Manning, Henry Edward, Cardinal, 295
Manning & Dalston, 154, 167
Mannynge, Edmunde, 220
Manorial records. *See* Accounts; Court Books; Court rolls; Maps & plans; Rentals; Surveys; and *see under* "Manorial and Local Affairs Papers" in Table of Contents
Mansfield, Daniel, 167
Mansfield, Earl of. *See* Murray, David
Manuche, Cosmo, 55
Maperton (Somerset), 100
Maps & plans, 103, 120–23, 132, 195, 245, 262–74 *passim.*, 278, 309, 363
Mar, Earl of. *See* Erskine, John
Marble, register of, 175
Marbury (Cheshire), 66
Marcham, Frank, 146, 303
Margaret of Anjou, Queen of Henry VI, 9
Margetson, James, 130
Marine Square [Wells Close Square] House (Middlesex), 67
Mark (Somerset), 261
Market Bosworth (Leics.), 98
Market Drayton (Salop.), 115
Market Marborough (Leics.), 98
Markfield (Leics.), 112
Markham, Gervase, 197
Markham, Sir Gryffin, 45
Markham, Joseph, 186
Markham family, 194
Marks Tay, 18

Marlborough, dukes of. *See* Churchill, John; Spencer-Churchill, John

Marlborough, Earl of. *See* Ley, Sir James

Marley (Sussex), 1–11 *passim.*

Marriage settlements, 19, 20, 27, 54, 59, 60, 64, 123, 188–89, 222, 241, 250–51

Marriages, Bill for the prevention of clandestine, 200

Marriott, Charles, 313

Marsh, Francis, Abp., 130, 251

Marshal (Sussex), 1

Marshall, George, 167

Marshall, John, 91

Marsley Park (Denbigh), 76

Marston, John, 30

Marsworth (Bucks.), 183

Martiau, Nicholas, 131

Martin, Elizabeth, 247

Martin, Sir Richard, 73

Martin, Thomas, 188

Martin, William [fl. 1696?–1756, British Admiral], 343

Martin, William [fl. 1814–26, of Stewards Hay, Leics.], 91

Martineau, James, 295

Martyn, Augustin, 209

Martyn, Catherine Horner Strangeways (Pearson), 167

Martyn, Mary Anne Fonnereau, 167

Martyn, Thomas, 200

Martyr Worthy (Hants.), 233, 258

Mary I, Queen of England, 73, 128, 177

Mary, Queen of Scots, 32, 84, 191, 245

Mary, Queen of George V, 364

Mary Louise Victoria, Princess, Duchess of Kent, 361

Maryland. 62, 73

Mason, Charles [fl. 1820–25, of London], 167

Mason, Charles [fl. 1848–51, timber merchant?], 167

Mason, George, 73

Mason, William, 91

Mason, William Monck, 254

Massachusetts, 309

Massachusetts Bay Company, 53

Master, Thomas, 31

Matchitt, Lydia, 126

Mathematics: commonplace book re, 140; treatise on, 31

Mathews, R., 332

Matthew, William, 252

Matthews, Matthew, 134

Maxfield (Sussex), 2, 4, 6

Maxwell, John, 347

Maxwell, Robert, 130

May, Sir Humfrey, 91

Maynard, William Lord, 18

Maynwaring, Arthur, 38, 73

Maynwaring, George, 332

Maynwaring, Katherine, 92

Mayo, viscountcy of, 243

Mayo, Co. (Ireland), 247

Measham (Derbys.), 96, 107

Meath, Co. (Ireland), 102, 119, 122, 248, 249

Meaux, John de, 124

Medals, of Sir John Rawdon, 103

Medicine: expenses for medical care, 154; in Navy, 318; recipes and prescriptions, 144, 203, 228, 300; typhus fever, 318; veterinary, 69; women in, 289. *See also: Post mortem* examinations

Mediterranean, British naval forces in, 343, 355

Medley, Henry, 343

Medows, Jemima (Montague), Lady, 335

Medstead (Hants.), 258

Meehan, Thomas, 167

Meggy & Chalk, 162

Melbourne (Derbys.), 82, 96, 107, 118, 142

Melton Mowbray (Leics.), 112

Melvill, Sir Peter Melvill, 285

Melville, David, 3rd Earl of Leven & 2nd Earl Melville, 328

Melville, Viscount. *See* Dundas, Robert Saunders

Mendip, Baron. *See* Ellis, Welbore
Mendip, Baroness. *See* Ellis, Anne (Stanley)
Mendip Hills (Somerset), mining in, 219
Menteith, Earl of. *See* Graham, William, 130
Menzies, Neill, 328
Mercers Company, 167, 177
Merchadine, Romano, 69
Merchant, Roderick, 328
Merchant Adventurers, 38, 73, 228
Merchants, 38, 287, 300, 354
Merionethshire, 35
Mersey & Irwell Navigation canal, 66
Messeruy, Daniel, 63
Messeruy, Maximillian, 63
Metaphysics, notes on medieval scholasticism and, 31
Meteorology, 228
Methodists, 80
Mevagissey (Cornwall), 179, 257, 269
Meverell, Mary, 15
Meverell, Samuel, 15
Meynell & Copleston, 167
Michael, James, 167
Michelmore, G. & Co., 366
Middle East, English travellers in, 345. *See also* Persia
Middleburgh (Sussex). *See* Battle
Middlesex, earls of. *See* Cranfield, Lionel; Cranfield, James
Middlesex: accounts for property in, 152, 230; concealed lands in, 68; deeds for property in, 68, 77, 99, 248, 259; maps and plans for, 271; Receiver of, 44; other, 68, 114, 179, 181, 236, 237, 238
Middleton, Christopher, 328
Middleton, John, 92
Middleton, Nathaniel, 126
Middleton, Thomas, 48
Middleton Plantation (Jamaica), 202, 245
Middlewich (Cheshire), 76
Mildenhall (Wilts.), 100, 116

Mildmay, Sir Walter, 36, 39, 73
Mildmay family, 242
Miles, Samuel, 92
Miles, William Augustus, 92
Milford Haven (Pembroke.), 31
Militia: in Buckinghamshire, 57, 61, 65, 70, 155, 192–93, 225–26; in Derbyshire, 136; in Hampshire, 244; in Hertfordshire, 57; in Leicestershire, 136; in Rutland, 136; other, 52, 65, 84, 346. *See also* Army; Array, commissions of; Musters
Mill, William, 41, 73
Millamarsh (Derbys.), 107
Millar, Samuel, 332
Miller, John [fl. >1707], 185
Miller, John [fl. 1842–51], 167
Millikan, Mrs. Robert A., 278
Mills, Thomas, 186
Mills, 82, 121
Milner, Isaac, 332
Milnes, Sir Robert Shore, 308
Milton, John, 48
Milton, Lord. *See* Fletcher, Andrew
Milton-under-Wychwood (Oxon.), 259
Milward, Robert, 92
Milward, Sir Thomas, 73
Minchenden House [Middlesex], 230
Minerals & mineralogy, 175, 190, 309
Mines & mining: alum, 58; coal, 82, 120, 123, 180, 323, 334, 346; copper, 39, 183; farm of, 38; lead, 68, 219; maps of, 269; Royal, 39; tin, 300; other, 230, 235
Minorca, 65, 66–67
Minshull, R., 13
Minshull, Sir Richard, 13, 14
Minshull family, 15
Minster (Cornwall), 96, 107
Mint, Royal, 37, 50, 58, 72, 296, 318–19. *See also* Coinage & currency
Mirabeau, Honoré Gabriel Riquetti, Comte de, 293

Missenden, Great & Little (Bucks.), 256
Mitchell, Logan, 292
Mitchelson, James, 328
Mitchelson, Samuel, 347
"Modus tenendi Parliamentum": (English), 29, 56; (Irish), 35
Moffett, Thomas, 333
Mohun, Charles, 5th Baron Mohun, 63
Moira, Countess of. *See* Rawdon, Elizabeth (Hastings), Countess of Moira & *suo jure* Baroness Hastings, Hungerford, Botreaux, & Moleyns, 80
Moira, earls of, 78, 132. *See* Rawdon, John; Rawdon-Hastings, Francis
Moira Colliery (Leics.), 82
Moira House (Dublin), 122
Mold, John, 167
Mold [Moughnutesdale] (Flint.), 76, 108
Molesworth, William, 347
Moleyns, John de, 126
Moleyns, barons, 78
Mollington (Oxon.), 259
Molloy, James Scott, 92
Molyneux, Samuel, 315
Molyneux, Sir Thomas, 5th Bart., 333
Mompesson, Sir Giles, 137
Monaghan, Co. (Ireland), 119, 129
Monck, George, 1st Duke of Albemarle, 92, 119, 128, 130
Moncton, Robert, 276
Monmouthshire: concealed lands in, 68; deeds for land in, 77; other, 46
Monpellier, 335
Monsey, Messenger, 335
Monsley, William Eaton, 92
Montagu, Dorothy (Fane), Countess of Sandwich, 335
Montagu, Edward, 333, 335
Montagu, Edward Wortley, 335
Montagu, Elizabeth (Charlton), 335

Montagu, Elizabeth (Robinson), 333–37
Montagu, John, 4th Earl of Sandwich, 328, 336
Montagu, Matthew, 4th Baron Rokeby, 336
Montagu, Richard, 337
Montagu, Richard, Bp., 48
Montague, Mary (Churchill), 247
Montague, viscounts, 11, 12. *And see* Browne, Anthony; Browne, Francis
Montfort family, 225
Montgomerie, Alexander, 9th Earl of Eglinton, 328
Montgomerie, John, 328
Montgomery, Hugh, 1st Earl of Mount-Alexander, 130
Montgomery, Nicholas, 118
Montgomery, Earl of. *See* Herbert, Henry
Montgomeryshire, 46
Monton (Lancs.), 76
Montresor, James Gabriel, 276
Montrose, Duke of. *See* Graham, James
Montrose, Marchioness of. *See* Bruce, Christian Leslie Graham
Moor, William, 328
Moore, ———, 59
Moore, James Carrick, 254
Moore, Mary, 186
Mordaunt, Henry, 2nd Earl of Petersborough, 219
More, Hannah, 331, 332, 336
More, Martha, 332
Moreton Morrell (Warwicks.), 152, 153, 180, 274
Morgan, Chandos Stuart Temple Henry, 167
Morgan, Charles [fl. 1685–86, Army officer], 92
Morgan, Charles [fl. 1694–96, Exchequer official?], 62
Morgan, Edward, 26
Morgan, Elizabeth Lydia Player (Brigstocke), 190
Morgan, G., 182

Morgan, George Manners, 155, 167, 174, 187, 188, 189, 190, 197
Morgan, Henry Charles, 188
Morgan, John [fl. 1728–29], 12
Morgan, John [fl. 1820], 92
Morgan, Thomas, 328
Morgan, Thomas Chandos Chardin, 167, 188
Morgan-Grenville [*formerly* Morgan], Luis Ferdinand Harry Courthope, 150, 167
Morgan-Grenville, Lady Mary, 195
Morgan-Grenville, Mary (Grenville), Baroness Kinloss of Stowe, 146, 150, 167, 189, 199
Morgan-Grenville, Richard George Grenville, Master of Kinloss, 151, 167, 178
Morgan-Grenville, Thomas, 199
Morgan-Grenville family, 155
Morgan-Grenville-Gavin, Thomas George Breadalbane, 167
Morin, James, 189
Morland & Co., 154
Morlands, Auriol & Co., 167, 254
Morley, George, 130
Morley, James, 92
Morley, John, 282
Morley, John, 1st Viscount Morley of Blackburn, 295
Mornay, Philip de, Seigneur du Plessis-Marly, 31
Morrice, George, 167
Morrice, J., 167
Morris family, 194
Morrison, Alexander, 292
Morrison, J., 167
Mort, Thomas, 337
Morton (Francis) & Co., 167
Morton (Henry J.) & Co., 167
Moseley, James, 73
Moss (S.) & Co., 167
Mossom, Robert, 131
Motton, Reginald de, 126
Moughnutesdale (Flint.). *See* Mold
Mould, Frederick, 167
Mould, William, 167

Mount-Alexander, Earl of. *See* Montgomery, Hugh
Mt. Etna (Sicily), 190, 194
Mountague, F. W., 168
Mountague, Ralph, 185
Mountjoy, Baron. *See* Blount, James
Mountjoy (Sussex). *See* Battle
Mountsfort (Warwicks.), 250
Mountsorrel (Leics.), 98, 112
Mousley, William Eaton, 92
Mousley & Barber, 168
Mowbray, Thomas, [Duke of Norfolk?], 132
Moylan, Francis, Bp., 254
Mudd, J & Sons, 199
Muddiman, Henry, 92
Mulgrave (Yorks.), 58
Mumby (Lincs.), 75, 77
Mumford, J. Aubrey, 168
Mumford & Son, 168
Munday, John, 168
Mundham (Norfolk), 114
Mundy, William, 240
Munro, George, 328
Munro, Sir Harry, 7th Bart., 328
Munro, Helen, 277
Murder, evidence in case re, 105
Mure, Sir William, Laird of Rowallan, 321, 323, 328
Mure family, 132, 321
Mure-Campbell, Flora, Countess of Loudoun. *See* Rawdon-Hastings, Flora (Mure-Campbell)
Mure-Campbell, James, 5th Earl of Loudoun. *See* Campbell, James Mure
Murray, Alexander, 7th Baron Elibank, 347
Murray, David, 2nd Earl of Mansfield, 92
Murray, Eustace Clare Grenville, 168
Murray, Frances Maria, 318
Murray, James, 2nd Duke of Atholl, 64, 328
Murray, John Fisher, 92

Murray, Patrick, 5th Baron Elibank, 347
Murray, Thomas, 168
Murray-Pulteney, Henrietta Laura (Pulteney), Countess of Bath, 347
Murray-Pulteney, Sir James, Bart., 347
Murton (Warwicks.), 68
Murton-cum-Hilton (Westmorland), 77
Museum Bookstore (London), 146, 344
Music: compositions, 32, 135, 194; instruments, 234; inventory of scores, 234; treatise on, 49
Muster rolls, 136, 226, 323
Musters (military): in Buckinghamshire, 57, 225; in Lancashire, 45; in Leicestershire, 136; in Rutland, 136; in Shropshire, 52; in Sussex, 12; other, 44, 52, 57, 297. *See also* Militia
Mutton, P., 73
Myers, Winifred, 341
Myllward, John. *See* Alexander [*alias* Myllward], John
Myngs, Christopher, 337
Mynors, Henry Eden, 273

Nairne, Sir David, 328
Nanfan, John, 288
Nantmel (Radnor.), 260
Nantwich (Cheshire), 76
Napier, James, 168, 276
Naples: British ambassador at, 310; geography of Bay of, 190
Napoleonic Wars: Admiralty affairs during, 155, 191–92; British naval operations during, 189, 283–86, 315–16, 338–39, 355, 356; map of actions in, 92; naval surgeon in, 318; Peninsular campaign, 363; other, 84, 345
Nash, J., 92
Nash, W. J., 168
Natal, Bp. of, 295
Nautical charts, 309. *See also* Derroteros

Navestock (Essex), 67
Navigation Acts, 228
Navy (Royal):
—by period: in 16th century, 34; in 17th century, 50, 60–61, 136, 225; in 18th century, 342–44; in Napoleonic wars, 191–92, 283–86, 315–16, 338–39, 355–56; in War of 1812, 301, 317
—by subject: administration of, *see* Admiralty; commissions in, 192, 365; diaries concerning, 189, 318, 364; finances of, 57, 225; Hydrographic Office, 284; impressed seamen, 61, 64, 184; medical care in, 318; Navy Office, 162; reports on state of, 34, 50, 61; signal books, 192, 306–07, 316; wages of officers and men in, 57; William IV in, 364; other, 162, 226, 283–84, 316, 344. *See also* Ships (of Royal Navy)
Navy (U.S.), 301
Neale, Francis, 73
Neale, Owen, 31
Near East, description & travel, 284
Needham, Mary (Shirley), Viscountess Kilmorey, 92
Needham, Thomas, 9th Viscount Kilmorey, 92
Nelson, George, 168
Nelson, Horatio, Viscount Nelson, 338–39
Nether Alstanton (Cheshire), 76
Nether Knutsford (Cheshire), 46, 76
Netherfield (Sussex). *See* Battle
Netherlands, 33–34, 49, 56–57, 62, 136. *See also* Holland
Netherseal (Derbys.), 96, 107
Nevill, H., 168
New England, proposed union of with New York, 62
New York, 62, 300, 304, 309
Newbold Verdon (Leics.), 98, 112
Newbury Farm (Essex), 13
Newby (Yorks.), 117

Newcastle, dukes of. *See* Cavendish, William; Holles, John; Pelham-Holles, Thomas
Newcastle-upon-Tyne (Northants.), 334
Newdigate, Sir Robert, 43
Newfoundland, 305, 343
Newhall, Richard Ager, 314
Newhaven, Viscount. *See* Cheyne, William
Newland (Cornwall), 107
Newnham, John, 185
Newport, Emmanuel, 220
Newport, Treaty of (1648), 52
Newsham, James, 250
Newsletters, 52, 64, 84, 281, 286
Newton, Anne, 277
Newton, Sir Isaac, accounts of executors of, 144
Newton (Yorks.), 101
Newton Blossomville (Bucks.), 183
Newton Corner, 121
Newton Harcourt (Leics.), 98, 112
Newton Montagu (Dorset), 108
Newton St. Loe (Somerset), 100
Newtown Linford (Leics.), 112
Nicholas, Sir Edward, 92
Nicholson, Sir Francis, 62, 73
Nickolls, Robert Boucher, 92
Nicol, Margaret. *See* Brydges, Margaret (Nicol)
Nicoll, John, 234
Nicolls, John, 231
Nile, map of mouth of the, 123
Noble, Francis, 92
Noel, Thomas, 2nd Viscount Wentworth, 135
Non-conformists. *See* Religious dissent
Norden, John, 31
Norfolk: deeds for lands in, 99, 259; elections in, 65; other, 114
Normanby, Duke of. *See* Sheffield, John
Normanby, Marchioness of. *See* Sheffield, Ursula (Stawell) Conway

Normandy, English administration of, 314
Normanton (Derbys.), 107
Normanton (Leics.), 109
Norrreys, Sir Edward, 27, 73, 125
Norreys, Francis, 2nd Baron Norreys of Rycote [*aftw.* 1st Earl of Berkshire], 27, 73
Norridge (Wilts.), 101
Norris, Sir John, 343
Norris & Sons, 168
North, Anne (Montagu), Baroness North, 340
North, Dudley, 4th Baron North, 340
North, Sir Francis, 58
North, Francis, 1st Baron Guilford, 339–40
North, William H., 168
North America: British in, 61–62, 301, 364; French in, 62. *See also* Canada; United States; West Indies
North Berwick, Lord. *See* Dalrymple, Hew, 1st Bart. & Lord North Berwick
North Cadbury (Somerset), 115
Northampton, Marchioness of. *See* Compton, Margaret (Douglas-Macleen-Clephane)
Northamptonshire: accounts of estates in, 152; deeds for lands in, 77, 99, 173, 259; maps of estates in, 271; other, 114, 179, 184, 217
Northamptonshire Record Office, Stowe manuscripts in, 147
Northend (Warwicks.), 180, 212, 217, 219
Northesk, Earl of. *See* Carnegie, David
Northey, W., 14
Northington, Earl of. *See* Henley, Robert
Northope (Flint.), 46, 76
Northumberland, Duke of. *See* Percy, Hugh
Northumberland, Earl of. *See* Percy, Algernon

Northumberland: deeds for lands in, 99, 248; other, 114
Northwich (Cheshire), 38, 46
Norton, Richard, 240
Norton (Radnor.), 260
Norton Bavant (Wilts.), 101
Norwich, recusants in bishopric of, 37
Norwich Union Fire Insurance Society, 155, 168
Nosworthy, Lyle, 277
Nottingham, Roger de, 8
Nottingham, earls of. *See* Finch, Heneage; Finch, Daniel; Howard, Charles
Nottinghamshire: deeds for lands in, 99; other, 47, 114–15
Nova Scotia (Canada), 224
Novels. *See* Literature and Literary papers
Noy, William, 46, 125
Nugent, Alison (Bridget), 251
Nugent, Ann, 250
Nugent, Anna (Craggs) Newsham Knight, 246
Nugent, Balthasar, 250
Nugent, Charles Edmund, 248
Nugent, Christopher, "14th" [3rd?] Baron Delvin, 251
Nugent, Christopher, *styled* Lord Delvin, 249
Nugent, Elizabeth (Drax) Berkeley, Countess of Berkeley and Countess Nugent, 246
Nugent, Emilia Plunkett, 246, 251
Nugent, Edmund, 249, 250 *(bis)*, 251 *(bis)*
Nugent, Garrett, 249
Nugent, Sir George, 1st Bart., 168, 250
Nugent, George Thomas John, Marquis of Westmeath, 168
Nugent, James, 247
Nugent, John, 247, 251
Nugent, Lawrence, 249 *(bis)*
Nugent, Lady Maria (Skinner), 168
Nugent, Mary Ann, 247, 250

Nugent, Mary Elizabeth. *See* Grenville, Mary Elizabeth (Nugent)
Nugent, Michael, 249 *(bis)*, 250
Nugent, Richard, 250
Nugent, Robert [fl. >1679, of Aughnegarron], 250
Nugent, Robert [fl. >1666, of Ballentullagh], 250
Nugent, Robert [of Bobsgrove], 247
Nugent, Robert [other than above?], 249–51 *passim.*
Nugent, Robert, 1st Earl Nugent, 149, 246–50 *passim.*
Nugent, Thomas, 249
Nugent, Thomas, 4th Earl of Westmeath, 252
Nugent, Baron. *See* Grenville, George Nugent, 2nd Baron Nugent
Nugent-Grenville, George, 2nd Baron Nugent. *See* Grenville, George Nugent
Nugent-Temple-Grenville, George, 1st Marquis of Buckingham. *See* Grenville, George Nugent-Temple-
Nugent-Temple-Grenville, Mary Elizabeth (Nugent), Marchioness of Buckingham. *See* Grenville, Mary Elizabeth (Nugent) Nugent-Temple-
Nutbourne (Sussex), 100

Oadby (Leics.), 98
Oakham (Notts.), 115
Oakley (Bucks.), 177, 256, 265
Oakthorpe (Leics.), 82, 98, 112
Oaths: of Allegiance, 45, 61, 65, 128, 142–43; of Supremacy, 143
O'Conor, Charles [1710–91], 252, 254
O'Conor, Charles [1764–1828], 200, 252, 254
O'Conor, Matthew, 254
O'Conor Don, Denis, 254
O'Conor Don, Owen, 254
Offices, lists and fees of, 279

Officials (municipal), lists of, 144
Ogilvie, William, 92
Ogilvy, James, 328
Ogilvy, James. 4th Earl of Findlater & 1st Earl of Seafield, 328
Ogilvy, James, 5th Earl of Findlater & 2nd Earl of Seafield, 328
Ogle, Thomas, 209
O'Gorman, Thomas le Chevalier, 254
O'Hara, James, Baron Kilmaine and 2nd Baron Tyrawley, 329
O'Hara, Patrick, 343
Old Malton (Yorks.). *See* Malton [Old Malton]
Oldcastle, Sir John, 44
Oldwicke (Bucks.), 211
Ollerton (Cheshire), 46, 76
Ollivant, Alfred, Bp., 313
Olney, Edward, 220, 222
Ombersley (Worcs.), 116, 262
O'Neill, Henry McToole, 131
O'Neill, Phelim, 131
Ongar (Essex), 13, 14, 17
Onslow, Denzell, 92
Onslow, Sarah Foote Lewis, 92
Opie, _____ [father of Richard & Nicholas], 221
Orcheston St. George (Wilts.), 101
Orcheston St. Mary (Wilts.), 101
Orde, James P., 340–41
Orde-Powlett, Thomas, 1st Baron Bolton, 342
Orderly books (military & militia), 192, 304–05
Ordnance, 44
Orkney, Earl of. *See* Hamilton, George
Ormonde, Duke of. *See* Butler, James
Orrell, Richard, 41
Orrery, Earl of. *See* Boyle, Roger
Orton Quartermarsh (Leics.), 98
Orton Saucy (Leics.), 98, 112
Osbaston (Leics.), 98
Osborn, Sir George, 4th Bart., 366
Osborn, James, 168
Osborne, Hugh, 51

Osborne, John, 127
Osborne, Peregrine, 2nd Duke of Leeds, 61, 73, 198, 225
Osborne, Thomas, 1st Earl of Danby & 1st Duke of Leeds, 56, 73
Osbourne, Ward & Co., 168
Osgathorpe (Leics.), 98, 112
Osleton (Derbys.), 96
Osney, Robert, 209, 358
Oswald Kirk (Yorks.), 212
Otterhampton (Somerset), 261
Over Knutsford (Cheshire), 46
Overalstanton (Cheshire), 76
Overseers of the Poor, 109, 216
Overton, F., 209
Ovington (Hants.), 258
Owen, George, 31
Owen, Sir Richard, 282
Owston (Leics.), 112
Oxford, Countess of. *See* Vere, Elizabeth (Trussell) de
Oxford, earls of. *See* Vere, John de; Vere, Edward de
Oxford Movement, 313
Oxford University, 36, 73, 84, 168, 177, 178, 290
Oxfordshire: deeds for land in, 100, 173, 211, 259; maps of estates in, 271–72; recusants in, 37; other, 179, 217, 218, 219
Oxlade, Jonathan, 168
Oxley, John, 168
Oxley & Son, 168
Oyer et terminer, commission of, 44

Packington (Leics.), 98, 109, 112, 118
Padbury (Bucks.), 211, 256, 265, 358
Page, Thomas, 168
Paine, John, 188
Paine, Sarah (Harvey), 187
Paintings: catalogues & inventories of, 103, 174, 175, 234; exhibition of, 353; in English homes, 340. *See also* Drawings & sketches
Pakeman, Simon, 126

Pakington, John Somerset, 1st Baron Hampton, 168
Palatinate, war in the, 49
Pall Mall House (London), accounts of, 152
Palles, Ignatius, 247
Palles, Jane, 251
Palles, Mary, 251
Palmer, Charles F., 92
Palmer, Sir Henry, 221
Palmer, Sir James, 185
Palmer, John, 223
Palmer, Mary, 188
Palmer, Philip, 188
Palmer, Phoebe, 188
Palmer, Sir Thomas, 188
Palmer, W. J., 168
Palmer, William [1803–85, theologian], 285
Palmer, William [fl. 1844–47, tenant at Stowe], 168
Palmes, William, 209
Panin, Nikita Petrovich, Count, 168
Pannyngrydge, "Westalls Book of," 11
Parfitt, Edmund, 168
Paris, description and travel, 334
Parish registers, 178, 191, 194, 216, 225
Parishes: assessment of for land taxes, 182; history of in Buckinghamshire, 183
Parker, J. H., 168
Parker, John, 41
Parker, John, Abp., 131
Parker, Matthew, Abp., 138
Parker, Samuel, 168
Parker, Theodore, 295
Parker, Thomas, 1st Earl of Macclesfield, 191
Parker, William, 168
Parker, Hayes, Barnwell & Twisden, 168
Parkinson, John, 168
Parliament:
—Acts (Statutes): 8, 9, 26, 29, 37, 38, 39, 44, 49, 56, 63, 137, 139, 198, 226

—Bills, 66, 200, 201, 244
—Committee for Buckinghamshire (in Civil War), 225
—Committee for Plundered Ministers in, 226
—diaries of, 279–80
—elections & electioneering: at Aylesbury, 198; for Ayrshire, 323; for Buckinghamshire, 59, 65, 68, 193, 208, 224; at Leicester, 111; for Leicestershire, 84; for Norfolk, 65; for Radnorshire, 365; at St. Mawes, 198; for Shropshire, 346; for Sussex, 193; for Warwickshire, 224; at Westminster, 307; at Winchester, 244; other, 84, 289, 346, 365
—House of Commons, 66, 72, 137, 226, 307
—House of Lords, 52, 72, 127, 137, 162, 226, 305, 307, 323
—impeachments in, 9, 49, 52, 56
—Journals of, 39, 127, 226, 307
—"Lords Standing Orders" [Remembrances for Order and Decency to be kept in the Upper House . . .], 56, 63, 138
—Members of, 49, 136, 137, 193, 198, 226, 235, 243, 244, 307
—petitions to, 30, 49, 57, 58
—proceedings in, 49, 57, 137, 279, 280, 298, 299, 307
—relations with Crown, 39–40, 52, 137, 226
—Rolls of, 39, 127, 226, 316
—speeches in, 26, 32, 39, 49, 63, 137, 198, 226, 244, 282, 298
—subsidies, 8, 38, 50, 58, 72, 88
—summonses to, 127
—treatise on, 280–81
—other, 26, 39–40, 49, 63, 72, 198–99, 244, 327
See also under Ireland; Scotland
Parnell, Thomas, 131
Parrott, Edmund, 169
Parrott, George, 156, 169
Parrott, Joseph [fl. 1765–1809], 169
Parrott, Joseph [fl. 1849–62], 169

Parry family, 194
Parslow, John, 366
Parslow, Thomas, 169
Parsons, John, 169
Parsons, Robert, 319
Partridge, W. G., 169
Paston, Robert, 1st Earl of Yarmouth, 65
Paston, W., 8
Patronage: ecclesiastical, 195, 200, 289, 303, 341; literary, 26, 28; military, 322, 365; political, 26, 33, 41, 51, 195–96, 289, 323, 341; university, 36, 50; in Ireland, 195, 196; in Wales, 51; other, 46, 54, 59, 156, 315
Paul, John, 169
Paul (Cornwall), 257
Paulet, Charles, 1st Duke of Bolton, 22, 60, 73
Paulet, Charles, 2nd Duke of Bolton, 60, 73
Paulet, Jane. *See* Egerton, Jane (Paulet)
Paulet, Lord William, 60, 209
Pawlett (Somerset), 180, 261, 273
Pawley, W., 19
Paxton, Bartholomew, 221, 267
Paxton, Jonas, 169
Paxton, Robert, 169
Paymaster for Annuities disbursed by Parliament, 246
Paymaster General of the Forces, 231, 244, 308
Payne, John, 169
Payne & Foss, 254
Pearce, John, 14
Peat, Thomas Henry, 92
Pécaut, Felix, 295
Peel, Sir Robert, 169
Peerage (English): arms & orders of, 28; creations, 33, 142; lists of, 43, 44, 332; rights of, 40. *See also* Baronage
Peerage (Irish), 51
Pelham, Catherine Cobbe, 92
Pelham, Henry, 92

Pelham-Holles, Thomas, 1st Duke of Newcastle-upon-Tyne and of Newcastle-under-Lyme, 67, 303, 329
Pellew, Edward, 1st Viscount Exmouth, 169, 285
Pemberton, John, 352
Pemberton (Lancs.), 77
Pembroke, earls of, 78. *And see* Herbert, Philip; Herbert, Henry
Penal laws, for Ashby de la Zouch, 109
Penbrugge, Margaret, 26
Pengelly (Cornwall), 107
Penhallow, Samuel, 288
Penhele (Cornwall), 96, 106
Peninsular Wars, 84, 363
Penistone (Yorks.), 262
Penn, Granville, 197
Penn, William, 58
Pennsylvania, 304–05
Penponds (Cornwall), 257
Penry, John, 26, 37
Pensford (Somerset.), 100
Pensions, accounts of, 11
Penton, Thomas, 169
Peplesham, John de, 7
Pepusch, John Christopher, 234
Pepys, Sir William Weller, Bart., 336
Percy, Algernon, 4th Earl of Northumberland, 102
Percy, Hugh, 2nd Duke of Northumberland, 92
Pering, Thomas, 126
Perkins, John [fl. >1697], 185
Perkins, John [fl. >1714], 185
Perranporth (Cornwall), 269
Perranzabuloe (Cornwall), 257
Perrot, Sir John, 45
Perry, Grace (Blake), 221
Perry, Jane, 169
Persia, 299, 364. *See also* Middle East
Persius, 29
Pery, Edmond Sexton, Viscount Pery, 341–42
Pescod family, 242

Pestell, Ellis Shipley, 92
Pestell, Thomas, 92
"Peterloo" riots, 202
Peters, Francis, 239
Petersborough, Earl of. *See* Mordaunt, Henry
Peterston (Norfolk), 259
Petherton, North (Somerset), 261
Petition of Right, 52
Petley, Thomas, 220
Petour, Vasse Le, 92
Petre, William, 2nd Baron Petre, 18
Petrie, Henry, 254
Pett, William, 20
Petty, Henry, 1st Earl of Shelburne, 105
Petty, Sophia (Carteret), Countess of Shelburne, 336
Petty, William, 1st Marquis of Lansdowne, 336
Petty-FitzMaurice, Henry Charles Keith, 5th Marquis of Lansdowne, 282
Petyr, John, 9
Petyr, Richard, 9
Pevensey (Sussex), 4, 6
Peverell, barons, 132
Peyton, Sir John, 36
Phellips, Sir Edward, 39
Philanthropists, 294–95. *See also* Charities
Philip II, King of Spain, 34
Philips, T. N., 121
Phillimore, Joseph, 169
Phillipps, Ambrose, 92
Phillipps, Sir Thomas, 2, 315
Phillips, Henry, 169
Phoenix Park (Ireland), 175
Photographs, 199
Physicians & surgeons, 318
Pickering, J., 169
Pickering (Yorks.), 101
Pickhill (Denbigh), 75
Pickmere (Cheshire), 76
Picton, William, 366
Piddocke, Leonard, 92
Pierce, Thomas, 92

Pierrepont, Evelyn, 1st Duke of Kingston, 73
Pierrepont, Evelyn, 2nd Duke of Kingston, 68
Pigot, Agnes, 69
Pigott, George Grenville Wandesford, 169
Pilgrim, C., 169
Pilgrim, G., 265
Pinchbeck (Lincs.), 113
Pipe Roll. *See under* Exchequer
Pipewell (Leics.), 98
Piracy & privateers, 33, 58, 61–62, 105, 252, 287, 296, 322
Pirton (Herts.), 97
Pitchcott (Bucks.), 183, 267
Pitchford, Samuel, 343
Pitman, Frederick, 92
Pitstone (Bucks.), 74
Pitt, Anne, 336. *See also* Grenville, Anne (Pitt)
Pitt, Hester (Grenville), Countess of Chatham & *suo jure* Baroness Chatham, 148, 188, 336
Pitt, Mary, 336
Pitt, William, 1st Earl of Chatham, 148, 188, 276, 359, 360
Pittillo, James B., 287
Place, Francis, 292
Placentia, British forces at, 65
Plantagenet, Edward, 2nd Duke of York, 28
Plantations, 202
Plants, register of, 175
Plate, inventory of, 66
Platel, Peter, 73
Plea Rolls, extracts from, 43
Plowden, Edmund, 30
Plumley (Cheshire), 46
Plundered ministers, Committee for, 216
Plunkett, Emilia. *See* Nugent, Emilia Plunkett
Plunkett, George Thomas, Bp., 254
Pluralities, list of (Leics.), 139
Plymouth (Devon.), 61
Pneumatology, 309
Poachers, lawsuit involving, 215

Pocock, Sir George, 342–44
Poetry, discourse on, 134. *See also* Literature & literary papers
Poges, Roger, 126
Pole, Catherine. *See* Hastings, Catherine (Pole)
Pole, Henry, Baron Montagu, 78
Pole, Margaret (Plantagenet), Countess of Salisbury, 118
Pole, Reginald, Cardinal, 78, 92, 138
Pole, William de la, Duke of Suffolk, 9
Poll books, 59, 66, 69
Poll lists, 224
Pollard, John, 209, 214
Political science & government, treatise on, 29, 55
Pollicott, Great &/or Little (Bucks.), 152, 178, 181, 216, 217, 263 *(bis)*
Polruan (Cornwall), 107
Polton, Thomas, Bp., 8
Pombal, Sebastian Jose de Carvalho y Mello, Marquez de, 329
Pompeii, plan of, 274
Pool, John, 233
Poole, John, 169
Poole, Margaret, 231
Poole, Robert, 209
Poole family, 231
Poole (Dorset), 223
Poor: lists of, 177, 178, 179; Overseers of the, 109, 216; proposals for aiding, 58; tax lists for, 106. *See also* Charities; Philanthropists
Poor laws (Elizabethan), 38
Pope, Beata (Poole), Countess of Downe, 340
Pope, Richard, 344
Pope, Sir Thomas, 3rd Earl Downe, 340
Popham, Sir Home Riggs, 120, 169
Popham, Sir John, 34, 37, 73
"Popish Plot," the, 320
Port, Dorothy. *See* Hastings, Dorothy (Port)

Port, Sir John, 79, 124, 139, 298
Poringland (Norfolk), 114
Porter, Anna Maria, 344
Porter, Endymion, 51
Porter, George, 14
Porter, George Richard, 285
Porter, Jane, 344
Porter, Mary (Scherbatoff), Lady, 345
Porter, Ogilvie, 345
Porter, Sir Robert Ker, 344
Porter, Thomas, 57
Porter family, 344
Porters, petition to Parliament from, 57
Portland, Duchess of. *See* Bentinck, Margaret Cavendish (Harley)
Portland, dukes of. *See* Bentinck, William; Cavendish-Bentinck, William Henry
Ports: Customs officials at, 306; Oaths of Allegiance administered at, 45; plans & sketches of, 121, 122, 123; survey of, in southern England, 208; treatise on, 32. *See also under* names of individual ports, e.g. London, Milford Haven, Portsmouth
Portsmouth (Hants.), 208, 223
Portugal: British envoy to, 67; British forces in, 244, 323, 363; map of, 123; relations with England, 314
Post, Christian Frederick, 276
Post mortem examinations, 144, 191, 242
Post Nati, case of the (Calvins Case), 36
Potter, Robert, 336
Pottinger, Henry, 143
Poulett, Ann, 189
Poulett, John, 4th Earl Poulett, 366
Povey, ——, 49
Povey, John, 288
Powell, Cranfield Spencer, 329
Powell, Nowell, 188
Powlett. *See* Paulet; Poulett

Pownall, Thomas, 276
Powys, Thomas Littleton, 4th Baron Lilford, 169
Poyntz, William Deane, 296
Praed, Helen (Bogle) Mackworth, 169
Pratt, Charles, 92
Pratt, John, 196
Pratt, John Jeffreys, 1st Marquis Camden, 169, 200
Pratt, Samuel Jackson, 336
Pratt, Walter Caulfield, 169
Prebend End (Bucks.), 178, 265
Press, freedom of the, 292
Presteigne (Radnor.), 260
Preston, S. Kerrison, 283
Preston, Thomas, 240
Preston Bissett (Bucks.), 256, 266
Prestonpans, battle of, 322
Prestwold (Leics.), 98
Prevost, Sir George, 308
Price, Henry, 233
Price, John, 169
Price, Priscilla, 73
Price, Robert, 59
Priddy (Somerset), 180, 234, 238, 261
Prime Minister: George Grenville as, 149, 155, 156; William Wyndham Grenville as, 149
Primerose, Hugh, 3rd Viscount Primerose, 329
Princes Risborough (Bucks.), 266
Pringle, Lady Elizabeth Maitland (Campbell), 169
Pringle, Henry, 366
Prinkham (Surrey). *See* Limpsfield
Prints, catalogues of, 174
Prior, Thomas, 131
Priscian, 29
Prisons & prisoners, 43, 44, 292
Privateers. *See* Piracy & privateers
Privy Council, 32, 36, 40, 44, 45, 50, 52, 61, 64, 65, 66, 72, 88, 142, 162, 209, 223, 242, 297, 308–09. *See also* Council (Kings)
Privy Council Office, 155

Privy Seal Office, 67, 72, 163
Probets, William, 169
Probus (Cornwall), 257
Proby, Lady Charlotte, 197
Proby, John Joshua, 1st Earl of Carysfort, 169
Proclamations (Royal), 32, 40
Prynne, William, 306
Psalters, 29
Public Record Office (London), 3
Publow (Somerset), 100
Puckering, Cisley, 225
Puckering, Sir John, 42
Puckle, Henry, 169
Puddlestown (Dorset), 97, 108
Puget, Peter, 169
Pugh, Edward, 240
Pukfet, W., 18
Pullen, Samuel, Abp., 131
Pulteney, Frances, Lady Pulteney, 336, 345
Pulteney, Harry, 336
Pulteney [*formerly* Johnstone], Sir William, 345–48
Pulteney, William, Earl of Bath, 336
Puritans. *See* Religious dissent
Puriton (Somerset), 234, 261
Pym, George, 137
Pym, John, 49
Pymme, William, 27
Pyx, trials of the, 50, 58, 63

Quainton (Bucks.), 256
Quakers. *See* Friends, Society of
Quantock Hills, 272
Quarter sessions, in Buckinghamshire, 68, 183. *See also* Justices of the Peace
Quebec, 291
Queen Anne's Bounty, 163, 199
Queen Camel (Somerset), 100
Queens County (Ireland), 119
Queensberry, Duke of. See Douglas, James
Quoitca, 359
Quorndon (Leics.), 98, 109, 112

Radclive (Bucks.), 178, 181, 183, 256, 266

Radnor., Old &/or New (Radnor.), 260

Radnorshire: accounts for estates in, 230; elections in, 365; other, 238

Radstock, Baron. *See* Waldegrave, William.

Radstoke (Somerset), 67

Radway (Warwicks.), 212, 219, 262

Rae, R. R., 169

Ragdale (Leics.), 112

Railroads: in Australia, 348; in England, 156, 201, 348; in France, 348; in India, 348; in Scotland, 348

Ralegh, Sir Walter, 45, 55, 281, 296, 297

Ramsay, George, 8th Earl of Dalhousie, 329

Ramsey (Hants.), 237

Randolph, Edward, 73, 288

Randolph, Francis, 54

Rant, Felina, 125

Ratby (Leics.), 112

Ratcliffe-upon-Soar (Notts.), 114

Rathmoylan [Rathmullen], (Ireland), 119, 122

Ratisbon, diplomatic reports from, 34

Raton, Agatha, 277

Ravens, Rodolphus, 31

Ravenscroft, Elizabeth. *See* Egerton, Elizabeth (Ravenscroft)

Ravenscroft, William, 74

Ravenstone (Leics.), 98, 112

Rawdon, Sir Arthur, 104, 131

Rawdon, Brilliana, 125

Rawdon, Dorothy, 131

Rawdon, Lady Dorothy (Conway), 131

Rawdon, Elizabeth (Hastings), Countess of Moira & *suo jure* Baroness Hastings, Hungerford, Botreaux, and Moleyns, 80, 92, 128

Rawdon, Sir George, 125, 128, 131

Rawdon, Sir John, 103, 119

Rawdon, John, 1st Earl of Moira, 80, 92, 119, 120, 121, 122, 126, 128, 131–32

Rawdon, Michael, 127

Rawdon, baronetcy of, 132

Rawdon (Yorks.), 101, 117

Rawdon-Hastings [*formerly* Abney-Hastings], Charles Edward, 2nd Baron Donington, 81

Rawdon-Hastings, George Augustus Francis, 2nd Marquis of Hastings, 80, 93, 122, 126

Rawdon-Hastings, Flora (Mure-Campbell), Marchioness of Hastings & *suo jure* Countess of Loudoun, 93, 95 n, 144

Rawdon-Hastings, Lady Flora Elizabeth, 93, 135

Rawdon-Hastings, Francis, 2nd Earl of Moira & 1st Marquis of Hastings, 80, 93, 95 n, 103, 105, 132, 135, 143

Rawdon-Hastings, Henry Weysford Charles Plantagenet, 4th Marquis of Hastings, 80

Rawdon-Hastings, Paulyn Reginald Serlo, 3rd Marquis of Hastings, 80

Rawlins. *See* Woodcote [*alias* Rawlins] (Oxon.)

Rawlinson, Dr., 49

Ray, William, 187

Rayne Parva (Essex), 258

Raynes, Thomas, 209

Raynham (Norfolk), 283

Ré, Isle of, 49, 297

Read, Thomas, 169

Reading (Berks.), 1

Reading, University of, 147

Reay, Baron. *See* Mackay, George

Recipes (medical & culinary), 144, 203, 228, 300

Records (public), *temp.* Elizabeth I and James I, 29

Recusants, 17, 37, 57, 61, 84, 227. *See also* Catholics

Redich, Hugh de, 68

Redmile (Leics.), 98, 112
Redruth (Cornwall), 269
Reeve, Richard, 329
Reeves, Edmund, 169
Reform movements & reformers: anti-slavery, 293, 331; ecclesiastical, 313; social & intellectual, 292, 295; womens suffrage, 295
Refugees, German, 65
Reid, Andrew, 93
Religious dissent, 37, 44, 57, 138–39, 200. *See also* Recusants
Religious tracts & treatises, 31, 48, 55, 139. *See also* Sermons
Remona, ———, 336
Rennell, James, 285
Rennie, Sir John, 348
Rent receipts, 106 n, 176, 178
Rentals & rent rolls, 6–7, 17–18, 27, 35, 46, 47, 54, 60, 67, 107–119 *passim.*, 139, 181–82, 218–19, 237–38
Rents, accounts of. *See under* Accounts
Repton, George Stanley, 349
Repton, Humphry, 349–50
Repton, John Adey, 350
Repton, William, 350
Repton (Derbys.), 96
Repton Charity School, 84, 139–40, 357
Requests, Court of. *See under* Courts
Reservoir Colliery (Derbys.), 120, 123
Retainers: Lord Hastings', 133; Viscount Montague's, 12
Revile & Thorne, 169
Reynold, John, 50, 74
Reynolds, Walter, Abp., 225
Rhetoric, 48
Rhulen (Radnor.), 260
Rich, Robert, 2nd Earl of Warwick, 102
Richard III, King of England, 142, 300
Richard, Duke of York, 9
Richardson, William Madox, 366

Richelieu, Armand Jean du Plessis, Cardinal, 139
Richmond, Duke of. *See* Stuart, Ludovic
Rickett, Thomas, 169
Rickmansworth (Herts.), 75
Ricraft, Josiah, 350
Ridge, John, 93
Ridgeway, Frances (Temple), Countess of Londonderry, 209
Ridgeway, Robert, 4th Earl of Londonderry, 209
Ridgeway, Weston, 1st Earl of Londonderry, 222
Ridgeway, Weston, 3rd Earl of Londonderry, 213
Ridgeway, William, 169
Ridley, Nevile, 93
Ridley (Cheshire), 76
Ridley (Denbigh.), 68, 76
Ridpath, George, 288
Rigaud, Pierre Francois de, Marquis de Vaudreuil-Cavagnal, 276
Riley, Charles, 249
Riley, Edmund, 249
Riley, John, 249
Rimswell (Yorks.), 101
Ringrose, George H., 169
Ringwood (Hants.), 108
Ripley (Hants.), 108
Rippingale (Lincs.), 113
Risdon, Tristram, 350
Risley, Christian (Temple), 209
Risley, John, 209, 215
Risley, William, 358
Ritchmont, Duncan, 329
River (Sussex), 100
Rivers, 19, 141
Rivers, earls, 242
Roads, 123, 141, 272, 273, 346
Robarts, Abraham George, 169, 188
Robarts, John, 74
Robertsbridge (Sussex), 2, 6, 11 (*bis*), 12, 13 (*bis*), 19
Robertson, Duncan, 170
Robertson, John, 329
Robethon, Jean de, 288

Robinson, ——, 315
Robinson, Charles, 336
Robinson, Elizabeth (Drake), 336
Robinson, Emma (Charlton) Cornwallis, 233
Robinson, George, 170
Robinson, Henry, 177, 215
Robinson, Mary (Richardson), 336
Robinson, Matthew, 336
Robinson, Morris, 336
Robinson, Richard, 1st Baron Rokeby, 336
Robinson, Robert, 336
Robinson, Thomas, 336
Robinson, Sir Thomas, 245
Robinson, Sir William, Bart., 336
Robinson, Sir William Rose, 170
Robinson-Morris, Matthew, 2nd Baron Rokeby, 336
Robson, Edward, 170
Robson, John, 170
Robson, Lightfoot & Robson, 154 (*bis*), 156, 170
Rochester, Earl of. *See* Hyde, Laurence
Rochester, recusants in bishopric of, 37
Rock (Worcs.), 262
Rock & Hawkins, Coach builders, 201
Rockford, Katherine, 188
Rockford Moyles (Hants.), 108
Rockingham Forest (Northants.), 39, 114
Rodgers, John, 93
Rodney Stoke (Somerset), 152, 180, 230, 234, 237, 239, 261, 273
Rogers, ——, 170
Rogers, Bridgett, 358
Rogers, Martha, 170
Rogier, Charles, 170
Rohan, Vicomte de. *See* Chabot, Louis William de Rohan
Rokeby, barons. *See* Robinson, Richard; Robinson-Morris, Matthew; Montagu, Matthew
Rolfe, Benjamin, 170

Rolls. *See* Compotus rolls; Court rolls; Homage rolls; Rent rolls; Subsidy rolls; Suit rolls
Roman Britain, 140, 290
Roman Catholic Church. *See* Catholics
Roman coinage, 351
Romney Marsh, 18
Romsey (Hants.), 258
Ronquillo, Don Pedro, 62
Rooke, Sir George, 61, 354
Roper, Anne (Temple), Viscountess Baltinglass, 209, 214, 215
Roper, Thomas, 2nd Viscount Baltinglass, 209, 214, 215, 226
Ropsley (Lincs.), 114
Roscoe, Frank, 277
Rose, Francis, 137
Rose, Henry, 206, 209, 213, 358
Rosenbach, A. S. W., 2, 288, 337
Ross, Lady Anne, 170
Ross, George [Agent for the independent companies in Scotland], 329
Ross, George [of Galstoun, Scotland], 329
Ross, James, 329
Ross, Sir James Clark, 170
Ross, Sir John, 350
Ross, William, 170
Rosse, William, 12th Baron Rosse, 329
Rosslyn, Earl of. *See* Wedderburn, Alexander
Rostherne (Cheshire), 47, 76
Rother river, 19
Rotherby (Leics.), 98, 112
Rothley (Leics.), 113
Rothschild, Baron Ferdinand de, 268
Roundell, H., 170
Rous, Sir John, 209
Rowallan, lairds of, 321
Rowden (Wilts.), 101
Rowe, J. Grindley, 170
Rowell, James, 170
Roxburgh, Jean, 277
Roy, John, 170

Royal African Company, 235, 245
Royal Agricultural Society of England, 170
Royal Geographical Society, 289
Royal Horticultural Society, 289
Royal Irish Academy, Stowe manuscripts in, 147, 253
Royal Society (London), 144, 284
Royle, Peter, 209
Ruabon [Denbigh.], 75
Ruddock, A. B., 313
Rudyerd, Sir Benjamin, 49
Rum production, 245
Rummens, Francis, 170
Russell, Francis, 105
Russell, John, 4th Duke of Bedford, 67
Russell, Rachel. *See* Egerton, Rachel (Russell)
Russell, Lord Wriothesley, 93
Russell, Wriothesley, 2nd Duke of Bedford, 22
Russia: English embassy to (1598), 34; English travellers in, 345; map of, 123; treatise on, 330
Ruthrebrugg Hundred, 8
Rutland, Duke of. *See* Manners, Charles
Rutland, Earl of. *See* Manners, Edward
Rutland: Deputy Lieutenants of, 84, 93; Lords Lieutenant of, 83–84, 86; muster rolls for, 136; other, 84, 115
Rutland Forest, 115
Ryde, ——, 270
Ryde, H. T., 170
Ryder, Sir Dudley, 126
Ryder, Nathaniel, Baron Harrowby, 126

S., J., 48
Sabin, John Edward, 170
Sacheverell, Mary (Hungerford) Hastings, 124
Sackville, Thomas, Baron Buckhurst, *(aftw.)* 1st Earl of Dorset, 41, 43, 73, 74

Sackville, Viscount. *See* Germain, George Sackville
Sadlers Company (Shrewsbury), admissions register of, 354
Sailors, 332
Sainsbury, William, 170
St. Agnes (Cornwall), 257, 269
St. Albans, Viscount. *See* Bacon, Francis,
St. Andre, Nathaniel, 315
St. Austell (Cornwall), 257
St. Christopher's, 252
St. Cleer (Cornwall), 257
St. Clement (Cornwall), 257
St. Columb Major (Cornwall), 257
St. Denis, —— de, 93
St. Erme (Cornwall), 257
St. Erth (Cornwall), 257
St. Ewe (Cornwall), 257
St. George, Oliver, 93
St. Harmon (Radnor.), 260
St. Hilary (Cornwall), 257
St. Issey (Cornwall), 257
St. John, Henry, 1st Viscount Bolingbroke, 237
St. John, Oliver, 102, 140
St. John, Oliver, 1st Viscount Grandison, 131
St. Just in Penwith (Cornwall), 257
St. Just in Roseland (Cornwall), 257
St. Keverne (Cornwall), 257
St. Levan (Cornwall), 257
St. Margaret's (Kent), 258
St. Mawes (Cornwall), 179, 181, 193 *(bis)*, 198, 249, 250, 257, 269
St. Neot (Cornwall), 257
St. Pauls Cathedral. *See* under London
St. Vincent, Earl of. *See* Jervis, John
Salehurst (Sussex), 6
Salford Hundred (Lancs.), 45
Salisbury, John, 35
Salisbury, Sir Robert, 35
Salisbury, Countess of. *See* Pole, Margaret (Plantagenet)
Salisbury, Earl of. *See* Cecil, Robert
Salisbury, Marquis of. *See* Cecil, Robert Arthur Talbot Gascoyne

Salisbury, recusants in bishopric of, 37
Sallord (Radnor.), 260
Salmon, George, 170
Saltford (Somerset), 234, 237, 239, 261
Salueme, Gerard, 44
Salusbury, Thomas, 93
Salzburg, charity for the poor of, 144
Sandars, Charles, 170
Sandars, Francis, 170
Sanden (Berks.), 95
Sanders, Henry, 170
Sandford St. Martin (Oxon.), 259
Sandford Orcas (Somerset), 13
Sandgate (Kent), 270
Sandlake (Sussex). *See* Battle
Sandleford Priory (Berks.), 334
Sandwich, Countess of. *See* Montagu, Dorothy (Fane)
Sandwich, Earl of. *See* Montagu, John
Sandys, Sir Edwin, 31, 137
Sandys, Henry, 209, 220
Sandys, Lady Margaret, 223
Sandys, Miles, 203, 209
Sandys family, 224
Sanitary Law Commission, 289
Saratoga (N.Y.), 344
Sardi, Alessandro, 351
Sark [Serch], island of, 36
Satire. *See* Literature & literary papers
Saul, Thomas, 276
Saunders, James, 170
Saunders, John, 186
Savage, T. W., 170
Savage, Thomas, *styled* Viscount Colchester, 54, 70, 74
Savile, George, 1st Marquis of Halifax, 55
Sawbridge, J. S., 170
Sawyer, Charles J., Ltd., 360
Sayer, Henry, 170
Schalick, John, 301
Scammel, William, 170
Scanderoon, naval battle at, 48

Scargill, John, 93
Scarsdale, Countess of. *See* Leke, Mary Lewis
Scarsdale, Earl of. *See* Leke, Robert
Schevez, Robert, 329
Scholasticism, notes on medieval metaphysics &, 31
Schrader, L. J., 288
Science, Academy of (France), 144
Scientists. *See* Grove, Henry; Beaufort, Sir Francis
Schools & education, 84, 116, 121, 139–40, 178, 190, 200, 289, 352, 357
Scotland: border with England, 36, 84; and Charles I, 52; church in, 139, 200, 223; Commissioners for Treating with England (1640), 50, 52, 74; description & travel, 334; etchings of, 194; Jacobite rebellions in, 322; Parliament of, 198; Privy Council, 329; railroads in, 348; Scott's history of, 351; self-government for, 281; trade & economy of, 228, 289; treatise on, 330; union with England, 32; other, 35–36, 346
Scott, Richard, 347
Scott, Sarah (Robinson), 336
Scott, Thomas, 186
Scott, Sir Walter, 315, 351
Scrope, John, 312
Scudamore family, 242
Seafield, earls of. *See* Ogilvy, James
Seamen: impressed, 61, 64; runaway, 62
Seaports. *See* Ports
Seaton, Jonathan, 177
Secretary at War, William Blathwayt as, 287
Secretary for War, Sir George Yonge as, 365
Secretary of State: William Blathwayt as, 287–88; George Grenville as, 149; Thomas Townshend as, 359. *See also* Foreign Secretary; Home Secretary
Sedgmoor (Somerset), 67

Sedlescombe (Sussex), 6
Seeley, John, 254
Segrave, A., 93
Segrave, Charles, 93
Seisdon Hundred (Staffs.), 69
Selby, Thomas James, 186
Selden, John, 29, 40, 48, 351
Sellick, Thomas, 170
Selwin, Charles, 93
Sendaye, Arthur, 31
Sennen (Cornwall), 257
Sergeante, Peter, 27
Serle, Ambrose, 351
Serlethorpe (Leics.), 98
Sermons, 31, 48–49, 54, 55, 59, 69, 138–39, 200, 227, 299, 318
Servants. *See under* Households (private); Wages
Seton, James, 329
Seven Years War, 191, 275, 291, 334
Sewell, Stephen John, 93
Sewers, bill re, 45
Seymour, Charles, 6th Duke of Somerset, 240
Seymour, Edward, Duke of Somerset, 32
Shackerstone (Leics.), 98
Shackleton, Abraham, 352
Shackleton, Elizabeth (Carleton), 352
Shackleton, Richard, 352
Shaftesbury, Earl of. *See* Cooper, Anthony Ashley
Shailer, T. H., 170
Shakerly, Alice, 222
Shalford (Essex), 258
Shalstone (Bucks.), 211, 256, 266, 271
Shannon, Charles Haselwood, 353
Sharp, Bartholomew, 310
Sharp, John, 57
Sharpe, J. C., 353
Sharpe, John, 93
Shaw, Sa., 93
Shaw, Tobias, 31
Shaw (Berks.), 236, 255
Shawe, John, 31
Sheep, sales of, 206
Sheepshed (Leics.), 98

Sheeron, John, 93
Sheffield, John, 1st Duke of Buckingham & Normanby, 63
Sheffield, Ursula (Stawell) Conway, Countess Conway & Marchioness of Normanby, 104
Shefford, John D., 170
Shelburne, Earl of. *See* Petty, Henry
Shelburne, Countess of. *See* Petty, Sophia (Carteret)
Sheldon, Gilbert, 131
Shelton (Leics.), 112
Shenley (Herts.), 108
Sheppeard, Mary, 185
Shepperd, Samuel, 170
Shepton Montague (Somerset.), 115
Sherbrooke, Sir John, 308
Sheridan, Richard Brinsley, 197
Sheriff Hutton (Yorks.), 101
Sheriffs: of Buckinghamshire, 208, 225, 227; of Essex, 20; in Welsh Marches, 51, 69; other, 44, 69
Sherington, Francis, 42
Sherington, Gilbert, 70, 74
Sherington family, 70
Sherwood Forest (Notts.), 115
Ship Money, 50, 52, 140–41, 208, 227–28, 306
Shipping, 13, 287, 332
Ships:
—design & building of, 301, 316
—lists & registers of, 50, 57, 136, 192
—of Royal Navy: "Aldborough," 342; "Aquilon," 283; "Bacchante," 318; "Blossom," 284; "Bridgewater," 342; "Burford," 342; "Canterbury," 342; "Cumberland," 343; "Fredericksteen," 284; "Lancaster," 337; "Latona," 283; "Namur," 342; "Peacock," 317; "Peloris," 318; "Phaeton," 283; "Prince George," 364; "Proserpine," 302; "Raleigh," 318; "Renown," 364; "Romney," 342; "St. Michael," 337; "Shrewsbury," 342; "Suth-

erland," 342; "Theseus," 355; "Tigre," 355; "Tromp," 318; "Victory," 337; "Woolwich" 283, 342
—of U.S. Navy, "Hornet," 317
—other: "Anna Eliza," 175; "Fortune," 355; "Friendship" of Bristol, 320; "Isabella," 350; "Katherine" of Bristol, 320; "Michael" of Bristol, 320; "Red Dragon," 349; "Victory," 351
Shipton-under-Wychwood (Oxon.), 259
Shirley, Sir Henry, 104
Shirley, Laurence, 93, 126
Shirley, Lewis, 93
Shirley, Mary (Levinge), Countess Ferrers, 93
Shirley, Sir Robert, 102
Shirley, Robert, 1st Earl Ferrers, 93, 134
Shirley, Washington, 2nd Earl Ferrers, 80, 103
Shirley family, 82, 84
Shotesham (Norfolk), 114
Shovell, Sir Clowdisley, 354
Shrewsbury, earls of. *See* Talbot, Francis; Talbot, George
Shrewsbury (Salop.), Sadlers Company of, 354
Shropshire: deeds for lands in, 77; election in, 346; Grand Jury for, 74; musters in, 52; Ship Money collected in, 50; other, 115
Shucklow (Bucks.), 183
Shute, Josiah, 49
Shuttleworth, Richard, 187
Shyrley, Anthony, 223
Sibbertoft (Northants.), 99
Sible Hedingham (Essex), 258
Sidney, Sir Philip, 29, 296, 333
Sierra Leone Colony, 293, 331
Signal books (naval), 306–07, 316
Sileby (Leics.), 98
Silverstone (Northants.), 211, 217, 259, 271
Simcoe, John Graves, 354
Simmons, J. Lintern, 170

Simmons, John, 170
Simmons, Joseph, 125
Simony, 37
Sinclair, Sir John, 1st Bart., 347
Sinfin (Derbys.), 107, 120
Singapore, inhabitants of, 143
Sithians (Cornwall), 257
Skeffington, Sir John, 131
Sketches. *See* Drawings & sketches
Skinner, Vincent, 40
Skirbeck (Lincs.), 75, 77
Skynner, Dr., 49
Slaley (Northumb.), 99
Slaney, Humphrey, 50
Slavery & slave trade: abolition of, 293, 331; in West Indies, 202, 245, 252; other, 287
Sligo, Co. (Ireland), 119
Slingsby, Sir Henry, 355
Slingsby (Yorks.), 117
Small, Edward H., 170
Small, Henry, 170
Smallman, R., 93
Smart, Ithiel, 93
Smelt, Leonard, 336
Smisby (Derbys.), 96, 107
Smith, Aaron, 143
Smith, Adam, 329
Smith, Elizabeth, 186
Smith, George D., 24, 315
Smith, Gerrit, 293
Smith, Henry [fl. >1704], 185
Smith, Henry [fl. 1840–66], 171
Smith, Hugh, 131
Smith, John, 63
Smith, John Spencer, 355
Smith, Kenelm, 214
Smith, Peter, 138
Smith, Sir Robert, 12
Smith, Thomas [fl. >1781, salt-carrier of Packington], 126
Smith, Thomas [fl. 1806–07, in Royal Navy], 171
Smith, Thomas H., 171
Smith, William, 329
Smith, William Edward, 93
Smith, William James, 171
Smith, Sir William Sidney, 355–56

Smith & Mammatt, 93
Smith, Mammatt & Hale, 93
Smith & Roberts, 171
Smith & Small, 171
Smith & Son, 171
Smithfield Club, 171
Smithsby, J., 93
Smuggling, 346
Smythe, Emily Anne (Beaufort), Viscountess Strangford, 284, 285
Snape, 46
Snee, Edmund, 171
Snigg, Sir George, 36
Snufnall (Salop.). *See* Idsall [*alias* Snufnall]
Society for the Promotion of Christian Knowledge [SPCK], 144, 174, 191
Society of Friends, 139
Solemn League & Covenant, 52, 228
Solicitor-General, 21, 305
Somerford (Hants.), 108
Somerford (Wilts.), 116
Somerset, Elizabeth (Berkeley), Duchess of Beaufort & *suo jure* Baroness Botetourt, 336
Somerset, dukes of. *See* Seymour, Edward; Seymour, Charles
Somerset, Earl of. *See* Carr, Robert
Somerset: accounts for estates in, 152, 230; concealed lands in, 68; deeds for lands in, 13, 77, 100, 233–34, 260–61; maps for lands in, 272–74; other, 115, 180, 219, 236–37, 238–39
Somerton (Somerset), 100, 115
Sommers, H., 15
Somodevilla y Bengoechea, Zeno de, Marques de la Ensenada, 93
Sondes, Anthony, 222
Sondes, Thomas, 220
Sopwith, Thomas, 348
Sorn Castle (Ayrshire), 323, 329
Sothebys of London, 24, 330, 345, 350, 352, 358
Sotheran & Co., 342
South America, sea coasts of, 309

South Pool (Devon), 97
South Sea Company, 11, 245, 246
Southam, John, 171
Southampton, Earl of. *See* Wriothesley, Henry
Southampton (Hants.), 236, 237
Southee, Robert, 171
Southern, James, 69
Southwark (Surrey), 261
Spa (Belgium), description of, 334
Spain: British forces in, 244, 363; British merchants in, 287; relations with Great Britain, 33–34, 41, 56, 314, 361; in West Indies, 34
Spanish Succession, War of the, 232
Sparke, Noel, 74
Sparkenhoe Hundred (Leics.), 112
Spearman, Alexander Young, 303
Spectres, treatise on, 31
Speen (Berks.), 255
Speidell, John, 31, 140
Spence, John, 171
Spencer, E., 35
Spencer, Sir Edward, 74
Spencer, Giles, 213, 220
Spencer, George John, 2nd Earl Spencer, 171
Spencer, Herbert, 295
Spencer, Sir Robert, 125
Spencer, Robert, 1st Baron Spencer of Wormleighton, 46, 212
Spencer, Thomas, 203
Spencer family, 28, 224
Spencer-Churchill, John, 7th Duke of Marlborough, 263
Spenser, Edmund, 51
Spooner, Catherine, 126
Spottiswood, James, Bp., 280
Spratley, Thomas, 213
Stackhouse, John, 191
Stael-Holstein, Baron Auguste Louis, 332
Stafford, Edward, 3rd Duke of Buckingham, 78
Stafford, Henry, 1st Baron Stafford, 356

Stafford, Henry, Duke of Buckingham, 9
Stafford, Marquis of. *See* Leveson-Gower, Granville, 1st Marquis of Stafford
Stafford (Staffs.), 116
Staffordshire: deeds for lands in: 77, 100, 173; other, 68, 116, 181
Stair, Countess of. *See* Dalrymple, Eleanor (Campbell) Primrose
Stair, earls of. *See* Dalrymple, John; Dalrymple-Crichton, William
Stamford, Heinrich Wilhelm von, 171
Stamford, Earl of. *See* Grey, Henry
Stamp Act, 308–09
Standbridge & Kaye, 171
Stanford Rivers (Essex), 17, 18
Stanforde, Sir William, 40
Stanhope, Arthur, 93
Stanhope, Charles [fl. 1655–1712, of Mansfield Woodhouse, Notts.], 93
Stanhope, Charles [d. 1759, son of the above], 93
Stanhope, Charles [1673–1760, Secretary of the Treasury], 94
Stanhope, Edward, 74
Stanhope, George, 6th Earl of Chesterfield, 268
Stanhope, Sir Henry Edwyn, 356
Stanhope, James Hamilton, 171
Stanhope, John, 131
Stanhope, Philip, 1st Earl of Chesterfield, 94, 140
Stanhope, Philip, 2nd Earl of Chesterfield, 140
Stanhope, Philip Dormer, 4th Earl of Chesterfield, 94, 356
Stanhope, Philip, 5th Earl of Chesterfield, 94
Stanhope, Thomas, 131
Stanley, Alice (Spencer), Countess of Derby. *See* Egerton, Alice (Spencer) Stanley
Stanley, Anne (Hastings), Countess of Derby, 124
Stanley, Arthur Penryn, 295

Stanley, Edward, 3rd Earl of Derby, 28
Stanley, Elizabeth. *See* Hastings, Elizabeth (Stanley)
Stanley, Ferdinando, 5th Earl of Derby, 27, 28, 79
Stanley, Lady Frances, 49
Stanley, Hans, 94
Stanley, Henry, 56
Stanley, Henry, 4th Earl of Derby, 47, 74
Stanley, Peter, 35
Stanley, Sarah (Sloane), 336
Stanley, Thomas, 2nd Earl of Derby, 28
Stanley, William, 6th Earl of Derby, 27
Stanley family, 27–28, 242
Stanley (Bucks.), 180
Stanmore, Great &/or Little (Middlesex), 179, 181, 229, 236, 237, 238, 259
Stannary Parliament, 300
Stansby, James W., 171
Stanton under Bardon (Leics.), 112
Stantonbury (Bucks.), 218, 256
Stanwix, John, 276
Staple Hundred, 8
Staples, Abel, 171
Star Chamber. *See under* Courts
Starkey, Ralphe, 29
Statues, list of, 144
Statute books, 29, 30, 113
Staveley, Christian, 94
Staveley, William, 94
Stebyn, Thomas, 10
Steeple Barton (Oxon.), 259
Steeple Claydon (Bucks.), 183
Stephen, James, 332
Stephen, Sir James, 332
Stephens, Simon, 9
Stephenson, Robert, 348
Stepney (Middlesex), 259
Stevens, Mrs. Norman F., 292
Stevens, William, 221
Stevens, William Bagshaw, 357
Stevenson, John, 329
Stewart, Robert, 171

Stewart, Sir William James, 329
Stilgoe, Nathaniel, 271
Stillingfleet, Benjamin, 336
Stillingfleet, J., 12
Stillingfleet, John, 94
Stockholt (Bucks.). *See* Akeley cum Stockholt
Stockingford (Warwicks.), 219
Stockland Bristol (Somerset), 261
Stockley Park (Staffs.), 116
Stogursey (Somerset), 180, 261, 274
Stoke, South (Oxon.), 259
Stoke Albany (Northants.), 99
Stoke Mandeville (Bucks.), 256, 266
Stoke Poges (Bucks.), 84, 96, 106
Stokenham (Devon.), 97, 107
Stokes, William, 125
Stone, Edward [fl. >1644], 185
Stone, Edward [fl. 1844–68], 171
Stoneferry (Yorks.), 101
Stoneham (Hants.), 258
Stoney Stanton (Leics.), 98, 112
Stoney Stratford (Bucks.), 183
Stony Middleton (Derbys.), 257
Storthwaite (Yorks.), 117
Stoughton, Thomas, 94
Stoughton (Leics.), 99
Stow, John, 357
Stowe [estate] (Bucks.), 151–54 *passim.*, 178, 194–218 *passim.*, 256, 266, 358
Stowe [parish] (Bucks.): churchwardens of, 216; parish registers for, 216; vicar of, 215
Stowe Clothing Club, 154
Stowe School, 154, 201
Stowey (Somerset), 261
Strafford, Countess of. *See* Wentworth, Anne (Johnson)
Strafford, Earl of. *See* Wentworth, Thomas
Strange, barons, 64, 132, 243
Strangford, Viscountess. *See* Smythe, Emily Anne (Beaufort)
Stratford, George, 222
Stratford Lodge, 266
Stratford de Redcliffe, Viscount. *See* Canning, Stratford

Stretton Dunsmore (Warwicks.), 212
Stringston (Somerset), 261
Strongfleete, Cuthbert, 45
Stuart, Andrew, 347
Stuart, John, 329
Stuart, John, 3rd Earl of Bute, 329
Stuart, Ludovic, 2nd Duke of Lennox & 1st Duke of Richmond, 209
Stuart, Sophia Frederica Christina (Rawdon-Hastings), Marchioness of Bute, 94
Stuart & Maxwell, 171
Stuberg, Svend Peter, 352
Sturge, Joseph, 293
Sturt, Charles, 94
Styford (Northumb.), 99
Subsidies, 8, 38, 50, 58, 72, 88. *See also* Taxes & taxation
Subsidy rolls, 38
Suffolk, Countess of. *See* Howard, Henrietta (Hobart)
Suffolk, dukes of, 132. *See also* Pole, William de la
Suffrage, women's, 295
Sugar production, 202, 245, 252
Suit rolls, 106 n, 109, 110, 112
Sulby (Northants.), 114
Summers, H., 15 *(bis)*
Sumptuary legislation, 28, 39, 45
Sundials, 55–56
Surrey, Earl of. *See* Howard, Henry
Surrey: deeds for lands in, 261; other, 7
Surveys (estate), 7, 17, 18, 108–19 *passim.*, 219, 239
Sussex, Duke of. *See* Augustus Frederick
Sussex: commission of array in, 10; concealed lands in, 68; deeds for lands in, 6, 13, 100, 173, 261; elections in, 193; other, 7, 11–12, 15–17, 47, 116, 193, 238, 250
Sussex Record Office, *See* East Sussex Record Office
Sutherland, John, 329
Sutherland, Patrick, 329

Sutherland, William, 17th Earl of Sutherland, 329
Sutherland, Duke of. *See* Leveson-Gower, George Granville
Sutherland Fencible Regiment, returns for, 66
Sutton, Henry, 273
Sutton (Norfolk), 99
Sutton (Notts.), 99
Sutton (Yorks.), 101
Sutton Bonnington (Notts.), 99
Sutton Maddock (Warwicks.), 75
Suttons Hospital (Charterhouse), 66
Swannington (Leics.), 99, 112
Swans, royal, 144, 279
Swanton, John, 8
Swarkestone (Derbys.), 96
Sweden, English trade in, 56
Sweet & Sutton, 171
Sweete, Walter, 185
Swinham (Dorset), 17
Swinton (Lancs.), 77
Swithland (Leics.), 113
Switzerland, map of, 123
Sybthorpe, Robert, 209
Sydney, Viscount. *See* Townshend, Thomas
Symes, Thomas [fl. 1665–67], 131
Symes, Thomas [fl. 1826–38], 171
Syresham (Northants.), 114, 179, 211, 259

Tacitus, 48
Talbot, Lady Barbara (Slingsby), 355
Talbot, Francis, 5th Earl of Shrewsbury, 357
Talbot, George, 6th Earl of Shrewsbury, 357
Talbot, James, 3rd Baron Talbot of Malahide, 171
Talbot, Mary (de Cardonnel), Countess Talbot, 336
Tamworth (Staffs.), 116
Tangiers, 56, 136
Tapestries, list of at Loudoun Castle, 103

Tarrant Grenville (Dorset), 179
Tarrant Launceston (Dorset), 179
Tarrant Monkton (Dorset), 179
Tarrant Rushton (Dorset), 179
Tatham, Thomas James, 171
Tatton (Cheshire), 26, 76
Taxes & taxation: clerical, 113; land, 11, 110, 111, 114, 118, 134, 182, 230; poem on, 134; poll, 134; receipts for payments of, 12, 18, 106, 176; other, 38, 50, 68, 106, 208, 287. *See also* Subsidies
Taylor, J. [fl. 1653], 18
Taylor, J. [fl. 1687–90], 210
Taylor, John, 186
Taylor, Robert, 292
Taylor, William, 171
Taymouth Castle (Scotland), 174, 175, 274
Teffont Evias (Wilts.), 101
Temple, Sir Alexander, 222
Temple, Anne (Halsey), Viscountess Cobham, 205, 221
Temple, Anne (Throckmorton), 204
Temple, Anne Sophia, 222
Temple, Anthony, 212
Temple, Christian (Leveson), Lady, 204, 213, 214, 221
Temple, Dorothy, 222
Temple, Elizabeth, 213, 222 *(bis)*
Temple, Frances, 222
Temple, Hester (Sandys), Lady, 203, 210, 212, 213, 214, 221, 357–58
Temple, John [1542–1603], 203, 206, 210, 212, 214, 220, 221
Temple, John [fl. >1632, brother of Sir Thomas Temple?], 220
Temple, John [fl. 1635–72, brother of Sir Richard Temple], 210
Temple, Sir John, 210
Temple, Katherine (Kendall), 358
Temple, Martha, 109
Temple, Maria, 222
Temple, Mary (Knapp), Lady, 204, 210
Temple, Miles, 210

Temple, Millicent, 212, 220
Temple, Nicholas, 221
Temple, Peter [d. 1578], 203, 206, 210, 214, 220, 223
Temple, Peter [1589–1657], 214
Temple, Sir Peter, 2nd Bart., 204, 206, 210–16 *passim.*, 221–27 *passim.*, 267
Temple, Sir Purbeck, 210
Temple, Sir Richard, 3rd Bart., 204–15 *passim.*, 221–27 *passim.*
Temple, Sir Richard, 7th Bart., 222
Temple, Richard, Viscount Cobham, 148, 181, 204–10 *passim.*, 221–26 *passim.*
Temple, Robert, 212, 220
Temple, Susan (Spencer), 203, 220
Temple, Thomas [b. 1604, son of Sir Thomas Temple], 210
Temple, Thomas [fl. 1673–89, surveyor of port of Weymouth], 210, 213
Temple, Sir Thomas, 1st Bart., 203, 206, 210, 213, 214, 215, 220, 223, 225, 357
Temple, William [d. >1706], 210, 221
Temple, countesses. *See* Grenville, Hester (Temple); Grenville-Temple, Anne (Chambers)
Temple, Earl. *See* Grenville-Temple, Richard
Temple-Nugent-Brydges-Chandos-Grenville, Richard. *See under* Grenville, Richard . . .
Tenison, Thomas, Abp., 302–03
Tennant family, 194
Terriers, 18
Terry, E., 171
Terry, E. & Son, 171
Terry, John, 171
Teversham (Cambs.), 96
Tew, Great &/or Little (Oxon.), 259
Teysdey, Thomas, 138
Thacker, Godfrey, 94
Thatcham (Berks.), 237
Thatcher, Abraham, 14
Thatcher, Ninian, 14

Theale Hundred (Berks.), 106
Theater (English), 314, 317, 319
Thicknesse, Ann (Ford), 359
Thicknesse, Elizabeth (Touchet), 359
Thicknesse, Maria (Lanove), 359
Thicknesse, Philip, 358–59
Thirty Years War, account of a battle in, 136
Thistlethwaite, Robert, 240
Thistlethwaite family, 239
Thomas, Sir Edmond, 15
Thompson, Henry Yates, 281
Thornborough (Bucks.), 178, 211, 216, 218 *(bis)*, 256, 267
Thornbrough, Sir Edward, 171
Thorne, Peregrine Francis, 347
Thornham (Norfolk), 259
Thornton, Thomas, 210
Thornton (Bucks.), 211, 256
Thornton (Leics.), 99
Thornton Dale (Yorks.), 101
Thorp Arch (Yorks.), 117
Thorpe, Henry, 171
Thorpe, Thomas, 2
Thoulstone (Wilts.), 101
Thringstone (Leics.), 99, 113
Throckmorton, Anne, 222
Throckmorton, Lady Anne (Lucas), 220
Throckmorton, Air Arthur, 220
Throckmorton, Mary, 188
Throckmorton, Sir Robert, 74
Thrussington (Leics.), 113
Thurlow, William, 171
Thynne, Francis, 29, 30 *(ter)*, 74
Tibbets, T., 74
Tibbetts, William Holliday, 171
Tidcombe, John, 94
Tildisley, Thurstan, 70
Tildisley family, 70
Tilehurst (Berks.), 106
Tillotson, John, Abp., 299
Tilston (Cheshire), 76
Tindal, Acton, 171
Tindal, Thomas, 171
Tindal & Baynes, 171

Tingewick (Bucks.), 178, 216, 256, 267
Tithe books, 12, 109
Tithes, 14, 47, 109, 113, 163, 196, 214
Tiverton (Somerset), 234, 239, 261
Tobago (West Indies), government & politics of, 346
Tods, Murray & Jamieson, 171
Tofino de San Miguel, Vincent, 123
Tolcarne (Cornwall), 179, 257, 269
Tomkins family, 191
Tomkinson, James, 233
Tomlinson, Josiah, 14
Tonge (Leics.), 99, 109
Tonyn, Patrick, 366
Toogood, William, 171
Topsell, Edward, 31
Torpurley (Cheshire), 76
Touchet family, 132
Touloun (France), 122
Tourneur, Timothy, 74
Tourville, ——, 347
Towcester (Northants.), 259
Tower of London, 44, 362
"Town and gown" disputes, 36
Townesend, George, 94
Townhill (Hants.), 237
Towns, list of in Bucks., 58.
Townsend, Samuell, 366
Townshend, George, 1st Marquis of Townshend, 329, 342
Townshend, Thomas, 198
Townshend, Thomas, 1st Viscount Sydney, 67, 359–60
Townshend family, 283
Traballefi, Jo. Gaetano, 144
Tracy, Paule, 210
Trade. *See under* Great Britain
Trade, Board of. *See* Board of Trade
Tradesmen, accounts with, 65, 230, 311, 358
Trafalgar, battle of, 338
Trammont (Ireland), 122
Transportation, 141–42, 201, 346, 348. *See also* Railroads; Roads
Travel journals 189–90, 191, 284, 302, 320, 350

Treaga [?Treagoe] (Cornwall), 218
Treasury, 163, 312. *See also* Exchequer
Tregair (Cornwall), 218
Tregavethan (Cornwall), 179, 211, 218, 269
Treherne, ——, 39
Treleven (Cornwall), 179
Trengoff (Cornwall), 107
Trent river, 122, 141
Trevecka College, Cambridge, 81
Trevelyan, Sir Charles Edward, 331
Trevelyan, Hannah More (Macaulay), Lady, 331, 332
Trevigowe (Cornwall), 107
Trewern (Radnor.), 260
Treyage (Cornwall), 257
Triennial Bill, 63
Trimleston, Baron. *See* Barnewall, Robert
Trinidad, treatise on, 330
Troy, John Thomas, Abp., 254
Truro (Cornwall), 250, 257
Truss, Thomas, 171
Tryvet, Nicholas, 29
"Ttesremos," Mr., 28
Tucker, Benjamin, 171
Tuder, William, 186
Tuite, James, 248
Tull, Susannah, 186
Tunbridge Wells (Kent), social life at, 334
Tunstall (Yorks.), 101
Turin, British chargé d'affaires at, 296
Turkey: description & travel, 284; relations with England, 364
Turkish language, documents in, 203
Turner, John, 210
Turner, W. J., 272
Turnpikes. *See* Roads
Tutbury (Staffs.), 100, 116
Tuxford & Sons, 172
Tweedy, Henry, 34, 74
Twisleton family, 242
Tylee, Edward, 94
Tyler, Francis Henry, 94

Tyley, Charles, 172
Typhus fever, in Ireland, 318
Tyrawley, Baron. *See* O'Hara, James
Tyrell, Sir Edward, 1st Bart., 210
Tyringham (Bucks.), 256
Tyrone, Co. (Ireland), 102, 119
Tytherington (Wilts.), 101
Tywardreath (Cornwall), 257

Udimer, 11
Ulster (Ireland): defense of, 20; land papers re, 250; Plantation of, 35, 50, 129
Uniforms (military), 283
Union Lodge Farm, 121
United Service Club, 270
United States: Abolitionist movement in, 293; Army of, 278; government of by England in Colonial period, 61–62, 84, 131, 155, 275, 305, 308–09, 321; Navy of, 301; privateers of, in Mediterranean, 296; railroads in, 348; Revolutionary War, 84, 132, 296, 304, 318, 332, 344, 346, 351, 354, 359; Society of Friends in, 352; War of 1812, 291, 301, 317. *See also under* names of individual states, e.g., California, Florida, New York
Universities, 36, 105, 235. *See also* Cambridge; Oxford
Uny Lelant (Cornwall), 96
Upton (Wilts.), 101
Upton Scudamore (Wilts.), 101, 116
Ure, Masterton, 347
Urren, Edward S., 172
Ussher, James, Abp., 131, 299
Usury, treatise on, 38, 301
Uthwatt, E. A., 172
Uthwatt, Richard, 188

Vallancey, Charles, 254
Valors, 118
Vanbrugh, Philip, 344
Vane, Charles William, 3rd Marquis of Londonderry, 172

Vane, Henry, 2nd Earl of Darlington, 348
Vane, Lucy (Jolliffe), Viscountess Vane, 94
Vanhattem, John, 234
Varcoe, Henry, 172
Varney, L., 199
Vaudreuil-Cavagnal, Marquis de. *See* Rigaud, Pierre Francois
Vaughan, Richard, 2nd Earl of Carbury, 54, 55, 74
Vaughan v. *Vaughan,* 51
Vaux, Edward, 4th Baron Vaux, 222
Vaynol estate (Caernarvons.), 60
Veaitch, Charles, 329
Venables, Catherine (Shirley), 94
Vanables, Peter, 125
Venables, Thomas, 74
Venice: British diplomats at, 67, 208; naval battle with England, 48
Vennor, Henry George, 290, 291
Vere, Edward de, 17th Earl of Oxford, 38, 71
Vere, Elizabeth (Trussell) de, Countess of Oxford, 117
Vere, John de, 13th Earl of Oxford, 10
Verney, Sir Harry, 2nd Bart., 172
Vernon, G. C., 172
Vernon, George, 94
Vernye, Sir Raphe, 210
Verse. *See* Literature & literary papers
Veryan (Cornwall), 257
Vesey, Elizabeth (Vesey) Handcock, 336
Veterinary medicine. *See under* Medicine
Viccars, Richard, 172
Victoria, Queen of England, 290, 360–61
Vienna: British ambassador at, 318; diplomatic reports from, 34
Villiers, George, 1st Duke of Buckingham, 74, 137, 210, 225, 298, 361
Villiers, George William Frederick, 4th Earl of Clarendon, 289

Villiers, William, 3rd Earl of Jersey, 186
Villiers (Co. Leix), 238
Villierstown (Co. Waterford), 238
Virginia, British investments in, 131
Virginia Company of London, 131
Visitations, episcopal, 8
Volcanoes, 310

W., W., etchings of Scotland by, 194
Waad, Sir William, 227
Waddesdon (Bucks.), 178, 256, 267
Wade, George, 94, 329
Wager, Sir Charles, 344
Wages: of estate labourers, 11, 82, 151, 153, 205, 230; of household servants, 47, 59, 82, 153–54, 230–31; of naval officers, 57
Wagner, Henry, 285
Waie, Elizabeth, 14
Wake, Johanna, 126
Wake, William, Abp., 20
Waldegrave, George, 5th Earl Waldegrave, 67
Waldegrave, Sir William, 208
Waldegrave, William, 1st Baron Radstock, 172
Waldegrave, Lady, 67
Wales: Council in the Marches of, 35, 51, 69, 72, 115; courts & legal matters in, 35, 51, 58; Egerton family lands in, 68; Herbert family lands in, 46; patronage in, 51; sheriffs in, 51, 69; other, 333
Walford, W., 172
Walker, Catherine, 329
Walker, Sir Edward, 361
Walker, George, 102
Walker, John, 105
Walker, Joseph Cooper, 254
Walkington (Yorks.), 101
Walkinshaw, Catherine, 94
Wallace, Charles William, 314
Waller, Elizabeth (Hogan), 214
Waller, John, 5
Waller, Thomas, 214
Wallingford, Viscountess. *See* Knollys, Mary (Law)

Wallis, John, 123
Wallop, Nether (Hants.), 258
Walpole, Robert, 285
Walrond, Edward, 74
Walsingham, Sir Francis, 33, 34, 39, 44, 74, 94, 362
Walter, James, 240
Walton, Sir George, 344
Wanting (Berks.), 60
Wappenbury (Warwicks.), 212
Wappenham (Northants.), 211, 259
War, Secretary at. *See* Secretary at War
War Office, 88, 163
War of 1812, 291, 301, 317
Warburton, Elizabeth, 46
Warburton, Peter, 46
Ward, Mary Augusta (Arnold), 295
Ward, Nicholas, 2nd Viscount Bangor, 105
Ward, Robert Palmer, 172
Warder, Chidiocke, 40, 74
Wardley Hall (Lancs.), 69
Wards and Liveries, Court of. *See under* Courts
Wards and wardships, 9, 15, 46
Ware, John, 186
Ware (Herts.), 97, 108
Warminster (Wilts.), 101
Warner, W. P., 172
Warren, Ambrose, 220
Warren, Sir John Borlase, Bart., 172
Wartter, William, 185
Warwick, Sir Philip, 362
Warwick, earls of. *See* Dudley, Ambrose; Rich, Robert
Warwickshire: accounts for estates in, 152; deeds for land in, 77, 100, 173, 212, 261–62; elections in, 224; maps of estates in, 274; other, 68, 116, 180, 217, 218, 219, 250
Wasey, William George, 344
Wasse (Yorks.), 212
Water Eaton (Oxon.), 106, 211, 217, 259
Water Stratford (Bucks.), 211, 256
Waterhouse, Noble, 210
Waterton, Thomas, 127

Waterworks, 19, 63
Watford (Herts.), 75
Watkins, Hooper, Baylis & Baker, 172
Watson, Thomas, Bp., 94
Wattell, T., 18
Wattlesworth, 18
Wauldby (Yorks.), 101
Webb, D. H., 172
Webb, John, 74
Webb, Mary, 212
Webb, Robert, 172
Webb, Thomas, 212
Webster, George, 19
Webster, Godfrey, 11, 15, 20
Webster, Sir Godfrey, 5th Bart., 2
Webster, Hugh, 19
Webster, J., 94
Webster, Jane, Lady, 2, 15, 20
Webster, John, 19
Webster, T., 14
Webster, Sir Thomas, 1st Bart., 2, 10–19 *passim.*
Webster, Sir Whistler, 2nd Bart., 2, 11–19 *passim.*
Webster, William, 19
Webster family, 19
Wedderburn, Alexander, 1st Earl of Rosslyn, 94
Wedderburn, Sir John, 6th Bart., 348
Wedmore (Somerset), 234, 238, 261
Weedon, John, 172
Weedon (Bucks.), 178, 181, 263, 267
Welbeck (Notts.), 115
Welford (Northants.), 99
Wellesbourne (Warwicks.), 250
Wellesley, Arthur, 1st Duke of Wellington, 172, 362–63
Wellesley, Richard, Marquis Wellesley of Norragh, 172, 364
Wellington, 1st Duke of. *See* Wellesley, Arthur
Wellow (Somerset), 115
Wellow, East (Hants.), 233, 236, 238, 258
Wellow, West (Wilts.), 237, 238, 262
Wells, Thomas, 172

Wells (Somerset), 261
Wells Close Square [Marine Square] (Middlesex), 67
Wellsebourne (Warwicks.), 250
Welsh, Jean, 329
Wembdon (Somerset), 261, 273
Wendover (Bucks.), 256
Wenlock, William, 74
Wentworth, Anne (Johnson), Countess of Strafford, 94
Wentworth, Benning, 276
Wentworth, Hugh, 329
Wentworth, Thomas, 53
Wentworth, Thomas, 1st Earl of Strafford, 49, 50–51
Wertlesham, John de, 7
West, Catherine (Bartlett), 336
West, Gilbert, 336
West, Richard, 222
West Florida, boundary of, 305
West Ham (Essex), 258
West Indies: British forces in, 301, 333, 343, 344; British government in, 61, 155, 252, 287; Brydges family interests in, 244–45; Grenville family interests in, 202; immigration to, 202; plantations in, 202, 244–45; slavery in, 202, 245, 252; Spain in, 34; voyage to, 320. *See also:* Jamaica; Leeward Islands; St. Christopher's; Tobago
West Kirby (Cheshire), 76
West Meath, Co. (Ireland), 119, 180, 248, 250, 262
Westbury (Bucks.), 178, 181, 211, 216, 218, 256, 267
Westbury (Somerset), 180, 238, 261
Westcott (Bucks.), 178, 256, 267
Westcott Barton (Oxon.), 259
Westham (Sussex), 6
Westmeath, Earl of. *See* Nugent, Thomas
Westmeath, Marquis of. *See* Nugent, George Thomas John
Westminster: elections at (1784), 307; vestry meetings in, 63
Westmoreland, 77

Weston Turville (Bucks.), 178, 256, 266 *(bis)*
Wethered, Owen Peel, 172
Wethered, Thomas & Sons, 172
Wethersfield (Essex), 258
Wettenhall, William, 27
Wexford, Co. (Ireland), 119
Whatley, Thomas, 172
Whatlington (Sussex), 6, 7, 8, 9
Whatton (Notts.), 115
Wheldale (Yorks.), 117
Wheler, Lady Catherine Maria (Hastings), 94
Wheler, Granville, 94
Wheler, Granville Hastings, 126
Whigs, history of, 225
Whistler, Gabriel, 20
Whistler, Henry, 2, 11, 14, 15, 19
Whistler, Mary, 11, 20
Whitbe, Thomas, 74
Whitchurch (Salop.), 66, 75
White, Archibald, 172
White, H. V., 120
White, Ignatius, Marquis de Albeville, 251
White, Thomas, 58
White Plains, battle of, 132
Whitefoord, Allan, 329
Whitefoord, Sir John, 2nd Bart., 330
Whithorn Priory (Scotland), 27, 77
Whitney, James, 172
Whittlebury (Northants.), 211, 259, 271, 311
Whittlebury Forest (Northants.), 312
Whitton, William, 172
Whitwick (Leics.), 99, 109, 113
Whitworth, Charles, Earl Whitworth, 172
Wicklow, Co. (Ireland), 119
Widdrington, Robert, 349
Wigg, Joan, 185
Wight, Isle of (Hants.), 237
Wigston Magna (Leics.), 113
Wike (Yorks.), 117
Wilbarston (Northants.), 99

Wilberforce, Albert Basil Orme, 295, 332, 336
Wilberforce, Robert Isaac, 313
Wilberforce, Samuel, Bp., 313
Wilberforce, William, 331
Wild, George, Bp., 131
Wilderly (Salop.), 46, 75
Wilds, William, 254
Wilkenson, William, 330
Wilkes, John, 334
Wilkins, Thomas, 67
Wilkinson, Abraham, 94
Willerby (Yorks.), 102
Willes, Edward, 210
Willes, Samuel, 94
Willesden (Middlesex), 259, 271
Willesley (Leics.), 113, 121
Willesthorne (Herts.), 68, 74, 75
William I, King of England, 278
William III, King of England, 62, 225
William IV, King of England, 94, 317, 338, 364
William I, King of the Netherlands, 172
William Augustus, Duke of Cumberland, 330
William Frederick, 2nd Duke of Gloucester and Edinburgh, 94
William of Echyngham, 8
William of Munceaus [Herstmonceaux?], 7
William of Pagula, 29
Williams, Sir Charles Hanbury, 312
Williams, Sir David, 36
Williams, Frances, 94
Williams, Lady Frances (Coningsby), 336
Williams, Henry, 172
Williams, John, Abp., 94
Williams, Sir Thomas, 34
Williams, Thomas J., 172
Williams, William Peere, 233
Williams, Sir William, 60
Willingdon (Sussex), 6
Willis, Browne, 69, 74
Willmere, John C., 172
Willoughby, Sir Francis, 105

Willoughby, Lord. *See* Hastings, Richard
Wills, 19, 20, 27, 28, 46, 54, 59, 60, 67, 68, 69, 105, 124–26, 185, 220–21, 240–41, 250
Willson, Alec J., 364
Wilmot, Nicholas, 94
Wilson, Edward [fl. >1707], 185
Wilson, Edward [fl. 1746], 330
Wilson, John, 172
Wilson, Lestock, 283, 285
Wilson, Samuel, 55
Wilson (Leics.), 109
Wiltshire: concealed lands in, 68; deeds for lands in, 100–01, 262; other, 116, 237, 238, 250
Winchelsea, Earl of. *See* Finch, Daniel
Winchelsea (Sussex), 6, 9
Winchendon (Bucks.), 178, 256, 268
Winchester (Hants.), 184, 236, 244
Winchester, recusants in bishopric of, 37
Winchester Fee (Honour of), 113
Windham, William, 172
Wing, Abraham, 172
Winnington, Sir Francis, 226
Winslow Association, 182
Winster (Derbys.), 107
Wistow (Leics.), 99, 113
Wither, George, 364
Witherell, S. D., 172
Wode (Sussex), 1, 5, 9
Wold Newton (Yorks.), 102
Wolfe, Anne, 241
Wolfe, James, 286
Wolfe, Theobald, 105
Wolfpits (Radnor.), 260
Wollaston (Northants.), 33, 54, 59, 75, 77
Wolley, Elizabeth (More) Polsted. *See* Egerton, Elizabeth (More) Polsted Wolley
Wolsey, Thomas, Cardinal, 292
Wolsingham (Durham), 257
Wolston (Warwicks.), 212
Women's rights, 295
Wonston (Hants.), 258

Wood, Charles Harris, 172
Wood, Edward H., 172
Wood, John, 365
Wood, Peter, 94
Wood, William [*temp.* James I, scholar], 31
Wood, William [fl. 1791–92, military paymaster], 94
Wood, William Page, Baron Hatherly, 313
Wood Eaton (Oxon.), 211, 259
Woodcote [*alias* Rawlins] (Oxon.), 99, 100, 116, 206, 217
Woodend (Northants.), 259
Woodham, John, 173
Woodham (Bucks.), 173, 256, 268
Woodhouse, James, 336
Woodhouse, John Thomas, 94
Woodhouse, Jonathan, 95
Woodhouse (Leics.), 99, 109, 113
Woodruffe, Benjamin, 95
Woods, Albert W., 285
Woods, accounts of keeper of, 4
Woodthorpe (Leics.), 99, 107
Woodville family, earls Rivers, 242
Woodward, William, 173
Wookey (Somerset), 261
Wool, sales of, 206
Wool trade, 296
Woolsthorpe (Lincs.), 99
Wootton Courtney (Somerset), 100
Worall Hundred, 38
Worcester, battle of, 228
Worcestershire: deeds for lands in, 101, 262; other, 116, 218, 238
Wordeley (Lancs.), 77
Worge, George, 11
World War II, 277, 314
Worleston (Cheshire), 76
Worlington (Devon.), 60
Worrall, William, 305
Worsley, Ellen, 70
Worsley, Sir Robert, 42
Worsley, Thomas, 42
Worsley (Lancs.), 42
Worth (Sussex), 18
Worthington (Leics.), 99

Worthyvale (Cornwall), 96
Wotton, Sir Edward, 206
Wotton, Edward, 1st Baron Wotton, 210
Wotton, Sir Henry, 48, 298
Wotton, Thomas [1521–87], 210, 214
Wotton, Thomas [fl. 1693–97], 95
Wotton Clothing Club, 154
Wotton House, 175
Wotton School, 201
Wotton Tramway, 156, 173
Wotton Underwood (Bucks.), 151–54, 173, 178, 181, 191, 218, 256, 268
Wrexham (Denbigh), 75
Wrey, Lady, 60, 74
Wrey, Sir Bourchier, 60
Wrey, Sir Christopher, 60
Wrey family, 60
Wright, Henry Clarke, 293
Wright, John [fl. 1627], 18
Wright, John [fl. 1764–66], 337
Wright, Sir Nathan, 95
Wright, Robert, 270
Wrightson, Michael, 95
Wriothesley, Henry, 3rd Earl of Southampton, 279
Writs, register of, 43
Wroxton (Oxon.), 340
Wyatt, John, 215
Wye (Kent), 1, 4
Wymarke, Edward, 74
Wyndham, Charles, 2nd Earl of Egremont, 330
Wyndham, Thomas, 179
Wynn, Charles Watkins Williams, 155, 173, 253, 254
Wynn, Elizabeth, 13, 14
Wynn, Sir Henry Watkin Williams, 173
Wynne, Peter, 34
Wynyard, William, 330

Yale, lordship of. *See* Bromfield & Yale
Yarmouth, Earl of. *See* Paston, Robert
Yarmouth (Norfolk), 114
Yelverton, Barbara (Yelverton) Rawdon-Hastings, 95
Yelverton, Sir Christopher, 39
Yelverton, Sir Hastings Reginald, 95
Yerrow, W., 274
Yonge, Sir George, 5th Bart., 365–66
Yonge, William, 330
York, Duchess of. *See* Cecily, Duchess of York
York, dukes of. *See* Richard, Duke of York; Frederick Augustus, Duke of York
York: proceedings at (1640), 52; waterworks at, 19
York Buildings Company, 235
York Castle, account of expenses at, 82
Yorke, Philip, 1st Earl of Hardwicke, 235, 303
Yorke, Philip, 2nd Earl of Hardwicke, 337
Yorkshire: concealed lands in, 68; deeds for lands in, 77, 101–02, 212, 262; maps of estates in, 122; other, 47, 117, 217, 219
Young, Alexander, 348
Young, Dr. Edward, 244
Young, John [fl. 1737–60, Army officer], 330
Young, John [fl. 1819, banker in India], 95

Zhary, Alexandre, 285
Zouche, Edward la, Baron Zouche, 35, 114
Zouche, barons la, 132